Contents

"The Gentle Voices of Teachers"

FRONTISPIECE. School of Tours: The Jerome frontispiece from the First Bible of Charles the Bald. Paris, Bibliothèque Nationale, MS lat. 1, fol. 3v. Photo: Paris, Bibliothèque Nationale.

"The Gentle Voices of Teachers"

Aspects of Learning in the Carolingian Age

EDITED BY

RICHARD E. SULLIVAN

OHIO STATE UNIVERSITY PRESS

COLUMBUS

✤

This work was performed under the sponsorship of the Board
of Trustees of Michigan State University and of the College of
Humanities at The Ohio State University.

Library of Congress Cataloging-in-Publication Data

"The gentle voices of teachers" : aspects of learning in the Carolingian
age / edited by Richard E. Sullivan.
    p. cm.
    Includes bibliographical references and indexes.
    ISBN 0-8142-0662-X. — ISBN 0-8142-0663-8 (pbk)
    1. Learning and scholarship—Europe—Medieval, 500–1500—
Congresses. 2. Carolingians—Congresses.   3. Civilization,
Medieval—Congresses. I. Sullivan, Richard Eugene, 1921–   .
AZ321.G46 1995
001.2′094—dc20   95-11557
                                                    CIP

Text and jacket design by James F. Brisson.
Type set in ITC Galliard by The Composing Room
of Michigan, Inc., Grand Rapids, Michigan.
Printed by Thomson-Shore, Inc., Dexter, Michigan.

9 8 7 6 5 4 3 2 1

Illustrations

Preface

In a poem written after his departure in 796 from his "cell," his "sweet, beloved dwelling" at the royal court at Aachen to assume leadership of the abbey of St. Martin of Tours, Alcuin said in praise of his former habitat: "In you the gentle voices of teachers could once be heard / expounding with their hallowed lips the books of Wisdom" (qtd. from Godman, *Poetry of the Carolingian Renaissance*, pp. 124–25). It is from his reflection on what was obviously a satisfying season in his illustrious career that the title of this book has been borrowed. Such an expropriation is entirely fitting, for the essays that constitute this volume are indeed primarily about the "voices of teachers" expounding on their search for the wisdom that would motivate and guide right action, a quest that played a major role in shaping the history of eighth- and ninth-century western Europe. The authors of these studies address many matters related to teaching and learning in the large sense: the milieu in which teaching and learning occurred; who, what, and how the masters tried to teach; what material and cultural resources they drew upon in their effort to discharge their responsibility in society; and the impact their efforts had on the world in which they practiced their magisterial métier.

In the final analysis, each of these essays speaks to a particular facet of Carolingian history that must always hold a central place in the attention of scholars seeking to understand that distant age: the revival of learning. With due allowance for poetic license, Alcuin very likely consciously chose to speak of the "gentle" voices who nurtured that renewal. He knew well enough, and modern historians know even better, that there was much about the Carolingian world, including affairs at the court in Aachen, that was anything but gentle. That world was filled with wars, murder, pillaging, oppression, injustice, intrigue, deceit, treachery—and almost everything else that might stand in opposition to gentleness. Contemporaries who described the Carolingian world talked much about these darker aspects of their society, and modern historians are often tempted to dwell at even greater length on such matters. Alcuin was surely aware that, in his violent world, the voices of the Carolingian masters sounded a different note, a note that provided whatever semblance of civility and whatever hope of improvement could be found in those times. And modern Carolingianists know equally well that unless they hear and comprehend the "gentle voices" of the masters of the eighth and ninth centuries, they will never fathom what was essential about Carolingian history or what constituted the vital heritage bestowed by that society on succeeding ages. It is the echo of those voices that the authors of these essays have listened for and attempted to translate into an idiom that has meaning for an audience living twelve centuries later, during another season when gentleness and civility are in short supply.

The studies that constitute the core of this book (chapters 2–7) derive from presentations that were originally made at a conference devoted to the general topic "Learning in the Age of the Carolingians," organized by the Center for Medieval and Renaissance Studies at The Ohio State University in February 1989. Since this symposium was intended to engage the interest and to expand the intellectual horizons of an audience of nonspecialists, each presenter consciously sought to frame his or her discourse on Carolingian learning in terms that would reflect solid scholarship expressed in an idiom that members of an educated audience could readily comprehend.

The reception accorded the papers suggested to the Center for Medieval and Renaissance Studies and to the presenters that their publication might serve a useful purpose in informing both scholars and general readers. In response to this decision to publish the essays, the authors modified their oral presentations in order to enrich and expand upon the original treatment and to provide the scholarly apparatus required to support their interpretations of various aspects of Carolingian cultural activity. In making these revisions, each author has attempted to honor the spirit of the original symposium by maintaining a level of discourse suitable to a general audience while at the same time rendering due attention to the latest and best scholarship concerned with Carolingian culture. To the six essays that constitute the core of this volume an introduction and a conclusion have been added, each especially prepared to focus attention on ideological and methodological issues affecting how contemporary scholars approach the Carolingian age, to highlight crucial concerns addressed by all the essays, to assess the results of this collective enterprise, and to chart the direction that future inquiry into Carolingian cultural history might take.

A selective bibliography of modern secondary materials, compiled from works cited by the several authors of the essays, has been appended. Its content perhaps needs a word of explanation. It combines two elements that may strike some as an odd mix.

The bulk of the works cited consist of studies devoted to various aspects of Carolingian cultural history in the proper sense of that term; the inclusion of such material needs little explanation. In no sense does this compilation provide a complete guide to the vast literature devoted to Carolingian thought and expression. The titles listed will, however, serve to demonstrate to experts the scholarly foundations undergirding the investigations that produced the studies included in this volume. More important, it is hoped that this component of the bibliography will provide a convenient guide to the basic literature that will be useful to those who are beginning the serious study of Carolingian history.

Interspersed with these items treating cultural history in a specific sense are works concerned with broad intellectual currents and historiographical issues, works that provide insight into how the past has been and is now viewed, that seek to open new vistas on how it should be reconstructed, and that try to clarify why contact with the past is important to the present world. The inclusion of this kind of bibliographical material in a work specifically devoted to Carolingian cultural history seems justified for a rather obvious reason: the nature of the past that historians discover and delineate is in crucial ways defined by the questions they ask about the past and the methods they use to recapture it. Those questions emerge from the way the world in which they live understands the human condition and the processes that determine the operation of human communities. Likewise, the techniques employed to explore the past are decisively shaped by what the contemporary world believes knowledge to be and how it is acquired. It follows that those who read what historians write about any segment of the past will have a fuller understanding of that past if they are aware of conceptual and methodological parameters encompassing historical inquiry in the contemporary world. In effect, the bibliography seeks to engage those who use it in a mutually interlocking intellectual process: learning what happened in the past and understanding how and why investigators arrive at that knowledge. Perhaps a greater awareness of the

latter dimension of historianship will serve to stimulate and enrich Carolingian studies.

Collectively, the authors of the essays in this volume wish to thank the
Center for Medieval and Renaissance Studies at OSU not only for spon-
soring the conference that occasioned these essays but also for its support
in seeing this volume into print. They are particularly in the debt of Dr.
Christian Zacher, who was director of the Center at the time the conference on Carolingian learning was held and the decision to publish this volume was made, and who since has become Associate Dean of the College
of Humanities at OSU. The counsel of Professor Joseph H. Lynch of the
Department of History at OSU was invaluable. The staff of the Center for
Medieval and Renaissance Studies provided invaluable assistance, especially in arranging the original conference. No less valuable was the support lent to this project by former Dean G. Michael Riley of the College of
Humanities at OSU and by Dean John Eadie of the College of Arts and
Letters at Michigan State University. The volume benefited greatly from
the expert guidance pertaining to numerous matters provided by the staff
of The Ohio State University Press, especially Charlotte Dihoff, Acquisi-
tions Editor, and Ruth Melville, Managing Editor. The authors are also
grateful for the suggestions offered by the members of the audience at the
conference.

As editor of this volume, I want to extend my special thanks to my colleagues. All of them listened with remarkable forbearance to suggestions
for changes to successive versions of their essays; the response to those
suggestions was invariably constructive (although not always what the editor expected). All accepted with good grace innumerable petty corrections
imposed in order to achieve stylistic uniformity and standardization of the
scholarly apparatus accompanying each essay. Most gratifying of all was
the effort of each author to achieve not only the highest scholarly standards possible in discoursing on some aspect of Carolingian learning but
also a lucid level of discourse suited to a general audience. That commit-
ment to scholarly excellence and to intelligibility has nurtured a sense of
gratification in being associated with this project—to hear again, as it
were, the "gentle voices of teachers" still searching for and propounding
the wisdom encased in ancient books.

East Lansing, Michigan   R.E.S.
January 1995

Abbreviations

CC cont. med.	Corpus Christianorum continuatio medievalis, vol. 1–. Turnhout, 1971–.
CCSL	Corpus Christianorum Series Latina, vol. 1–. Turnhout, 1953–.
LC	*Libri Carolini sive Caroli Magni capitulare de imaginibus*, ed. Hubert Bastgen, MGH, Concilia 2, Supplementum (Hannover, 1924).
Mansi, *Concilia*	J. D. Mansi, *Sacrorum conciliorum nova et amplissa collectio*. 53 vols. Paris, 1901–27; reprinted, Graz, 1960–61.
MGH	**Monumenta Germaniae Historica**
Capit.	Legum Sectio II: Capitularia regum francorum, 2 vols.
Concilia	Legum Sectio II: Concilia, vol. 2: *Concilia aevi Karolini*, parts 1 and 2.
Epp.	Epistolae merovingici et karolini aevi, vols. 3–6.
Poetae	Poetae latini aevi carolini, vols. 1–4.
SS	Scriptores, 32 vols.
SS rer. Germ.	Scriptores rerum Germanicarum in usum scholarum separatim editum.

PG   J. P. Migne, Patrologiae cursus completus: Series graeca. 161 vols. Paris, 1857–66.

PL   J. P. Migne, Patrologiae cursus completus: Series latina. 221 vols. Paris, 1844–64.

Settimane   Settimane di studio del Centro italiano di Studi sull'alto medioevo, vol. 1–. Spoleto, 1955–.

Introduction:
Factors Shaping Carolingian Studies

RICHARD E. SULLIVAN

his volume has a relatively straightforward objective. It seeks to describe what happened in certain interrelated realms of intellectual and artistic life during a period commonly called the Carolingian age, an era conventionally described as spanning roughly the eighth and ninth centuries. Whether for good or bad, historians seeking to discover and account for what occurred at any particular moment in the past are never entirely free to sail their own sea. They must navigate a space where powerful direction is given to their course by prevailing winds and relentless currents set in motion by the efforts of some of their scholarly predecessors to give shape and meaning to the past. At the same time their landfall is rendered unpredictable by flotsam and jetsam cast adrift when the efforts of other precursors seeking to make sense out of the same historical problems ran aground on uncharted shoals created by changing views concerning how the past should be addressed and what was important about it. This nautical metaphor is particularly applicable to historians who concern themselves with the realm of intellectual and artistic history, an arena of historical investigation that has encountered conspicuously stormy waters during recent times. In commenting on the cliché that "history has many mansions," Dominick LaCapra, one of the more perspicacious commentators on the current state of intellectual history, observed in 1985 that "today social history tends to occupy many of the mansions and intellectual history a number of shacks."[1]

Unfortunately, the history of the historiography of Carolingian cultural life still remains unwritten, a lacuna that makes it difficult for contemporary Carolingian scholars to know and understand their roots.[2] No claim is made to fill that lacuna in this introductory essay. However, a few reflections formulated in broad terms touching on some of the major ideological and methodological factors that have decisively conditioned the approach to study of Carolingian cultural history in the past might provide a useful backdrop for the essays that will follow. Moreover, a look backward can perhaps provide some sense of the direction that investigation of Carolingian cultural history might or should take in the future.[3] More important still, such an overview may compel Carolingianists to ask whether they need to reassess their conceptual and methodological posture in the light of current intellectual and ideological trends in order to sustain the vigor of their enterprise and to retain the interest of the considerable segment of contemporary society drawn toward the past that has meaning for them.

❖

First of all, it is important to remind readers having some familiarity with Carolingian cultural history and to alert those who are venturing into that realm for the first time that the historians who have been there before them fashioned a scholarly terrain with a particular configuration. It was shaped by scholars whose inquiries were given a special conceptual orientation by their focus on the phenomenon of cultural renewal. That phenomenon can be defined broadly as quickened and redirected activity in thought and expression that derives its prime impetus and fundamental shape from a conscious turning to an earlier cultural tradition in search of models that will allow the creation of cultural artifacts capable of animating the minds and spirits of a particular collectivity, the members—or at least some members—of which perceive themselves to be restrained and confined by a deficient cultural milieu. The processes involved in the appropriation of tradition; its transformation into new patterns of thought, expression, feeling, and behavior; and the propagation of those new patterns through the fabric of society have provided historians with organizing and explanatory tools through which they have sought to frame the total history of selected cultural communities. Indicative of the seductiveness of that concept is the fact that a code word has come into use as a standard term in the conceptual vocabulary of historians to designate that cultural phenomenon that involves shaping something new out of what is ancient: *renaissance*. Although distressingly imprecise in its meaning and sometimes used in such an indiscriminate fashion as to cause genuine anguish among those who cherish preciseness in the language of historical discourse, the term *renaissance* has been attached to various moments and diverse situations in the past as a cue for all concerned to take special notice.[4]

Perhaps to a greater extent than has been the case for any other historical era, the cultural revival that occurred during the Carolingian period has served for a very long time as a prime focal point around which the study of that age has been given shape. As David Ganz astutely observes in his concluding chapter in this volume, "the medieval legend of Charlemagne . . . had little to say about education and learning until that legend became the property of historians."[5] It may be that that particular perspective on Carolingian history began to take on substance in a world being shaped by another renaissance, that of the fourteenth and fifteenth centuries. Although many who lived during the eighth and ninth centuries were keenly aware that cultural *renovatio* constituted a central element of their effort to renew society as a whole, their sense of their own unique intellectual and artistic accomplishments had a relatively short-lived impact on the historical consciousness of western European society. With the benefit of hindsight it is not difficult for today's historian to demonstrate that during the period extending from the tenth to the fourteenth century a wide assortment of cultural leaders depended on the cultural capital accumulated during the Carolingian age as the basis for a variety of intellectual, literary, and artistic endeavors. However, those who lived during those centuries perceived the Carolingian era from perspectives that had little apparent relationship to intellectual and artistic activity. They remembered the Carolingian age in terms of the *translatio imperii* or the articulation of the basic concepts of papal monism or the point of origin (real or fictive) of noble lineages or the delineation of the prototype Christian prince or the definition of the consummate holy warrior or the formation of the chivalric ideal or the shaping of a unique art style.[6]

Eventually, as institutional and mental patterns changed in the later Middle Ages, these once fruitful images of the Carolingian accomplishments were eroded, and for the most part that era lost its relevance to the central concerns of the later medieval world. As a result and with hardly a demurrer, the Carolingian era was folded into what by the sixteenth century came to be called the "middle age" located between the "ancient age" and the "modern age." As interpreted and judged by a succession of humanists, religious protesters, minions of the Enlightenment, and disciples of the cult of progress, that "middle age" was transformed into a "dark

age" serving as a foil against which to measure not only the glories of antiquity but also the liberating enlightenment of the "new" and "modern"
epoch. In the eyes of many caught up in the dreams of emergent modernism the entire Middle Ages, including the Carolingian period, needed to
be studied because "it is necessary to know the history of that age only to
scorn it," as Voltaire wrote in his *Essay on the Manners and the Spirit of
Nations.*[7]

However, in an intellectual environment that in general looked darkly
on the Middle Ages, there emerged a tradition that viewed Carolingian
cultural activity, especially education, in a positive light. Numerous intellectual luminaries of the sixteenth, seventeenth, and eighteenth centuries
attested to this positive evaluation, as Ganz shows in the study already
cited. What inspired this particular interest among a variety of cultural
leaders who otherwise shared a negative view toward medieval civilization
is not entirely clear.[8] Perhaps various activities central to Carolingian
cultural history struck a resonant chord in the minds of postmedieval intellectuals deeply engaged in comparable endeavors: appropriating the Greco-
Roman classics, purifying Christianity, cultivating the powers of reason,
and improving the human lot. Whatever the explanation, there can be no
question that well before the emergence of modern historianship in the
nineteenth century the idea that Carolingian history was essentially about
educational reform and cultural renewal became firmly entrenched in the
historical consciousness of western Europe's intelligentsia.

That emphasis in reading the Carolingian record received powerful re-
inforcement from the revolutionary changes that affected historical studies
in the nineteenth century. Among other things those new approaches to
the reconstruction of the past began to deliver medieval civilization from
its long entombment in the limbo defined by the dark age concept and to
provide a more objective and positive recognition of its major accomplishments. While the rediscovery—or as some would have it, the "invention"[9]
—of the Middle Ages was nourished by a variety of impulses, the prime
force generating a fundamental reassessment of the Middle Ages was the
growing conviction shaped during the nineteenth century that nothing in
the present could be understood without knowing how it came to be, that
the true nature of current institutions, ideas, techniques, and values could
only be comprehended by reconstructing their history. This historicizing
of thought, powerfully reinforced by concurrent evolutionist trends in the
concepts governing the biological and physical sciences, initiated a pas-
sionate search among those concerned with the "human" sciences for the
origins of all aspects of human existence. From that starting point could be

reconstructed a history of every facet of human endeavor, which alone could reveal how things came to be what they now were and, in so doing, provide a valid, true understanding of present reality.

More often than not the quest for the roots of nineteenth-century western European civilization led back to the Middle Ages. As a consequence, that epoch grew to seem less distant and less dark; indeed, it became the fertile seedbed from which had emerged most of what really counted on the nineteenth-century scale of values—nation states, representative government, legal systems, the bourgeoisie, European expansion, commerce, capitalism, vernacular languages and literatures, universities, and technology. In general terms, historians argued that those facets of western European civilization had their origins in the period between about 1000 and 1350—the High Middle Ages. Such a definition of the medieval past that counted left the Carolingian era still entrapped in a truncated "dark age" whose history held only a modest interest.[10]

Although the main thrust of nineteenth-century investigations of the Middle Ages tended to slight the Carolingian age, there was one dimension of that period that nineteenth-century practitioners of the genetic approach to the past were no more able to disregard than were earlier historians. That had to do with the cultural revival of the Carolingian period. Increasing familiarity with the sources treating Carolingian history that resulted from the intensified emphasis on source collection and from evolving techniques of source criticism provided a prime stimulant to inquiry oriented in that direction. Looming large in the vocabulary employed by Carolingian writers to describe their own world were certain key terms: *renovatio*, *reformatio*, and *regeneratio*. While not necessarily equivalent in meaning and while often employed in a context bespeaking aspiration rather than achievement, these terms left the indelible impression that Carolingian history was about cultural revival. As the activities associated with these terms became better known and understood, historians were increasingly persuaded that Carolingian cultural achievements had something fundamental to do with both the Carolingian world itself and the future course of European cultural life. That realization led to what may be called, without undue flippancy, the act of establishment of modern Carolingian studies.

In 1839 a French literary historian, J.-J. Ampère, was emboldened to characterize the Carolingian cultural achievement as a "renaissance." Ampère justified such nomenclature not only on the basis of his assessment of the quantity and quality of the literary output of Carolingian writers but also on his detection in Carolingian cultural activity of certain generic features that struck him as comparable to the fundamental characteristics of other more famous renaissances, especially the "great" one of the fourteenth and fifteenth centuries.[11] That the cultural revival of the Carolingian age was of sufficient importance to be called a renaissance served as an open invitation to a variety of scholars to investigate the era in search of whatever else from its history might have been as creative and significant in the total record of human achievement as were the fruits of the Carolingian cultural *renovatio*. In a general sense the tremendous outpouring of scholarship during the last century and a half treating all aspects of Carolingian civilization has never strayed far from its fundamental mooring—cultural revival in all its aspects as pivotal to an understanding of Carolingian history.

Although the concept of a renaissance, formulated on the basis of what happened in the realm of cultural activity, has enjoyed a long reign in shaping the approach of Carolingianists to their era, modern scholars have increasingly come to realize that its usefulness as a conceptual tool is surrounded by formidable problems.[12] As a consequence of what has sometimes been called the renaissance debate, few scholars would now employ the term as did Ampère or, somewhat later, Jacob Burckhardt to provide a conceptual frame within which the entire history of a particular era could be fitted in a meaningful fashion. The declining faith in the heuristic value of the renaissance concept has stemmed in part from the obvious fact that it rests on assumptions about the roles of thought and expression as indicators of dynamism in a society or as determinants shaping collective human behavior that find little support in the historical record. More significantly, it has been argued persuasively that history based on such dubious assumptions is bound to be bad history, faulted in many ways—by its too great concern with superstructure at the expense of deepseated, enduring structures that give basic shape to life; by its undue preoccupation with elites and their "high" culture to the neglect of "little people" and the realms where they lived their silent, unlettered, culturally unadorned lives; by its esoteric focus on abstractions that are difficult to define in objective terms and to relate to the social fabric generally; by its unconscionable neglect of the extent to which cultural artifacts serve as tools of oppression.

For a variety of reasons, then, the venerable renaissance concept has gradually lost much of its potency as an intellectual construct around which all the elements required to formulate an interpretation of the Carolingian age can be arranged and made to cohere. And yet the idea lingers as a dimension of Carolingian historiography. Almost without exception books surveying the history of world civilizations, the history of western civilization, the history of the Middle Ages, the history of the early Middle Ages, and even the history of the Carolingian age feature a section specifically designated "the Carolingian renaissance."[13] Perhaps all of this could be dismissed as lip service to tradition. But one cannot be certain. A very recent and highly sophisticated book bears a title that certainly evokes the renaissance specter: *Carolingian Culture: Emulation and Innovation*. With such a title it is not surprising that the volume's first chapter is entitled "Introduction: The Carolingian Renaissance."[14] And Carolingianists should be mindful that not too long ago an often-cited article argued that "the Carolingian period is, from the cultural point of view, a potential hotbed of controversy" because "no one . . . has presented an adequate analysis of the relationship between Carolingian culture and the Renaissance problem in general, nor of the methodological problems associated with this relationship."[15] After "some exploratory suggestions about the Carolingian 'renaissance' as an historical conception," the author found reason to affirm that "the Carolingian was possibly the most significant, because the most pioneering 'renaissance' of all."[16] Obviously, the renaissance concept has not gone away completely as a factor in Carolingian historiography.

❖

The chapters that constitute this book are rooted in the fundamental insight that generated the renaissance approach to the Carolingian world, namely, the idea that the Carolingian cultural revival was a phenomenon of central importance not only to the Carolingian era but also to the total stream of western European history. However, this statement should not be taken to mean that their authors are fixed in a traditionalist, conservative posture. Their researches and interpretations have been enriched and reshaped by various intellectual developments that moved beyond the conceptual boundaries defined by the renaissance approach to Carolingian cultural history.

Contemporary treatments of Carolingian cultural history have been indelibly marked by scholarly endeavors shaped by the fundamental canons defined during the nineteenth century to guide the exploration of the past. Although that approach, sometimes called "scientific" historianship, has been seriously challenged during the twentieth century on a variety of fronts, its powerful impact on the methods employed to discover the past, on the intellectual processes utilized to discern meaning from the historical record, and on the techniques employed to produce a comprehensible reconstruction of the past are still discernible in the historical enterprise.

Awareness of that heritage from the nineteenth century is essential to understanding the current state of Carolingian studies.

A central tenet of scientific history was the need to go to the historical record left behind by past human activity in search of the essential evidence for reconstructing the past; "no documents, no history" was its motto. As self-evident as this point appears, it posed a problem: that of gaining access to authentic versions of the sources in which traces of what happened in the past were recorded. The response to this challenge was provided by a number of scholars who worked in a variety of ways to make available in usable form the primary sources relevant to Carolingian history. Preeminent in the ranks of those engaged in this undertaking were those who sought to recover the written texts relating to the Carolingian era. That enterprise began to gather momentum as early as the seventeenth century and eventually took on an existence of its own, involving a highly specialized, complex, and arduous procedure carried out by specialists trained in institutions established specifically to develop skills appropriate to the collection and editing of texts.[17] The process required a search in diverse repositories for manuscripts surviving from the Carolingian age or containing copies of texts that had originated in that age; the determination of the provenance and history of each manuscript; the collation of several versions of the same text; the application of philological, paleographical, and codicological criteria to establish an authentic, original version of each text; and the publication in printed form of the edited product.

Modern scholars encounter the most visible memorials celebrating the individual labors of hundreds of manuscript collectors and text editors in the form of multivolume printed collections of texts that constitute what is probably the most prized bequest of the nineteenth-century scholarly establishment to posterity. Especially precious to those studying the Carolingian cultural revival are the documents that found their way into such exemplary collections as the Acta Sanctorum, the Monumenta Germaniae Historica, and J. P. Migne's Patrologia Latina. No less important than the editing and publishing of written texts has been the effort to collect other kinds of primary source material mirroring Carolingian cultural activity: seals, coins, inscriptions, liturgical objects, jewelry, manuscript illuminations, sculptures, paintings, tools, household furnishings, and so forth. Most of these physical objects ended up in museums where they were displayed in settings that allowed easy access by researchers and where descriptive catalogues were prepared to facilitate their use.

The same development in historical inquiry that since the beginning of the nineteenth century has focused the attention of historians on the collection, editing, and publication of the sources gave powerful impetus to a second fundamental intellectual activity that has occupied a central place in historical inquiry over much of the last two centuries and has left an indelible mark on how all aspects of the past, including Carolingian cultural history, have been viewed. That activity involved what in old-fashioned parlance was called source criticism. In simplest terms, source criticism involved making the mute records surviving from the past yield concrete data that would permit the historian to reconstruct what actually happened in the past.

The critical approach that evolved during the nineteenth century rested on certain basic points that still command the respect of most scholars involved in decoding the sources of Carolingian cultural activity as a crucial aspect of reconstructing what happened in that realm of Carolingian society. Cultural artifacts produced by men and women living in the Carolingian age were approached as creations consciously constructed with the intent of saying something comprehensible to someone about the external realities that constituted the Carolingian world. The historian's task was to extract from the source what that message was. This required that the historian determine the literal meaning of the words set down in written texts and of the images created by artists, an endeavor that required that the critic be cognizant of and true to the linguistic and visual idiom prevailing in the world in which the source was created. Beyond that the historian qua critic sought to determine to what extent the formal literary or artistic genre utilized by the creator of the cultural artifact was instrumental in giving shape to the message contained therein.

Given the role played in the study of Carolingian culture by the renaissance concept, it has been especially important for Carolingianists to ascertain the extent to which the artifacts created by their Carolingian informants were influenced by pre-Carolingian models, from which they derived the words, images, ideas, and techniques of expression utilized to convey their message. An effective critic of Carolingian sources needed to use whatever means were at his or her disposal to discover to what extent the witness being tested was able and willing to report accurately what was happening. To a considerable degree this aspect of source evaluation depended on the critic's ability to locate the witness precisely in a specific political, social, economic, religious, and cultural context. And it behooved the critic who wanted to extract the truth from a Carolingian source to inquire about what its creator intended in fabricating the artifact under scrutiny. This critical posture presumed that a detached, objective "cross examination" of cultural artifacts from these perspectives would allow the historian to accumulate factual data that at some point would reach a critical mass sufficient to allow the historian to put together a narrative account that would make clear what happened in the Carolingian world and explain why things occurred as they did.[18]

The sustained application of these critical principles to a wide range of sources surviving from the Carolingian world produced a huge corpus of critical commentary on the nature and meaning of literary and nonliterary sources surviving from the Carolingian era. Whatever one judges the value of this body of critical comment to be, it remains a factor in determining how the Carolingian past is approached and understood. Serious students of Carolingian culture can disregard it only at their peril.

Hand in hand with the recovery of source materials and the increasingly refined and sophisticated critical assessment of their meaning went a third major activity that was given its basic configuration by concepts of historianship defined in the nineteenth century. Using the data provided by a critical decoding of the primary sources scholars undertook to reconstruct what happened on the cultural scene during the Carolingian age, to write the history of cultural life in an idiom that would permit someone from the present to relive vicariously what took place in another segment of time. As defined by the canons of scientific history, effective reconstruction of the past involved arranging verifiable evidence in a sequential order in a fashion that would simultaneously portray the progress of events that marked the changes that occurred within a chronological framework and explain why and how these changes occurred. Sound historianship enjoined that the historian allow nothing to enter into the reconstructed past that was not rooted in the historical record; especially anathematized was the presence of the historian in the past. In re-creating a meaningful account of what happened in the past, historians had to make choices about the relative significance of the many pieces of data wrested from the sources. Within the frame of reference prevailing in the nineteenth century, it was generally accepted that political actions shaped by the decisions of highly visible political leaders entrusted with the direction of the affairs of nations constituted the basic framework within which the historical process worked.

While the ideal toward which the historian aspired was a universal narrative that would embrace all human activity as it actually was and explain all change as it flowed from the actions and decisions of human agents, the practicalities surrounding the discovery of the past required more limited spheres of research and reconstruction. As the nineteenth century progressed, the sweeping narratives of earlier times gave way to more modest endeavors to reconstruct small pieces of the past: the monograph made its appearance. The efforts of those preparing studies narrow in chronological and subject-matter scope were nourished by a faith that each limited bit of research and reconstruction would constitute a contribution to the eventual creation of the universal history. As a consequence, investigation of Carolingian cultural history came to be marked by a division of labor to produce diverse forms of inquiry that still continue to frame the efforts of scholars. The lives and creative activities of individual Carolingian writers and artists were reconstructed in detail. Particular cultural events, such as the composition of a particular book, the construction of a building, the founding and evolution of a school, the collection of a library, or the activities of a scriptorium or atelier, were described and analyzed. Efforts were made to discern the contextual setting within which cultural development occurred. This concern worked in two complementary directions: the search for factors in the larger historical setting that influenced cultural development and the assessment of the impact of intellectual and artistic activities on society in general.

With the passage of time the effort to reconstruct the history of Carolingian cultural life increasingly assumed a configuration that responded to the specialized disciplinary concerns that were evolving to give structure to modern historianship as its practice became increasingly carried on by professionals working in academic settings. Separate cadres of scholars concentrated their attention ever more narrowly and sharply on specific facets of Carolingian culture: education, literature, art, architecture, theology, philosophy, law, political theory, music, and so forth. The fragmentation of Carolingian cultural history proceeded even further: for example, the history of education produced specialized studies of each of the seven liberal arts; the history of law was reconstructed in terms of Roman, Germanic, canon, and customary law; and the history of literature led to separate treatments of poetry, letters, histories, and biographies. While sometimes resulting in distortions arising from the imposition on Carolingian cultural artifacts of disciplinary categories that represent modern intellectual constructs foreign to the Carolingian mental world, the disciplinary compartmentalization of Carolingian cultural history has generally been salutary. It allowed scholars to bring discipline-specific methodological techniques, explanatory models, and accumulations of knowledge to bear on source materials in a way that gave new depth and increased comprehensibility to the reconstruction of Carolingian thought and expression. It permitted the fashioning of manageable narrative accounts and analytical treatments devoted to specific areas of cultural activity that with some degree of certainty provided a measure of what the Carolingians accomplished.

However, the balkanization of Carolingian cultural history raised formidable challenges that still face Carolingianists. It has tended to mute scholarly discourse across the almost impermeable barriers that stake out modern disciplinary domains in a way that has veiled the interconnections and commonalities at work in Carolingian cultural activity. And it has constantly reminded Carolingianists of the vision rooted not only in their nineteenth-century background but also in the entire Western historiographical tradition: the need to formulate syntheses seeking to describe and explicate in a holistic fashion the entire range of phenomena associated with the Carolingian cultural achievement. To date the realization of that vision has proved elusive.[19]

The massive effort on the part of past historians whose methodology and objectives were shaped by concepts developed during the nineteenth century to collect the sources, submit them to rigid critical scrutiny defined in a particular way, and utilize the data extracted from them to write the history of Carolingian culture has provided contemporary historians with a huge storehouse of information and interpretive insights about Carolingian intellectual and artistic history. As the twentieth century progressed, opinion gradually began to divide on whether the fruits of historical investigation shaped by nineteenth-century concepts of reconstructing the past provide a crucial nutrient for the history that is currently being and in the future will be written or constitute an obfuscating screen that blocks meaningful access to the "real" Carolingian past. Perhaps it is safe to say that the majority of contemporary Carolingianists place a high value on what their scholarly forebears passed on to them and turn to that inheritance as an indispensable foundation upon which further inquiries into Carolingian cultural history must be based. But even those who see this scholarly heritage in a less-favorable light must still take it into account, if only, as a contemporary Voltaire might put it, to scorn it.

❈

While the central thrust of the scholarship devoted to Carolingian cultural activity has been shaped primarily by the interactive play of knowledge and understanding produced by source collection and editing, source criticism, and historical reconstruction, the rather dispassionate, almost scientific environment defined by these pursuits has been subject to other forces that have had a significant bearing on the shaping of Carolingian cultural history. Conditioned by a variety of factors at work in the larger social setting with which historians worked, these forces have created powerful intellectual currents that have blown across the scholarly world from different directions and at varying velocities to assert a decisive influence on the reconstruction of the history of the Carolingian era. Since echoes of earlier ideological and methodological concerns still resonate in Carolingian scholarship and since intellectual developments of more recent vintage play a decisive role in defining what presently is and in the future will be central to the study of Carolingian cultural life, these issues deserve at least brief attention in our effort to provide an introduction to the historiography of Carolingian cultural history.

Perhaps the simplest way to alert readers to the ideological and intellectual forces presently affecting historical inquiry is to consider briefly the impact on the study of Carolingian culture resulting from the massive changes that have occurred in recent times with respect to how history is conceived and how the past is reconstructed. In a very real sense those new approaches have emerged from a wide range of political, economic, social, intellectual and psychological forces that have played on and reshaped the modern mentality in general.[20]

Amid the ferment surrounding contemporary approaches to the exploration of the past one point has remained constant: "no documents, no history." However, that anchor point of traditional historiography has taken on new dimensions in recent times. While the heroic age of the collection, editing, and publication of primary sources for the Carolingian period undoubtedly lies in the past, the work is not yet complete. As will be evident in the notes appended to the chapters in this volume, the search for still-undiscovered written documents and the editing and reediting of texts remain the concern of many Carolingianists.[21] So also does the effort to discover and describe all manner of Carolingian objets d'art.[22] The adaptation of modern technology to serve scholarly ends has yielded a rich harvest in terms of the accessibility and management of Carolingian source materials. Through the wonders of modern photography and printing techniques, accurate representations of most material objects of Carolingian provenance have been made conveniently accessible to all Carolingianists in their local libraries or even their private studies. Electronic data retrieval systems are in the course of development that allow rapid searches of the corpus of Carolingian written and visual sources that would formerly have required years of effort on the part of the individual scholar. These developments will serve as a reminder to those exploring Carolingian cultural activity that they must always be on the alert for newly discovered sources of information as well as improved versions of those already known.

However, it is no longer so certain that Carolingian cultural history can continue to view sources from the traditional perspective that survives as a heritage from the nineteenth century. The potential of computer technology in the management of data opens up possibilities of grouping written and visual texts for a synchronic treatment and quantifying data included in them; both approaches may produce new insights about Carolingian history.[23] Concepts have emerged in the realm of modern textual criticism that have compelled historians of medieval cultural history to wonder about their long-standing trust in the primacy of modern edited texts. Indeed, there are reasons to consider that the heroic, much-applauded efforts of a long succession of text editors—typified by the Bollandists or the editors of texts published in the Monumenta Germaniae Historica—who have carried out an elaborate process of conflation of many manuscripts to produce what were claimed to be authentic *Urtexte* have in fact resulted in artificial versions of the essential written witnesses to what happened in the cultural realm. Perhaps it is the unique surviving manuscript that deserves the historian's prime attention as he or she searches for evidence of what actually happened. In their anxiety to produce an *Urtext* of a particular work of a single author, earlier editors of Carolingian texts were not always attentive to the codices, the florilegia, in which many individual texts of different provenances were consciously combined by someone for some purpose. From the perspective of what constitutes a valid source, these composite cultural artifacts may have something unique to say that goes beyond the message of any of the discrete pieces included in them: that matter has only begun to be addressed in Carolingian scholarship.

To such concerns must be added the issue of what constitutes legitimate sources relative to Carolingian cultural history. For a long time Carolingianists have depended on a selected corpus of written texts to provide the data that reveal the nature of the Carolingian revival of learning and its influence on society in general. Without questioning the value of that corpus of material as a window into the Carolingian cultural world defined in a certain way, Carolingianists familiar with recent developments in historical thinking relative to how culture is conceptualized are compelled to ask whether other kinds of sources have something to say about Carolingian thought and expression. It has become increasingly obvious that visual "texts" tell much about Carolingian cultural life that not only complements literary sources but also provides different insights into what that life was really about. There are reasons to suspect that the same could be said of "audio" texts from the Carolingian age; that is, music texts. Historians are now compelled to accept that ritual actions surrounding Carolingian political and religious life are redolent with signifiers that give access to the Carolingian mentality. Perhaps they must go even further. Modern anthropological and psychological studies have suggested that almost any social act—for example, a coronation ceremony, a marriage celebration, the drawing up of legal documents, a burial rite, treating the ill, stealing relics—can serve as a "text" that tells the investigator of the past how people thought and felt, thereby serving as a useful source relative to the cultural life of any period in the past. What all of this means is that now and in the future investigators of Carolingian cultural life must once again ask themselves what their predecessors asked: what are the sources available that will allow the reconstruction of Carolingian cultural history, and how can access be gained to this material? The response will be much more complex than has been true traditionally.

If defining what constitutes a legitimate source for Carolingian cultural history has become increasingly problematic, even more unsettled are issues related to the evaluation of sources and the extraction of information about the past from them; that is, the problem of source criticism. The mere evocation of certain names will almost certainly raise concerns— perhaps even panic—among Carolingianists accustomed to relying on the vast body of traditional source criticism as a guide to the reading and interpretation of Carolingian sources. Among those individuals are Ferdinand de Saussure, Claude Lévi-Strauss, Jacques Derrida, Jacques Lacan, Hans-Georg Gadamer, Roland Barthes, Paul de Man, Northrup Frye, and Michel Foucault. Out of their diverse concerns with the functioning of the human mind, the nature and function of language, and the complexities surrounding human discourse these seminal figures have opened vast new vistas on the treatment of texts and have posed numerous unresolved challenges in terms of discerning their meaning.[24] Their collective efforts have raised disturbing questions for Carolingian historians concerning the sufficiency of their traditional critical approach and the relevance of new schools of criticism to their explorations of Carolingian cultural life.

There can be little doubt that Carolingian cultural historians have been less dramatically affected by evolving theories of criticism than have scholars concerned with other segments of medieval cultural development. For instance, one will not find in Carolingian scholarship the equivalent of the conscious efforts to apply the critical canons propounded by New

Criticism, structuralism, semiotics, deconstruction, psychoanalytical criticism, feminist criticism, reader reception theory, and the "new historicism" featured so prominently in the works of scholars concerned with the writings of Chrétien de Troyes, Chaucer, William Langland, Dante, or William de Lorris and Jean de Meun, or with the creations of late-medieval and Renaissance artists.

While this comment may suggest that Carolingianists are incurably traditionalist and old-fashioned in their critical stance toward their sources, it does not reflect the whole truth. A close scrutiny of the critical approach currently taken toward literary and nonliterary sources would reveal that Carolingianists have felt and reacted to various influences emanating from the roiling currents that have shaped postmodernist theories and practices relating to the nature, reading, and interpretation of texts. Perhaps they were forced to take note of the voices that have dominated modern critical theory because of the ominous threat implicit in the central message of that body of theory: in its major thrust modern critical theory has pushed relentlessly toward the dehistoricizing of texts; toward detaching them from any specific historical context and authorial intention; and toward making them objects of scrutiny independent of time, place, or circumstance of creation. The ultimate consequence of this development is, of course, the effacement of the past.

Carolingian scholars have reflected the impact of modern critical theory by their expanded awareness that texts must be seen as self-contained entities to be understood on their own terms rather than as treasure troves of data to be plundered for discrete "facts" about what happened in the past. Greater attention has been paid to the internal forms, structures, and strategies that are involved in the production of meaning in a text, an angle of attack that adds new dimensions to understanding texts beyond what was previously possible when attention focused primarily on the text's "factual" content. This sensitivity to the text as a unique, self-defining entity has made contemporary Carolingianists somewhat more hesitant than were their predecessors in treating the language of texts as a simple reflection of external reality.

As a consequence of structuralist views of texts, it has become more difficult to explicate a source in terms of the context that presumably produced it. Obversely, a critic is compelled to exercise greater caution in assuming that a text can tell its reader what that context was. Critical acumen among Carolingianists has been sharpened by what modern literary and artistic criticism has to say about how a text is brought into existence.

That lesson suggests caution in being satisfied with the traditional view that a cultural artifact is the product of an agent consciously moved by an intention to combine form and language to formulate a message the essence of which is the replication of some external reality.

Aside from providing new insights into the nature and structure of texts, modern critical theories have had much to say about the interpretation of texts: how meaning is extracted from texts, what that meaning consists of, and its relationship to some external order of reality. Carolingianists have shown that they have learned from this facet of modern criticism that decoding texts calls for an advance beyond a methodology defined essentially in philological terms to an interdisciplinary approach involving insights drawn from linguistics, psychology, philosophy, anthropology, and semiotics.

The emphasis on textuality inherent in modern critical theory has raised the intriguing possibility that texts create their own meaning that has no relevance to anything beyond the text. Contemporary Carolingian source criticism certainly reflects the expanded awareness of the nature of language as a system of codes whose meaning derives from the relation of one code to another that has flowed from modern structural linguistics and semiotics. In their approach to texts, contemporary Carolingian critics have been influenced by what modern reception theory says is involved in reading or viewing a text and about the relationship between text and audience as a dimension of ascertaining meaning. And finally, from the chaos wrought by deconstructionist views on the interpretation of texts, historians dealing with Carolingian texts have become more cautious in laying claim that some order of incontestable, timeless, universally intelligible meaning can be drawn from a text. The complexities that surround the discernment of the meaning of a text have raised questions about traditional concepts of causality, change, human agency, and social determinism as comprehensible dimensions of the historical process.

All of these developments in Carolingian source criticism flowing from the impact of recent trends in critical theory and practice have at once enriched and made more problematic the efforts of Carolingianists to pursue the critical function required to get to a particular past through the traces it deposited in the form of various kinds of texts. Perhaps the time has come for a collective effort among all concerned with Carolingian cultural history to take stock of where they stand in terms of their critical posture toward their sources. Such a stocktaking might involve a more rigorous evaluation of the limitations implicit in their traditional critical methodology and an objective assessment of the possibilities offered by contemporary critical theory and practice to enlarge what the texts can be made to say.

No less formidable than the issues concerning what constitutes a valid historical source and how the historian goes about decoding sources are highly charged questions about what is the meaningful past, how one best proceeds to reconstruct it, and why anyone should make the effort. The vast upheavals that have altered the mental landscape of most of the world as the twentieth century has progressed have radically reshaped views on these matters fundamental to historianship and substantially redefined the agenda of historians. The impact of these developments, which are inextricably related to changing ideological concerns, is of crucial importance in defining where the focus of Carolingian cultural history is located and assessing the results of inquiry into that realm of the past.

It would not, of course, be difficult to demonstrate that previous scholars studying Carolingian cultural history were affected by values and beliefs prevailing in the world in which they worked. The scholarly record is replete with examples illustrating the link between ideology and historical inquiry. The rationalism of the Enlightenment cast a negative coloration on Carolingian cultural activity because of the religious framework within which it found expression. The early Romanticists and a long succession of their ideological heirs, who persisted in seeking Camelot, found relief from the horrors of capitalism, industrialism, technology, materialism, and individualism in what they discerned as the organic, collective, emotional, and populist aspects of medieval society. Positivism rooted in experimental science exercised a powerful influence on how Carolingian historical sources were read, on what could be extracted from those sources as legitimate historical "facts," and on what governed an objective reconstruction of the past as it actually was. Philosophical idealism oriented scholarly inquiry toward a search for a zeitgeist that would provide the center of gravity around which Carolingian thought and expression revolved and toward dialectical imperatives that shaped the ideational underpinnings of cultural communities.

Such prominent features of nineteenth-century thought as the idea of progress, historicism, and deterministic materialism provided different and often conflicting modes of explanation to account for change in the Carolingian cultural scene and contrasting norms to measure the advance—if any—that stemmed from Carolingian cultural renewal. The epistemological tenets undergirding nineteenth-century natural science emboldened some historians to approach any segment of the past in search of empirical evidence that would form the basis of general laws governing human activity. Bourgeois cultural values played a decisive role in defining what constituted high culture in past societies. Confessional positions and concerns dividing Protestants and Roman Catholics put significant twists on defining the all-important nexus between Carolingian religious life and its intellectual and artistic life; the progressive secularization and demythologizing of thought added new complexities to that issue. Various political movements, such as liberalism, socialism, communism, nazism, and fascism, acted as prisms through which the Carolingian world was variously viewed. Nationalist sentiments influenced the tone and content of the scholarly treatment of Carolingian culture. Lurking not far below the surface of nationalist ideology were racist ideas from whose baleful influence not even Carolingianists were immune.

While remnants of older ideological positions are still embedded in the scholarly discourse on all aspects of Carolingian history, their importance has been muted by more recent intellectual trends that have posed a new range of issues concerning what constitutes history and how the historian should address the past. Although the differences between the "old" and the "new" history may not be as radical as some of the proponents of either faction have claimed,[25] and although some of what not so long ago was trumpeted as new history has begun to show signs of aging, it is important for anyone interested in the past to have some sense of the prime ideological and methodological forces currently giving shape to the investigation and understanding of the past, including Carolingian cultural history.

Contemporary historical consciousness has been radically reshaped by what might be called a major intellectual revolution that had its roots in the nineteenth century but that has impacted upon the Western world with special force since World War I in redefining how human nature and human behavior are understood. This transformation is perhaps best mirrored in the works of a series of seminal thinkers, including especially Friedrich Nietzsche, Karl Marx, Sigmund Freud, Max Weber, Albert Einstein, Edmund Husserl, Martin Heidegger, Ludwig Wittgenstein, Emile Durkheim, Lévi-Strauss, Foucault, and Derrida, and of a legion of natural scientists who have rewritten contemporary understanding of the ways in which physical and biological factors condition human behavior. Collectively these figures have added the decisive pieces needed to complete the process of dethroning human beings from their long-standing central place in the universe, a decentering process that perhaps began with Galileo and extended through Newton to Darwin, Freud, and Einstein but whose full implications were veiled until fairly recently by such landmarks of modernism as Cartesian rationalism and empirical science.

In more specific terms, these shapers of the postmodern intellectual environment and designers of the postmodern man/woman have cast serious—if not fatal—doubts on the efficacy of reason as a uniquely human power capable of discerning an order of objective truth by which the universe operates and of making choices within that framework that would permit human affairs to unfold in a pattern beneficial to the human lot. They have, as some postmodern thinkers might put it, made suspect all forms of logocentrism and cast doubt on almost everything that such systems claimed were human capacities.

In a universe where the power of human reason and the boundaries of human freedom were being progressively pruned back it became increasingly imperative for those concerned with human affairs to find alternative ways of accounting for human behavior. Those who honestly faced the implications of the dethronement of reason had to give serious thought to the need for abandoning any idea that human destiny was shaped by conscious choices formulated on the basis of knowledge and applied by human will acting through institutional processes—primarily political—specifically shaped to determine collective well-being. Explanations of human conduct had to be sought in terms of impersonal forces not immediately amenable to rational human control—modes of economic production; deep-seated social structures; enduring mind-sets; unconscious instincts embedded in the human psyche; immobile systems of discourse through which the meaning of human existence and action is shaped and shared; even pure chance.

The central place given to such forces in determining human destiny brought to the fore new ways of grouping human beings into meaningful communities—groupings based on class, wealth, ethnicity, gender, family, marginality, ideology, and so on—that took precedence over the traditional political definitions of communities. This reconfiguration of social groupings gave new importance to various types of behavior that left hardly recognizable the traditional human being defined as a rational political animal. The redefinition of social structures and behavioral patterns brought into prominence new power relationships whose essence was shaped by control of material resources or by modes of discourse from which emerged ideologies capable of controlling human activity by manipulating conscious desires and subconscious urges. The potency of various structurally defined determinants of human relationships was such that it reduced to insignificance mere "events," interpreted as products of human choices, that once seemed so decisive in chartering the course of human affairs; equally fruitless was any effort to explain human affairs by stringing together in sequential order these meaningless events. Thinkers of all kinds found it increasingly difficult to define any grounds for establishing a basis of truth that could be verified by criteria external to the minds that thought it and the language codes that expressed it; relativism in various forms began to permeate the realms of knowledge, morals, and values.

These new readings on the human condition were accompanied by a steady erosion of confidence that the human species was moving in any discernible direction. In a real sense, the emergence of postmodernism has been accompanied by the end of the long-standing faith that humanity was advancing toward a more perfect state. Perhaps the nineteenth-century idea of progress, increasingly discredited on philosophical grounds and by the multiple horrors that scarred the twentieth-century landscape, and "vulgar" Marxism, increasingly revealed to be a manifesto guaranteeing economic regression and political oppression, represented the last manifestations of a teleological view of the human condition.

As new and different definitions of the nature and behavior of contemporary human beings were forged, it was only natural that these new perceptions were projected onto efforts to understand human activities in the past. The result has been a proliferation of schools of historical inquiry, each representing an effort to extract from the changing concepts of basic human nature and the social order a new response to how the past should be addressed and a revision of how to interpret the meaning and significance of past human activities. A brief comment on some of those schools that have asserted a particularly seminal influence on contemporary historiography will help to highlight some of the major intellectual trends affecting Carolingian historiography.

A long succession of revisionists have given a significant role to material forces, chiefly economic and climatic, as decisive determinants of human destiny. Perhaps Marxist historians have systematized this approach most cogently in their effort to explain the past in terms of a struggle between classes forged by the system of economic production prevailing at a particular moment. That approach gave a central place in historical inquiry to material conditions, to social groups either dominant or oppressed by virtue of their location in the prevailing system of production, to cultural and religious superstructures through which those in power maintained their mastery, and to an inexorable dialectic rooted in these conditions, which provided the dynamic in historical development.[26] In due course the characterization of the human mind and its working articulated by Freud and his followers was applied to the past. Psychohistory opened challenging new possibilities for discerning the motives for human actions, for explaining individual and collective behavior, and especially for assessing the impact, often unperceived, of various impersonal phenomena on the human psyche.[27] Drawing on models provided by key social scientists who played major roles in the above-noted redefinition of human nature, another group of historians devised a structuralist approach that attempted to analyze and explain the past in terms of the influence exercised on human activity by deep-seated, long-lasting structures defined by social organization, economic activity, biological factors, behavioral patterns, and systems of belief.

Although in some forms structuralism tended to impose a mechanistic pattern on human life so powerful as to make moot attempts at the explanation of human affairs, past or present, structuralism's value to historians was given credibility, a particular focus, and widespread publicity by the *Annales* school, which since World War II has exercised a decisive influence on historiography, especially in France.[28] Although far from constituting a cohesive scholarly community, a long succession of *annalistes* produced a rich body of research that placed special emphasis on utilizing various forms of quantification in describing and analyzing structures and articulated a conceptual framework through which the working of structures in the human setting could be described and analyzed. That paradigm involved structures of the *longue dureé* viewed as virtually immobile (e.g., climate, geological features, and forms of agricultural exploitation); cyclical forces of middle duration bringing changes *(conjonctures)* in the economic and social structures controlling the human condition—changes that the historian can measure by systematic quantitative soundings of economic and social structures at regular intervals (e.g., measuring such factors as prices, birth and death rates, and levels of economic productivity); and short term events marking the day-by-day unfolding of life, usually political events. Since *Annales* historians felt that event history had no significant bearing on human affairs, they argued that traditional narrative history—characterized by reconstructing history in terms of a sequence of events, each of which served to explain what came next—was useless in terms of determining what really happened.

Currents of thought and fields of interest emanating chiefly from the *Annales* school—but supported by concepts held by Marxists and psychohistorians and constantly reinforced by ideas and methodologies derived from the social sciences and philosophy—resulted in what has often been called the "new history" or the "new social history," a kind of history that since World War II has commanded the central attention of professional historians and has been on the cutting edge of new approaches to the past.[29] While the full range of this kind of history is too complex to capture in a brief statement, its essential features are fairly clear. It postulates the centrality of deeply rooted economic, social, and mental structures emerging from the material base of society as determining forces in shaping the past. The prime task of the historian is to describe and analyze these structures. Access to them depends upon asking a new range of hypothetical questions about the past, questions which for the most part are derived from theories postulated by social scientists concerning contemporary society.

To answer those questions relating to the structural features of past societies and their affect on human activity, social historians have sought to exploit a variety of new sources of information about the past and have deployed an armory of new techniques for decoding these sources in quest for new data about the past. This "opening" of the past has revealed a greatly enlarged cadre of people and a vastly expanded range of human activities that have played roles in history that have heretofore been neglected. The resultant history "from the bottom up"—focusing on how "little people" operated within the basic structures in which their lives were encased—has cast serious doubt on the veracity of the "old" history, with its emphasis on the activities of political elites and their "high civilization," narrow conceptual approach, and constrained methodology.

Although sometimes given a combative edge by the political commitments and egalitarian values of its advocates, the new social history has certainly given the past a new look. Especially important have been the new social groupings brought into view as important contributors to the human endeavor and the new range of activities thought worthy of the attention of historians and their audiences. In some cases these new social groupings have become major foci of inquiry in their own rights; women's history, family history, and the history of ethnic groups come to mind. The broadened range of subjects that contemporary social historians have deemed worthy of attention—illustrated by such matters as the history of sexuality, insanity, play, criminality, childhood, the imagination, dreams, melancholy, monastic maledictions, pornography, death, sodometries, and even rhubarb—has provided an immensely expanded sense of what has counted in shaping human destiny. It is indeed to their credit that social historians consider no group and no form of human activity from the past too insignificant or too inconsequential to deserve the historian's attention.

This modest survey of prominent schools of thought in contemporary historiography certainly runs the risk of oversimplifying what drives the contemporary approach to the past. It mutes the infinite nuances of thought that have existed among the members associated with each school and obscures the points of intersection in the approaches advocated by each school. Most important of all, it fails to call attention to the widespread reservations held by practicing historians to the claims of any and all of the schools just noted. In fact, at this point in time, one could argue that a reaction has set in against the central conceptual positions shared by all these schools of thought.

Materialistic and psychological determinants seem less decisive than "vulgar" Marxists and avant garde psychohistorians would have it. "Immobile" structures appear more malleable than ardent structuralists once claimed. "Events" and their perpetrators attract more attention than some would have once allowed. Political history may have almost as good a future as its past. Elites of all kinds may have at least a modestly respectable place in history's many mansions; all things in Clio's realm may not be ipso facto equal. There may be a reality beyond whatever it is that exists in the human mind, and individuals may have something to say that does tell the attentive ear what that reality is. Yet despite the complexities that it veils, our brief summary of the state of historical studies at the present does make a point: the past looks different today than it did not too long ago, and the future of the past appears to be something other than what historians two generations ago would have surmised. Historians of the Carolingian era must be aware of these currents of thought if they are to reconstitute a past that has any meaning to their audience.

❧

While the various efforts to view the past from fresh perspectives defined by recent interpretations of human nature and the human condition speak in one way or another to all ages and all aspects of the past, certain developments in recent historical thought and practice relate more directly to the history of cultural activity and thus to our concern with Carolingian cultural history.

Some historians continue to have an interest in what has been called "the history of ideas," a venerable enterprise defined roughly as the study of the content, impact, and transmission of certain major intellectual concepts that have repeatedly engaged the minds and stimulated the creative efforts of those recognized by their contemporaries as "thinkers" (philosophers, theologians, belletrists, even historians). These historians have not had an easy road in recent times; their efforts have been criticized for being elitist, detached from the reality created by economic and social structures, irrelevant in a world where rationalistic inquiry is viewed with suspicion.

However, perhaps this kind of cultural history is not completely obsolete; perhaps "big" ideas, somewhat removed from the street, and the cultural artifacts in which they find expression are still important. For example, it seems fairly clear that certain "major" literary, philosophical, and religious texts have played a decisive role in the past as vehicles through which the members of particular groups in particular societies have gained access to a coherent ensemble of aspirations, sentiments, and values that have united them, set them apart from other groups in the same society, and moved them to actions that changed the course of events.

Although the psychoanalytic procedures pioneered by Freud have not been as fruitful as some once claimed in penetrating the thought world of cultural figures from the past, insights derived from psychology are useful to cultural historians in their efforts to reconstruct collective mentalities and measure how shared beliefs and values influence behavior. Marxist historians have constantly compelled cultural historians to be mindful of the processes through which the material conditions in any past society influence cultural activity and have forced historians at least to consider how cultural "superstructures" can serve as factors in shaping the power structure in a society.

Recently, several more sharply focused approaches to cultural history have emerged to enliven and enrich the field. Particularly fertile and challenging has been what is called the history of mentalities (*l'histoire des mentalités*),[30] defined initially by historians associated with the *Annales* school and inspired by their passion for social history. Generally eschewing the thought patterns and cultural forms associated with "high" culture, historians of mentalities have sought to reconstruct the systems of thought shared by collectivities and serving as prime forces shaping the mental and psychological environments within which the lives of ordinary people unfolded. Often unarticulated and operating below the level of consciousness within the collectivity affected by them, these thought patterns have tended to be long-lasting and repetitive in their impact on behavior. For historians of mentalities, access to the ingredients that constituted collective mentalities depends less on interpreting literary texts and formal

works of art than on decoding rituals, gestures, symbols, myths, supersti-
tions, taboos, oral language usages, folklore, games, and informal educa-
tive practices associated with the socialization process.

As befits the *Annales* approach in general, historians of mentalities often
seek to quantify the evidence contained in such sources and arrange it seri-
ally, so as to chart the changing patterns—the *conjonctures*—affecting collective mentalities. They also seek to locate the collective mental patterns
existing at any particular moment in history on the contemporary socio-
economic grid in a fashion that will illuminate interactions between social,
economic, and mental structures. Such concerns have prompted historians
of mentalities to explore the creation, implantation, and circulation of elements that constituted collective mentalities. And such inquiries have constantly expanded the realm that could properly be embraced by *l'histoire des
mentalités*; perhaps the term "history of popular culture" more accurately
defines the field as it has evolved. This expansion has led to efforts to establish the boundaries between "high" and "popular" culture and to assess the
interactions between the two realms—or, in some cases, to inquire
whether there is any distinction. In all its manifestations, the history of
mentalities has greatly expanded contemporary understanding of what
constitutes culture and how cultural factors affect the working of any human society in all its diverse components.

Perhaps even more challenging to contemporary historians of culture
are the complex ramifications surrounding what has come be called the linguistic turn in the broad field of sociocultural history. In what amounted
to a revolution in the approach to social and cultural history, a revolution
rooted in the seminal work of Saussure, *Cours de linguistique générale*
(1916), this movement brought language and discourse to center stage as
prime factors in shaping the fabric of the social order and determining human behavior.[31] In fact, among the most ardent champions of this new
approach to language, defined as a system of codes through which meaning is created and transferred, came to be viewed as the prime constitutive
force in shaping all levels of human consciousness, all forms of human
bonding, and all types of human action. Across a kaleidoscopic trajectory
highlighted by endeavors now labeled semiotics, structuralism, poststructuralism, and deconstruction—a course that in some sense has culminated
in the works of Jacques Derrida and Michel Foucault—the "linguistic
turn" has posed a wide range of problems for historians of culture.[32]

Beyond identifying the linguistic structures that make possible all forms
of human discourse upon which social interaction depends, cultural historians marching to the beat of modern linguistic and communication the-

ory have been compelled to reexamine how cultural artifacts come into being, a task that involves not only the activity of the ostensible creator but also the audience, who in the act of receiving the text play a role in creating it. Given the way language is understood in modern linguistic theory, the role of texts in representing some external reality has become problematic to the point where some theorists of language would deny any connection between the message of a text and external reality. Such concerns raise serious problems concerning the relationship between context and text; especially problematic for cultural historians is the long-standing assumption that the context within which a text originated serves as a prime factor in constructing its meaning. Equally problematic has become the matter of ascertaining the intentions of the creators of a cultural artifact and assessing the importance of such intentionality in the message a text conveys. Vexing issues involving the relationship between orality and literacy have had to be addressed.[33] As noted earlier in this chapter, modern critical theory has surrounded the quest for meaning in cultural artifacts with obstacles that have made some cultural historians doubt whether any fixed meaning can be attached to texts, a conclusion that raises questions about the ultimate validity of cultural history.[34]

There are indications that many aspects of the history of mentalities, popular culture, and language and communication theory in particular, and of Marxist and *Annales* history in general, are converging to create still another approach to cultural history, one that has been called the new cultural history.[35] While still a field of investigation that remains fluid in terms of its objectives and methodology, most practitioners of the new cultural history would probably agree that it seeks to avoid the reductionism implicit in treatments of cultural life by Marxists and *annalistes,* who generally have tended to make cultural phenomena derivative from and dependent on economic or social factors operating in a society, and to transcend the essential lack of coherence and the randomness that characterizes the seemingly endless range of topics that, under the rubric "cultural history," comes under scrutiny by historians of mentalities and popular culture.

The new cultural history seeks to establish the determinative role of cultural factors in shaping human affairs, especially in terms of defining the power relationships that prevail in a society. Relying heavily on concepts drawn from cultural anthropology, the new cultural historians view culture in terms much broader than has been traditional for cultural historians. They see culture as embracing a wide range of actions, which express in allegorical or symbolic form some order of meaningful message with which members of society can collectively identify. Culture defined in this way might include social acts (e.g., riots, parades, or marriage ceremonies), written texts (e.g., saints' lives, political tracts, novels dealing with gender issues, or popular songs), visual representations (e.g., public building programs, styles in clothing, or material objects related to religious worship), or mechanisms involved in the circulation of cultural artifacts (e.g., educational practices, book production, and literacy). Obviously the context that produces cultural artifacts of this kind embraces the entire spectrum of collective life—political, economic, social, and religious. The task of the cultural historian is to read the meaning inscribed in these kinds of cultural texts for those who encountered them in a particular historical setting and to discern the impact of that message in determining social consciousness and behavior.

The new cultural historians draw heavily on techniques provided by contemporary literary criticism to guide their efforts to decode what such cultural texts mean to those "reading" them and to determine what the text does to its recipients. In general their efforts aim less at defining structures undergirding cultural communities than at understanding how cultural artifacts emerge out of a particular ambience and influence the way people act in a particular historical setting. In this sense, the cultural dimension of a society's existence takes on central importance in explaining what holds the society together and in accounting for what initiates the numerous events marking its movement through time. Within the conceptual framework posited by the new cultural history, the traditional dichotomy between elite and popular culture tends to lose its relevance; all cultural artifacts and activities potentially become a part of a network of symbolic expressions of how a society conceives itself and its activities. The approach expands without trivializing what is embraced by the concept of culture and elevates cultural activity conceived in this broader sense to the level of active agent in any human setting in a way that promises to put cultural historians near the center of the scene in accounting for what happened in the past and how it happened. To some Carolingianists that may not seem to be a revolutionary insight, but in many respects the new cultural history offers a salvific antidote from the nihilistic approach to cultural artifacts implicit in some contemporary schools of thought.

❖

Anyone looking to Carolingian history in search of an arena that could serve as a model in which these developments—shaping recent historical thought generally and affecting the treatment of cultural history in particular—were applied to produce radical changes in approaches or interpretation will likely be disappointed. Practitioners of cultural history defined in these terms have found more hospitable arenas in the late-medieval world of Montaillou; in early modern times when witchcraft had its best days; in the eighteenth-century world that discovered madness; in fin de siècle Vienna, where the road to the postmodern world was charted, and in the media industry in America, where that same road ended. But even though new approaches to cultural history have not found a prime focal point in the Carolingian age, the total weight of ideological developments over the last half century has brought subtle changes to the study of Carolingian culture.

The revisionist mentality that has characterized modern historical thought and practice—in part a consequence of an effort to purge mind-sets rooted in earlier ideological positions—has had its impact on Carolingian cultural history primarily in terms of establishing how the Carolingian cultural achievement is perceived to fit into a larger historical context. The psychic shock produced by the world wars of the twentieth century—catastrophes that many came to view as the consequences of crass materialism, ideological dogmatism, hypernationalism, and blatant racism rooted in nineteenth-century ideologies—sired a countervailing wave of transnationalism and cosmopolitanism. From this revised ideological perspective it seemed more productive to abandon debates over whether one should speak of Charlemagne or Karl der Grosse in order to enshrine the great Carolingian as *Europae Pater*, whose role in establishing a cultural community provided benefits that might be emulated in the twentieth century.[36] Modern scholarship has devoted a good deal of energy to demonstrating the contribution of Carolingian cultural activity to unifying Europe in the eighth and ninth centuries, thereby providing a base for European community in future centuries.[37] The role of religion as a formative force in Carolingian cultural history has been reevaluated in light of the spirit of ecumenism that has flowed from the moral outrage stemming from the Holocaust, the agenda defined by Roman Catholic *aggiornamento*, growing awareness in an increasingly interdependent world of religious systems other than the Judeo-Christian, and new insights into the nature of religious experience in general provided by modern social sciences.

Recent developments in historical thought have also given scholars concerned with Carolingian history cause to reconsider their definition of the periodization framework within which they fit the Carolingian period. In line with nineteenth-century concepts of what was central in reconstructing the past, the Carolingian age has long been defined in political terms:

it was a discrete, self-standing temporal entity given its own identity by the activities of the rulers of a single dynasty, which ascended to power in the early eighth century and fell from grace at the beginning of the tenth. From the perspective of cultural history, this periodization scheme never provided an entirely comfortable fit as a consequence of the association of Carolingian cultural history with a renaissance concept. The very idea of a Carolingian renaissance made no sense unless Carolingian cultural activity was connected with some prior cultural system that could be "reborn"; likewise, if the renaissance typology meant anything, then a Carolingian renaissance must have shared something with subsequent renaissances— Ottonian, twelfth-century, Italian, Northern European.

The famous Pirenne thesis, which since World War II has loomed large in Carolingian historiography, ostensibly buttressed the traditional politi- cally defined periodization scheme by positing a decisive break in the his- torical continuum in the middle of the eighth century at the very moment that marked the accession of the Carolingian dynasty to power. However, it is well to recall that Pirenne's argument was based on evidence derived primarily from economic history, which, when Pirenne's seminal book was published in 1937, was a relatively new arena of historical inquiry in which developments proceeded at a pace and for reasons quite indepen- dent of political affairs.[38] In positing a disjunction in history in the eighth century resulting from the rupture of Mediterranean unity by the Muslim intrusion, the Pirenne thesis oriented Carolingian cultural historians to- ward a search for the new, unique, and formative aspects in Carolingian intellectual and artistic life that would mark the "birth of Europe" and throw light on what the product of that blessed event would grow up to become.

The appearance of Pirenne's seminal book in a sense marked the rising impact exercised by the *Annales* school and the new social history on the study of late antiquity and the early Middle Ages. Concerned chiefly with deep-rooted, slowly changing structures, historians working within the conceptual framework staked out by these approaches began to lay the foundations for a periodization scheme that folded Carolingian history into an expanding temporal framework stretching roughly from the end of the fourth to the end of the tenth century. Such an approach focused on identifying and describing common structures that defined the human scene across the entire period. The same approach provided grounds for arguing that there occurred a radical transformation of the basic structures affecting society beginning around 1000, which in effect marked the be- ginning of a new epoch in European history that had little to do with the Carolingian age except to end it.[39]

Some schools of historical thought have argued the need to go even further in extending the time frame within which meaningful Carolingian history should be embraced. Their adherents have read the central features of Carolingian history in terms that make that age part of a vast, unchanging epoch given its common configuration by "feudal modes of production" or "preindustrial social structures" or "primitive (or at best archaic) mentalities."[40]

The end result of these adjustments in temporal sight lines, shaped by changing ideological perspectives affecting historical studies, has been to mute the uniqueness of the cultural activity traditionally associated with a particular royal dynasty. As one especially vocal advocate of repositioning the Carolingian age in the historical continuum put it, the Carolingian revival was an episode without consequence, a feeble stirring of a society still locked in a position of "fetal dependence," awaiting the beginning of "le 'vrai' Moyen âge" about A.D. 1000.[41] One can hardly mistake the thinly veiled invitation embedded in this formulation to partake in the dismantling of at least one renaissance, which heretofore had enjoyed a long career![42] In any case, these shifting views on where the Carolingian age fits into the historical continuum demonstrate anew that attempts to divide the past into temporal segments as a heuristic tactic essential in making sense out of historical inquiry assert a powerful influence on what is discovered.

Changing concepts of historical inquiry have certainly played a significant role in expanding the present view of what constituted the essential elements of Carolingian cultural life. For a long time the investigation of Carolingian cultural activity tended to be defined within parameters established by political and ecclesiastical history. Meaningful cultural life involved whatever developed as a response to the official program set forth by Carolingian rulers, especially Charlemagne, and the Church to bring about a *renovatio* of society. Carolingian culture defined in these terms focused attention on royal, episcopal, and monastic legislation; schools and their curricula; libraries; scriptoria; artistic ateliers attached to or patronized by the royal court; and the production and explication of standardized texts. Key cultural figures involved an elite who were ostensibly identified with the royal court and its cultural policy.[43]

While few contemporary Carolingianists would diminish the importance of the royal and ecclesiastical policies and the particular cultural activities they engendered in shaping the Carolingian cultural environment, all would insist that the definition of culture must be extended beyond what was sanctioned by royal policy. In response to the philosophical premises that undergird the history of mentalities, the history of popular culture, and the new cultural history, Carolingianists today have posited a whole new range of activities as subjects appropriately subsumed under the mantle of Carolingian culture. In seeking to decode the meaning of cultural monuments traditionally viewed as instrumentalities explicable in terms of official cultural policy, Carolingian cultural historians have discerned levels of meaning and modes of expression having little if any relevance to official culture; the result has been an enriched understanding of the sophistication and originality of what in contemporary parlance would be called Carolingian high culture. Cultural artifacts that marked departures from "official" Carolingian ideological positions have been given closer scrutiny as integral parts of the entire cultural setting, and the creators of such aberrant cultural expression have earned new honor in the galaxy of significant cultural leaders. The result has been a heightened sense of the complexity and diversity of Carolingian culture.

What constitutes Carolingian culture has been given new dimensions by a willingness among scholars to acknowledge a new array of actors as culture creators and bearers: holy men, preachers, noble warriors, women, seekers of patronage, ecclesiastical power brokers, polemicists, members of "textual communities."[44] Activities involving rituals, displays of symbols, and veneration of material objects have been given a significant place in the delineation of meaningful cultural activity. The important place accorded language and discourse in cultural life by modern linguists and anthropologists is reflected in Carolingian cultural history by the effort to assess the impact of illiteracy, orality, and bilingualism on Carolingian culture and society. The possibilities of quantifying some aspects of Carolingian life as a guide to fuller understanding of the implantation and impact of ideas have been explored; examples include the accumulation and circulation of books, frequency of the occurrence of iconographic motifs, traffic in relics, common themes utilized in the definition of saintliness, and recurrent patterns in language usage.

Prompted by the critical importance accorded to material conditions in life by modern historiography, especially by Marxist and structuralist historians, Carolingian cultural historians have given greater attention to the interrelationships between material conditions and cultural activity. Yet to be measured is the potential impact on the exploration of Carolingian culture that might emerge from the agenda of current advocates of multiculturalism and cultural diversity engendered by ethnicity, religion, race, and gender.[45]

As the array of activities and actors deserving of attention by Carolingian cultural historians has expanded, so also have the range of evidence they put into play in reconstructing Carolingian cultural history and the techniques they employ to decode that evidence. Note has been made earlier of the impact felt in the criticism of Carolingian sources resulting from recent approaches to literary criticism. What is equally noteworthy are the new kinds of evidence upon which Carolingianists rely in their explorations of cultural life. This development is in part a response to the general thrust in twentieth-century historiography to expand what counted as legitimate witnesses to past human activity; but it is also a by-product of the resourcefulness of Carolingian historians seeking answers to new questions posed by ideological developments affecting the general field of cultural history.

While never losing sight of what traditional sources such as official documents (e.g., capitularies, diplomas, or royal instructions) and literary texts (representing intellectual artifacts consciously crafted to serve cultural purposes, e.g., theological tracts, scriptural exegeses, educational manuals, histories, letters, liturgical books, or collections of laws) tell about their age, Carolingian historians have grown increasingly adept at extracting information from a more diverse body of sources. They have probed the meaning of art works of all kinds to produce fresh insights into the content of Carolingian culture and how its meaning was transmitted. Symbolic acts associated with public ceremonies and religious rituals have yielded expanded perceptions of how Carolingians thought and what they thought about. Poetry, saints' lives, and moral tracts, instead of serving as texts to be culled for "facts" relative to Carolingian political, economic, social, or ecclesiastical history, have become mirrors reflecting the emotional dimensions of Carolingian society and revealing the value system that gave direction to the lives of an entire society. Material objects originally fabricated to support daily life and its routine round of activities have yielded insights into such important ingredients of cultural life as tastes, relations between human beings and nature, attitudes toward death, and concepts of pleasure and pain. In short it no longer suffices to depend on a relatively narrow body of written texts to reconstruct cultural history. A much more diverse body of evidence must be brought into play in order to see Carolingian culture for what it was.

When added together, these diverse trends perhaps justify concluding that a new Carolingian cultural history is in the making, a history crafted in large part in response to powerful ideological forces that have combined during the last half century to redefine how the past is approached. Awareness of what is involved in this development will serve as a reminder that the reconstruction of the cultural history of the Carolingian era has always been something more than a dispassionate, objective pursuit of the "noble dream" of scientific history aimed at delineating, in the Rankean sense, the past as it actually was. In important ways the cultural history of that distant age has been contemporary history, seeking to employ knowledge of what happened in the past as a medium through which to speak intelligibly to issues that living historians and their living audiences have thought significant in a context defined by their current intellectual vision, their societal concerns, and their system of values. It has been that quest for meaning within the context of the present that has given vitality, excitement, and even passion to what might otherwise be sterile discourse on a dead past. By the same token it has been that search for the relevance of Carolingian cultural life to an ever changing present that has generated new issues and new challenges of sufficient magnitude to require the constant rewriting of Carolingian cultural history.

❖

The exploration of Carolingian cultural life has been affected by another set of factors. Appearances to the contrary, historians do not operate exclusively in the realm defined by ideas and their interplay; they also live and work—along with almost everyone else—in a social milieu shaped by institutional patterns, material resources, professional practices, group mores, and personal concerns. This volatile realm generates its own subtle forces determining the way historians work and shaping the products of their investigation. What transpires in that space, which probably deserves to be called the sociology of historical scholarship, needs greater attention than it is given by those seeking to understand the dynamics of historical inquiry.

In the context of the historiography of Carolingian cultural life, only one small but highly significant aspect of that larger subject warrants comment. That has to do with the composition of the scholarly community concerned with Carolingian cultural history. Until well into the twentieth century that community was dominated by continental Europeans, particularly by French-, German-, and Italian-speaking scholars, predominantly male, whose national identities, education, social status, institutional attachments, cultural values, and gender provided a distinctive perspective from which to view the past. Then within a brief span of time, especially the decade or two after World War II, the community of Carolingianists began to expand numerically and reflect a changing ethnic and gender mix, a process that has continued unabated. That trend has manifested itself in the increasingly transnational composition of congresses devoted to Carolingian history and in the authorship of the contributions made to multi-authored syntheses treating Carolingian culture noted above. Even more noteworthy is the fact that the annual bibliographies chronicling the progress of Carolingian studies have increasingly recorded significant studies by Spanish, Scandinavian, Polish, Russian, Japanese, and above all English and North American scholars.[46] Most important of all is the increasing number of women who have assumed a significant role in the study of the Carolingian age.

Given the temporal, spatial, and cultural remoteness of the Carolingian world from many of the new participants in Carolingian studies, why this universalizing of Carolingian studies has occurred raises intriguing questions. It goes without saying that the increasing presence of women in the community of Carolingianists is in large part a salutary consequence of the struggle defined by the feminist movement in general and of the demonstrated capability of female scholars to perform in an exemplary fashion once given a chance to do so. Certainly the quest of many Europeans to find their common roots after the trauma resulting from political, economic, and ideological divisiveness of the late nineteenth and early twentieth centuries encouraged scholars from European nations to seek out each other and listen to one another.

The restricted boundaries of the Eurocentered scholarly world were increasingly erased by the intensification of scholarly exchange made possible by technological advances permitting speedy, affordable travel, the subsidization of research by public agencies and private foundations, and the rapid transfer of information made possible by a variety of technological advances. The scholarly diaspora that occurred just before, during, and immediately after World War II had an especially significant impact on Carolingian studies, particularly in the Anglo-American world.[47] But perhaps above all else the universalizing of Carolingian studies owed most to the maturation of historical consciousness on a global scale and the onset of some remarkable scholarly entrepreneurship in support of Carolingian studies exercised in settings other than a continental European space bounded in rough terms by interlocking spheres of influence emanating from Paris, Berlin, and Rome.

The universalizing of the scholarly community concerned with Carolingian studies poses an intriguing issue: what has been the effect of this development on that enterprise? While that question has not been addressed in a systematic way, one suspects that closer inquiry would unearth some notable points that would tell a great deal about the recent course of Carolingian historiography.[48] The expanding cadre of Carolingian scholars includes individuals whose education and professional training differ in marked ways from that of the scholarly circle that traditionally dominated Carolingian studies. Many of those who have joined the ranks of Carolingianists during the last two generations have emerged from a social milieu that has endowed them with concerns, values, and perspectives contrasting sharply with those of earlier generations of Carolingianists. Their scholarly and teaching functions have been situated in institutional settings that have demanded that they speak to audiences whose interests in the past and levels of susceptibility to historical insights have been quite different from those audiences to whom earlier Carolingianists spoke. Their spatial, cultural, and emotional distance from a scholarly community that formerly carried the torch for old Francia allowed some salutary head clearing.

All of these sociological factors surrounding the changing composition of the community of Carolingian scholars have combined to create a yeasty brew that has broadened, deepened, redirected, and—perhaps most important—enlivened inquiry into the nature and significance of Carolingian cultural life. The future of Carolingian studies will undoubtedly depend in crucial ways on how the bonds uniting that diverse community are cultivated and expanded and in what ways the unique insights rooted in diverse economic, social, ethnic, gender, and educational backgrounds that characterize the modern scholarly community and its audiences are brought to bear on a particular segment of the past.

❖

The studies that follow seek to treat selected aspects of Carolingian cultural history in a way that will simultaneously utilize the rich scholarly tradition just described and respond to new conceptual and methodological challenges as the point of departure for an attempt to rewrite that history. Each chapter seeks consciously to make its readers aware of the *état de question* on the matter it treats; each can be read by those beginning their venture into Carolingian history as a convenient summation of the prevailing scholarly consensus on what is known and understood about that subject. No less consciously each study attempts to move current knowledge and understanding of Carolingian cultural activity onto a new plane; already established specialists in Carolingian cultural history may find reasons in these essays to reevaluate and perhaps even readjust their current views.

Those reading these chapters should be alert for the devices employed by their authors to achieve the dual end of summarizing existing scholarly positions and advancing to new levels of understanding. These strategies include the following: approaching established scholarly positions with respectful skepticism; rereading the historical sources in search of historical data heretofore undetected in them; reformulating the questions to which the sources are asked to speak; rearranging and recombining the factual data revealed by the sources into new narrative and analytical patterns; reinterpreting the signification of the surviving historical record in the light of new analytical and conceptual tools that expand the comprehension of the processes affecting human societies; rearranging surviving data into narrative and analytical treatments that provide new levels of comprehension and explanation of what happened in the past. The judicious pursuit of such scholarly operations is not apt to produce quantum leaps into new terrain; the chapters that follow are not fundamentally revisionist in intent or result. Rather they seek to expand incrementally upon what is known and understood about a segment of the past. To the extent that each study achieves this objective it contributes an ingredient that is absolutely essential to the sustenance of vitality in historical scholarship: the constant establishment of new vantage points from which the process of reconstructing the past can proceed.

While each chapter has its own unique contribution to make to the rewriting of the history of different aspects of Carolingian cultural activity, collectively these studies are linked by central concerns that give them cohesion. Without consciously seeking to do so, each author has brought to the fore certain points that are echoed by the other authors. These shared views come into focus in a way that reveals where the cutting edge of scholarly endeavor relative to Carolingian culture is now located and that provides indications of the direction in which inquiry about Carolingian thought and expression is currently moving. The common grounds undergirding the collaborative enterprise represented by this volume are well worth noting at this point as a means of focusing attention on what is most essential in the studies taken collectively.

First, all of the chapters point up the crucial importance of approaching Carolingian cultural activity in terms of the specific historical context in which any particular activity occurred. The repeated sounding of this note in matters pertaining to education, artistic expression, scriptural exegesis, musical practice, and theological discourse strongly suggests that future scholars treating Carolingian cultural activities will pay greater attention to Carolingian history in the broadest sense than was the case with their predecessors. Such a shifting of perspective may counteract the recent vogue of detaching all matters that have anything to do with thought, expression, and communication in any form from any context beyond language itself. And it may mute the prevailing tendency to treat cultural phenomena within a framework defined primarily by the abstract, detached, universalized concepts and categories that surround contemporary disciplinary thought and practice.

To respond to this evolving perception of what constitutes the appropriate contextual framework for describing and explaining intellectual and artistic life, Carolingian cultural historians will perforce need to immerse themselves more deeply in the general history of the Carolingian age. No less significantly, historians of all facets of the Carolingian world will need to be sensitive to the relevance of their investigations to Carolingian cultural life. In brief, these chapters collectively suggest that when the Carolingian age is discussed in the future, its cultural history will increasingly constitute an integral part of the total picture rather than an appendage to the larger historical setting, sometimes tacked on as an afterthought little related to the main scene.

Second, the essays in this collection highlight the fruitfulness of an interdisciplinary approach to Carolingian cultural activity, thereby suggesting that future research should and most likely will give greater importance to that approach. As is implicit in the points made in my comments on the context of Carolingian cultural activity, the new level of understanding of cultural life that can flow from interrelating cultural history with political, economic, social, and religious history will by definition depend upon interdisciplinary inquiry. Even more important are the insight and the understanding that can result from expanded dialogue among the practitioners of the scholarly disciplines whose focus is primarily on cultural activity: literature, art, music, theology, philosophy, linguistics, education.

The studies in this volume abound in examples of such fruitful cross fertilization. John J. Contreni's treatment of educational practice throws light on the content and form of literary composition and shows that an understanding of the basic characteristics of Carolingian literature illuminates what was learned and how. Bernice M. Kaczynski and Lawrence Nees show how creations in the visual arts clarify the meaning of literary texts and how literary texts explicate the motifs and forms given expression in the visual arts. Richard L. Crocker demonstrates how liturgical needs, spiritual concerns, and the organizational structures of monastic and canonical communities help to explain how and why a borrowed musical tradition was adapted and reshaped. Thomas F. X. Noble shows how political ideology takes on new meanings when concepts rooted in theology and scriptural exegesis are brought to play and how esoteric theological precepts find fresh relevance in shaping effective political polemic and molding historical consciousness. Such examples provide persuasive evidence that any scholar investigating a particularized aspect of Carolingian cultural activity needs not only to know what colleagues concerned with other facets of cultural life are doing but also that he or she should become more familiar with how others do their work.

Third, the studies in this volume are marked in a special way by a concern on the part of their authors for how the products of the Carolingian cultural revival were actually utilized. This interest goes beyond defining how the creators of cultural artifacts or those who patronized their activities intended such creations to be used and minimizes the tendency among cultural historians to elevate the phenomena they explore into an esoteric realm beyond the mundane, often messy, and not always inspiring terrain where most human activity transpires. Instead, these chapters focus attention on the impact that specific aspects of learning and artistic expression had on the real world of the eighth and ninth centuries. How an individual master in a particular school taught and what individual students learned emerge from Contreni's rereading of the historical record. How music was performed by real people in real churches becomes evident in Crocker's study. How scriptural exegetes and manuscript illuminators applied interpretive techniques to specific biblical passages and with what precise results come into clear focus in Kaczynski's essay dealing with how an unlikely figure became a cultural hero in a new age. The ways in which visual artists and theologians utilized their métiers to make statements about real political situations are set forth in concrete terms by Nees and Noble. Especially illuminating to many students of the Carolingian world will be the ways in which Crocker, Kaczynski, Nees, and Noble make music, art, and theology bear witness to the realities of the Carolingian world. Their studies suggest that a new day is at hand for a fruitful dialogue among those who have trouble dealing with a real problem, both Carolingian and modern: what is the relationship between the written word and the visual image?

In its total effect, the emphasis given in these chapters to the uses to which cultural activity were put adds a dimension of concreteness to cultural life. And it opens significant channels for integrating every facet of cultural life into the total fabric of Carolingian society in ways that make thought and expression more central and more relative to that society than has often been the case in past treatments of Carolingian intellectual and artistic life. Without assuming a position of stridency in advocating any particular school of thought about cultural history, the authors of the chapters that follow have demonstrated that thought and expression are indeed close to the lifeblood that nourishes any community at any moment in history.

Fourth, these studies produce results that when taken together highlight the uniqueness of the Carolingian cultural accomplishment in terms that reinforce the claim that the Carolingian period deserves to be viewed as a discrete segment of the historical continuum. The basis of that claim hinges on how any society responds to what is probably the crucial factor in shaping its destiny: the reception and use of tradition. In one way or another each chapter highlights the unique and creative ways in which the entire Carolingian cultural establishment—school masters, students, writers, scriptural exegetes, artists, cantors, liturgists, theologians, political polemicists, even patrons—appropriated and adapted components of an inherited cultural tradition to serve the complex, constantly changing, and newly discovered needs of a particular society.

Like many of their predecessors, the authors of these studies are aware of the ongoing need to discover what components of that tradition were recovered during the Carolingian age, how that process proceeded, and what of the recovered treasure was transmitted to later ages. But beyond that remains a more fundamental issue: what happened to that tradition? If one can judge by what emerges from the studies in this volume, the Carolingian cultural establishment reworked, reinterpreted, and rearranged major segments of that inheritance to create a wide range of unique cultural artifacts that had a significant impact on the way life was understood and how an entire society arranged its collective existence. It is that achievement that defines the uniqueness of the Carolingian cultural renewal. In brief, it would seem that the concept of renaissance is returning to center stage to provide the interpretive model that gives focus and direction to the description, analysis, and explanation of Carolingian cultural life.

Finally, there may be discernible in these essays a glimpse of the scholarly paths that must be taken to fill a major lacuna in Carolingian studies as a whole: the absence of a synthetic treatment of Carolingian cultural life that provides a holistic picture of what happened in that spectrum of Carolingian society. To meet that need requires a kind of treatment beyond what currently passes for synthesis: manuals that patch together a panoramic picture describing what happened in different realms of cultural activity;[49] histories treating in relative isolation discrete aspects of Carolingian cultural activity;[50] and collections of studies dealing with selected aspects of cultural activity at particular moments in Carolingian history.[51] The chapters that follow suggest what needs to be done to reach a new level of synthesis.

Carolingianists must work together to fashion treatments of Carolingian cultural activity derived from a firm grasp of a myriad of discrete cultural events, each understood in terms of its unique context. Interconnections linking diverse facets of cultural activity must be established on firmer ground as a means of identifying overarching themes that give shape to proper synthesis. Specific cultural developments must be synchronized more precisely in chronological terms so as to detect development on the entire cultural scene. Activities related to learning, thought, and expression must be integrated more closely into the total pattern of Carolingian society in search of a fuller understanding of how cultural phenomena affected all aspects of Carolingian life. Conceptual paradigms that are helpful in defining the general processes involved in cultural creativity and dissemination need to be applied by design to the total array of cultural activities as a means of imposing a comprehensible order on what is otherwise inchoate.

In short, scholars interested in Carolingian cultural history need to dedicate part of their collective effort to a special kind of intellectual enterprise consciously aimed at knitting together all that they know and understand about every individual facet of cultural activity into a single picture that retains the identity of each piece while enhancing its significance by locating it in a larger setting that has its own order of meaning. That will be a formidable task, but to sense its demands may represent a significant step toward achieving a holistic reconstruction of what was really involved in the Carolingian revival of culture.

All of which brings us back to where we started. This book seeks to describe and explain what happened in selected realms of intellectual and artistic life during the eighth and ninth centuries. Need we think that what happened then—a mind-boggling twelve centuries ago—means nothing? Before anyone whose mind is open to any enterprise that might allow a better understanding of the human condition responds, he or she must read on. What follows may—indeed, will—help resolve issues that are of fundamental importance to how any intelligent person responds to the world in which we all live and how any society sustains its civility: What does the past mean? Why is that meaning of importance?

Notes

1. Quoted by Russell Jacoby, "A New Intellectual History?" p. 406. Suggestive on the current travails of intellectual history are Dominick LaCapra and Steven L. Kaplan, eds., *Modern European Intellectual History: Reappraisals and New Perspectives*; Donald R. Kelley, "Horizons of Intellectual History: Retrospect, Circumspect, Prospect"; Anthony Pagden, "Rethinking the Linguistic Turn: Current Anxieties in Intellectual History"; David Harlan, "Intellectual History and the Return of Literature"; and David A. Hollinger, "The Return of the Prodigal: The Persistence of Historical Knowledge."

2. For some provocative reflections on this problem, see the chapter by David Ganz in this volume. Also helpful is Arnold Angenendt, *Das Frühmittelalter: Die abendländische Christenheit von 400 bis 900*, pp. 24–52.

3. No attempt will be made in this essay to cite examples of scholarly studies that illustrate the general points being made concerning Carolingian historiography; such an effort would produce a scholarly apparatus that would quickly get out of hand. References will be confined to selected studies that help to elucidate the historiographical issues under discussion.

4. Suggestive on the variety of situations to which the term *renaissance* has been applied are Derek Baker, ed., *Renaissance and Renewal in Christian History*; and Warren Treadgold, ed., *Renaissances before the Renaissance: Cultural Revivals of Late Antiquity and the Middle Ages*.

5. See chap. 8 in this volume.

6. Suggestive on this theme are Robert Folz, *Le Souvenir et la légende de Charlemagne dans l'empire germanique médiéval*; Wolfgang Braunfels, et al., eds., *Karl der Grosse: Lebenswerk und Nachleben*, vol. 4: *Das Nachleben*, ed. Braunfels and Percy Ernst Schramm; Werner Goez, *Translatio Imperii: Ein Beitrag zur Geschichte des Geschichtsdenkens und der politischen Theorien des Mittelalter und der frühen Neuzeit*; Walter Ullmann, *The Growth of Papal Government in the Middle Ages: A Study in the Ideological Relation of Clerical to Lay Power*; Folz, *L'Idée d'empire en occident du Ve au XIVe siècle*; *The Cambridge History of Medieval Political Thought, c. 350–c. 1450*, ed. J. H. Burns; Timothy Reuter, ed., *The Medieval Nobility: Studies on the Ruling Classes of France and Germany from the Sixth to the Twelfth Century*; Carl Erdmann, *Die Entstehung des Kreuzzugsgedankens*; Reto R. Bezzola, *Les Origines et la formation de la littérature courtoise en occident (500–1200)*; R. R. Bolgar, *The Classical Heritage and Its Beneficiaries from the Carolingian Age to the End of the Renaissance*; and Kenneth John Conant, *Carolingian and Romanesque Architecture, 800 to 1200*.

7. "Il ne faut connaitre l'histoire de ces temps-là que pour la mépriser." Voltaire, *Essai sur les moeurs et l'esprit des nations*, chap. 94, 12:123.

8. This is a topic that would bear closer examination by those interested in early modern European intellectual history. Suggestive are Siegfried Epperlein, "Karl der Grosse in der deutschen bürgerlichen Geschichts-schreibung"; Arno Borst, "Das Karlsbild in der Geschichtswissenschaft vom Humanismus bis heute"; Rosamond McKitterick, "The Study of Frankish History in France and Germany in the Sixteenth and Seventeenth

Centuries"; and Nikolaus Staubach, "'Das grossen Kaisers kleiner Sohn': Zum Bild Ludwigs des Frommen in der älteren deutschen Geschichtsforschung."

9. I borrow the terminology—although not necessarily the argument—of Norman F. Cantor, *Inventing the Middle Ages*.

10. One suspects that an expanding awareness of this growing "isolation" of the Carolingian age in the total stream of European history was in part the explanation for a series of books appearing in the middle decades of the twentieth century that attempted to define the early Middle Ages as an epoch with its own unique character; illustrative are H. St. L. B. Moss, *The Birth of the Middle Ages, 395–814*; Christopher Dawson, *The Making of Europe: An Introduction to the History of European Unity*; C. Delisle Burns, *The First Europe: A Study of the Establishment of Medieval Christendom, A.D. 400–800*; J. M. Wallace-Hadrill, *The Barbarian West, 400–1000*; William Carroll Bark, *Origins of the Medieval World*; Richard E. Sullivan, *Heirs of the Roman Empire*; and Archibald R. Lewis, *Emerging Medieval Europe, A.D. 400–1000*. (A comparable list of works in German and French could be compiled.) Perhaps that concern persists; see Judith Herrin, *The Formation of Christendom*; Angenendt, *Das Frühmittelalter*; and Roger Collins, *Early Medieval Europe, 300–1000*.

11. J.-J. Ampère, *Histoire littéraire de la France avant le douzième siècle*, 3:31–33.

12. For some illuminating reflections on this issue, see Wallace K. Ferguson, *The Renaissance in Historical Thought: Five Centuries of Interpretation*; Erwin Panofsky, *Renaissance and Renascences in Western Art*; Karl F. Morrison, "The Church, Reform and Renaissance in the Early Middle Ages"; G. W. Trompf, "The Concept of the Carolingian Renaissance"; Janet L. Nelson, "On the Limits of the Carolingian Renaissance"; and Anita Guerreau-Jalabert, "La 'Renaissance carolingienne': Modèles culturels, usages linguistiques et structures sociales."

13. Perhaps this is changing. For example, Pierre Riché, whose efforts to illuminate Carolingian cultural activity have put all Carolingianists in his debt, in his *Les Carolingiens: Une famille qui fit l'Europe*, pp. 310–42 (pp. 325–59 in the English trans.), acknowledges the conventionality of the term "renaissance carolingienne" but chooses to discuss Carolingian cultural activity in terms of "la premier grand épanouissement de la culture européene" ("the first great flowering [?] of European culture" [p. 311; p. 326 in the English trans.]), a culture for which the Carolingians cannot take sole credit. Likewise, Collins, *Early Medieval Europe*, pp. 280–86, subsumes his discussion of Carolingian cultural activity under the rubric "the ideological programme" [of Charlemagne], a discussion prefaced by some remarks on the inadequacy of the term "Carolingian renaissance" to characterize what was essential in Carolingian cultural activity.

14. Rosamond McKitterick, ed., *Carolingian Culture*; the first chapter, by Giles Brown, is found at pp. 1–51.

15. Trompf, "The Concept of the Carolingian Renaissance," pp. 6, 7.

16. Ibid., pp. 7, 25.

17. Some indication of the magnitude of that task relative to Carolingian

written texts is provided by Bernhard Bischoff, "Panorama der Handschriftenüberlieferung aus der Zeit Karls des Grossen." For the full picture,
see E. A. Löwe, *Codices Latini Antiquiores: A Palaeographical Guide to Latin
Manuscripts Prior to the Ninth Century*. The best description of the total
corpus of Carolingian literary sources is Wilhelm Wattenbach, Wilhelm
Levison, and Heinz Löwe, *Deutschlands Geschichtsquellen im Mittelalter:
Vorzeit und Karolinger*.

18. The confidence generated in the nineteenth century that source criticism in
this positivist sense could be reduced to an exact science is illustrated by the
handbooks on methodology produced for historical researchers. The most
famous of these were Ernst Bernheim, *Lehrbuch der historischen Methode*, and
Charles-Victor Langlois and Charles Seignobos, *Introduction aux études
historiques*; both of these works went through many editions. In the same
vein was the development of a special kind of training facility to develop the
skills required to pursue effectively the challenges posed by source criticism.
That instrument was the historical "seminar," developed first in German
universities and then imitated widely elsewhere. Invaluable insight into the
challenges still facing source critics working in this rather traditional mode
can be gleaned from the many studies published under the editorship of
Léopold Genicot in an ongoing series entitled Typologie des sources du
moyen âge (Turnhout, 1972–). Each volume in this series (more than sixty
have now been published) deals with a separate genre of source materials,
seeking to identify its unique features, describe the kind of information that
can be gleaned from it, and highlight the methodological problems inherent
in utilizing the genre. Although the series deals with types of sources drawn
from the entire medieval period, many of the individual studies deal
specifically with types of sources characteristic of the Carolingian period.

19. Worth noting are five efforts to provide a synthetic treatment of Carolingian
cultural activity that have been made during the last four decades. Taken
together they provide a fundamental point of departure for the study of
Carolingian cultural history. Two of them represent efforts to see Carolingian cultural life in its entirety. In 1953 the first of the annual conferences
sponsored by the Centro Italiano di Studi sull'Alto Medioevo was devoted
to Carolingian cultural life; the results were published as *I problemi della
civiltà carolingia*. Most recent is the collection of essays edited by Rosamond
McKitterick, *Carolingian Culture*. The other three sought to provide overall
characterizations of Carolingian culture at particular moments. The 1960s
witnessed the appearance of the landmark collaborative work *Karl der Grosse:
Lebenswerk und Nachleben*, ed. Wolfgang Braunfels, et al. Volume 2, *Das
geistige Leben*, ed. Bernhard Bischoff, and volume 3, *Karolingische Kunst*, ed.
Braunfels and Hermann Schnitzler, focused on Carolingian cultural life. On
a somewhat lesser scale were two significant collections of studies attempting
to provide an overview of cultural life in the times of Charles the Bald and
Louis the Pious: Margaret T. Gibson and Janet L. Nelson, eds., *Charles the
Bald: Court and Kingdom*; and Peter Godman and Roger Collins, eds.,
Charlemagne's Heir: New Perspectives on the Reign of Louis the Pious (814–

840). Despite the many virtues of these works, most scholars would probably agree that they leave something to be desired as syntheses.

20. Helpful in providing some sense of these complex developments are the following works: Jacques Le Goff and Pierre Nora, eds., *Faire de l'histoire*; Georg G. Iggers and Harold T. Parker, eds., *International Handbook of Historical Studies: Contemporary Research and Theory*; Michael Kammen, ed., *The Past Before Us: Contemporary Historical Writing in the United States*; Ernst Breisach, *Historiography: Ancient, Medieval and Modern*, pp. 268–411; Iggers, *New Directions in European Historiography*; Leonard Krieger, *Time's Reason: Philosophies of History Old and New*; Peter Burke, ed., *New Perspectives on Historical Writing*; and Henry Kozicki, ed., *Developments in Modern Historiography*.

21. Of special interest to Carolingianists in terms of the reediting of important written texts is the ongoing project undertaken by Benedictine Abbey of Steenbrugge and Brepols Publishers of Turnhout, Belgium, to create what has been heralded as a "new Migne" containing new editions of previously edited texts that will meet modern editorial standards. The newly edited texts most relevant to Carolingian studies are appearing in two series, entitled Corpus Christianorum, Series Latina, and Corpus Christianorum, Continuatio Mediaevalis (full citation given in List of Abbreviations). Hardly less noteworthy is the ongoing effort of the Monumenta Germaniae Historica to make available editions of key Carolingian sources; the progress of the editing activities of the MGH is chronicled in the annual volumes of *Deutsches Archiv für Erforschung des Mittelalters.*

22. Much of what represents new source material in this area depends on the work of archaeologists. Unfortunately, there is no convenient study that provides a general overview of the present state of Carolingian archaeological investigations, particularly as they relate to cultural history, and that suggests what the future agendum of that enterprise might be. Although their emphasis is primarily on economic conditions, some sense of the possibilities can be gleaned from the following works: Franz Petri, ed., *Siedlung, Sprache und Bevölkerungsstruktur im Frankenreich*; Herbert Jankuhn, *Einführung in die Siedlungsarchäologie*; Jankuhn and Reinhard Wenskus, eds., *Geschichtswissenschaft und Archäologie: Untersuchungen zur Siedlungs-, Wirtschafts-, und Kirchengeschichte*; Joachim Werner and Eugen Ewig, eds., *Von der Spätantike zum frühen Mittelalter: Aktuelle Probleme in historischer und archäologischer Sicht*; Richard Hodges and David Whitehouse, *Mohammed, Charlemagne, and the Origins of Europe: Archaeology and the Pirenne Thesis*; and Klaus Randsborg, *The First Millennium A.D. in Europe and the Mediterranean: An Archaeological Survey*. Although not everyone will agree with all its authors' conclusions, the magnificent work of Walter Horn and Ernest Born, *The Plan of St. Gall: A Study of the Architecture and Economy of, and Life in a Paradigmatic Carolingian Monastery*, illustrates how archaeological evidence can illuminate Carolingian cultural history. Also suggestive is Carol Heitz, *La France pré-romane: Archéologie et architecture religieuse du haut moyen âge du IVe siècle à l'an mil.*

23. Developments in this area are occurring on so many diverse fronts that it is difficult to get a firm fix on the present state of the art, especially for one whose understanding of and competence in electronic data management have progressed about as far as Charlemagne's competence in writing. Some sense of the potential of computer technology for Carolingianists can be gained from the computerized word lists being prepared for each of the texts now published in the Corpus Christianorum series. Each of these elaborate indexes will eventually be combined to create a common thesaurus of all the Latin fathers that will open vast opportunities for comparing their ideas, tracing influences, and charting changes in thought patterns. But perhaps the impact of computer technology illustrated by this example will be dwarfed by more far-reaching consequences affecting the way people think and communicate their thoughts; on this possibility, see, e.g., Mark Poster, *The Mode of Information: Poststructuralism and Social Context.*

24. I have found the following useful introductions to the vast and confusing arena of modern literary criticism and linguistic theory: D. W. Fokkema and Elrud Kunne-Ibsch, *Theories of Literature in the Twentieth Century: Structuralism, Marxism, Aesthetics of Reception, Semiotics*; Jonathan Culler, *On Deconstruction: Theory and Criticism after Structuralism*; Terry Eagleton, *Literary Theory: An Introduction*; John E. Toews, "Intellectual History after the Linguistic Turn: The Autonomy of Meaning and the Irreducibility of Experience"; and Lee Patterson, *Negotiating the Past: The Historical Understanding of Medieval Literature.* See also the essays collected in a special issue of *Speculum* under the general title "The New Philology," ed. Stephen Nichols. For the visual arts, see E. H. Gombrich, *Ideals and Idols: Essays on Values in History and in Art*; Hans Belting, *The End of the History of Art?*; David Freedberg, *The Power of Images: Studies in the History and Theory of Response*; Francis Haskell, *History and Its Images: Art and the Interpretation of the Past*; and, more sharply focused on the early Middle Ages, the essays in *Testo e immagine nell'alto medioevo.*

25. Illustrative of issues at stake in this debate are Gertrude Himmelfarb, *The New History and the Old*; Peter Novick, *That Noble Dream: The "Objectivity Question" and the American Historical Profession*; and *"AHR Forum*: The Old History and the New."

26. There is a huge literature on the Marxist interpretation of history; helpful are William H. Shaw, *Marx's Theory of History*; G. A. Cohen, *Karl Marx's Theory of History: A Defence*; Melvin Rader, *Marx's Interpretation of History*; Paul Q. Hirst, *Marxism and the Writing of History*; S. H. Rigby, *Marxism and History: A Critical Introduction*; and Paul Wetherly, ed., *Marx's Theory of History: The Contemporary Debate.*

27. Useful on this subject are Bruce Mazlish, ed., *Psychoanalysis and History*; Jacques Barzun, *Clio and the Doctors: Psycho-History, Quanto-History, and History*; D. E. Stannard, *Shrinking History: On Freud and the Failure of Psychohistory*; Peter Loewenberg, *Decoding the Past: The Psychohistorical Approach*; Peter Gay, *Freud for Historians*; Geoffrey Cocks and Travis L. Crosby, eds., *Psycho/History: Readings in the Method of Psychology, Psychoanalysis, and History*; William McKinley Runyan, ed., *Psychology and*

Historical Interpretation; and Mazlish, *The Leader, the Led, and the Psyche: Essays in Psychohistory.*

28. The *Annales* school is so called after the journal that, since its founding in 1929 under the title *Annales d'histoire économique et sociale* (changed after World War II to *Annales: Economies, Sociétés, Civilisations*), has been the showcase for *Annales* scholarship. For the main features of *Annales* history, see Le Goff and Nora, eds., *Faire de l'histoire*; Traian Stoianovich, *French Historical Method: The Annales Paradigm*; Lynn Hunt, "French History in the Last Twenty Years: The Rise and Fall of the *Annales* Paradigm"; François Dosse, *L'histoire en miettes: Des "Annales" à la "nouvelle histoire"*; and Philippe Carrard, *Poetics of the New History: French Historical Discourse from Braudel to Chartier.*

29. Insightful introductions to this subject are provided by Jacques Le Goff, et al., eds., *La Nouvelle histoire*; and Theodore K. Rabb and Robert I. Rotberg, eds., *The New History, the 1980s and Beyond: Studies in Interdisciplinary History*. The works cited in n. 20, above, also provide useful information.

30. For brief descriptions of this approach see Le Goff, "Les Mentalités: Une Histoire ambiguë"; Philippe Ariès, "L'Histoire des mentalités"; and Volker Sellin, "Mentalität und Mentalitätgeschichte."

31. Any attempt to provide a suitable bibliography covering this development is beyond the scope of this study. Helpful are the works cited in nn. 20 and 24, above, to which should be added LaCapra and Kaplan, eds., *Modern European Intellectual History.*

32. It is not entirely clear to me whether historians have as yet made a sure fix on the importance of the ideas of Derrida and Foucault in shaping historical inquiry concerning culture. Anyone wishing to tackle this subject might begin with the writings of these authors, especially Derrida, *Of Grammatology*, and Foucault, *The Archaeology of Knowledge*. There is a massive literature that seeks to respond to this challenge; useful to me have been E. M. Henning, "Archaeology, Deconstruction, and Intellectual History"; Allan Megill, *Prophets of Extremity: Nietzsche, Heidegger, Foucault, Derrida*; and Megill, "The Reception of Foucault by Historians."

33. Insightful on these issues are Walter J. Ong, *The Presence of the Word: Some Prolegomena for Cultural and Religious History*; Eric Havelock, *Origins of Western Literacy*; Brian Stock, *The Implications of Literacy: Written Language and Models of Interpretation in the Eleventh and Twelfth Centuries*; Harvey J. Graff, *The Legacies of Literacy: Continuities and Contradictions in Western Culture and Society*; Jack Goody, *The Interface between the Written and the Oral*; McKitterick, *The Carolingians and the Written Word*; Stock, *Listening for the Past: On the Uses of the Past*; and Michel Banniard, *Viva Voce: Communication écrite et communication orale du IVe au IXe siècle en occident latin.*

34. Insight into the relationship between currents in modern literary criticism and cultural history are explored by Hayden White, *Metahistory: The Historical Imagination in Nineteenth-Century Europe*; White, *Tropics of Discourse: Essays in Cultural Criticism*; Frank Lentricchia, *After the New Criticism*; LaCapra, *History and Criticism*; Derek Attridge, Geoff

Bennington, and Robert Young, eds., *Post-structuralism and the Question of History*; Bryan D. Palmer, *Descent into Discourse: The Reification of Language and the Writing of Social History*; and Thomas Brook, *The New Historicism and Other Old-Fashioned Topics*.

35. The best introduction is Hunt, ed., *The New Cultural History*. In her introduction to this collection, Hunt suggests the convergence of various approaches in the new cultural history in these terms: "Are we headed here for . . . an ending that promises reconciliation of all contradictions and tensions in the pluralist manner most congenial to American historians?" (p. 22). A seminal figure in shaping the approach of the new cultural history has been the American anthropologist Clifford Geertz, especially in his *The Interpretation of Cultures: Selected Essays*, in which he wrote a kind of manifesto for the new cultural history: "Believing with Max Weber, that man is an animal suspended in webs of significance he himself has spun, I take culture to be those webs, and the analysis of it to be therefore not an experimental science in search of law but an interpretative one in search of meaning" (p. 5). For English speakers, perhaps the kind of history produced by Robert Darnton, Natalie Zemon Davis, Carl Schorske, and Peter Gay will serve to illustrate the new cultural history.

36. The discussion of this issue found its way into print under the title *Karl der Grosse oder Charlemagne? Acht Antworten deutscher Geschichtsforscher*, a work that reflects many of the worst features of Nazi German nationalism. The nomenclature used by Charlemagne's contemporaries designating him "father of Europe" has been brought to our attention by Donald A. Bullough, "*Europae Pater*: Charlemagne and His Achievements in the Light of Recent Scholarship."

37. Riché voiced this sentiment touchingly in his dedication to *Les Carolingiens*: "Pour mes enfants et mes petits-enfants, citoyens de l'Europe du troisième millénaire" (p. 7).

38. Pirenne's seminal work *Mohammed and Charlemagne* is still worth reading, especially by those just venturing into the world of the Carolingians. The effort to evaluate Pirenne's thesis has produced a vast literature. For recent assessments of the state of the question, see Hodges and Whitehouse, *Mohammed, Charlemagne, and the Origins of Europe*; *La Fortune historio-graphique des thèses d'Henri Pirenne*; and Léopold Genicot, "'Mahomet et Charlemagne' après 50 ans."

39. For some remarks on this issue, and a guide to essential literature treating it, see Sullivan, "The Carolingian Age: Reflections on Its Place in the History of the Middle Ages," pp. 279–87.

40. For some examples illustrating this approach, see Perry Anderson, *Passages from Antiquity to Feudalism*; Chris Wickham, "The Other Transition: From the Ancient World to Feudalism"; Arno Borst, *Lebensform im Mittelalter*; and A. J. Gurevich, *Categories of Medieval Culture*. Indications of new interpretive models shaped by this approach are often found in the articles dealing with the early Middle Ages published in *Annales: Economies, sociétés, civilisations*, *Past and Present*, and *Frühmittelalterliche Studien*.

41. Robert Fossier, *Le Moyen Age*, 2:6.

42. The scholars who in increasing numbers feel comfortable treating Carolingian history within this expanded periodization scheme have been slow to find a captivating name for this new age. However, the direction in which their thinking is moving is suggested by the nomenclature attached to several research institutes under whose aegis some of the most significant research on the Carolingian age has been produced during the last thirty years: the Centro Italiano di Studi sull'Alto Medioevo of Spoleto, the Institut für Frühmittelalterforschung of the University of Münster, the Centre de Recherche sur l'Antiquité Tardive et le Haut Moyen-Age of the University of Paris X-Nanterre. The impact of the Spoleto Centro in shaping this new approach can be measured not only by what has been published in its journal, *Studi medievali* (3rd ser., vol. 1, 1960, et seq.), but also by the volumes containing papers read at the annual Spoleto Settimane, where the international cardinalate of early medieval studies has been gathering for forty years to exchange wisdom about the early medieval world. Hardly less influential have been the studies published in *Frühmittelalterliche Studien* (vol. 1, 1967, et seq.), the scholarly organ of the Münster Institut für Frühmittelalterforschung. Still another journal, *Early Medieval Europe* (vol. 1, 1992, et seq.), devoted to the history of the period extending from the fourth to the eleventh century, promises to serve as a forum for studies that will give clearer definition to that era as a distinctive period in a larger chronological continuum.

43. For more on this point, see chap. 2 in this volume.

44. I refer to "textual communities" as defined by Brian Stock in *The Implications of Literacy* and *Listening for the Past.*

45. Suggestive of the implications for medieval studies of an interpretative approach defined in such terms are the articles collected in a special issue of *Speculum* under the title "Studying Medieval Women: Sex, Gender, Feminism," ed. Nancy F. Partner. See also Hans-Werner Goetz, ed., *Weibliche Lebensgestaltung im frühen Mittelalter.*

46. The influx of American scholars into Carolingian studies is a little surprising in view of strictures uttered early in the twentieth century by an eminent American medievalist to the effect that the history of the early Middle Ages had been so thoroughly investigated that there remained little left to do, a sentiment repeated a half century later by another noted American medievalist; see Bark, *Origins of the Medieval World*, p. 5.

47. In this connection one thinks of the impact on Carolingian studies of such migrant scholars as Wilhelm Levison, Walter Ullmann, Ernst Kantorowicz, and Luitpold Wallach.

48. Some interesting comments on this matter as it pertains to the historical profession in America are provided by Novick, *That Noble Dream.*

49. An enduring monument in English of this kind of synthesis is M. L. W. Laistner, *Thought and Letters in Western Europe, A.D. 500 to 900* (orig. pub. 1931). Equally enduring is Erna Patzelt, *Die karolingische Renaissance* (orig. pub. 1924). Briefer attempts at synthesis are a common feature of larger studies of Carolingian history; useful recent examples include the following: Theodor Schieder, ed., *Handbuch der europäischen Geschichte*, 1:568–79,

622–32; McKitterick, *The Frankish Church and the Carolingian Reforms, 789–895*; McKitterick, *The Frankish Kingdoms under the Carolingians, 751–987*, pp. 140–68, 200–227; Riché, *Les Carolingiens*, pp. 310–42 (pp. 325–59 in the English trans.); Michel Rouche, "The Carolingian Renewal"; Angenendt, *Das Frühmittelalter*, pp. 304–52, 432–57; and Johannes Fried, *Der Weg in die Geschichte: Die Ursprünge Deutschlands bis 1024*, pp. 263–96.
50. Typical works of this nature are cited in chapter 2, n. 21.
51. See n. 19, above, for examples of such works.

2

The Context of Cultural Activity in the Carolingian Age

RICHARD E. SULLIVAN

Among other things this volume is intended to demonstrate—and perhaps even to provide reason for celebrating—the efficacy of scholarly collaboration in illuminating complex phenomena that occurred in the past. It stands to reason that fruitful collaboration depends in part on a common point of reference that can be shared both by cooperating scholars and by those who are informed by their investigations. This chapter is intended to help define such a common ground. It will seek to achieve this end by focusing attention on the larger setting within which a particular historical phenomenon—the cultural revival of the Carolingian age—took shape. It will be assumed that that setting had a significant bearing on the shape the Carolingian cultural renewal took. At least in theory, such a contextual framework should establish a matrix within which various aspects of Carolingian intellectual and artistic activity can be interrelated with some degree of coherence and posit issues that will stimulate further investigation of that subject. To create such a framework requires keeping a focus on the large picture, formulating generalizations, and making bold statements—all scholarly operations surrounded by considerable peril. Such risks seem justified in terms of the ends this chapter seeks to serve in providing a meaningful setting for the more sharply focused studies of Carolingian cultural activity that follow it.

It will not have escaped the attention of most readers, especially Carolingianists, that there are troublesome ambiguities surrounding any attempt to discourse on the context shaping Carolingian cultural activity. Rooted in the very terms selected for the title of this chapter, they need to be identified, and some explanation must be offered concerning what position will be taken on them.

The conscious selection of the singular term *context* as the focus of this essay implies that it is possible to define a single, consistent, all-embracing framework within which to treat the Carolingian cultural renewal. Although such a goal is worth pursuing, we have seen in the previous chapter that a long scholarly tradition has produced several different contextual paradigms within which to consider Carolingian thought and expression. Viewed from a global perspective these diverse approaches are noncomplementary and even contradictory. For anyone familiar with scholarly gamesmanship, this situation offers a golden opportunity for what is particularly alluring to the contemporary scholar: the fabrication of a radical revisionist position on a significant historiographical issue. There will be no response to that siren call in this essay; it is more Protean than Promethean in spirit. Its aim is to suggest how the well-established and fecund contextual approach that presently shapes scholarly scrutiny of Carolingian cultural activity might be expanded, enriched, and refined in ways that will add new dimensions to an interdisciplinary approach to Carolingian culture. It seeks not to fix what needs no fixing but to supply reagents that will increase the potency of an already powerful contextual brew that currently drives the exploration of Carolingian thought and expression.

Another ambiguity embedded in the title of this chapter involves the term *cultural activity*. Readers have a right to assume that this term has a specific meaning that will allow them to focus on a particular subject matter or process. However, they must be warned that Carolingianists are very latitudinarian about the term. Their catholicity is exemplified by the titles of the chapters included in this volume. For Carolingianists, cultural life embraces such disparate topics as education, biblical exegesis, art, music, book production, polemics, and ideology. That is only a small sample of what Carolingianists subsume under the rubric cultural activity, as would be obvious from even a glance at any bibliography attempting to provide a general guide to the study of Carolingian thought and expression. It can be argued that, in the interest of conceptual clarity, Carolingianists should be more precise in ascribing a meaning to cultural activity. That issue will not be addressed in this study. Whatever has survived from the period extending from the early eighth to the early tenth century, in whatever form, as an articulated expression of thought for whatever purpose, will be considered to be a legitimate component of the Carolingian world of culture.

There are even problems associated with the use of "Carolingian" as an adjectival qualifier of "cultural activity." Much of what is called Carolingian culture was a possession shared with earlier and later ages. No one was more aware of or satisfied with this fact than the Carolingians themselves. When Alcuin wrote "I wish to follow the footsteps of the holy fathers, neither adding to nor subtracting from their most sacred writings,"[1] he was voicing the almost universally shared opinion that his age and all generations that followed would be served best by repossessing and safeguarding a sacred and ageless heritage that would be sullied by attaching to it a modifier implying singular possession. Thus, when modern scholars speak of "Carolingian" cultural activity, they must necessarily involve themselves with identifying and explaining what was particular, innovative, and creative about an enterprise whose agents, in the eighth and ninth centuries, perceived themselves as taking possession of and utilizing a fully sufficient cultural heritage. As the title of a recent book so felicitously put it, modern scholars concerned with Carolingian culture must wrestle with *nova antiquitas et antiqua novitas*.[2]

The context sought in this chapter is one that will help to explain how and why Carolingians modified and adapted an inherited cultural heritage. At a time when powerful intellectual currents are modifying traditional periodization paradigms, propounding new interpretive modes that alter how the Carolingian age is understood, and perhaps even threatening to obliterate the era as a discrete segment of the total historical continuum,[3] it is especially critical that Carolingian scholars focus their attention on the uniqueness of the Carolingian age as a means of grasping the import of its accomplishments. Such an objective will be central to this search for the context of the Carolingian cultural renewal.

With the flanks and rear properly guarded, it is time to face the central issue. In setting the context for Carolingian intellectual and artistic life there is a strong temptation to dwell on features of the Carolingian age that impeded thought and expression. Quite aside from the vestiges of the venerable concept of the dark ages, which still gives a negative cast to the modern historical consciousness about anything medieval, the Carolingian record is replete with factors that seem antithetical to the nurture of culture: constrained material resources, anemic societal infrastructures, massive illiteracy, brutality of manners, endemic violence, adherence to diverse and deeply ingrained "primitive" mind-sets running counter to the light of learning. Woven into the very fabric of Carolingian thought was a dark thread of fear and uncertainty that productive and useful cultural activity could not be sustained. That concern was exemplified by a somber observation written in the 840s by Walahfrid Strabo in the prologue of his revision of the *Life of Charlemagne* by Einhard (or Eginhard):

> Of all the kings Charlemagne was the most eager diligently to search for wise men . . . and he thereby made the entire kingdom which God had entrusted to him in a state of darkness and, so to speak, of virtual blindness radiant with a blaze of fresh learning, hitherto unknown to our barbarism. . . . But now once more the pursuit of scholarship is falling back into decline; the light of wisdom is less loved, and is dying out in most men.[4]

A diligent searcher in the Carolingian record can find abundant anecdotal evidence suggesting a superficial, transient dimension to the Carolingian effort to nurture learning and expression. What, for instance, is one to think of a cultural renewal whose chief architect provided in his will that his "great collection of books" should be sold to help the poor?[5] Could not learning have been better served by a royal mandate founding an *Institutum ad Romanum gubernandum* as a repository for the royal library? The importance of learning in the Carolingian world seems somehow diminished by a passage penned by one of its most notable champions, Abbot Lupus of Ferrières. In one of his letters he reports that in his efforts to win back some property, he was tempted to imitate the ancients by "turning to the artifice of erudition," but then decided that would be fruitless. As he put it: "If Vergil himself were to return now and expend all the skill of his three works to win hearts, he would not find a single reader among our contemporaries."[6] How deflating it is to read William of Malmesbury's account of the ultimate fate of one of the most learned of all Carolingians, John Scottus Eriugena. That account says first that John left Francia for England. Does not that fact alone speak volumes about the state of learning in the Carolingian world? Then it reports that John's English students stabbed him to death with their pens because he made them think.[7] The troubles faced by teachers in England obviously predate our generation!

But let us abandon this negative approach. To pursue it further would only result in shaping a contextual framework founded on a riddle: how could cultural life flourish in a world that had nothing working in its favor? A more positive approach is required to account for the fact that intellectual and artistic life did blossom.

⁕

In a study that seeks to enrich and refine current approaches to the context of the Carolingian cultural revival, a logical starting point requires at least a brief excursus on the prevailing contextual framework within which Carolingian thought and expression are examined. As befits any discourse on Carolingian culture, a short exegesis on a scriptural passage will provide the fundamental touchstone to that issue. In Isaiah 9:1–3 we read:

> The people who walked in darkness have seen
>   a great light;
> Upon them who dwelt in the land of gloom
>   a light has shown.
> You have brought them abundant joy and great
>   rejoicing;
> They rejoice before you as at the harvest, as
>   men make merry when dividing the goods.

Every Carolingianist will immediately recognize the metaphorical sense of these words. Those living in darkness were the eighth-century Franks, the land of gloom was Gaul. The great light that came upon them was the light of Christian learning. The "you" who brought abundant joy was Charlemagne, the "philosopher of liberal studies,"[8] the new David who "love[d] to understand the hallowed knowledge of the ancients . . . and to ponder the secrets of holy wisdom."[9] Those who rejoiced at the harvest were an array of Carolingian scholars, poets, clerics, and even lay magnates whose world was made so "radiant with the blaze of fresh learning, hitherto unknown to [their] barbarism"[10] that "the modern Gauls or Franks came to equal the Romans and the Athenians."[11] And those who make merry while dividing the spoils are modern Carolingianists, who, a century and a half ago, came into a priceless benefaction: their own renaissance to describe, explain, and even gloat over.[12]

This playful exegetical exercise comes amazingly close to characterizing the contextual framework that currently shapes the study of Carolingian cultural activity.[13] There was a demonstrable darkness afflicting Gaul during the seventh and eighth centuries, marked among other things by a deterioration of education, expression, religious life, and manners.

Awareness of the encroaching darkness and its political and religious implications,[14] an awareness perhaps nurtured by models of active learning establishments in the Lombard kingdom, Anglo-Saxon England, and Ireland, produced decisive, consciously taken action without which any comprehensible history of Carolingian cultural activity is unthinkable. That action took the form of a public mandate formulated in the late 780s and early 790s by Charlemagne, a ruler deeply concerned with the welfare of his subjects and supported in his aspiration to improve their condition by a court circle that included learned figures from foreign lands where the light of learning burned more brightly than in Francia.[15] Among modern scholars the centrality of Charlemagne's mandate has understandably and rightly provided powerful impetus to treat Carolingian cultural life in the context of public policy. This contextual framework has given prominent place to describing the royal promotion of cultural renewal through legislation and patronage and to assessing the reciprocal impact of the consequent intellectual and artistic activity on the political and religious actions and the consciousness of the Carolingian power establishment.

Given the fact that the nurture of cultural life was elevated to the level of public policy by Charlemagne and was accepted as such by many in the royal circle,[16] it follows that the meaning of the royal mandate has been of central importance in establishing a context within which to approach the Carolingian cultural revival. The search for that meaning has produced a widely shared scholarly consensus: as perceived by Charlemagne and his cohorts, what Frankish society needed to dispel the darkness was to rediscover and apply the "norms of rectitude" that had been formulated and written down in a past age to guide individual and collective Christian behavior.[17] Access to those salvific norms became a critical public issue to which the only response was the encouragement of learning activities. From the perspective of modern scholarship, the reception of tradition became a key component in defining the contextual framework that guided the investigation of Carolingian cultural life. The result has been a vast body of scholarship concerned with how, when, under what circumstances, and to what effect the Carolingian world received a literary and artistic heritage formulated in a distant past.

This contextual framework—featuring a mandate imposed from above by public authority directing cultural activity toward the recovery from the past of norms that would correct and renew society—quite understandably assumed another crucial dimension. Evidence abounds to indicate that Charlemagne and his collaborators were painfully aware that the late eighth-century Frankish world was ill-equipped either to seek or re-

ceive the saving wisdom from the past, which was enshrined in an imposing written corpus. Only education dedicated to improving Latin literacy
offered that world a solution to its disability. As a consequence, education
became the central element of the Carolingian cultural endeavor. And educational issues have provided a major focus for the modern scholarly effort
devoted to the investigation of Carolingian culture. A case could be made
that in relative terms more attention has been given to the role of education in Carolingian society than has been the case for any other era in history. Especially prominent has been the effort to elucidate the creation and
evolution of the educational infrastructure: schools, textbooks, teaching
techniques, scriptoria, libraries, and writing systems. Related concerns include the impact of the educational system on the reception of tradition,
the response of the educational establishment to expanding intellectual
horizons resulting from the absorption of ancient texts, and the impact
of education on the intellectual and creative activities of those involved
in it.[18]

Another important contextual consideration emerges logically from an
approach to Carolingian cultural activity that is fixed on the conscious
public policy that aimed at serving the public weal by recovering traditional wisdom through the instrumentality of education. Scholars have
been prompted to ask what was recovered and how that legacy was utilized.[19] These issues have played a major role in the scholarly treatment of
Carolingian cultural life. The writings of various learned individuals and
the artifacts produced by architects, painters, and sculptors of the Carolingian age have been scrutinized in minute detail in search of answers to
these problems.[20] Various facets of Carolingian cultural life—including
especially the liberal arts in general, grammar and rhetoric, literature, theology and philosophy, political theory and law, ecclesiology, and art[21]—
have been analyzed in terms of the sources undergirding them and the
modifications imposed on these sources by the learned establishment seeking to achieve a *renovatio*. Studies conducted within such a context have
provided cogent demonstrations of the unique and distinctive characteristics and accomplishments of the Carolingian cultural effort. Equally important, this line of investigation has established the grounds upon which
Carolingianists could claim that their era left a significant *Nachleben* giving
shape to post-Carolingian intellectual and artistic life in western Europe.

It can even be argued that the broad contextual framework just delineated has governed the scholarly treatment of the terminus ad quem of
Carolingian cultural history. Unfortunately, one of the perils of periodization schemes involves the need to bring to closure what the paradigm

defines as a unique and distinctive segment in the total continuum of historic time. If there was something that legitimately can be called the Carolingian cultural achievement, then whatever that was must have come to an end. Although the problem of defining the end of the Carolingian age in all its aspects confronts Carolingianists with increasing difficulty,[22] a well-established tradition among historians of the Carolingian intellectual and artistic effort prompts them to end their story early in the tenth century. In arriving at that closure, they speak in contextual terms with which we are already familiar. They sadly note that after 877 the guidance and support extended to cultural activity as a matter of public policy by a Charlemagne or a Charles the Bald gave way to the feeble efforts of what Edward Gibbon called "the dregs of the Carlovingian race . . . a crowd of kings alike deserving of oblivion."[23] With rare exceptions the secularized bishops and abbots of the tenth century were incapable of the cultural vision of their predecessors, who had been prime patrons of learning and art. The educational infrastructure upon which Carolingian learning had been built was eroded by the second wave of external invaders, civil disturbances, and the diversion of ecclesiastical resources into secularized activities centered on building local power bases. The increasingly feudalized world dictated behavioral norms considerably different from the "norms of rectitude" appropriate to a Christian commonwealth defined by Christian learning. The late Carolingian cultural establishment became too set in its ways and too constricted in its intellectual tools to sustain the impetus that originally created it or to respond to the changing world that it had helped shape. In short, Carolingian culture was a victim of the very contextual factors that had once energized it.[24]

Some will undoubtedly charge, probably with good cause, that this characterization of the contextual framework within which modern scholars have approached Carolingian cultural life is overly simplified and excessively schematized. However, by way of summarizing our point, it would not be too far from the mark to argue that most modern treatments of Carolingian intellectual and artistic life fit into—and are given meaning by—a contextual approach that can be given precise articulation in the following terms: The Carolingian cultural renewal was a phenomenon shaped and driven by a conscious public policy aimed at serving the public weal by utilizing education to recover and transmit behavioral norms defined in the distant past. Its achievements can best be assessed in terms of the capacity of its agents to capture, adapt, and apply that tradition in ways that modified the behavioral patterns of a troubled, "backward" society seeking to renew itself.

Perhaps indicative of the general acceptance of and satisfaction with this contextual framework is the fact that the scholarly world concerned with Carolingian cultural life has been remarkably free from disagreements, such as those surrounding the meaning of Charlemagne's imperial coronation, the nature of the Carolingian economy, or the status of the Carolingian nobility. The only note of discord in that community has been an occasional scuffle over whether the Carolingian cultural achievement should be described as a renaissance or a *renovatio*. Did its impetus and achievement center on a rebirth of humanistic culture akin to that of the classical world or on a renewal of society in a moral and spiritual sense? Probably most Carolingianists would join François L. Ganshof in dismissing this distinction as a matter of semantics having little to do with the most fundamental aspects of Carolingian cultural life.[25]

Viewing current Carolingian scholarship in broad terms, there seems no compelling reason to challenge a contextual framework that has served so fruitfully in promoting, guiding, and integrating the study of Carolingian culture or to propose a new one. Perhaps, however, scholars concerned with various aspects of Carolingian thought and expression might profitably consider expanding and refining the contextual approach that presently frames their collective effort. In what follows some suggestions are offered pointing in that direction. No claim of originality is made in identifying certain contextual considerations that might stimulate new lines of investigation and produce new levels of understanding of Carolingian culture. Most of what will be said derives from a general reading of recent Carolingian scholarship devoted to Carolingian society as a whole.[26] The important issue is whether these borrowed insights might add fruitful dimensions to the ways in which scholars are presently inclined to approach Carolingian cultural history.

❈

In defining the context within which they pursue their investigations, Carolingianists concerned with cultural history should consider the need to expand their chronological framework, especially backward. They have long been accustomed to accepting a periodization model that hinges on a decisive turning point in historical development in the middle of the eighth century. Such an approach came easily in the light of the dramatic events in 751 that replaced "do-nothing" Merovingian kings with a vigorous new dynasty that made things happen. That chronological perspective was given persuasive conceptual substance by the famous Pirenne thesis, which entered the full light of day with the publication of Henri

Pirenne's *Mahomet et Charlemagne* in 1937. Pirenne argued that as a consequence of Muslim expansion the unity of the Mediterranean world was
ruptured in the middle of the eighth century, a development that ended
the ancient world and marked the beginning of a new, medieval pattern of
civilization unique to western Europe. In a fundamental sense, the Pirenne
thesis tempted and even convinced many Carolingianists to think that
what happened before about 750 was of minor concern to them as they
sought to delineate the "new" order that began to take shape at a decisive
turning point in history. However, in the half century since the Pirenne
thesis began to assert a decisive influence on Carolingian studies, an ever
increasing body of evidence has been amassed indicating that many essential aspects of Carolingian history can only be explained in terms of civili-
zational patterns that preexisted the so-called dawn of a new age. In brief,
Carolingianists have increasingly had to learn to cope with continuities
rather than to feast on discontinuities.[27]

Scholars concerned with Carolingian culture have, of course, been sensitive to this need to expand their chronological sights backward in time
for a simple reason: a fundamental dimension of Carolingian cultural activity involved the reception of a tradition embedded in earlier literary and
religious texts, art works, and musical compositions from which the Carolingian world felt separated to its peril. Especially crucial were the literary
and religious texts. Modern scholars all know well enough who, in the eyes
of the Carolingians, represented that tradition: God's writ enshrined in
Scripture; a select group of pagan Latin authors; a circle of late antique
religious Fathers, including especially Ambrose, Jerome, Augustine, Boethius, Cassiodorus, Benedict of Nursia, Gregory the Great, and Isidore of
Seville; the Christian poets of late antiquity; and the compilers of liturgical, pedagogical, and legal texts.[28] The models in the visual arts and music
are likewise fairly obvious. On the surface, the challenge facing modern
scholars has seemed simple and straightforward. Their task has been to determine who among the Carolingians took what from that storehouse of
tradition, how the recipients understood what was received, to what use
the acquired wisdom was put, and with what consequences in terms of the
history of thought and expression.

However, any effort to understand the processes involved in the transmission and reception of tradition has another crucial dimension. The
modern scholar is an active agent in reconstructing those processes and in
weighing their consequences. How he or she understands and interprets
the elements of tradition under consideration is a decisive ingredient in
elucidating its transmission to and reception by the Carolingian world.

This reformulation of the well-worn truism that the past is always seen through the prism of the present poses a fundamental methodological question about the treatment of Carolingian cultural life. Have modern scholars been sufficiently sensitive to the role played by their own comprehension of the tradition being absorbed by the Carolingian world in their analysis and explanation of its reception? Have they been sufficiently rigorous in examining their understanding of the authorities who represented the tradition in question to see whether it needs to be refurbished? Or have they been content to treat the sources of authority with which learned Carolingians engaged themselves as fixed quantities, the import of which is a matter of common knowledge and complete consensus? When assessing Hrabanus Maurus's dependence on Isidore of Seville in composing his *De rerum naturis*, evaluating how the disputants in the quarrel over predestination wrestled with the views of Augustine, tracing the extent to which John Scottus Eriugena borrowed from Pseudo-Dionysius in fashioning his *Periphyseon*, or assessing the dependence of the Carolingian architects who designed the new church at Aachen on Byzantine models found in Italy, have Carolingianists proceeded as if everyone knows exactly what Isidore or Augustine or Pseudo-Dionysius or Byzantine artists meant?

While any generalization on this issue is likely to be misleading, there are grounds for concluding that those investigating Carolingian culture seldom face these issues. The consequence is their tendency to proceed as if the tradition being received was a fixed entity, leaving them only to measure how much and how well learned Carolingians appropriated that constant and fixed store of accumulated learning.

As an antidote for this constricting disability it seems obvious that scholars concerned with Carolingian cultural activity must come to view various components of the tradition that nurtured Carolingian learning and expression as entities in perpetual flux, constantly being redefined and reinterpreted by those who make a speciality of investigating and interpreting them and their creators. To cope with that situation will require that Carolingianists expand the chronological context within which they approach Carolingian culture in ways that will make them participants in a larger scholarly universe than has conventionally been perceived as the Carolingian world. In more specific terms, they must become aware of what their colleagues studying the pre-Carolingian world, especially that of late antiquity and the early Middle Ages, are doing to illuminate the meaning of the tradition upon which so much Carolingian thought and expression depended. They must absorb as part of their own mental equipment what is being revealed by modern scholarship about the sense of the cultural artifacts to which the Carolingians turned for their intellectual and artistic sustenance, and they must let the light of that scholarship, dealing with what they too often perceive to be another and different age, shine constantly on their efforts to elucidate Carolingian cultural activity. To cite but a few examples by way of illustrating the point, when Carolingian scholars are discussing the reception of the Rule of Benedict or of Gregory the Great or of Isidore of Seville or of Boethius, they must be certain that they have found and absorbed the works of Adalbert de Vogüé, Carole Straw, Jacques Fontaine, Henry Chadwick, and Jerold C. Frakes.[29]

While the expansion of the temporal context backward to embrace several centuries preceding the Carolingian age will add a needed ingredient to the investigation of Carolingian learning, there still remains the problem of fixing the specific context marking the inception of a distinctive chapter in the history of culture that can be called "Carolingian." In considering this issue scholars need to foreshorten their backward look in order to center attention more rigorously on the eighth century. As already noted, the prevailing contextual approach to Carolingian culture has focused on a conscious policy choice made by Charlemagne at a specific moment in the late eighth century to promote cultural activity of a special kind in the service of a particular politico-religious program intended to renew society. Those who shape their approach to Carolingian cultural life within that context have been willing to consider certain eighth-century preconditions that shaped Charlemagne's cultural program. They note such factors as the availability of men of learning from parts of western Europe where local "renaissances" had recently occurred; the inception of a reforming mentality reflected in religious legislation of Pepin III and Carloman; the impact of missionary figures such as Willibrord, Boniface, Pirmin, and Kilian; and certain activities of Pepin, which some have argued prefigured his son's actions with respect to cultural life.[30] However, on the whole, these preconditions for the revival of Carolingian cultural activity have not been judged decisive in giving shape and form to Carolingian culture. With his usual directness, Walter Ullmann put the point unequivocally: "It was in pursuit of [Charlemagne's] educational policy—exclusively a royal measure and carried through at royal expense—that the literary and cultural phenomenon of a Carolingian Renaissance emerged."[31]

Without diminishing the decisive role played by Charlemagne in giving shape to Carolingian cultural life, Carolingianists need to ask whether there existed in the eighth-century Frankish world forces—other than the royal will that stimulated cultural activity and gave it a particular thrust and substance—that sometimes complemented and sometimes ran counter to the royal renaissance. They need to escape the tyranny asserted over all aspects of Carolingian historiography by a mind-set existing since Carolingian times, which has tended to see everything before and after Charlemagne as either prelude or postlude. Major problems face anyone seeking a contextual perspective on issues related to cultural life during the decades preceding Charlemagne's accession,[32] an era almost as difficult to view on its own terms as is the reign of Louis the Pious.[33] But at least scholars concerned with Carolingian culture should open their minds to the possibility that the entire eighth century should be embraced within the contextual framework they employ as the setting for the Carolingian cultural effort. Perhaps Pope Gregory II knew something that modern scholars have overlooked when, in a letter written to Emperor Leo III in 732, he observed that the civilized East appeared to be returning to savagery and violence while the previously savage and barbarian peoples of the West were becoming civilized![34]

❖

Having considered the advisability of adjusting the temporal framework within which Carolingian cultural life is treated, let us shift our attention to another arena. In the search for contextual factors affecting Carolingian thought and expression, it is perhaps time to ask again whether scholars have given sufficient attention to the full range of interests and aspirations of certain power groups as factors affecting the development of Carolingian cultural life.[35] That issue was especially critical during the eighth century, when power relationships were being redefined under circumstances of considerable flux, which compelled competing interests to seek new modes of defining and legitimating their position.

One might begin with the challenges faced by the Carolingian dynasty itself. Not the least of those concerns was the matter of the dynasty's legitimacy. Although the status of the Carolingian family had been open to challenge from the time of Pepin of Herstal's victory at Tertry in 687, the issue became especially critical as a consequence of Pepin III's deposition of the last "long-haired king" in 751 to clear the way for his ascendancy to the throne and then, not long after, the even more audacious elevation of Charlemagne to the imperial office in 800, acts that smacked of usurpation. Modern scholars have been inclined to argue that election by "the people" (that is, by the *potentes*) and ecclesiastical approval in the form of ritual anointment—buttressed by the unique political abilities of Pepin

III and Charlemagne and by booty fortuitously gained from military victories—sufficed to legitimate the new dynasty.

However, it is far from certain that Pepin and Charlemagne were fully confident that the fate of the *stirps karolinorum* was assured by acclamations of the "people," religious rites, personal political skills, and unpredictable campaigns against the likes of the Aquitainians, Muslims, and Saxons. Their ongoing concern for legitimacy reverberates through the history of the last half of the eighth century. It was reflected in various events: Pepin's poignant request to Pope Zacharias before his deposition of the last Merovingian for guidance in defining upon what the authority to rule was based;[36] the measures taken by Pope Stephen IV during his visit to Francia in 754 to foreclose on future dynastic changes by threatening with anathema anyone who sought to disinherit Pepin's heirs;[37] Pepin's troubles with his half brother Grifo and with his brother Carloman and his sons after Carloman's abdication to become a monk;[38] Charlemagne's attempt to appropriate the Merovingian heritage by giving his twin sons born in 778 names unique to the Pippinid family tradition, Louis (Clovis) and Lothair (Clothair);[39] Charlemagne's consternation with the rebellion in 792 involving his bastard son, Pepin the Hunchback, who "conspired with certain of the Frankish leaders who had won him over to their cause by pretending to offer him the kingship;"[40] and Charlemagne's concern about the meaning of two eclipses that preceded and followed the death of his son Pepin in 810.[41]

Given these uncertainties about the position of the new dynasty, Pepin III and Charlemagne needed above all else to establish their suitability (*idoneitas*) to rule, to provide qualitative dimensions to what Einhard in almost the opening words of his *Life of Charlemagne* described as the "useless royal title" (*inutile regis nomen*) of the last Merovingians. There were various options that would serve this end: royal prowess on the field of battle; strengthening the bonds of kinship and personal dependence; effective management of royal resources; exemplary personal conduct; administrative assertiveness; and mustering the powers of the Church to curry God's special favor.

Pepin and Charlemagne eschewed none of these possibilities. But surely they must have sensed that poets, historians, artists, liturgists, and exegetes could serve to exalt their accomplishments and thereby demonstrate the fitness of their royal line. The feats of their chief models, Solomon and David, were celebrated in the written word and the visual image, as were those of Constantine. The service rendered to some of their Merovingian predecessors by the panegyrics of Venantius Fortunatus was not unknown in the eighth century.[42] The support given by men of learning to the Lombard monarchy provided a model closer at hand.[43] Pepin spent time at the Lombard court in his youth,[44] and Charlemagne turned there for one of the first scholars he recruited, Paul the Deacon, already famous for his historical works and panegyric poems lauding the Lombard rulers.[45]

Soon after 751 the record begins to reflect the light of learning focusing ever more sharply on celebrating the attributes and achievements of those bearing the seed of Arnulf in a way that highlighted their suitability to exercise lordship over the *populus christianus*. A succession of popes discoursed in learned terms on the divine blessing that would fall on Pepin and Charlemagne for their service to St. Peter's "peculiar people."[46] The liturgy of the Church began to be adapted to provide for glorification of the king, and so did the symbols surrounding the royal office and the exercise of power.[47] Chronicles took shape to assure the selective presentation of the passing events in a way that cast the best light on the newly elected royal family.[48] A learned monk at Saint-Denis formulated a prologue for a recension of the Salic law that exalted the Franks as an illustrious race instituted by God and especially their equally illustrious leaders, who since Clovis had worked under the inspiration and protection of Christ to fulfill the divine plan.[49] The papacy matched this lofty characterization of the Franks and especially of their rulers by likening their accomplishments to a new Israel.[50]

Military victories took on special dimensions at the hands of writers, as evidenced by Pope Hadrian's panegyric written following Charlemagne's victory over the Lombards,[51] by the poem entitled *Carmen de conversione Saxonum* composed in 777 at a moment that was apparently assumed to be a decisive turning point in the Saxon wars,[52] and by the verses written to honor Charlemagne's victory over Duke Tassilo of Bavaria in 787. In that last poem the anonymous "Hibernicus Exul" poses a question and receives an answer that offers an important clue to a force giving shape to cultural life. "Do tell me, what is the value of my poetry?" asks the poet, to which the Muse replies that "sweet-sounding praises to the king" are a gift greater than the "enormous load of silver and of gleaming gold" offered by "leading men of the world," a gift that "will remain for all time!"[53] By the 790s many aspects of court life, especially the poetic production of figures like Alcuin, Theodulf of Orléans, and Angilbert, suggest that Charlemagne was almost as interested in learned men who could and would sing his praises as he was in the renewal of Christendom.[54] When Angilbert proclaimed that "David loves poetry . . . David loves poets," there can be little doubt that the royal sentiment stemmed in part from gratitude

for what men of letters had done to define the suitability of the Carolingians to rule.[55]

The theme of *laudatio regis* remained central to cultural life throughout
the entire ninth century, especially in poetry, letters, "mirrors for princes,"
history, biography, and art.[56] Although valiant efforts have been made to
translate this facet of Carolingian learning into the nobler idiom of ministerial kingship and theocratic political theory,[57] it has the unmistakable
odor of literary and artistic effort in the service of a noble family never
quite certain of its hold on a usurped crown. Indeed, one suspects that it
was only in the world of learning that Walahfrid Strabo could find assur-
ance for the categorical affirmation he made in a poem written in 829:
"The ruling dynasty will never fail in its seed / Until in His brilliance the
King appears in a cloud of belching fire!"[58] Scholars need to give closer
attention to the impact that this concern for defining the suitability of
the *stirps karolinorum* for rulership had on Carolingian learning, letters,
and art: on the selection of sources from the storehouse of tradition; on
the adaptation of those sources; on the choices made in literary and artistic forms; on language patterns; on the sensibilities of belletrists and artists in search of patronage; and on historical consciousness. Attention to
these matters might give many aspects of Carolingian cultural activity a
different look.

Another power group in the Carolingian world whose relationship to
cultural activity needs reconsideration is the episcopacy. Raising this issue
is in no sense intended to imply that the Carolingian episcopacy has suf-
fered scholarly neglect. Episcopal involvement in all aspects of Carolingian
life has been investigated in great detail, with special emphasis having been
given to the role of bishops as agents of royal power and religious reform.
That scholarship has not overlooked the episcopal role in the revival of
culture both in general terms and in terms of individual bishops.[59] However, the major thrust of the modern scholarly treatment of the episcopacy
as a force shaping the world of culture has tended to highlight the bishops
as agents engaged in carrying out the royal cultural program, an approach
that has left little room for ascribing an independent role to the episcopacy
in shaping the Carolingian cultural *renovatio*.[60]

Perhaps that approach needs to be reevaluated, especially in light of
changing perspectives on developments during the eighth century.[61] It has
become increasingly clear that from early in that century there developed
in the Christian world considerable tension, if not a crisis, involving a
quest for the locus of authority that would provide direction and cohesion
for Christian society.[62] In dealing with this issue, Carolingian scholarship

has focused attention chiefly on the evolution of two responses: papal monism and ministerial kingship (with due attention to the sustenance these fledgling concepts drew from the vestiges of imperial ideas of lordship of the late Roman Empire still claimed in Byzantium). A third possibility needs to be given greater prominence in elucidating this crucial issue, which would remain central to discussions of governance of Christian society far beyond the eighth century: there existed a venerable tradition ascribing to the episcopacy, acting collegially in council, the right to direct Christian society.[63]

A case can be made that from at least the middle of the eighth century there was clearly present in the Frankish world an impulse on the part of the episcopacy to reclaim that right by articulating a rationale and engaging in a course of action that would justify the entrustment of ultimate authority to the college of bishops, who by virtue of their office were collectively *clarissima mundi luminaria*, as one Carolingian capitulary put it.[64] The revival of this collective episcopal consciousness manifested itself in several ways during the eighth century: renewed episcopal collaboration in church councils after a long hiatus; the positive reaction of the episcopacy to the expanding efforts of the Pippinids to involve bishops in public life under royal direction; episcopal involvement in the change of dynasties; episcopal participation in missionary activity; the less-than-enthusiastic reaction of the Frankish episcopate to the Roman-inspired reform program of Boniface; the quest for episcopal solidarity reflected in the establishment of a prayer brotherhood at the Council of Attigny in 762; and the efforts to reestablish the corporate structure of the clergy reflected in the legislation of the early reforming councils of Pepin III and Carloman and in Chrodegang's *Regula canonicorum*.[65]

Despite the fact that the papal, monarchical, and episcopal concepts of authority often overlapped and interpenetrated one another during the Carolingian age, they all involved an issue fundamental to the shaping of the Carolingian cultural revival. At stake was control of the traditions that defined by whom, through what means, in what ways, and to what ends Christian society should be directed.[66] It almost goes without saying that cultural activities of various kinds were of crucial importance in recovering and interpreting those traditions. There seems to be clear evidence that key figures in the episcopal establishment had realized that connection at least as early as the time when the royal program of cultural revival was launched. The careers of Boniface, Willibrord of Utrecht, Chrodegang of Metz, and Lul of Mainz and the enactments of the earliest reforming councils seem to bear witness to this realization. The promotion of learning and the shaping of its content thus became a basic concern of the episcopacy as a facet of its effort to define its corporate place in a renewed Christian society.

Especially crucial to the bishops' collective aspirations was the control of traditions dealing with what constituted right belief, right cult practices, right morality, right discipline, and right expression, for these were the realms where tradition most clearly afforded primacy to the episcopacy. Likewise, as was patently clear to the ninth-century episcopacy—represented by such redoubtable figures as Agobard of Lyons and Hincmar of Reims—the management of these realms in particular assured a decisive role in controlling Christian society. Even more important, these were matters of central concern to the world of culture in the Carolingian age. Unless modern scholars take into account the aspirations of the Carolingian episcopacy in their efforts to establish the context of Carolingian cultural activity, they are apt to overlook and misconstrue vital aspects of Carolingian cultural life concerned with education, theology, canon law, liturgy, music, art, and architecture.

In setting the context for Carolingian cultural endeavor there may be the need to give greater attention to still another power group in Carolingian society: the aristocracy. Although the political and social status of the Carolingian aristocracy has been explored in great detail in recent years,[67] that group has not received a very positive press from investigators of Carolingian cultural life. The image of the Frankish *potentes* in the face of the Muses was set in stone in Theodulf's verse portrait of the noble courtier Wibod: a brawny, big-bellied, loud-talking, ill-gaited figure whose only reaction to displays of learning and literary prowess was to shake his thick head, cast dark looks, and rain threats on poets when they were not around. As Theodulf pointed out, the only creature worse than this late eighth-century Frankish Babbitt was an Irish expatriate claiming to be learned.[68]

Perhaps this picture is distorted and misleading. There were signs already evident in the eighth-century Frankish setting suggesting that the aristocracy nurtured traditions, felt needs, and had aspirations that could be served by cultural activity conceived in its broadest sense. It should not be forgotten that the Carolingian dynasty had its roots in the aristocratic world; without questioning the efficacy of unction, even papal unction, one might reasonably assume that its bestowal did not instantly reconstruct the family's mentality. Might not the interest in cultural activities shown by the early Carolingians reflect a concern shared by others of the social stratum from which the Pippinids emerged? Charles Martel did break a long-standing tradition by sending his son Pepin to Saint-Denis for his education rather than to a noble court.[69] Another of his sons, Jerome, is reported to have made a copy of the life of his ancestor, Bishop Arnulf of Metz, when he was only nine years old, a feat requiring at least some education.[70] A brother of Charles Martel, Count Childebrand, and his son, Nibelung, played a part in preparing the continuation of the chronicle attributed to Fredegar, a cultural enterprise that undoubtedly served the interests of all the heirs of *stirps karolinorum*.[71] The court of Pepin III was the scene of a variety of activities reflecting a concern with cultural issues.[72]

Evidence of aristocratic interest in culture was not confined to a single family of noble origin. Boniface's visit to a nunnery at Pfalzel in 723 provided the occasion for the noble abbess's grandson, Gregory, the future bishop of Utrecht, to read aloud from a Latin text. Although the young aristocrat had difficulty in explaining the text he read, he was able to comprehend the saint's commentary.[73] The letters addressed to the Frankish aristocracy by the papacy during Pepin III's reign, including one allegedly written by St. Peter himself, seem to presuppose aristocratic responsiveness to learned discourse.[74] A recent study has reminded us that during the early years of Charlemagne's reign—the incubation period of the royal cultural program—the court was dominated by noble laymen.[75] At least in its initial stages, the royal educational program envisaged schooling for lay aristocrats;[76] perhaps the reprimand that, according to the monk of Saint Gaul, Charlemagne heaped upon young nobles who neglected their studies reflects at least some involvement in education by members of that class.[77]

Almost without exception the first generation of native Frankish men of learning, exemplified by Einhard and Angilbert, derived from aristocratic families, suggesting approval of pursuit of learning as an activity befitting noble status.[78] Two of the early literary products of the Carolingian renaissance, Alcuin's *De virtutibus et vitiis Liber* and Paulinus of Aquileia's *Liber exhortationis*,[79] were composed for *homines laicos*, Count Wido of Brittany and Duke Erich of Friuli. In one of his letters, Alcuin commended Erich for his zeal in reading Scripture.[80] In another Alcuin indicated that members of the laity posed questions about the interpretation of Scripture.[81] The fact that Charlemagne thought it important to put into writing the vernacular songs of noble society suggests some cultural sensitivity among aristocrats.[82] Toward the end of the Carolingian period, Otfrid of Weissenburg lamented that the Franks had not taken the trouble to write down the "webs they wove from their wordhoard"; by implication, something had been going on among aristocrats that was culturally valuable.[83]

Nobles collected and patronized art, gathered libraries, and even wrote books, as witnessed by Einhard, Angilbert, Nithard, and most notably the noble lady Dhuoda.[84]

These disparate bits of evidence, indicating that from the eighth century onward the Carolingian aristocracy was more than a culturally inert collection of self-serving individuals and power-seeking kin groups, raise an intriguing possibility. Those of a cynical bent of mind might argue that the Carolingian clerical order sought to exclude the aristocracy from the world of literate culture as a part of its effort to establish its ascendancy. In the case noted above, Alcuin was not comfortable with the knowledge that members of the laity were thinking about the meaning of Scripture without benefit of clergy; one can at least wonder if fear of heterodoxy was his only concern. Nor should we forget that the monastic reforms of Benedict of Aniane tried to restrict aristocratic access to monastic education,[85] and that Louis the Pious openly spurned the "heathen poetry" that appealed to his father and his aristocratic followers.[86]

It is not impossible that these two pillars of clerical culture were applying cultural sanctions against a class whose members were a factor to be reckoned with in the struggle for control of minds that highlighted the reign of Louis the Pious.[87] Perhaps the threat to the learned clerics seeking ascendancy at Louis's court was exemplified by the empress Judith, whose aristocratic background equipped her with cultivated tastes in literature and music. Could it have been that her cultural sophistication enhanced her influence and convinced many clerics that their lot would have been more secure if the reputation of this cultured Jezebel could be ruined?[88]

These reflections suggest that modern scholars may neglect significant aspects of Carolingian cultural life unless they keep the Carolingian aristocracy within their sights as they address issues bearing on Carolingian culture. Obviously, with few exceptions, aristocrats were not creators of cultural artifacts; rather, they were consumers. The evidence suggests that they constituted an audience responsive to many of the currents central to intellectual, literary, and artistic activity: the search for a definition of authority; the concern for the meaning of history; the interest in reconstructing the deeds of saints and warriors; the attempt to define the content of education; the quest for moral norms; the search for proper ways of worship; and the awareness of the pleasures and benefits to be derived from literature, art, and music. Those who promoted the official program of cultural renewal, as well as those who were the creators in intellectual and artistic life, must surely have been aware of the aristocratic audience. It remains to explore more deeply how the existence of that audience influenced the thought and expression of cultural leaders. And that exploration must not disregard the signs that during the ninth century the aristocracy may have been denied a place in the mainstream of cultural development by a clerical *ordo* bent on exploiting cultural forces as instruments of power. There is a possibility that the outcome of that cultural warfare left the unlettered and unrefined aristocracy in a position where it eventually had to develop its own cultural life, one that manifested itself in the eleventh and twelfth centuries in chivalric behavior and the flowering of vernacular literature.

Finally, there is the world of the monks. Many Carolingianists may be taken aback by the suggestion that the relationship between monasticism and Carolingian cultural life needs to be reconsidered. They will rightly point out that the role of monasticism in the Carolingian renaissance has been explored in great depth;[89] the result of that intense investigation has tempted many scholars to equate Carolingian culture with monastic culture.[90] But for all its richness, that scholarship leaves one with the sense that there is still something missing in the assessment of the role of monasticism in shaping Carolingian culture.

Modern scholarship has approached Carolingian monastic culture in what might be characterized as a reactive mode. Almost without exception, monastic cultural activities are described and evaluated as responses to the royal cultural program. The cultural heroes who served as abbots— Alcuin, Hrabanus Maurus, Paschasius Radbertus, Lupus of Ferrières, Hilduin, Walahfrid Strabo, Smaragdus—are portrayed as veritable royal ministers of culture. The monastic establishments over which they exercised their stewardship emerge as workshops where were worked out the details implicit in the official cultural program. This approach is not wrong; it is simply inadequate. It fails to consider whether there was a dynamism in the Carolingian monastic establishment capable of giving a unique and particular shape to the world of culture. Put in terms of defining the context of Carolingian cultural life, the crucial question is this: were there dimensions to Carolingian monasticism that gave it an independent interest in and unique capacity for creative cultural activity beyond the cultural objectives dictated by the royal, episcopal, and aristocratic power structure?

An answer to this question is far from clear, in part because of the limitations of modern scholarship in its portrayal of Carolingian monasticism in institutional terms. That scholarship has failed to produce a convincing picture of what Carolingian monasticism was and what drove it.[91] In its main thrust it has left a negative picture of monastic life and institutions. Monasticism emerges as a kind of directionless avatar buffeted by royal and aristocratic manipulation, misdirected by ambitious and greedy lay abbots, overburdened with wealth and worldly concerns, befuddled by a tentative comprehension of the tradition defining the ascetic ideal and how to achieve it, and plunged into uncertainty and tension by the royal effort to impose on the monastic establishment *una regula et una consuetudine*. In brief, modern scholars find little of significance in the Carolingian phase of monastic history; sometimes those describing Carolingian monasticism seem almost impatient to get on to the tenth-century reforms that excised the rot afflicting the Carolingian monastic establishment.[92]

Perhaps a clearer picture of Carolingian monasticism would emerge if it were approached within a larger temporal framework. Such an approach suggests that the Carolingian era marked a crucial stage in the evolution of western monasticism. It was a time of transition between two contrasting concepts of the place of monasticism in the economy of salvation and in Christian society. Prior to the Carolingian age monasteries were viewed as isolated enclaves, outside the larger Christian community, where individuals worked their way toward perfection free from relationships with the world, which by its nature was irreparably corrupt and inevitably corrupting. Such a conception of the monastery produced different institutional forms: the hermit cell; the transplanted desert of Lérins; the place made magic by the presence of a holy person; the transient camp of the Irish *peregrinus*, with his evanescent following of spiritual groupies; the school for the service of God of Benedict of Nursia. But these models shared a common characteristic: each separate establishment stood alone, needing nothing from other monastic communities or from society at large in order to pursue the strenuous business of opening conduits to the divine, through which grace flowed to select individuals who established their eligibility for that grace by severing all ties with the world. Perhaps in the total perspective of western European monastic history, the period from 400 to 700 can be characterized as an age during which the monastic quest for perfection was organized on an autarkic principle.

Beyond the Carolingian age, say by the year 1000, one encounters a different monastic world. The monks, while still living in individual establishments, now constitute collectively an *ordo* discharging a special role vital to the salvation not only of individual monks but of the total Christian community. The bonds knitting together the members of the *ordo* of monks have been consciously fashioned: a common constitution, a standard regimen of activity, a uniform pattern of worship, a shared mode of interacting with ecclesiastical and political authorities, and a consistent message to the entire Christian community. That new conception of monasticism was mirrored in the Cluniac order and given sharper focus by the new monastic movements of the twelfth and thirteenth centuries. Borrowing again from the language of political economy, monasticism had been collectivized and socialized.

In many ways the Carolingian age appears to be the decisive period in the revolutionary transition from autarkic to collectivized monasticism. The dynamic element in Carolingian monastic life was the search for means that would allow all monks to identify with each other as a distinct component in the Christian community and to define a collective role for monks in the total economy of salvation. An essential corollary in realizing these ends was a reformulation of the traditionally negative ascetic view toward the world in ways that envisaged its goodness and perfectibility. Many aspects of Carolingian monastic life—ranging from involvement of monastic communities in public administration, to concern for the management of monastic property, to the formation of prayer brotherhoods, to the attempt to impose a common rule—make better sense when viewed from this perspective than when treated as reactions to royal, episcopal, or aristocratic pressures of various kinds.

It required neither a great leap of consciousness nor royal ordinances to prompt the monastic world to see that the nurture of cultural activity could be a powerful instrument in the cause of collectivization and socialization of monasticism. In fact, the efficacy of learning as an instrument of personal spiritual advancement was well ingrained in the autarkic monastic world. All that was needed was to extend learning's function to serve the ends of collectivization and socialization. Mastering a common language, writing and speaking according to standard grammatical rules, reading and singing the office from uniform texts, seeking spiritual sustenance from common sources, exchanging reactions to these texts, correcting each other's views on the interpretation of texts, and sharing common visual symbols all served to knit the society of monks together and to make visible and palpable their collective existence. Cultural endeavors also served to develop essential skills promoting the socialization of monasticism. Such activities prepared monks to serve teaching, pastoral, missionary, and administrative roles, all vital functions permitting monks to claim a share in the salvation of society as partners with other agencies in the secular world.

The Carolingian record is replete with evidence that cultural enterprises did serve these ends in the monastic world. That evidence compels one to conclude that, in setting the context for Carolingian cultural life, modern scholars must allow a large place for a unique influence on thought and expression exercised by monks seeking a means to identify with other monks and trying to articulate a distinct role for monasticism in a world no longer satisfied with autarkic monastic communities, where an other-worldly troop spoke to no one but God and then only in an esoteric language appropriate to individual salvation.

⁂

These reflections on possible interrelationships between cultural life and the interests and aspirations of key groups in Carolingian society should serve as a reminder that Carolingian cultural activity in all its forms cannot be divorced from the realities of that age. That point is no less apparent when the search to define the context of Carolingian culture is shifted from particularized interest groups to more generalized aspects of Carolingian society. Such a shift of focus opens wide vistas related to political, social, and economic conditions as factors affecting cultural activity. Considerations of space preclude venturing into these areas in order to focus attention on somewhat more elusive facets of the Carolingian scene that influenced the shaping of cultural life.

The first such topic involves Carolingian religious sensibility and spirituality. In a capitulary issued in 811, Charlemagne posed a poignant question to his bishops, abbots, and counts: "Are we really Christians?"[93] This query should serve as a reminder that a powerful concern of the Carolingian age was a search for the meaning of the Christian experience, both in a collective and an individual sense. That spiritual quest must be given a central place in any attempt to understand the context within which Carolingian cultural life evolved.

Contemporary scholars face formidable obstacles in assessing Carolingian spirituality as a factor influencing culture. Part of the problem lies in a modern value system that makes it difficult to envisage a constructive interaction between the realm of the spirit and that of the intellect. Another difficulty stems from the inadequate picture provided by current scholarship of the spiritual dimensions of the Carolingian world. As one scholar has put it, "the history of the development of Carolingian religious sensibility has yet to be written."[94] Proof of that observation is evident in recent histories of Christian spirituality, which are uniformly thin and tentative on the essence of being a Christian in the Carolingian age.[95] As a consequence, those investigating Carolingian thought and expression receive little help in attempting to weave spiritual factors into the contextual fabric that shapes their approach to cultural life.

There are grounds for arguing that this constricted view of Carolingian spirituality is a by-product of the conventional approach to the Carolingian religious *reformatio* and the way cultural activity has been linked to that endeavor. Carolingian religious renewal has been treated primarily as a magisterial enterprise involving the imposition on society of norms formulated on high by ministerial kings and authoritative bishops, who called into their service agents equipped with the tools of learning that enabled them to extract the norms encased in a well-defined tradition.[96] The specific terms of this legislated reform were given expression in capitularies, conciliar acts, episcopal decrees, canonical collections, liturgical manuals, homiliaries, and penitentials. From this body of prescriptive material, modern scholars have formulated a statement of what the Carolingian age perceived as the essence of being a Christian. With such a definition in hand, the main task remaining in terms of characterizing the spiritual climate of the Carolingian world has been to assess how a prescribed Christianity was received by the society whose salvation was being engineered. The record makes it painfully clear that the authoritarian reformers met almost insurmountable obstacles in persuading their world to accept and live by the prescribed norms of religious rectitude. From this fact it follows that Carolingian society in general was not very Christian and that the age was not particularly significant in the history of Christian spirituality.

It would be not only perverse but also erroneous to dismiss the Carolingian effort to canonize what it meant to be a Christian or to consider inconsequential the efforts of Carolingian authorities, backed by the learned world, to impose a mandated religiosity on a spiritually deficient society. However, overemphasis on that approach veils a deep-seated urge in Carolingian society to seek dimensions of religious experience beyond the acceptance of a few basic credal formulations and the observance of prescribed cult practices. A fuller awareness of that urge is absolutely crucial to the study of Carolingian cultural life because Carolingian spiritual seekers had a profound trust in learning as a source of spiritual fulfillment.

Not ascetic practice, mystical illumination, or even magisterial prescription were sufficient in the search for holiness; books were fundamental. "Only letters are immortal and ward off death, only letters in books bring the past to life . . . and reveal everything in the world that is, has been, or may chance to come in the future," as Hrabanus Maurus put it in one of his poems. Alcuin avowed that in the presence of books, "nothing was lacking that was needed for religious life and the pursuit of knowledge." The value of books for spiritual life was more than the musings of a spiritual elite. The *Admonitio generalis* warned that faulty books led to bad praying among all Christians, a conviction echoed by Theodulf of Orléans in a capitulary directed to the clergy of his diocese, who were exhorted to remember that only reading and prayer were effective in repelling the devil and vice and in nurturing virtue and gaining eternal life.[97]

Perhaps the key to a greater sensitivity to the Carolingian quest for and anxiety about what being a Christian entailed lies in the quandaries posed by the Carolingian effort to appropriate and apply religious tradition. While many Carolingians would have agreed with Alcuin when he wrote, "I wish to follow the footsteps of the holy fathers, neither adding to or subtracting from their most sacred writings,"[98] others were fully aware, as another author (probably Florus of Lyons) put it, that they lived in a "modern" age,[99] which confronted them with religious problems unique to their time for which neither Scripture nor the Fathers offered clear answers.

Nowhere did those inconsistencies and contradictions become more evident than when Carolingian scholars grappled with dogmatic issues.[100] The same Florus reminded contemporaries of the challenge facing "moderns": it was easy for "the devoted and simple reader" to become confused by "the great and multiple arguments" of Augustine.[101] The Carolingian age knew and appreciated the Augustinian idea that God's plan unfolded over time, with each generation responsible for interpreting that plan to fit its particular situation.[102] Some learned Carolingians might complain, as did Alcuin, that a scourge on their age involved those who took "pleasure in making up a new terminology for themselves and who [were] not content with the dogma of the holy fathers."[103] But others could also appreciate with equal conviction the spiritual gain that might be gleaned from such inventiveness, from heeding Irenaeus's admonition that tradition "was not transmitted in writing, but by the living voice."[104] John Scottus Eriugena put it this way: "Just as the art of poetry, by means of imaginary fables and allegorical likenesses, develops moral and cosmological interpretations to rouse human minds . . . so theology, like a poetess, employs imaginary inventions to adopt Holy Scriptures to the capacities of the intellect."[105]

It was apparently this same disturbing view that led to the charge that Amalarius of Metz drew his controversial views on the liturgy from within his own spirit.[106] Gregory the Great's strictures against the study of grammar on the grounds that the same language cannot praise both Christ and Jupiter[107] haunted more than one Carolingian scholar seeking to reconcile pagan learning with Christian belief.[108] There are suggestions in the sources that learned men, such as Alcuin, Theodulf, and Paschasius Radbertus, were uneasy with a legalistic and formalistic approach to Christian life; they envisioned a teaching church whose pastors would find within their own spirits the words and actions required to heal tainted souls in a world beset by its own particular spiritual afflictions.[109]

These random examples point to a deep-seated tension in Carolingian religious consciousness, rooted in a disturbing uncertainty about what it meant to be a Christian and how any member of Christian society could advance in holiness. Awareness of that tension should caution against assuming that Carolingian religious sensibilities and spiritual aspirations can be encapsulated in some kind of Tridentine formulation derived from and sanctioned by a tradition recaptured in a mechanical way by a learned resort to authorities. Rather, the deeply felt uncertainties about the essence of Christian life must be factored into any consideration of how culture was put to the service of religious *renovatio*, defined in terms ranging from instructing the simplest *rusticus* to unraveling the mysteries of the eucharist and the Trinity, from converting pagans to determining the proper use of images. Modern scholars must ask to what extent the spiritual concerns of learned souls seeking to be better Christians and to make their world more Christian conditioned the choice of literary and artistic authorities to which they looked, their interpretation of these sources, the emphases they chose to give to particular themes embedded in their authorities, the words and images they used to convey their ideas about tradition, and the way their guidance was received by the population of the Carolingian world.

The key to these riddles probably will not be found in capitularies and conciliar acts; the answer lies in the "tough" stuff in the Carolingian corpus of sources: scriptural exegeses, theological tracts, sermons, poetry, histories, letters, songs, iconography, building designs, liturgical texts, and a wide range of symbolic acts, associated with the affairs of daily life. No less crucial will be an effort to read these texts in new ways, especially from perspectives provided by modern concepts shaping theories of language and the sociology and psychology of religion. Although the answers about Carolingian religious sensibility are far from clear, one thing seems certain: if modern scholars do not keep the spiritual yearnings embedded in such sources central to their treatment of Carolingian cultural life, they are apt to overlook some of the prime forces motivating thought and expression and to miss some of the most significant originality of the Carolingian cultural achievement.

✣

If any scholar were to follow the suggestion to give closer attention to Carolingian spiritual values as a factor affecting the context within which Carolingian cultural life unfolded, he or she would quickly be reminded of another broad contextual issue that has a bearing on the Carolingian cultural world. The investigation of Carolingian religious sensibilities—or, for that matter, any other aspect of Carolingian life—would quickly reveal that there were complex problems surrounding written and spoken languages during the Carolingian age. Every Carolingianist has learned from frequent, often frustrating, recourse to the lexicons of Ducange or Niermeyer how imprecise and fluid language usage was among Carolingians trying to express themselves in Latin about almost any facet of their individual and collective lives. The Carolingian world itself was aware of its language problems, as evidenced especially by the well-documented concerns among its leaders with improving reading capabilities, establishing a common grammar and orthography, correcting faulty texts, finding means to transmit religious messages to audiences who spoke no Latin, and even improving the language employed in public administration.[110]

This evidence points to a contextual situation of crucial importance to the history of the eighth and ninth centuries. The Carolingian world was faced with something bordering on a crisis in communication. That crisis was the product of the need to find a common mode of communication to serve what was envisaged as a political-religious-cultural commonwealth the members of which were becoming increasingly separated by language differences. The seriousness of that problem was dramatically revealed in the famous incident in 842, when "Louis [the German] and Charles [the Bald] came together in the city once called Argentaria, but now in the vulgar language called Strasbourg, and swore oaths, set down below, Louis in the Romance and Charles in the German language. And before they swore, they spoke to the assembled people, one in the German and the other in the Romance language."[111] This episode points up what investigators of the history of European languages have made clear. By the Carolingian age, spoken and written Latin was evolving along lines that placed barriers in the way of understanding and communicating a cultural heritage encased in classical forms of that language.[112]

That same age was a crucial period in the development of diverse, increasingly exclusive branches and subbranches of spoken Germanic and Romance languages.[113] A concern for bridging the language gap is evident in the Carolingian record: for instance, Charlemagne's efforts to "learn foreign languages";[114] his putting into writing of the ancient poems, preparing a grammar of his native language, and giving the months and the winds new names in his own tongue;[115] Lupus of Ferrières's dispatch of three of his pupils to Prüm to learn German, a step "so necessary nowadays that nobody except the idle neglect it";[116] and the efforts to utilize spoken vernacular languages as vehicles of written expression.[117]

Without going so far as does one scholar who recently argued that the Carolingians invented something called medieval Latin to resolve this communication problem,[118] it seems imperative that modern scholars be sensitive to the fact that Carolingian cultural life evolved in a context marked by flux in written and spoken language and by a concern on the part of Carolingians that the media might determine the message. Modern scholars must forgo the luxury of taking for granted that even learned Carolingians understood each other with certainty and precision. Rather, they must assume that uncertainties about language colored every aspect of thought and expression. They must take into account that the way Latin was learned may have shaped how it was used. They must leave open the possibility that language difficulties colored the reception of ancient authorities. They must ask whether the way a particular author wrote was affected by his perception of the linguistic capabilities of the intended audience. They must inquire whether language problems limited the distance a learned person could go in pursuing any intellectual issue or aesthetic urge, especially one calling for a vocabulary of abstraction.

Such baffling issues, rooted in the larger context within which Carolingian culture evolved, demand from modern scholars a special sensitivity to language and communication techniques and strategies; perhaps their capacity to deal with these problems would be enhanced by greater familiarity with modern linguistic and communication theory.[119] How blessed it might have been for modern scholars had Boniface and Alcuin set the world on course to what appears to be its ultimate language destiny by insisting that the Franks could not gain salvation without learning Anglo-Saxon!

※

In setting the context for Carolingian cultural life, it is always crucial to keep in mind that its many components were crafted by individuals. Modern scholars have certainly been aware of this aspect of Carolingian cultural activity; they have supplied their readers with careful assessments of various factors surrounding the external, public lives of the leading participants in Carolingian learning: their social status, training, offices, and connections. Dare one suggest that scholars should go further? Perhaps in setting the context of Carolingian thought and expression they should expand their treatment of individuals to include certain aspects of the human psyche to the extent that that elusive entity is known. This suggestion is not intended to open a new frontier for psychohistory. The point to be made is much more modest. It is simply to propose that, in defining their contextual parameters, investigators of Carolingian cultural life might be well served by keeping in mind two rather simple considerations relating to human behavior. First, they should remember that there appear to be facets of the human psyche, relating to personal fulfillment, that condition behavior of all kinds. For example, people seem possessed of an urge to improve their status, seek beauty, laugh, establish intimate contacts with others, imagine, and locate themselves in time and place. Second, scholars should not forget that cultural activity defined in its broadest terms— reading, writing, talking, thinking, singing, and drawing—can serve as an instrumentality through which these psychic urges are unleashed and realized.

There are facets of the Carolingian cultural scene that suggest such personal psychic urges were instrumental in giving shape and tone to thought and expression. A quest for personal advancement certainly played a part in the uses to which a long succession of Carolingian poets—including Angilbert, Alcuin, Theodulf, Ermoldus Nigellus, Walahfrid Strabo, and Sedulius Scottus—put learning and artistry in their quest for the patronage of kings, bishops, abbots, and nobles.[120] One suspects that inner urges released by learning had some part in shaping the flights of imagination encountered in Carolingian poetry, hagiography, history writing, manuscript illumination, vision literature, and even forgeries. Does it not require an interplay of learning and imagination to explain Walahfrid Strabo's portrayal of Charlemagne, "the master of the mighty Roman people," standing rooted to the spot in hell, while "opposite him was an animal tearing at his genitals," his reward for defiling "his good deeds with foul lust"?[121] Or the enchanting picture of St. Brigid hanging her laundry on trembling sunbeams, which bore their dripping burden as if it were attached to a strong rope?[122] Or Sedulius Scottus's eulogy to a wether?[123]

An inner personal urge to laugh must have prompted the flashes of humor that lace otherwise somber Carolingian literature. Modern scholarship has demonstrated that the Carolingian learned world faced a serious and onerous task in fashioning suitable grammar textbooks, a task involving the reception and appropriation of Donatus, Priscian, and Martianus Capella and the selection and elucidation of suitable illustrative passages from classical authors in a way that, in Bede's words (borrowed from Virgil), would allow learners "to pluck the flowers and fruits," while remaining on the alert for the "chill snake lurk[ing] in the grass."[124] But it took an individual with both learning in grammar and a sense of humor to put such weighty matters into perspective. Such was the author who lamented that because he had lost all hope in life and found his soul troubled, he took his grammar book to the market in order to sell it so that he could buy a couple of drinks, only to find that "no one would buy it or even look at it."[125] The learned John Scottus Eriugena must have released some kind of inner genie when he wrote his epitaph for Hincmar of Reims: "Here lies Hincmar, a thief and a mighty miser; one noble deed he managed, that he died."[126] It would take a congress of eminent psychiatrists to explain what prompted Hucbald of Saint-Amand to write a poem of 146 lines on baldness *(Egloga de Calvis)*, every word of which began with the letter *c*.[127]

When one reads Carolingian letters or poetry, it is hard to avoid concluding that an inner urge for affective ties added a dimension to learned discourse; as one author put it, "little verses" helped to fortify the force that "embraces dear ones divided in body but conjoined by love in their minds."[128] Some personal aesthetic sense certainly helped to give shape to such monuments to learning as Walahfrid Strabo's *De cultura hortorum* or Ermoldus Nigellus's description of the church and palace at Ingelheim.[129]

These random examples suggest that Carolingian culture was shaped and colored by factors somewhat distant from the somber theme that dominates much of modern discussions, namely, culture as an instrument that permitted Charlemagne and his "splendid dynasty" to "cause innumerable peoples to achieve supreme salvation."[130] Carolingian cultural expression in all its forms had a human dimension stemming from the personalities of those involved in its development. Unless that dimension is given place in the contextual framework within which cultural activity is considered, modern scholars may be impeded from discerning some of the most fundamental features of the Carolingian achievement. Taking into account the psyches of intellectuals and artists as factors in cultural life has not deeply troubled cultural historians dealing with fin de siècle Vienna or Edwardian England. Why not utilize it as a contextual tool in seeking to enrich our understanding of the Carolingian renaissance?

❋

In weaving a contextual tapestry capable of enriching the study of Carolingian cultural life one ultimately faces a disconcerting problem rooted in chronology in both its diachronic and synchronic dimensions. That problem can be formulated in terms of what most would probably agree is a fundamental proposition about historianship. The essence of reconstructing the past involves a double operation: capturing what the situation was at any given moment and charting what happened beyond that moment to produce new situations along a linear continuum. To particularize that axiom, a comprehensible history of the phenomenon called the Carolingian cultural renewal must unfold in a way that illuminates the state of culture at any moment and describes and explains change over time.

A case can be made that modern scholarship has not met this condition. It has not fashioned an adequate reconstruction of the diachronic dimension of Carolingian cultural life defined in broadest terms. One would be hard pressed to direct readers to a synthetic treatment of Carolingian cultural life that would permit them to comprehend in a holistic way the difference between the cultural world of the early eighth century and that of the early tenth century. Equally lacking are studies that provide a panoramic picture of the cultural scene at any one moment.[131]

As a substitute for a comprehensive history of Carolingian culture as it evolved over time, one has to be content with topical treatments of various facets of Carolingian cultural life, each arranged on a chronological basis: histories of education, theology, political theory, law, poetry, architecture, iconography, and so forth. Sometimes such treatments are lumped together in a single volume; more often each topic is the subject of a separate study.[132] Such works make only a minimal effort to interconnect or synchronize the several changing strands of Carolingian cultural activity. Nor are their authors always careful in asking whether the topical categories into which they partition Carolingian cultural activity are entirely appropriate to the Carolingian world. Taken together, all of these works provide only pieces of a mosaic that do not fall together to constitute a meaningful design.

Why, it may be asked, has the immense scholarly effort devoted to Carolingian cultural activity failed to produce an effective intellectual and cultural history of the age? Why is there no treatment that charts the continuous movement in the world of culture viewed globally from some beginning to some end, while still allowing the film to be stopped at any point to frame a synchronic portrayal of the world of culture? Are the sources too meager? Are Carolingianists too specialized? Are they incompetent? Is Carolingian "culture" a concept so amorphous that its history is impossible? None of these explanations is very persuasive.

Rather, the difficulty lies in a contextual situation not always taken into account by historians of Carolingian cultural life. In a unique way and to an unusual degree Carolingian cultural activity was a creature of circumstance. Almost any cultural artifact of the era was the product of a unique and particular circumstance. Each such artifact makes sense only in the particular context that produced it. To paraphrase an expression recently abroad in the political realm, the Carolingian cultural landscape was filled with a thousand points of circumstance, each of which constituted the essential context within which cultural life unfolded.[133]

The reason why Carolingian cultural activity was so much a product of an infinite array of particular circumstances seems fairly obvious. Intellectual and creative activity developed in an ambience in which cultural life had no independent institutional basis, intellectuals and artists had no discrete status, there was no concept of an independent function for learning and expression, and there was no self-standing conceptual framework for the structuring of cultural endeavor. Schools were not conceived as institutions to promote creative cultural activities; they were places for teaching skills with a wide societal application. If schools contributed to cultural life, it was a consequence of some special circumstance. Masters were not intellectuals devoted by profession to the cultivation and advancement of learning. If their efforts advanced cultural life, it was because some unique circumstance provided such an outcome. Bishops, abbots, and abbesses were not founders, directors, and fund-raisers for advanced institutes or universities with clearly delineated cultural missions. They were individuals with multiple, diverse, and particular agenda who exercised their talents and spent their resources in the service of cultural life in order to respond to a particular situation at a particular moment. Libraries were not collections of books crafted to promote a preconceived vision of learning and its ends. They were fortuitously shaped collections that might serve the enhancement of cultural life if the circumstances permitted. In short, what counted across the entire Carolingian scene in terms of cultural activity were particular circumstances, discrete conditions, and special situations that might give impetus and shape to thought and expression.

It is this absence of an independent structural and conceptual framework for cultural activity that challenges modern scholars in their effort to fashion an account of Carolingian intellectual and cultural history that is cohesive both diachronically and synchronically. They have no institutional and conceptual template around which to structure their treatment of the Carolingian cultural effort. This lacuna is not a product of scholarly inadequacy; it stems from the fact that no such template existed in the Carolingian world. To write a holistic cultural history of the Carolingian period requires the ferreting out of the particular circumstances that produced every individual facet of cultural life and a concurrent effort to establish within a chronological framework linkages with other cultural "events" shaped by equally unique circumstances.

There are encouraging signs that modern scholarship is increasingly cognizant of the need to investigate Carolingian culture in the context of particular circumstances. It would be possible to compile an impressive list of recent studies of individual cultural figures, schools, libraries, scriptoria, texts, and monastic centers that emphasize the particular, localized contextual factors affecting each of these aspects of cultural life.[134] It is becoming increasingly possible to take a position at a particular moment in the Carolingian age from which one can catch a panoramic view of the diversity of cultural activity occurring simultaneously and discern the complex network of interactions of varying degrees of intensity affecting cultural development in a global sense. Continued awareness of the diverse contextual situations shaping the development of Carolingian cultural life remains the best hope for progress toward a total history of Carolingian culture.

Raising the issue of the global configuration of Carolingian culture prompts one final observation on the context affecting Carolingian thought and expression. Anyone who is familiar with the history of the entire Mediterranean world in the eighth and ninth centuries cannot help being struck by contextual similarities in the Western European, Byzantine, and Islamic worlds that may have important cultural implications.[135] There were changes of dynasties in each realm, each requiring special rationalization. There were highly charged struggles concerning the locus of authority in each society. There were religious reforms everywhere. There was a palpable quickening of learning in Anglo-Saxon England, Ireland, the Lombard kingdom, the Byzantine empire, the Muslim empire, and in Francia. There were building booms in Rome, Pavia, Constantinople, Baghdad, and Aachen. There were administrative reforms in many different centers.

Perhaps all these congruencies mean nothing in setting the context for Carolingian cultural life. But maybe, just maybe, they are signs of a historical season during which something was in the air that sparked new levels of human endeavor on a global scale. Pending a more profound inquiry, perhaps the point can best be formulated in question form. Was the quickening of Carolingian cultural life a part of a larger cultural movement whose contours were molded by a contextual framework embracing several civilizations? Having reached a particular stage in their historical evolution, did all of the heirs of the Roman Empire, of Greco-Latin culture, and of Hellenistic religious syncretism encounter a common set of challenges that could only be met by a return to a religious-cultural heritage formulated in late antiquity? With apologies for an impertinent paraphrase, perhaps there would have been no Charlemagne without the Abbasids and the Isaurians. If so, then a rich harvest of understanding might accrue to scholars willing to explore Carolingian culture in a comparative context informed by simultaneous developments in cultural life in Byzantium and Islam.

⁜

In concluding this exploration of the context of Carolingian cultural life it should be said that there remain many other aspects of Carolingian society that deserve attention as factors affecting Carolingian cultural activity. In the original plan of this study the intent was to explore the implications for thought and expression of such additional contextual matters as these: the challenge placed before learning by the existence in the Carolingian world of what the anthropologists call elements of a primitive mentality; the tensions between elite and popular culture; the expanded spatial and temporal awareness resulting from the extension of the Carolingian political sway and from a changing historical consciousness; the regionalism and ethnic rivalries endemic in the Carolingian world; the dependence on memorization and orality in acquiring and transmitting learning; the utilization of authoritative texts in fragmentary form.

To keep the chapter within reasonable bounds it was necessary to trust that Heiric of Auxerre (ca. 841–975) spoke the truth when he wrote, "To have begun something is already a little part of completing it."[136] The purpose of the chapter was not so much to be all-embracing as it was to heighten awareness that the treatment of Carolingian cultural life might be enriched by expanding the contextual framework within which scholars approach it. Perhaps what has been said will serve as an invitation to scholars primarily concerned with Carolingian cultural history to expand their knowledge of the totality of Carolingian society in search of factors that influenced cultural activity. Equally important, perhaps these reflections will remind Carolingianists engaged in the investigation of any aspect of Carolingian society to be sensitive to the possibility that whatever they discover may have ramifications that can help advance the understanding of Carolingian cultural life in all its forms.

Notes

1. "In omnibus huiusmodi quaestionibus sanctorum sequi patrum vestigia desidero, nihil addens vel minuens illorum sacratissimis litteris." "A Letter of Alcuin to Beatus of Liébana," ed. Wilhelm Levison, in Levison, *England*

and the Continent in the Eighth Century (The Ford Lectures), p. 322. The same sentiment was expressed in a letter sent to the Frankish bishops from the Council of Frankfurt in 794; see *Concilia aevi karolini*, no. 19, ed. Albert Werminghoff, MGH, Concilia, pt. 1 (Hannover and Leipzig, 1906), p. 156.

2. Elisabeth Dahlhaus-Berg, *Nova Antiquitas et Antiqua Novitas: Typologische Exegese und isidorianisches Geschichtsbild bei Theodulf von Orléans.*

3. In addition to the remarks on this subject in the preceding chapter, see, e.g., Richard E. Sullivan, "Changing Perspectives on the Concept of the Middle Ages"; and Sullivan, "The Carolingian Age: Reflections on Its Place in the History of the Middle Ages."

4. *Eginhard, Vie de Charlemagne*, ed. and trans. Louis Halphen, 4th ed., rev. and corrected, Les Classiques de l'histoire de France au moyen âge (Paris, 1967), p. 106 (English trans. from Peter Godman, *Poetry of the Carolingian Renaissance*, pp. 33–34).

5. *Eginhard, Vie de Charlemagne*, chap. 33, ed. Halphen, p. 98. Such was probably not the fate of Charlemagne's library; see Bernhard Bischoff, "Die Hofbibliothek unter Ludwig dem Frommen."

6. *Servati Lupi Epistulae*, no. 44, para. 5, ed. Peter K. Marshall, Bibliotheca Scriptorum Graecorum et Romanorum Teubneriana (Leipzig, 1984), p. 57 (English trans. from *The Letters of Lupus of Ferrières*, no. 48, trans. Graydon W. Regenos, pp. 66–67).

7. *Willelmi Malmesbiriensis monachi Gesta regum Anglorum*, bk. 2, chap. 122, ed. Thomas Duffus Hardy, 2 vols., Publications of the English Historical Society (London, 1840), 1:189–90. The same story is repeated in other works of William; for references, see Maïeul Cappuyns, *Jean Scot Erigène: Sa vie, son oeuvre, sa pensée*, pp. 252–53.

8. *Beati Alcuini Adversus Elipandum Toletanum Libri IV*, bk. 1, chap. 16, PL 101:251: "philosophus in liberalibus studiis."

9. *Angilberti (Homeri) Carmina*, no. 2, ed. Ernst Dümmler, MGH, Poetae 1 (Berlin, 1881), p. 360, lines 15–17 (English trans. from Godman, *Poetry*, pp. 113–15).

10. Quoted above; see n. 4.

11. " . . . ut moderni Galli sive Franci antiquis Romanis et Athenienibus aequarentur." *Notkeri Balbuli Gesta Karoli Magni Imperatoris*, bk. 1, chap. 2, ed. Hans F. Haefele, MGH, SS rer. Germ., new ser., 12 (Berlin, 1959; repr. Munich, 1980), p. 3 (English trans. from *Einhard and Notker the Stammerer: Two Lives of Charlemagne*, trans. Lewis Thorpe, p. 95).

12. The expression "Carolingian renaissance" was first given prominence by J.-J. Ampère, *Histoire littéraire de la France avant le douzième siècle*, 3:31–33.

13. No attempt will be made to provide a full bibliographical guide to the extensive body of scholarship upon which the following assessment of the current contextual framework shaping the study of Carolingian learning is based.

14. Awareness of that "crisis" is clearly reflected in the following eighth-century sources: *The Fourth Book of the Chronicle of Fredegar; with Its*

Continuations, ed. and trans. J. M. Wallace-Hadrill, Medieval Classics (London and New York, 1960); *Die Briefe des heiligen Bonifatius und Lullus*, ed. Michael Tangl, 2nd ed., MGH, Epistolae Selectae 1 (Berlin, 1955) (English trans., *The Letters of Saint Boniface*, trans. Ephraim Emerton, Records of Civilization, Sources and Studies 31 [New York, 1940]); *Concilia aevi karolini*, nos. 1–2, 4, 6, 8–11, 13, ed. Werminghoff, MGH, Concilia, pt. 1, pp. 1–7, 33–36, 45–50, 54–63, 72–73; and MGH, Capit., nos. 10–18, ed. Alfred Boretius, vol. 1 (Hannover, 1883), pp. 24–43.

15. The key documents are the *Admonitio generalis* of 789 and the *Epistola de litteris colendis* written sometime during the 790s; see MGH, Capit., nos. 22, 29, ed. Boretius, 1:52–62, 78–79 (English trans. of the *Admonitio generalis* in P. D. King, *Charlemagne: Translated Sources* [Kendal, 1987], pp. 209–20, and of the *Epistola de litteris colendis* in H. R. Loyn and John Percival, *The Reign of Charlemagne: Documents on Carolingian Government and Administration*, pp. 63–64). A stimulating discussion on the launching of this program is provided by Wolfram von den Steinen, "Der Neubeginn." See also Giles Brown, "Introduction: The Carolingian Renaissance."

16. For example, in his *Egloga* the poet Moduin of Autun has an old poet rebuke an aspiring young poet in this fashion: "Publice nulla canis, nulli tua carmina digna" [you say nothing of public events, your poetry satisfies no one]; for that reason everyone, including "precipuus . . . David," spurns the aspirant's "hideous verse"; text and trans. from Godman, *Poetry*, p. 192, lines 33–36.

17. For a full treatment of the Carolingian sense of "the norms of rectitude," see Josef Fleckenstein, *Die Bildungsreform Karls des Grossen als Verwicklichung der norma rectitudinis*.

18. The best guides to Carolingian education are Emile Lesne, *Histoire de la propriété ecclésiastique en France*, vol. 4: *Les Livres, "scriptoria" et bibliothèques du commencement du VIIIe à la fin du XIe siècle*, and vol. 5: *Les Ecoles de fin du VIIIe siècle à la fin du XIIe siècle; La scuola nell'occidente latino dell'alto medioevo*; and Pierre Riché, *Les Ecoles et l'enseignement dans l'Occident chrétien de la fin de Ve siècle au milieu du XI siècle* (not available for this chapter is a new edition of this work entitled *Ecoles et enseignement dans le haut moyen âge: Fin du Ve siècle–milieu du XIe siècle*, 2nd ed. [Paris, 1989]).

19. On the problem of recovering tradition in the early Middle Ages, see Yves M.-J. Congar, *Tradition and Traditions: An Historical and a Theological Essay*; Karl F. Morrison, *Tradition and Authority in the Western Church, 300–1140*; *La cultura antica nell'occidente latino dal VII all'XI secolo*; and Norbert Kamp and Joachim Wollasch, eds., *Tradition als historische Kraft: Interdisziplinäre Forschungen zur Geschichte des früheren Mittelalters*.

20. Examples of such studies focusing on individuals include the following: Alain Stoclet, *Autour de Fulrad de Saint-Denis (v. 710–784)*; Wolfgang Edelstein, *Eruditio und Sapientia: Weltbild und Erziehung in der Karolingerzeit: Untersuchungen zu Alcuins Briefen*; Luitpold Wallach, *Alcuin and Charlemagne: Studies in Carolingian History and Literature*; Deng-Su I,

L'opera agiografica di Alcuino; Dahlhaus-Berg, *Nova Antiquitas et Antiqua Novitas*; Giuliana Italiani, *La tradizione esegetica nel Commento ai Re di Claudio di Torino*; Fidel Rädle, *Studien zu Smaragd von Saint-Mihiel*; Otto Eberhardt, *Via Regia: Die Fürstenspiegel Smaragds von St.-Mihiel und seine literarische Gattung*; Elisabeth Heyse, *Hrabanus Maurus' Enzyklopädia "De Rerum Naturis": Untersuchungen zu den Quellen und zur Methode der Kompilation*; Maria Rissel, *Rezeption antiker und patristischer Wissenschaft bei Hrabanus Maurus: Studien zur karolingischen Geistesgeschichte*; Jean Devisse, *Hincmar, Archevêque de Reims, 845–882*; Jean Jolivet, *Godescalc d'Orbais et la Trinité: La Méthode de la théologie à l'époque carolingienne*; Jean-Paul Bouhot, *Ratram de Corbie: Histoire littéraire et controverses doctrinales*; R. Savigni, *Giona di Orléans, una ecclesiologia carolingia*; Cappuyns, *Jean Scot Erigène*; Werner Beierwaltes, ed., *Eriugena: Studien zur seinen Quellen, Vorträge des III. Internationalen Eriugena-Colloquiums, Freiburg im Breisgau, 27.–30. August 1979*; Gangolf Schrimpf, *Das Werk des Johannes Scottus Eriugena im Rahmen des Wissenschaftsverständnisses seiner Zeit: Einführung zu Periphyseon*; John J. O'Meara, *Eriugena*; Goulven Madec, *Jean Scot et ses auteurs: Annotations érigéniennes*; Dermot Moran, *The Philosophy of John Scottus Eriugena: A Study of Idealism in the Middle Ages*; Ulrich Rudnick, *Das System des Johannes Scottus Eriugena: Eine theologisch-philosophische Studie zu seinem Werk*; and Willemien Otten, *The Anthropology of Johannes Scottus Eriugena*.

21. For example, on the liberal arts in general, see Josef Koch, *Artes Liberales von der antiken Bildung zur Wissenschaft des Mittelalters*; Günter Glauche, *Schullektüre im Mittelalter: Entstehung und Wandlungen des Lektürekanons bis 1200 nach den Quellen dargestellt*; Detlef Illmer, *Formen der Erziehung und Wissensvermittlung im frühen Mittelalter: Quellenstudien zur Frage der Kontinuität des abendländischen Erziehungswesens*; Riché, *Education and Culture in the Barbarian West, Sixth through Eighth Centuries*; and *La cultura antica nell'occidente latino*.

On grammar and rhetoric, see, e.g., James J. Murphy, *Rhetoric in the Middle Ages: A History of Rhetorical Theory from Saint Augustine to the Renaissance*; and Louis Holtz, *Donat et la tradition de l'enseignement grammatical: Etude sur l'"Ars Donati" et sa diffusion (IVe–IXe siècle) et critique*.

Illustrative on literature are Max Manitius, *Geschichte der lateinischen Literatur des Mittelalters*, vol. 1: *Von Justinian bis zur Mitte des zehnten Jahrhunderts*, pp. 243–718; M. L. W. Laistner, *Thought and Letters in Western Europe*, A.D. 500 to 900, pp. 251–386; Reto R. Bezzola, *Les Origines et la formation de la littérature courtoise en occident (500–1200)*, vol. 1: *La Tradition impériale de la fin de l'antiquité au XIe siècle*, pp. 86–224; and Franz Brunhölzl, *Geschichte der lateinischen Literatur des Mittelalters*, vol. 1: *Von Cassiodor bis zum Ausklang der karolingischen Erneuerung*, pp. 241–506.

Examples on theology and philosophy include *The Cambridge History of Later Greek and Early Medieval Philosophy*, ed. A. H. Armstrong, pp. 518–33, 565–86; Jaroslav Pelikan, *The Christian Tradition: A History of the*

Development of Doctrine, vol. 3: *The Growth of Medieval Theology (600–1300)*; John Marenbon, *From the Circle of Alcuin to the School of Auxerre: Logic, Theology, and Philosophy in the Early Middle Ages*; and Marenbon, *Early Medieval Philosophy (480–1150): An Introduction*, pp. 43–89.

Illustrative of the point with respect to political theory are Robert Folz, *L'Idée d'empire en occident du Ve au XIVe siècle*, pp. 11–46 (pp. 3–35 in the English trans.); H.-X. Arquillière, *L'Augustinisme politique: Essai sur la formation des théories politiques du moyen-âge*; Paola Maria Arcari, *Idee e sentimenti politici dell'alto medioevo*; Walter Ullmann, *The Carolingian Renaissance and the Idea of Kingship: The Birkbeck Lectures, 1968–1969*; Marta Cristiani, *Dall'unanimitas all'universitas da Alcuino a Giovanni Eriugena: Lineamenti ideologici e terminologia politica della cultura del secolo IX*; Hans-Werner Goetz, "Regnum: Zum politischen Denken der Karolingerzeit"; and *The Cambridge History of Medieval Political Thought, c. 350–c.1450*, ed. J. H. Burns, pp. 83–338 (with extensive bibliography).

On law, see Paul Fournier and Gabriel Le Bras, *Histoire des collections canoniques en occident depuis les Fausses Décrétales jusqu'au Décret de Gratian*; Schafer Williams, *Codices Pseudo-Isiodoriani: A Palaeographico-Historical Study*; Horst Fuhrmann, *Einfluss und Verbreitung der pseudoisidorischen Fälschungen: Von ihrem Auftauchen bis in die neure Zeit*; Hubert Mordek, *Kirchenrecht und Reform im Frankenreich: Die Collectio Vetus Gallica, die älteste systematische Kanonenssammlung des fränkischen Gallien: Studien und Edition*; Raymund Kottje, *Die Bussbücher Halitgars von Cambrai und des Hrabanus Maurus: Ihre Überlieferung und ihre Quellen*; Arnold Bühler, "Capitularia Relecta: Studien zur Entstehung und Überlieferung der Kapitularien Karls des Grossen und Ludwig des Frommen"; and Mordek, "Karolingische Kapitularien."

On ecclesiology, see Morrison, *The Two Kingdoms: Ecclesiology in Carolingian Political Thought*; Congar, *L'Ecclésiologie du haut moyen âge de saint Grégoire le Grand à le désunion entre Byzance et Rome*; and Brigitte Szabô-Bechstein, *Libertas Ecclesiae: Eine Schlüsselbegriff des Investiturstreits und seine Vorgeschichte, 4.–11. Jahrhundert*.

For the visual arts, see Wolfgang Braunfels, et al., eds., *Karl der Grosse: Lebenswerk und Nachleben*, vol. 3: *Karolingische Kunst*, ed. Braunfels and Hermann Schnitzler; Jean Hubert, Jean Porcher, and Wolfgang Fritz Volbach, *L'Empire carolingien*; Florentine Mütherich and Joachim E. Gaehde, *Carolingian Painting*; Carol Heitz, *L'Architecture religieuse carolingienne: Les Formes et leurs fonctions*; Heitz and Jean Roubier, *Gallia Praeromanica: Die Kunst der merowingischen, karolingischen und frühroma- nischen Epoche in Frankreich*; Marcel Durliat, *Des barbares à l'an mil*; Heitz, *La France pré-romane: Archéologie et architecture religieuse du haut moyen âge du IVe siècle à l'an mil*; and C. R. Dodwell, *The Pictorial Arts of the West, 800–1200*. Not available was "L'Art et la société à l'époque carolingienne: Actes des XXIIIe Journées romanes de Cuxa."

For brief overviews of music in the Carolingian era, see Susan Rankin, "Carolingian Music"; and Morrison, "'Know Thyself': Music in the Carolingian Renaissance." For longer treatments, see Richard Crocker and

David Hiley, eds., *The Early Middle Ages to 1300*; and Helmut Möller and Rudolf Stephan, eds., *Die Musik des Mittelalters*.

22. On this issue, see Sullivan, "The Carolingian Age," pp. 285–87.

23. Edward Gibbon, *The History of the Decline and Fall of the Roman Empire*, 5:292.

24. For examples of this interpretation, see Gustave Schnürer, *L'Eglise et la civilisation au moyen âge*, 2:9–177; and Jacques Paul, *L'Eglise et la culture en occident, IXe–XIIe siècles*, 1:256–92. It becomes increasingly difficult to sustain this position in the face of recent scholarship; for a convenient summary, see John J. Contreni, "The Tenth Century: The Perspective from the Schools." For fuller treatments, see Heinrich Fichtenau, *Lebensordnungen des 10. Jahrhunderts: Studien über Denkart und Existenz im einstigen Karolingerreich*; and *Il secolo di ferro: Mito e realtà del sec. X*.

25. For a succinct summary of this debate and a basic bibliography (including the reference to Ganshof's remark), see Contreni, "Inharmonius Harmony: Education in the Carolingian World," pp. 81–84. To Contreni's bibliography should be added the following: Anita Guerreau-Jalabert, "La 'Renaissance carolingienne': Modèles culturels, usages linguistiques et structures sociales"; Janet L. Nelson, "On the Limits of the Carolingian Renaissance"; Heitz, "Renaissances éphémères du haut moyen âge (VIIe–XIe siècles)"; and Lawrence Nees, *A Tainted Mantle: Hercules and the Classical Tradition at the Carolingian Court*, pp. 3–17 (with special emphasis on art history).

26. Considerations of space make it impossible to acknowledge in what follows all of the scholarly literature that has contributed to the points that will be made. Any reader interested in a basic reading list on the Carolingian world might turn to Theodor Schieder, ed., *Handbuch der europäischen Geschichte*, vol. 1: *Europa im Wandel von der Antike zum Mittelalter*, ed. Theodor Schieffer, pp. 527–632; or to Arnold Angenendt, *Das Frühmittelalter: Die abendländische Christenheit von 400 bis 900*, pp. 461–87. The best guides to current scholarly work on Carolingian cultural history are Claudio Leonardi, et al., eds., *Medioevo latino: Bulletino bibliografico della cultura europea del secolo VI al XIII*; and the "Bibliographie" published in each issue of *Revue d'histoire ecclésiastique*.

27. For this point, see Sullivan, "The Carolingian Age," pp. 281–85, nn. 29–37. To the references cited there should now be added F. M. Clover and R. S. Humphreys, eds., *Tradition and Innovation in Late Antiquity*; and Jacques Fontaine and J. N. Hillgarth, eds., *Le Septième Siècle: Changements et continuités/The Seventh Century: Change and Continuity*.

28. The Carolingian world had this list well in mind, as is evident in a poem by Theodulf of Orléans; *Theodulfi Carmina*, no. 45, ed. Dümmler, MGH, Poetae 1:543–44 (English trans. in Godman, *Poetry*, pp. 168–71).

29. Adalbert de Vogüé, *Le règle de saint Benoît*, vol. 7: *Commentaire doctrinal et spirituel*; Carole Straw, *Gregory the Great: Perfection in Imperfection*; Fontaine, *Isidore de Séville et la culture classique dans l'Espagne wisigothique*; Henry Chadwick, *Boethius: The Consolations of Music, Logic, Theology, and Philosophy*; and Jerold C. Frakes, *The Fate of Fortune in the Early Middle Ages: The Boethian Tradition*.

30. Suggestive on this point are Riché, *Education and Culture*, pp. 305–499; Wallace-Hadrill, *The Frankish Church*, pp. 143–80; Heinz Löwe, ed., *Die Iren und Europa in früheren Mittelalter*; Levison, *England and the Continent in the Eighth Century*; Theodor Schieffer, *Winfrid-Bonifatius und die christliche Grundlegung Europas*; Timothy Reuter, ed., *The Greatest Englishman: Essays on St. Boniface and the Church at Crediton*; Georges Kiesel and Jean Schroeder, eds., *Willibrord, Apostel der Niederlande, Gründer der Abtei Echternach: Gedenkgaben zum 1250. Todestag des angelsächsischen Missionars*; Angenendt, *Monachi Peregrini: Studien zu Pirmin und den monastischen Vorstellungen der frühen Mittelalters*; *St. Kilian:1300 Jahre Martyrium des Frankenapostel*; L. K. Walter, *St. Kilian: Schrifttums-Verzeichnis zu Martyrium und Kult des Frankenapostel und zur Gründung des Bistums Würzburg*; Riché, "Le Renouveau culturel à la cour de Pépin III"; Hubert, "Les Prémisses de la renaissance carolingienne au temps du Pépin III"; Hubert Mordek, "Kanonistische Aktivität in Gallien in der ersten Hälfte des 8. Jahrhunderts: Eine Skizze"; and David Ganz, "The Preconditions for Caroline Minuscule."

31. Ullmann, *The Carolingian Renaissance*, p. 3.

32. Symptomatic of this difficulty is the fact that a scholar could recently write, "No one work covers this difficult transitional period." See Wallace-Hadrill, *The Frankish Church*, p. 428. Some potentially fruitful suggestions are contained in the various essays in *I problemi dell'occidente nel secolo VIII*.

33. The reign of Louis the Pious is beginning to receive more serious attention; see François L. Ganshof, "Louis the Pious Reconsidered"; Thomas F. X. Noble, "Louis the Pious and His Piety Reconsidered"; Rudolf Schieffer, "Ludwig 'der Fromme': Zur Entstehung eines karolingischen Herrscherbeinamen"; Godman, "Louis 'the Pious' and His Poets"; and esp. Peter Godman and Roger Collins, eds., *Charlemagne's Heir: New Perspectives on the Reign of Louis the Pious (814–840)*.

34. Jean Gouillard, "Aux origines de l'iconoclasme: La Témoignage de Grégoire II?" provides the best edition of Gregory's letter with a French translation; the passage cited is at p. 297. The authenticity of this letter is open to question; see Hans Grotz, "Beobachtungen zu den zwei Briefen Papst Gregors II. an Leo III."; Grotz, "Weitere Beobachtungen zu den zwei Briefen Papst Gregors II. an Kaiser Leo III."; and Helmut Michels, "Zur Echtheit der Briefe Papst Gregors II. an Kaiser Leon III."

35. For some illuminating reflections on the relationship between power and culture, see Michael Mann, *The Sources of Social Power*, vol. 1: *A History of Power from the Beginning to A.D. 1760*.

36. *Annales regni Francorum*, anno 749, ed. Friedrich Kurze, MGH, SS rer. Germ. (Hannover, 1895), p. 8 (English trans. in *Carolingian Chronicles: "Royal Frankish Annals" and Nithard's "Histories,"* trans. Bernhard Walter Scholz with Barbara Rogers [Ann Arbor, Mich., 1970], p. 39).

37. As recounted in the "Clausula de unctione Pippini regis," most recently edited by Alain J. Stoclet, "La 'Clausula de unctione Pippini regis': Mises en point et nouvelles hypothèses," pp. 2–3.

38. These matters are treated in detail in Heinrich Hahn, *Jahrbücher des fränkischen Reiches, 741–752*; and Ludwig Oelsner, *Jahrbücher des*

fränkischen Reiches unter König Pippin. See also G. Wolf, "Grifos Erbe, die Einsetzung König Childerichs III. und der Kampf um die Macht: Zugleich Bemerkungen zur karolingischen 'Hofhistoriographie.'"

39. Jörg Jarnut, "Chlodwig und Chlothar: Anmerkungen zu den Namen zweier Söhne Karls des Grossen." It is not inconceivable that such an action resulted from uneasiness felt by Charlemagne upon reading a letter from Cathwulf written about 775 that raised the specter of failure because the Frankish king had too few columns to support the fortress of God; see *Epistolae variorum Carolo Magno regnante,* no. 7, ed. Dümmler, MGH, Epp. 4 (Berlin, 1895): "Paucas firmiter columnas, ut timeo, castra Dei tecum habes sustenare" (p. 503).

40. *Eginhard, Vie de Charlemagne,* chap. 20, ed. Halphen, p. 62 (English trans. from *Einhard and Notker the Stammer,* trans. Thorpe, p. 75). For details, see Sigurd Abel and Bernhard Simson, *Jahrbücher des fränkischen Reiches unter Karl dem Grossen,* 2:39–52.

41. *Dungali Scotti Epistolae,* no. 1, ed. Dümmler, MGH, Epp. 4:570–78. For further remarks on this episode, see Karl Ferdinand Werner, "*Hludowicus Augustus*: Gouverner l'empire chrétien—idées et realités," pp. 28–29.

42. Peter Godman, *Poets and Emperors: Frankish Politics and Carolingian Poetry,* pp. 1–38.

43. For an overview of cultural activity at the Lombard court in the eighth century see Bezzola, *Les origines et la formation de la littérature courtoise,* 1:24–33; and Riché, *Education and Culture,* pp. 336–45, 399–415.

44. *Pauli Historia Langobardorum,* bk. 6, chap. 53, ed. L. Bethmann and G. Waitz, MGH, Scriptores rerum langobardicarum et italicarum saec. VI–IX (Hannover, 1878), p. 183.

45. On Paul's career, see Karl Neff, ed., *Die Gedichte des Paulinus Diaconus*; Manitius, *Geschichte der lateinischen Literatur,* 1:257–72; and von den Steinen, "Karl und die Dichter," pp. 67–73.

46. That note is struck in nearly every letter in the *Codex Carolinus,* ed. Wilhelm Gundlach, MGH, Epp. 3 (Berlin, 1892), pp. 476–657.

47. Ernst H. Kantorowicz, *Laudes Regiae: A Study in Liturgical Acclamations and Mediaeval Ruler Worship,* pp. 1–111; C. A. Bouman, *Sacring and Crowning: The Development of the Latin Ritual for the Anointing of Kings and the Coronation of an Emperor before the Eleventh Century*; Percy Ernst Schramm, *Kaiser, Könige und Päpste: Gesammelte Aufsätze zur Geschichte des Mittelalters,* esp. vols. 1 and 2; Michael J. Enright, *Iona, Tara, and Soissons: The Origin of the Royal Anointing Ritual*; Donald A. Bullough, "'Imagines Regum' and Their Significance in the Early Medieval West"; Michael McCormick, *Eternal Victory: Triumphal Rulership in Late Antiquity, Byzantium, and the Early Medieval West,* pp. 328–87; and Nelson, "The Lord's Anointed and the People's Choice: Carolingian Royal Ritual."

48. Examples include *Annales regni Francorum,* ed. Kurze (pp. 57–125 in the English trans.); *Liber historiae Francorum,* ed. Bruno Krusch, MGH, Scriptores rerum Merovingicarum 2 (Hannover, 1888), pp. 215–328 (English trans., *Liber historiae Francorum,* ed. and trans. Bernard Bachrach [Lawrence, Kans., 1977]); *The Fourth Book of the Chronicle of Fredegar,* ed.

and trans. Wallace-Hadrill; *Pauli Warnefridi Liber de episcopis mettensibus*, ed. George Heinrich Pertz, MGH, SS 2 (Hannover, 1829), pp. 261–70; and *Annales Mettenses priores*, ed. Bernhard Simson, MGH, SS rer. Germ. (Hannover and Leipzig, 1905). For a discussion of the propagandistic aspects of these works, see Halphen, *Etudes critiques sur l'histoire de Charlemagne*, pp. 3–142; Hartmut Hoffmann, *Untersuchungen zur karolingischen Annalistik*; Helmut Beumann, *Ideengeschichtliche Studien zu Einhard und anderen Geschichtsschreibern des früheren Mittelalters*; Irene Haselbach, *Aufstieg und Herrschaft der Karlinger in der Darstellung der sogenannenten Annales Mettensis priores: Ein Beitrag zur Geschichte der politischen Ideen im Reich Karls des Grossen*; Ganshof, "L'Historiographie dans le monarchie franque sous les mérovingiens et les carolingiens: Monarchie franque unitaire et Francie Occidentale"; and Richard A. Gerberding, *The Rise of the Carolingians and the "Liber Historiae Francorum."*

49. *Lex Salica: 100-Titel Text*, ed. Karl August Eckhardt, MGH, Leges, Sectio 1, Leges Nationum Germanicarum 4, pt. 2 (Weimar, 1969), pp. 4–6. For a translation of the prologue, see *The Laws of the Salian Franks*, trans. Katherine Fischer Drew, Middle Ages Series (Philadelphia, 1991), p. 171.

50. *Codex Carolinus*, no. 39, ed. Gundlach, MGH, Epp. 3:551–52.

51. *Versus Libris Saeculi Octavi Adiecti*, no. 3, ed. Dümmler, MGH, Poetae 1:90–91.

52. Ed. Dümmler, MGH, Poetae 1:380–81. For a recent edition with a German translation, see Karl Hauck, *Karolingische Taufpfalzen im Spiegel hofnaher Dichtung: Überlegungen zur Ausmalung von Pfalzkirchen, Pfalzen und Reichsklöstern*, pp. 62–67. See also Dieter Schaller, "Der Dichter des *Carmen de conversione Saxonum*."

53. *Hibernici Exulis Carmina*, no. 2, ed. Dümmler, MGH, Poetae 1:395–99 (trans. from Godman, *Poetry*, pp. 175–79).

54. See Godman, *Poets and Emperors*, pp. 43–92; Alfred Ebenbauer, *Carmen Historicum: Untersuchungen zur historischer Dichtung im karolingischen Europa*, vol. 1, pts. A and B, pp. 1–97; Bullough, "*Aula Renovata*: The Carolingian Court before the Aachen Palace (Raleigh Lecture on History, 1985)"; Henry Mayr-Hartung, "Charlemagne as a Patron of Art"; and McKitterick, "Royal Patronage of Culture in the Frankish Kingdoms under the Carolingians: Motives and Consequences."

55. *Angilberti . . . Carmina*, no. 2, ed. Dümmler, MGH, Poetae 1:360: "David amat versus . . . David amat vates" (lines 2–3). The chapters by Lawrence Nees and Thomas F. X. Noble contained in this volume provide compelling evidence of the ways in which art and theological discourse were shaped to sustain the fitness of the Carolingians to rule.

56. An illuminating study might emerge from an effort to view this theme on the evidence provided in various forms of cultural expression, following the model so brilliantly carried out with respect to poetry by Godman, *Poets and Emperors*.

57. For examples of this tendency, see Hans Hubert Anton, *Fürstenspiegel und Herrscherethos in der Karolingerzeit*; Eberhardt, *Via Regia: Der Fürstenspiegel*

Smaragds von St.-Mihiel und seine literarische Gattung; and Nelson,
"Kingship and Empire."

58. "Deficiet quorum sceptrum de semine numquam, / Donec in ignivoma
veniet rex nube coruscans!" Walahfrid Strabo, *De imagine Tetrici*; text and
trans. from Godman, *Poets and Emperors*, p. 141. Hrabanus Maurus
expressed a similar sentiment in praising Louis the Pious; see *De laudibus
sanctae crucis*, PL 107:145–46: "Sicque eius sobolis laeta propago /
Succedens maneat sceptra tenendo, / Donec saecula sua iura tenebunt / Et
terrae solidus permanet orbis." For a more recent edition with a French
translation of this passage, see *Raban Maur, Louanges de la Sainte Croix*,
text and trans. Michel Perrin, L'Image et le mot (Paris and Amiens, 1988),
p. 170.

59. On this issue in general, see, e.g., Riché, *Les Ecoles et l'enseignement*; and
McKitterick, *The Frankish Church and the Carolingian Reforms, 789–895*,
pp. 1–154. Illustrative on individual bishops are the works of Dahlhaus-
Berg, Italiani, Heyse, Rissell, Devisse, and Savigni (cited n. 20, above). See
also Egon Boshof, *Erzbischof Agobard von Lyon: Leben und Werk*; Gerhard
Schneider, *Erzbischof Fulco von Reims (883–900) und das Frankenreich*; Dag
Norberg, *L'Oeuvre poétique de Paulin d'Aquilée: Edition critique avec
introduction et commentaire*; Raymund Kottje and Harald Zimmerman,
eds., *Hrabanus Maurus: Lehrer, Abt und Bischof*; Kottje, *Die Bussbücher
Halitgars von Cambrai und des Hrabanus Maurus*; introduction to *Amalarii
episcopi Opera liturgica omnia*, ed. John Michael Hanssens, vol. 1; Allen
Cabaniss, *Agobard of Lyons: Churchman and Critic*; Eugen Ewig,
"Beobachtungen zur Entwicklung der fränkischen Reichskirche unter
Chrodegang von Metz"; and Heinz Dopsch and Roswitha Ruffinger, eds.,
*Virgil von Salzburg: Missionär und Gelehrter: Beiträge des internationalen
Symposiums von 21.–24. September 1984 in der Salzburger Residenz*.

60. Perhaps modern scholars concerned with the episcopal role in cultural life
have had their attention diverted by the complaints of Carolingian bishops
about the burdens placed on them by royal demands. For example, the
constrictive impact of royal demands on the intellectual life of bishops was
well expressed in a letter written by Claudius, bishop of Turin, complaining
about the adversities he encountered in attempting to write a commentary
on Paul's letters to the Corinthians; see *Claudii Taurinensis episcopi Epistolae*,
no. 6, ed. Dümmler, MGH, Epp. 4:601, lines 16–22 (English trans. in
Pierre Riché, *Daily Life in the World of Charlemagne*, trans. McNamara,
p. 86).

61. A major problem facing those seeking to evaluate the role of the episcopacy
in any particular aspect of the Carolingian world is the lack of an adequate
synthetic treatment of the Carolingian episcopacy, comparable to such
treatments as Martin Heinzelmann, *Bischofsherrschaft in Gallien: Zur
Kontinuität römischer Führungsschichten vom 4. bis zum 7. Jahrhundert*; or
Georg Scheibelreiter, *Der Bischof in merowingischer Zeit*. A promising
beginning in filling that lacuna is Michael Edward Moore, "A Sacred
Kingdom: Royal and Episcopal Power in the Frankish Realm (406–846)."

62. The studies on political theory, law, and ecclesiology cited in n. 21, above,
treat this issue in detail.

63. Treated in detail in Hermann Josef Sieben, *Das Konzilsidee der alten Kirche*; see also Moore, "A Sacred Kingdom," chaps. 1–3.

64. MGH, Capit., no. 22, ed. Boretius, 1:53, line 32. Suggestive on this theme are Morrison, "The Church, Reform and Renaissance in the Early Middle Ages"; Anton, "Zum politischen Konzept karolingischer Synoden und zur karolingischen Brüdergemeinschaft"; Wilfried Hartmann, "Vetera et nova: Altes und neues Kirchenrecht in den Beschlüssen karolingischer Konzilien"; and Moore, "A Sacred Kingdom," chaps. 4–7.

65. For an excellent summary of renewed episcopal collaboration in church councils, see Hartmann, *Die Synoden der Karolingerzeit im Frankenreich und in Italien*, pp. 37–96.

    Important recent studies on the episcopacy's reaction to the Pippinids' efforts include Arno Borst, ed., *Mönchtum, Episkopat und Adel zur Gründungzeit des Klosters Reichenau*; Friedrich Prinz, "Der fränkische Episkopat zwischen Merowinger- und Karolingerzeit"; Heinzelmann, "Bischof und Herrschaft vom spätantiken Gallien bis zu den karolingischen Hausmeieren: Die institutionallen Grundlagen"; and Reinhold Kaiser, "Königtum und Bischofsherrschaft im frühmittelalterlichen Neustrien."

    For recent discussions of episcopal involvement in the dynastic change, see Werner Affeldt, "Untersuchungen zur Königserhebung Pippins: Das Papsttum und die Begründung des karolingischen Königtum im Jahre 751"; Stoclet, "La 'Clausula de unctione Pippini regis'"; Enright, *Iona, Tara, and Soissons*; David Harry Miller, "Sacral Kingship, Biblical Kingship, and the Elevation of Pepin the Short"; and Matthias Becher, "Drogo und die Königserhebung Pippins."

    On episcopal participation in missionary activity, see Kurt Dietrich Schmidt and Ernst Wolf, eds., *Die Kirche in ihrer Geschichte: Ein Handbuch*, vol. 2, Lieferung E: *Geschichte des Frühmittelalters und der Germanenmission*, by Gert Haendler; *La conversione al cristianesimo nell'Europa dell'alto medioevo*; Knut Schäferdieck, ed., *Die Kirche der früheren Mittelalter*, Kirchengeschichte als Missionsgeschichte, ed. H. Frohnes, et al., vol. 2, pt. 1; *Cristianizzazione ed organizzazione ecclesiastica delle campagne nell'alto medioevo: Espanzione e resistenze*; Alain Dierkens, "Pour une typologie des missions carolingiennes"; Sullivan, *Christian Missionary Activity in the Early Middle Ages*; and James C. Russell, *The Germanization of Early Medieval Christianity: A Sociohistorical Approach to Religious Transformation* (with excellent bibliography).

    On Boniface's difficulties see Jarnut, "Bonifatius und die fränkischen Reformkonzilien (743–748)"; and Heinz Joachim Schüssler, "Die fränkische Reichsteilung von Vieux-Poitiers (742) und die Reform der Kirche in den Teilreichen Karlmanns und Pippins: Zu den Grenzen der Wirksamkeit des Bonifatius."

    On the quest for episcopal solidarity, see Karl Schmid and Otto Gerhard Oexle, "Voraussetzung und Wirkung des Gebetsbundes von Attigny."

    On the reforming councils, see Carlo de Clercq, *La Législation religieuse franque: Etude sur les actes de conciles et les capitulaires, les statuts diocésians et les règles monastiques*, vol. 1: *De Clovis à Charlemagne (507–814)*; Ferdinand

Lot and Robert Fawtier, eds., *Histoire des institutions françaises au moyen âge*, vol. 3: *Institutions ecclésiastiques*, by Jean-François Lemarignier, Jean Gaudemet, and Guillaume Mollat, pp. 7–48; Hartmann, *Die Synoden der Karolingerzeit*, pp. 37–96, 406–22; *Saint Chrodegang*; and Ferminio Poggiaspalla, *La vita comune del clero dalle origini alla riforma gregoriana*. Perhaps a better understanding of the mentality and collective aspirations of the Carolingian episcopacy could be gleaned from a close scrutiny of the legislative enactments of several prominent bishops; these texts are in the process of being edited by the MGH; see *Capitula episcoporum*, pt. 1, ed. Peter Brommer (Hannover, 1984). Brommer provides a list of existing editions of these texts (p. ix).

66. Morrison, *Tradition and Authority*, pp. 3–264, is the fundamental work on this issue.

67. Excellent summaries of the main thrust of this scholarship include Léopold Genicot, "La Noblesse dans la société médiévale: A propos des dernières études aux terres d'empire"; K. Leyser, "The German Aristocracy from the Ninth to the Early Twelfth Century: A Historical and Cultural Sketch"; Heinzelmann, "La Noblesse du haut moyen âge (VIIIe–XIe siècles): Quelques problèmes à propos d'ouvrages récents"; Jane Martindale, "The French Aristocracy in the Early Middle Ages: A Reappraisal"; Hans K. Schulze, "Reichsaristokratie, Stammesadel und fränkische Freiheit: Neuere Forschungen zur frühmittelalterlichen Sozialgeschichte"; Constance B. Bouchard, "The Origins of the French Nobility: A Reassessment"; Goetz, "'Nobilis': Der Adel im Selbstverständnis der Karolingerzeit"; Werner, "Du Nouveau sur un vieux thème: Les Origines de la 'noblesse' et de la 'chevalerie'"; Genicot, "La Noblesse médiévale: Pans de lumière et zones obscures"; and Genicot, "La Noblesse médiévale: encore!"

68. For the text of Theodulf's description of Wibod with an English trans., see Godman, *Poetry*, pp. 160–61, lines 205–12; the description of the despicable "Scottelus" follows, lines 213–34.

69. *Pippini, Carolomanni, Caroli Magni Diplomata*, no. 8, ed. Engilbert Mühlbacher, MGH, Diplomata karolinorum 1 (Hannover, 1906): "donamus . . . ad monasterium beati domnis Dioninsiae, ubi enotriti fuimus" (p. 13, lines 6–7).

70. *Versus Libris Saeculi Octavi Adiecti*, no. 1, ed. Dümmler, MGH, Poetae 1:89.

71. *The Fourth Book of the Chronicle of Fredegar*, ed. and trans. Wallace-Hadrill, pp. 102–3.

72. Riché, "Le Renouveau culturel."

73. *Liudgeri vita Gregorii abbatis Traiectensis*, chap. 2, ed. O. Holder-Egger, MGH, SS 15, pt. 1 (Hannover, 1887), pp. 67–68.

74. *Codex carolinus*, nos. 5, 9, 10, ed. Gundlach, MGH, Epp. 3:487–88, 498–503.

75. Bullough, "*Aula renovata*."

76. That seems to be the implication of chap. 72 of the *Admonitio generalis*; see MGH, Capit., no. 22, ed. Boretius, 1:59–60. Suggestive on this issue are Riché, "Recherches sur l'instruction des laïcs du IXe au XIIe siècle"; and McKitterick, *The Carolingians and the Written Word*, pp. 211–70.

77. *Notkeri Balbvli Gesta Karoli Magni Imperatoris*, bk. 1, chap. 3, ed. Haefele, pp. 4–5 (English trans. in *Einhard and Notker the Stammerer*, trans. Thorpe, pp. 95–96).

78. On laymen in the court circle of Charlemagne, see Bezzola, *Les Origines et la formation de la littérature courtoise*, 1:88–119.

79. *Alcuini de virtutibus et vitiis Liber*, PL 101:613–38; and *Sancti Paulini patriarchiae Aquileiensis Liber exhortationis*, PL 99:197–282.

80. *Alcvini sive Albini Epistolae*, no. 98, ed. Dümmler, MGH, Epp. 4:142.

81. Ibid., no. 136, pp. 205–10.

82. *Eginhard, Vie de Charlemagne*, chap. 29, ed. Halphen, p. 82.

83. The original text can be found in *Otfrids Evangelienbuch*, ed. Oskar Erdmann, 4th ed., Altdeutsche Textbibliothek 49 (Tübingen, 1962), p. 7. A translation of and commentary on the passage in question is provided by Francis P. Magoun, Jr., "Otfrid's *ad Liutbertum*," p. 886. The felicitous reading quoted in my text is suggested by McKitterick, *The Frankish Church*, p. 185.

84. On nobles collecting art, see Riché, "Trésors et collections d'aristocrates laïques carolingiens"; and Herbert L. Kessler, "A Lay Abbot as Patron: Count Vivian and the First Bible of Charles the Bald."

   On libraries, see Riché, "Les Bibliothèques de trois aristocrates laïcs carolingiens."

   On writings by nobles: Einhard's literary gem was, of course, his *Life of Charlemagne* (see n. 4, above, for a Latin ed.; for an English trans., see n. 11, above). Further proof of his high level of literacy are his letters, *Einharti Epistolae*, ed. Karl Hampe, MGH, Epp. 5 (Berlin, 1899), pp. 105–49; and *Translatio et Miracula sanctorum Marcellini et Petri auctore Einhardo*, ed. G. Waitz, MGH, SS 15, pt. 1, pp. 238–64. Angilbert's skills as a writer were manifested in his poetry; see *Angilberti (Homeri) Carmina*, ed. Dümmler, MGH, Poetae 1:355–81. Nithard earned his place in the world of Carolingian letters as a historian; see *Nithardi Historiarum Libri IV*, ed. Reinhold Rau, in *Quellen zur karolingischen Reichesgeschichte*, pt. 1, Ausgewählte Quellen zur deutschen Geschichte des Mittelalter 5 (Berlin, n.d.), pp. 385–461 (English trans. in *Carolingian Chronicles*, trans. Scholz, pp. 129–74). For Dhuoda, see *Dhuoda, Manuel pour mon fils*, ed. Riché, Sources chrétiennes 225 (Paris, 1975) (English trans., Dhuoda, *Handbook for William: A Carolingian Woman's Counsel for Her Son*, trans. Carol Neel, Regents Studies in Medieval Culture [Lincoln, Nebr., and London, 1991]).

85. MGH, Capit., no. 170, chap. 45, ed. Boretius, 1:346.

86. *Thegani vita Hludowici imperatoris*, chap. 19, ed. Rau, in *Quellen zur karolingische Reichsgeschichte*, pt. 1, p. 226, lines 29–30.

87. These issues are treated brilliantly with extensive bibliographies in the articles by Werner, Nelson, Josef Semmler, Boshof, Stuart Airlie, and Johannes Fried in *Charlemagne's Heir*, ed. Godman and Collins, pp. 3–204, 231–74.

88. On Judith's cultural talents and interests, see Bezzola, *Les Origines et la formation de la littérature courtoise*, 1:162–63; and esp. Elizabeth Ward, "Caesar's Wife: The Career of the Empress Judith, 819–829"; and Ward,

"Agobard of Lyons and Paschasius Radbertus as Critics of the Empress Judith."

89. No attempt can be made here to provide an adequate guide to that scholarship. A general bibliographical orientation is provided by Giles Constable, *Medieval Monasticism: A Select Bibliography*. See also the bibliographies provided by Wallace-Hadrill, *The Frankish Church*, pp. 429–40; and Riché, *Les Ecoles et l'enseignement*, pp. 418–40.

90. For example, Jean Leclercq, *The Love of Learning and the Desire for God: A Study of Monastic Culture*.

91. Indicative of this problem is the slight attention given to monasticism as an institution in general manuals treating Carolingian church history; recent examples illustrating this point include Hubert Jedin, ed., *Handbuch der Kirchengeschichte*, vol. 3: *Die mittelalterliche Kirche*, pt. 1, *Vom kirchlichen Frühmittelalter zur gregorianischen Reform*, by Friedrich Kempf, et al., pp. 3–29, 62–196, 294–364 (pp. 3–25, 54–173, 258–319 in the English trans.); McKitterick, *The Frankish Church* (the term *monasticism* does not appear in the index to this study); Wallace-Hadrill, *The Frankish Church*, pp. 123–419; Paul, *L'Eglise et la culture en occident*, 1:103–21; and Angenendt, *Das Frühmittelalter*, pp. 401–19. The limitations on our understanding of Carolingian monasticism are made especially clear by such efforts at synthesis as Philibert Schmitz, *Histoire de l'ordre de Saint Benoît*, 1:15–134; *Il monachesimo nell'alto medioevo e la formazione della civiltà occidentale*; and Jean Décarreaux, *Moines et monastères à l'époque de Charlemagne*.

The most illuminating work done recently on Carolingian monasticism has been by Josef Semmler; see esp. the following: "Les Statuts d'Adalhard de Corbie de l'an 822" (with A. E. Verhulst); "Karl der Grosse und das fränkische Mönchtum"; "Episcopi potestas und karolingische Kloster-politik"; "Pippin III. und die fränkischen Klöster"; "Mönche und Kano-niker im Frankenreich Pippins III. und Karls des Grossen"; "Benedictus II: Una regula—una consuetudo" (esp. important); "Le Souverain occidental et les communautés religieuses de IXe au début du XIe siècle"; and "Bene-diktinische Reform und kaiserliches Privileg: Zur Frage des institutionellen Zusammenschlusses der Klöster um Benedict von Aniane."

However, Semmler's studies do not provide a holistic picture of Caro-lingian monasticism. Fruitful new approaches to the place of monasticism in Carolingian society are suggested by Prinz, *Frühes Mönchtum im Fran-kenreich: Kultur und Gesellschaft in Gallien, den Rheinlanden und Bayern am Beispiel der monastischen Entwicklung (4. bis 8. Jahrhundert)*; Otto Gerhard Oexle, *Forschungen zu monastischen und geistlichen Gemeinschaften im west-fränkischen Bereich: Bestandteil des Quellenwertes "Societas et Fraternitas"*; Prinz, ed., *Mönchtum und Gesellschaft im Frühmittelalter*; Raymund Kottje and Helmut Maurer, eds., *Monastische Reform im 9. und 10. Jahrhundert*; Prinz, "Grundzüge der Entfaltung des abendländischen Mönchtums bis zu Karl dem Grossen"; Prinz, "Kirchen und Klöster als literarische Auftrag-geber"; F. Büll, "Die Klöster Frankens bis zum IX. Jahrhundert"; Semmler,

"Le Monachisme occidental du VIIIe au Xe siècle: Formation und réformation"; McKitterick, "Le Rôle culturel des monastères dans les royaumes carolingiens du VIIIe au Xe siècle"; Jacques Stienon, "Quelques réflexions sur les moines et la création artistique dans l'occident du haut moyen âge (VIIIe–XIe siècle)"; and Oexle, "Les Moines d'occident et la vie politique et sociale dans le haut moyen âge."

92. One scholar put the point with special clarity in a recent work: "Le monachisme a déjà une longue histoire au moment où les rois francs soumettent à leur autorité la plus grande partie de l'Europe occidentale. Aussi la vie monastique est-elle, dans l'Empire, autant un héritage du passé que le fruit de la renaissance carolingienne"; see Paul, *L'Eglise et la culture en occident*, 1:103. The negative perspective on Carolingian monasticism is represented with particular vigor by such studies as Lorenz Weinrich, *Wala, Graf, Mönch und Rebell: Die Biographie eines Karolingers*; Karl Suso Frank, "Vom Kloster als schola dominici servitii zum Kloster als servitium imperii"; and Brigitte Kasten, *Adalhard von Corbie: Die Biographie eines karolingischen Politikers und Klostervorstehers*. Other examples include Karl Voigt, *Die karolingische Klosterpolitik und die Niedergang des westfränkischen Königtums: Laienäbte und Klosterinhaber*; Prinz, *Klerus und Krieg im früheren Mittelalter: Untersuchungen zur Rolle der Kirche beim Aufbau der Königsherrschaft*; Joachim Wollasch, *Mönchtum des Mittelalters zwischen Kirche und Welt*; Ludolf Kuchenbuch, *Bäuerliche Gesellschaft und Klosterherrschaft im 9. Jahrhundert: Studien zur Sozialstruktur der Familie der Abtei Prüm*; Franz J. Felten, *Äbte und Laienäbte im Frankenreich: Studie zum Verhältnis von Staat und Kirche im früheren Mittelalter*; Felten, "Herrschaft des Abtes"; Kuchenbuch, "Die Klostergrundherrschaft im Frühmittelalter: Eine Zwischenbilanz"; Dieter Hägermann, "Die Abt als Grundherr: Kloster and Wirtschaft im frühen Mittelalter"; Herbert Zielinski, "Die Kloster- und Kirchengründungen der Karolinger"; and Jean-Pierre Devroey, "'Ad utilitatem monasterii': Mobiles et préoccupations de gestion dans l'économie monastique du monde franc."

93. MGH, Capit., no. 71, chap. 9, ed. Boretius, 1:161.

94. McKitterick, *The Frankish Church*, p. 158, n. 5.

95. For example, one notes the slight attention given to Carolingian spirituality in Jean Leclercq, François Vandenbroucke, and Louis Bouyer, *La Spiritualité du moyen âge*, pp. 91–122 (pp. 68–94 in the English trans.); and André Vauchez, *La Spiritualité du moyen âge occidental: VIIIe–XIIe siècles*, pp. 9–32. That this subject may be opening up for more serious study informed by new approaches is suggested by the essays contained in *Segni e riti nella chiesa altomedievale occidentale*; and *Santi e demoni nell'alto medioevo occidentale (secoli V–XI)*; and by such studies as Sibylle Mähl, *Quadriga Virtutum: Die Kardinaltugenden in der Geistesgeschichte der Karolingerzeit*; J.-C. Poulin, *L'Idéal de la sainteté dans l'Aquitaine carolingienne*; Nikolaus Staubach, "'Cultus divinus' und karolingische Reform"; F. Chiovaro, et al., eds., *Histoire des saints et de la sainteté chrétienne*, vol. 4: *Les Voies nouvelles de la sainteté, 605–814*, ed. Riché, and

vol. 5: *Les Saintetés dans les empires rivaux, 815–1053*, ed. Riché; Yvette Duval, *Auprès des saints corps et âme: L'Inhumation "ad sanctos" dans la chrétienté d'orient et d'occident du IIIe au VIIe siècle*; Frederick S. Paxton, *Christianizing Death: The Creation of a Ritual Process in Early Medieval Europe*; *Les Fonctions des saints dans le monde occidental (IIIe–XIIIe siècle): Actes du colloque organisé par l'Ecole française de Rome avec le concours de l'Université de Rome 'La Sapienza,' Rome, 27–29 octobre 1988*; Rudi Künzel, "Paganisme, syncrétisme et culture religieuse populaire au haut moyen âge: Réflexions de méthode"; Valerie I. J. Flint, *The Rise of Magic in Early Medieval Europe*; and Russell, *The Germanization of Early Medieval Christianity*. What light may be cast on Carolingian spirituality by those scholars enthralled with the quest for "popular religion" remains problematic; for a sampling of studies shaped by this approach, see the bibliography provided by Sullivan, "The Carolingian Age," p. 284, n. 36; or by Jean Chélini, *L'Aube du moyen âge: Naissance de la chrétienté occidentale: La Vie religieuse des laïcs dans l'Europe carolingienne (750–900)* (Chélini's citations are not always accurate).

96. This point could be illustrated by the treatment of Carolingian religious reform in such standard works as Emile Amann, *L'Epoque carolingienne*, pp. 24–32, 71–93, 210–17, 255–66, 345–66; Jedin, ed., *Handbuch der Kirchengeschichte*, vol. 3: *Die mittelalterliche Kirche*, pt. 1, pp. 3–29, 62–196, 294–364 (pp. 70–78, 157–73, 258–319 in vol. 3 of the English trans.); Wallace-Hadrill, *The Frankish Church*, pp. 258–303; and Chélini, *L'Aube du moyen âge*.

97. For Hrabanus's words, see Godman, *Poetry*: "Grammata sola carent fato, mortemque repellunt, / Praeterita renovant grammata sola biblis / . . . Sunt, fuerant, mundo venient quae forte futura, / Grammata haec monstrant famine cunta suo" (p. 248, lines 9–10, 13–14; trans. on p. 249). Alcuin felt confident that in the presence of books nothing was lacking in terms of the religious life; see *Alcuini Epistolae*, no. 281, ed. Dümmler, MGH, Epp. 4: "dum sedebamus . . . inter librorum copias . . . quibus nihil defuit, quod relegiosae vitae . . . deposcebat" (p. 439, lines 23–26). See also the admonition of Bishop Theodulf of Orléans to his clergy in *Erstes Kapitular*, chap. 2, ed. Peter Brommer, MGH, Capitula Episcoporum, pt. 1 (Hannover, 1984): "Haec sunt enim arma, lectio videlicet et oratio, quibus diabolus expugnatur. Haec sunt instrumenta, quibus aeterna beatitudo acquiritur. His armis vitia comprimuntur, his alimentis virtutes nutriuntur" (p. 105). The *Admonitio generalis* warned that bad books led to bad praying; see MGH, Capit., no. 22, ed. Boretius, 1:59, line 42, to 1:60, line 7. Suggestive on this matter is Peter Dinzelbacher, "Die Bedeutung des Buches in der Karolingerzeit."

98. See n. 1, above.

99. *Sancti Remigii Lugdunensis episcopi De tribus epistolis Liber*, chap. 8, PL 121:1002. Although Alcuin might not have liked the implications of "modernity," others were not especially disturbed. The anonymous "Hibernicus Exul" wrote with respect to the poetry of his day: "Priscis quae extant tempora praeferimus"; *Hibernici Exulis Carmina*, no. 5, ed.

Dümmler, MGH, Poetae 1:400, line 10. And "Poeta Saxo" wrote in his poetic account of the deeds of Charlemagne: "Ob hoc, mirificos Karoli qui legeris actus, / Desine mirari historias veterum" (text with trans. in Godman, *Poetry*, p. 342, lines 653–54).

100. This point is brought out clearly by Pelikan, *The Christian Tradition*, vol. 3.
101. *B. Augustini sententiae . . . colligente Amulone episcopo Lugdunensi*, Praefatio, PL 116:106–7: " . . . ut devotus et simplex lector, ne magnis et multiplicibus praedicti Patris [Augustine] disputationibus fugetur, vel etiam profunditate ac perplexitate tantarum questionum deterreatur aut perturbetur." That this was a real problem is clearly demonstrated by an appeal made to Alcuin by the sister and the daughter of Charlemagne, asking him to prepare a commentary on the Gospel of John that would help them to escape the confusion they faced in trying to cope with the writings of Augustine; see *Alcuini Epistolae*, no. 196, ed. Dümmler, MGH, Epp. 4:323–25.
102. Morrison, *Tradition and Authority*, esp. pp. 155–253.
103. "A Letter of Alcuin to Beatus of Liébana," ed. Levison, in Levison, *England and the Continent in the Eighth Century*: "Qui nova nunc gaudent [fingere] verba sibi / Nec sunt contenti sanctorum dogmate patrum" (p. 322, lines 15–16).
104. *Sancti Irenaei episcopi Lugdunensis et martyris Contra Haereses Libri Quinque*, bk. 3, chap. 2, PG 7:846: "Non enim per litteras traditam illam, sed per vivam vocem."
105. *Iohannis Scoti Erivgenae Expositiones in ierarchiam coelestem*, chap. 2, pt. 1, ed. J. Barbet, CC cont. med. 31 (Turnholt, 1975): " . . . quemadmodum ars poetica, per fictas fabulas allegoricasque similtudines, moralem doctrinam seu physicam componunt ad humanorum animorum exercitationem . . . ita theologia, ueluti quedam poetria, sanctam scripturam fictis imaginationibus ad consultum nostri animi et reductionem a corporibus sensibus exterioribus" (p. 24, lines 142–49; English trans. from Godman, *Poetry*, p. 59).
106. *Concilia aevi karolini*, no. 57 C, chap. 3, ed. Werminghoff, MGH, Concilia, pt. 2 (Hannover, 1908), p. 778.
107. *S. Gregorii Magni Registrum Epistularum Libri XIV*, bk. 11, no. 34, ed. Dag Norberg, 2 vols., CCSL 140, 140A (Turnholt, 1982), 140A:922. Perhaps most Carolingians encountered Gregory's view on this point in his commentary on Job; see *S. Gregorii Magni Moralia in Job Libri XXXV*, Praefatio, ed. Marc Adriaen, 3 vols., CCSL 143, 143B, 143C (Turnholt, 1979–85), 143:8–24.
108. For good summaries treating this concern, see Roberto Giacone, "Giustificazione degli 'Studia liberalia' dalla sacralizzazione alcuiniana all'immanentismo di Giovanni Scoto Eriugena"; and Riché, *Les Ecoles et l'enseignement*, pp. 247–84.
109. Suggestive on this point are Bullough, "Alcuin and the Kingdom of Heaven: Liturgy, Theology, and the Carolingian Age"; McKitterick, *The Frankish Church*, pp. 53–58; and Morrison, *The Mimetic Tradition of Reform in the West*, pp. 121–35.

110. These matters are central to all treatments of the Carolingian renaissance; good surveys are provided by Riché, *Les Ecoles et l'enseignement*, pp. 47–118, 187–344; and McKitterick, *The Carolingians and the Written Word*.

111. "Lodhuvicus et Karolus in civitate quae olim Argentaria vocabatur, nunc autem Strazburg vulgo dicitur, convenerunt et sacramenta, quae subter notota sunt, Lodhuvicus Romana, Karolus vero Teudisca lingua iuraverunt. Ac sic ante sacramentum circumfusam plebem, alter Teudisca, alter Romana lingua alloquuti sunt." *Nithardi Historiarum Libri IV*, bk. 3, chap. 5, ed. Rau, in *Quellen zur karolingischer Reichsgeschichte*, 1:438. The texts of the oaths are recorded in the two languages in ibid., p. 440 (English trans. of this material provided in *Carolingian Chronicles*, trans. Scholz, pp. 161–63).

112. Suggestive on this complex issue are Lot, "A quelle époque a-t-on cessé de parler latin?"; Carlo Battisti, "Latini e germani nella Gallia del nord nei secoli VII e VIII"; Norberg, "La Développement du Latin en Italie de Saint Grégoire le Grand à Paul Diacre"; Herbert Grundmann, "*Literatus—illiteratus*: Der Wandlung einer Bildungsnorm von Altertum zum Mittelalter"; Norberg, "A quelle époque a-t-on cessé de parler latin en Gaule?"; Carlo Alberto Mastrelli, "Vicenda linguistiche del secolo VIII"; Gustavo Vinay, "Letteratura antica e letteratura latina altomedievale"; Christine Mohrmann, "Die Kontinuität des Lateins vom 6. bis zum 13. Jahrhundert"; Norberg, "Latin scolaire et latin vivant"; Fontaine, "De la pluralité à l'unité dans le 'latin carolingien'?"; Fontaine, "La Naissance difficile d'une latinité médiévale (500–744): Mutations, étapes et pistes"; Holtz, "Le Retour aux sources de la latinité du milieu du VIIIe s. à l'an mil"; Michael Richter, "A quelle époque a-t-on cessé de parler latin en Gaul? A propos d'une question mal posée"; Mark van Uytfanghe, "Histoire du latin, protohistoire des langues romanes et histoire de la communication: A propos d'un recueil d'études, et avec quelques observations préliminaires sur le débat intellectuel entre pensée structurale et pensée historique"; McKitterick, *The Carolingians and the Written Word*, pp. 1–22; Heinz Thomas, "Frenkisk: Zur Geschichte von *theodicus* und *teutonicus* im 9. Jahrhunderts"; and Jean Meyers, "Le Latin carolingien: Mort ou renaissance d'une langue?" Considerable light is thrown on the evolution of Latin in late antiquity and the early Middle Ages by the papers presented at several recent international conferences, the proceedings of which are published under the title *Latin vulgaire—latin tardif*; to date the proceedings of the first meeting, held at Pécs in 1985; the second meeting, at Bologna in 1988; and the third meeting, held at Innsbruck in 1991, have been published. Longer treatments include Erich Auerbach, *Literary Language and Its Public in Late Antiquity and the Early Middle Ages*, pp. 83–179; Norberg, *Manuel pratique du latin médiéval*, pp. 13–67; and Christine Mohrmann, *Etudes sur le latin des chrétiens*.

113. For a brief orientation, see Lot, "Quels sont les dialectes romans que pouvaient connaître les Carolingiens?"; and Riché, *Les Ecoles et l'enseignement*, pp. 306–9. A fuller treatment is provided by Philippe Wolff,

Les Origines linguistiques de l'Europe occidentale, pp. 7–137 (pp. 7–138 in the English trans.).

114. *Eginhard, Vie de Charlemagne*, chap. 25, ed. Halphen, p. 74. The seriousness of the Carolingian concern about the learning of languages has been highlighted by recent studies of the fate of Greek in the Carolingian world; see esp. Michael W. Herren, ed., *The Sacred Nectar of the Greeks: The Study of Greek in the West in the Early Middle Ages*; Bernice M. Kaczynski, *Greek in the Carolingian Age: The St. Gall Manuscripts*; and Walter Berschin, *Greek Letters and the Latin Middle Ages: From Jerome to Nicholas of Cusa*, pp. 102–71.

115. *Eginhard, Vie de Charlemagne*, chap. 29, ed. Halphen, pp. 82–84. On Carolingian language policy, see Werner Betz, "Karl der Grosse und die Lingua Theodisca"; Bischoff, "Paläographische Fragen deutschen Denkmäler der Karolingerzeit"; Michael Richter, "Die Sprachenpolitik Karls des Grossen"; and Dieter Geuenich, "Die volkssprachige Überlieferung des Karolingerzeit aus der Sicht des Historikers."

116. *Servati Lupi Epistulae*, no. 70, para. 2, and no. 91, para. 5, ed. Marshall, pp. 73, 89; in thanking Markward, abbot of Prüm, for his efforts, Lupus wrote: "linguae vestrae pueros nostros fecistis participes, cuius usum hoc tempore pernecessarium nemo nisi nimis tardus ignorat" (letter 70).

117. For brief summaries on this point, see Laistner, *Thought and Letters in Western Europe*, pp. 362–86; McKitterick, *The Frankish Church*, pp. 184–209; Wallace-Hadrill, *The Frankish Church*, pp. 377–89; and Cyril Edwards, "German Vernacular Literature: A Survey." Fuller treatments are provided by Joachim Heinzle, ed., *Geschichte der deutschen Literatur von den Anfängen bis zum Beginn der Neuzeit*, vol. 1: *Von den Anfängen zum hohen Mittelalter*, pt. 1, *Die Anfängen: Versuche volkssprachiger Schriftlichkeit im frühen Mittelalter (ca. 700–1050/60)*, by Wolfgang Haubrichs; and Walter Haug and Benedikt Konrad Vollmann, eds., *Frühe deutsche Literatur und lateinische Literatur in Deutschlands, 800–1150* (a rich collection of texts with a German trans.).

118. Roger Wright, *Late Latin and Early Romance in Spain and Carolingian France*.

119. Utilizing the approaches illustrated by, e.g., Walter J. Ong, *The Presence of the Word: Some Prolegomena for Cultural and Religious History*; Jack Goody, ed., *Literacy in Traditional Societies*; Brian Stock, *The Implications of Literacy: Written Language and Models of Interpretation in the Eleventh and Twelfth Centuries*; Eric A. Havelock, *The Muse Learns to Write: Reflections on Orality and Literacy from Antiquity to the Present*; Harvey J. Graff, *The Legacies of Literacy: Continuities and Contradictions in Western Culture and Society*; Stock, *Listening for the Past: On the Uses of the Past*; and Michel Banniard, *Viva Voce: Communication écrite et communication orale du IVe au IXe siècle en occident latin*. The issues that need to be addressed on this matter are cogently stated by D. H. Green, "Orality and Reading: The State of Research in Medieval Studies." This problem is complicated by recent developments touching theories and practices of literary criticism;

suggestive of the issues posed for Carolingian scholars by these developments are the remarks made in the preceding chapter in this volume, and the bibliography cited there.

120. As brilliantly demonstrated by Godman, *Poets and Emperors*; also suggestive is McKitterick, "Royal Patronage of Culture."

121. From his *Visio Wettini*; the text and translation here is from Godman, *Poetry*, pp. 214–15. The critical edition of this work is by Dümmler, MGH, Poetae 2 (Berlin, 1884), pp. 301–33; for the text accompanied by an English trans., see D. A. Traill, *Walahfrid Strabo's "Visio Wettini": Text, Translation, and Commentary*.

122. From a poem by an Irish author, Colman; text and translation from Godman, *Poetry*, pp. 278–79.

123. Text and translation in Godman, *Poetry*, pp. 292–301; another translation can be found in *Sedulius Scottus, On Christian Rulers and the Poems*, no. 41, trans. Edward Gerard Doyle, pp. 140–43.

124. *Bedae in Cantica Canticorum Libri VI*, ed. D. Hurst, in *Bedae Venerabilis Opera*, pt. 2, *Opera Exegetica* 2B, CCSL 119B (Turnholt, 1983), p. 168. Bede quotes from Virgil's third Ecologue; see William Berg, *Early Virgil* (London, 1974), p. 44, lines 92–93.

125. Cited by Riché, *Daily Life in the World of Charlemagne*, trans. McNamara, p. 175. A study of the Carolingian sense of humor would be cause for celebration; suggestive on the subject is Irven M. Resnick, "*Risus Monasticus*: Laughter and Medieval Monastic Culture."

126. Text and translation from Godman, *Poetry*, pp. 306–7.

127. Hucbald of Saint-Amand, *Egloga de Calvis*, ed. P. von Winterfeld, MGH, Poetae 4 (Berlin, 1899), pp. 267–71.

128. From a poem by Walahfrid Strabo; text and translation from Godman, *Poetry*, pp. 216–17.

129. Walahfrid Strabo, *De cultura hortorum*, ed. Dümmler, MGH, Poetae 2:335–50 (English trans., *Walahfrid Strabo, Hortulus*, trans. Raef Payne, commentary by Wilfrid Blunt, Hunt Facsimile Series 2 [Pittsburg, Pa., 1966], pp. 24–65). On Ermoldus Nigellus: *Ermold le Noir: Poème sur Louis le Pieux et Epîtres au roi Pépin*, ed. and trans. Edmond Faral, Les classiques de l'histoire de France au moyen âge 14 (Paris, 1932), pp. 156–67 (English trans. of part of this passage in Godman, *Poetry*, pp. 251–55). Suggestive of the insights that might flow from a more personalized approach to Carolingian sources dealing with cultural life is Contreni, "The Carolingian School: Letters from the Classroom."

130. From the "Poeta Saxo's" account of the deeds of Charlemagne; text and trans. in Godman, *Poetry*, pp. 342–43.

131. The challenge faced in establishing a synchronic view of Carolingian learning is well illustrated in such recent works as Braunfels, et al., eds., *Karl der Grosse*, vols. 2–3; Margaret T. Gibson and Janet L. Nelson, eds., *Charles the Bald: Court and Kingdom*; Godman and Collins, eds., *Charlemagne's Heir*, pp. 489–687; and McKitterick, ed., *Carolingian Culture*.

132. A multiple-treatment example is illustrated by Laistner, *Thought and Letters*

in Western Europe, pp. 189–386. Examples of single-topic studies are cited in n. 21, above.

133. I claim no originality in applying this terminology to the Carolingian cultural scene; Bezzola, *Les Origines et la formation de la littérature courtoise*, described Carolingian literature as "un littérature de circonstance" (1:128).

134. For suggestive guides to scholarly works illustrating this approach, see the bibliographies in Riché, *Les Ecoles et l'enseignement*, pp. 418–40; Wallace-Hadrill, *The Frankish Church*, pp. 428–39; Sullivan, "The Carolingian Age," pp. 295–97, nn. 54–57; and Ganz in chap. 8 of this volume, n. 54.

135. For this idea, see Riché, "Epilogo." See also Judith Herrin, *The Formation of Christendom*, pp. 291–487; Robert Fossier, et al., *Le Moyen âge*, vol. 1: *Les Mondes nouveaux*, pp. 189–501 (pp. 179–529 in the English trans.); and Roger Collins, *Early Medieval Europe, 300–1000*.

136. Quoted by Godman, *Poetry*, p. 80.

3

The Pursuit of Knowledge in Carolingian Europe

JOHN J. CONTRENI

O how sweet life was when we used to sit at leisure
amid the book boxes of a learned man, piles of books,
and the venerable thoughts of the Fathers; nothing
was missing that was needed for religious life and the
pursuit of knowledge.

—ALCUIN

Alcuin's nostalgic lament, written by a worried master to a former pupil traveling in distant and pestilent Italy *(Italia firma)*, captures the essence of learning in the early Middle Ages.[1] Written sometime between 793 and Alcuin's death in 804, this touching portrait of the life of scholarship, with its emphasis on tranquility, close personal bonds between master and student, and communion with great minds, might have been written in any medieval century. But Alcuin was writing in the Carolingian century at a time when education and learning were being radically transformed.

Alcuin, an Anglo-Saxon born around 730 and educated at York, represents part of that transformation. Many like him who had been educated in the cathedral and monastic schools of England, Ireland, Spain, and Italy no doubt had been destined to replace their own masters. Instead, as adults they found themselves transplanted to the kingdoms of the Franks, where their learning, pedagogical skills, and books were put to a new task. That task, the effort to harness the quiet pursuit of religious life and wisdom to broad social reform, forced Carolingian leaders to think about schooling and how it might be used to achieve their goals.

Two documents issued in the name of Charlemagne (ca. 742–814), one in March 789 and the other sometime during the 790s, might well be considered the manifestos of the Carolingian educational reform movement. The *Admonitio generalis* and the *Epistola de litteris colendis*, both of which bear the impress of Alcuin's mind, provide good starting points for a foray into the world of Carolingian schools.[2]

The *Epistola de litteris colendis* was directed to the monasteries of the Carolingian realms. This brief letter was prompted by the poor literary quality of letters monks had been sending to the royal court. The evident piety of the monks was poorly served by their clumsy prose. Charlemagne was convinced that monks had to be schooled in the study of *litterae*, Latin letters, in order to understand the message of the Scriptures and to be able to convey its spiritual meaning to others:

> For we want you, as befits the soldiers of the Church, to be inwardly devout and outwardly learned, pure in good living and scholarly in speech; so that whoever comes to see you in the name of God and for the inspiration of your holy converse, just as he is strengthened by the sight of you, so he may be instructed also by your wisdom, both in reading and chanting, and return rejoicing, giving thanks to Almighty God.[3]

The *Admonitio generalis*, as its title implies, was a more far-reaching document. Addressed to all the ranks of the clergy and secular leaders alike, it drew its inspiration from the example of Josiah, the Hebrew king who corrected his wayward people and restored them to the "words of the book of the law" (2 Kings 22:11). Josiah became a model of Carolingian kingship—later in the ninth century, Charlemagne's grandson, Charles the Bald (823–77), would be depicted in an illustration in his Psalter as a king in the tradition of Josiah and Theodosius—another lawgiver.[4] In the context of the *Admonitio generalis*, the example of Josiah was evoked just before the presentation of eighty-two articles that were intended "to correct what is erroneous, to cut away what is inadmissible, to strengthen what is right."[5] Fifty-nine of the eighty-two articles derive from the *Dionysio-Hadriana*, a collection of canons that Charlemagne had requested from Pope Hadrian I (r. 772–95). Amid the canons addressing clerical discipline, encouraging the observance of the Sabbath, and inveighing against sin and abuses of all kinds, one specifically obliged monks and priests to conduct themselves in a praiseworthy manner and to establish schools

> that many may be drawn to God's service by their upright way of life and they may gather and associate to themselves not only children of

servile condition but also the sons of freemen. And let schools for teaching boys the psalms, the *nota*, singing, computation and grammar be created in every monastery and episcopal residence. And correct catholic books properly, for often, while people want to pray to God in the proper fashion, they yet pray improperly because of uncorrected books. And do not allow your boys to corrupt them, either in reading or in copying; and if there is need to copy the gospel, Psalter or missal, let men of full age do the writing, with all diligence.[6]

These two documents prompt several observations about the nature of Carolingian educational reform policy. First, its focus was almost exclusively on the clergy or those intended for the clerical state. One might also observe the rudimentary and practical nature of the recommendations in the two documents: emphasis fell on the proper understanding and use of language; on mastery of Tironian notes, chant, and computus or calculation; and, of course, on proper manuscript copying. Most significant of all, these documents were intended to establish kingdom-wide policy—the *Admonitio generalis* by its very nature and also by the requirement that every cathedral and monastery establish schools, and the *Epistola de litteris colendis* by the injunction that copies be sent to all bishops and monasteries. Cassiodorus planned to establish a school in Rome in the sixth century; the Council of Vaison (529) ordained the creation of rural schools; and the Rules of Benedict, the Master, and other monastic founders made provisions for teaching and learning. Individual secular leaders also encouraged learning in the early Middle Ages, but the Carolingian documents are unique both in their scope and in the consistent royal and episcopal impetus that animated them.[7]

How did it all turn out? Some have been so impressed by the achievement of the late eighth and the ninth centuries that they have argued that a renaissance resulted in the Frankish lands. A little more than 150 years ago in 1839, Jean-Jacques Ampère coined the phrase "Carolingian renaissance." More recently Pierre Riché mapped out two renaissances—one during the reign of Charlemagne and a second one, more original than the first, during the reign of Charles the Bald in the third quarter of the ninth century. Some have seen the renaissance in education and intellectual life as part of a much larger package, the reform of society as a whole. Others have rightly underscored the limits of the Carolingian achievement and have stressed the disjunction between policies, programs, and ideals on the one hand, and results on the other.[8]

There can be no doubt, however, that the schools of Carolingian Europe, given the central position accorded them in the Carolingian educational program, flourished. Monasteries and cathedrals served as the principal centers where reforms in copying were carried out, where libraries were built up by the deliberate efforts of patrons and collectors, where new teaching manuals were created for new students, and where masters were recruited to supervise and direct the teaching of youth. Two school texts emanated from this charged environment and describe clearly the focus of Carolingian education and its goals.

The first is Hrabanus Maurus's treatise, *On Clerical Training*. Hrabanus (ca. 780/4–856) wrote this handbook when he was a teacher at the monastery of Fulda in response to the insistent urgings of his brothers, who were preparing for the priesthood. They wanted their teacher to take the notes he had written out on individual sheets of parchment and put them together in one volume. The first part of the treatise introduced students to the Church, the ecclesiastical grades, vestments, the sacraments—especially baptism and the Eucharist—and to the Mass. The second section provided a handy précis of the divine office, the liturgical year, feast days, hymns, the Bible, and basic prayers and blessings, and heresies. The final section outlined what priests in training ought to know, "Quid eos scire et habere conueniat, qui ad sacrum ordinem accedere uolunt." What they ought to know was, essentially, the liberal arts curriculum—grammar, rhetoric, dialectic, mathematics, arithmetic, geometry, music, astronomy, and the "philosophical" books.[9]

In Hrabanus Maurus's scheme, his chapters on the arts were bracketed by others that stressed the relationship between wisdom and charity and emphasized the acquisition and practice of virtue. The master also gave future priests helpful hints on preaching and recommended that they modify the style of their message for their audience. Education seen from the perspective of Hrabanus Maurus was essentially Christian and practical in purpose. Much of the third book of *On Clerical Training* consists of a pastiche of earlier guides to learning—notably Augustine's *On Christian Doctrine*, but also Gregory the Great's *Pastoral Care*, Cassiodorus's *Institutes of Divine and Secular Learning*, and Isidore of Seville's *Etymologies*. These texts, prepared in different times and for different audiences, found new life and a new audience in the ninth century when woven together by the Fulda master.

Notker of Saint Gall's guide to the foremost commentators on Scripture is another text that can stand both as a product and index of Carolingian educational practice.[10] Notker (ca. 840–912) prepared his survey of biblical exegetes for his former pupil Bishop Salomon of Constance (ca. 860–919/20). The reading program that he set out is heavily dependent on the work of the church fathers—Augustine, Jerome, and Gregory the Great—but also recommends Isidore of Seville, Alcuin, and Hrabanus Maurus.

The study and comprehension of Scripture were the ultimate goals of Carolingian education. Although modern observers of the Carolingian scene may be dazzled by the philosophic brilliance of a John Scottus Eriugena (ca. 810–ca. 877), the exegetical prowess of a Paschasius Radbertus (ca. 790–860), the poetical sophistication of a Theodulf of Orléans (ca. 760–821), or the classical humanism of a Lupus of Ferrières (ca. 805–ca. 862), what united these scholars of different talents and interests and their confreres was the absolute centrality of the Bible in their intellectual life. Notker's guide to the authorities one needed to consult to comprehend the Bible reflects the preeminence of biblical studies in Carolingian schools and the maturation of Carolingian biblical studies—a program complete with a list of authors had been erected around the Bible.[11]

Texts such as those of Hrabanus and Notker, however, can be deceptive. In their prescriptive nature they suggest a calm, orderly approach to learning and intellectual life in the Carolingian period. Reality of course was much different. While Carolingian teachers and their charges may have started from the same general intellectual presuppositions—a Christian spiritual worldview; the centrality of the sacred writings; enormous respect for the Fathers; and general acceptance of classical, pagan authors in the canon—what they came up with on their own was often widely divergent and sometimes the source of great anxiety in the world of Carolingian schools. While one master might lash out at the misplaced fondness of Irish scholars for the syllogism and an Irishman might accuse a Saxon of not knowing his Augustine, those who reflected more deeply on the matter concluded that many different streams flowed into the river of Christian wisdom and that there were, in fact, different "philosophical" schools. Harmony, in other words, was illusory, discord was systemic.[12]

Any attempt to explore the more prosaic world of Carolingian schooling inevitably reaches the same conclusion. Conventional treatments of Carolingian education center on the arts in somewhat schematic fashion. In reality, application of the program was spotty and everywhere unequal. Everything depended on the material and human resources available. Individual interests and talents no doubt played their part as well. Nevertheless, it is possible to present a panoramic view of studies in Carolingian schools across the ninth century while keeping inevitable differences and variety in mind. The survival of actual schoolbooks that masters and students used will lend detail to the panorama by revealing the specific educational experiences of individual Carolingian masters and students.

❖

The word *schola* had a long tradition in late antiquity and the early Middle Ages. It could refer to a group of any sort, from craftsmen, to cantors, to warriors. The monastery, in Benedict's famous phrase, could be called a "school" for the service of God.[13] By the late eighth and ninth centuries, *schola* came also to mean a grouping of students or disciples around a master pursuing studies that were at once academic and spiritual. The school itself, the place where studies took place, was ill defined. It could be a separate room in a monastic complex, such as the exterior school depicted in the Plan of Saint Gall.[14] It could also be located in a separate building, such as the one mentioned in a charter of 767 at Lucca and the novice's cloister in the Saint Gall Plan, or even in a garden, such as the one in which Fulbert of Chartres taught early in the eleventh century.[15] Hermits were known to teach in their isolated locations where the material surroundings must have been very spartan. At the opposite extreme, school could be held in the royal palace, where under the Carolingians, monarch and master could engage in intellectual conversation, debate, and witty repartee on a whole range of subjects.[16]

Most of the schools in Carolingian Europe about which something is known were associated with monasteries and cathedrals. More than seventy left some evidence of their activities.[17] The most numerous schools of all, those at the parish level, are the least well known. Carolingian bishops in their directives to their priests throughout the ninth century showed themselves faithful to the call for education at the parish level.[18] It was at this level, after all, where the reform of society had to begin, with rural priests serving as the point men, the "soldiers of the Church" (in the words of the *Epistola de litteris colendis*) of the new society. In his statutes for his priests, Archbishop Herardus of Tours (r. 855–66) bid them to establish schools for the training of priests and to have on hand corrected books.[19] Bishop Theodulf of Orléans counseled his priests to read and pray, for reading and prayer were the most effective weapons in overcoming the devil and winning eternal life. He also required them to maintain schools where the children of the faithful might come to learn their letters. Priests were not to charge for this tuition, but were to offer it freely in a spirit of love.[20]

In the face of political turmoil and competing demands for resources, it must always have been a struggle for dedicated bishops to maintain schools. When Fulco (r. 883–900) became archbishop of Reims at the end of the ninth century, he found the schools for the rural clergy and even the cathedral canons in plain disarray. He restored them by recruiting to Reims two of the leading masters of his day, Remigius of Auxerre (ca. 841–ca. 908) and Hucbald of Saint-Amand (ca. 850–930), and even by teaching himself. If the schools of Reims, one of the richest and most powerful ecclesiastical provinces in the Carolingian realms, led such problematic existences, what must the situation have been like in less fortunate bishoprics?[21] Furthermore, when Remigius of Auxerre and Hucbald of Saint-Amand answered Fulco's call, the schools of Reims gained at the expense of those at Auxerre and Saint-Amand.

No document takes us inside a parish school, so we cannot gauge how far priests struggling to maintain themselves and their buildings were faithful to the injunctions of their superiors. The few surviving inventories from rural parishes indicate that the resources for education were rudimentary indeed.[22] The occasional books mentioned in the inventories were either liturgical or books of canons, homilies, and penitentials obviously intended for the priest's own use. The kind of schooling the local priest provided was not book learning. His task was to impart religious instruction to his parishioners. Perhaps in the process he taught children how to write by forming letters on pieces of slate or wax tablets. Further instruction at this level would have prepared them with the skills they needed to enter the "literate community" that Rosamond McKitterick has reconstructed from the study of charters.[23] But the primary purpose of schooling at the parish level was to initiate young people into the community of belief. That community came together in the celebration of the liturgy, in which it was expected that the laity would participate actively. Abbot Angilbert of Saint-Riquier (ca. 755–814), in his *ordo* for the Ascension Day rogations, specified that the inhabitants of the seven towns surrounding Saint-Riquier would form up in ranks in an elaborate procession with the monks. Boys and girls were to sing the Lord's Prayer as they processed behind their banners and crosses.[24]

Some of these students may have gone on to cathedral or monastery schools for further training. Theodulf of Orléans suggested this possibility when he gave license to his priests to send their relatives, if they wished, to the cathedral school at Orléans or to one of the local monastic schools.[25] Archbishop Hincmar of Reims (ca. 806–82) in this way launched the education and clerical career of his sister's son, the future Bishop Hincmar of Laon (ca. 835/38–879).[26] It would be fascinating to know something of the social backgrounds of students in Carolingian monastic and cathedral schools. The *Admonitio generalis* did direct priests to teach the sons of free men as well as the sons of men in servile condition.[27] But what does this passage mean? That the children of unfree parents usually received schooling from monks and priests? Or that clerical leaders were being told not to assume that the sons of free parents, those who were wealthy and perhaps had clerical and aristocratic ties, were necessarily educated? Although two archbishops of Reims, Ebbo (r. 816–35) in the ninth century and Gerbert (ca. 945–1003; later Pope Sylvester II), in the tenth, emerged from humble beginnings and Paschasius Radbertus, the learned abbot of Corbie, was an orphan, it would stretch the evidence to suggest that education in the Carolingian world opened up paths to advancement to those with humble social backgrounds.

We would also like to know more about the education of women, but the surviving evidence tilts overwhelmingly toward the experiences of male students and masters. It may be, as Suzanne Wemple has suggested, that Carolingian efforts to cloister religious women more closely limited their creative scholarly activity and with it the survival of evidence that would throw light on the schooling of girls.[28] Nevertheless, if Carolingian women with the remarkable exception of the noble laywoman Dhuoda, were not writers, as Christians they had to participate to some extent in the literate culture of the Carolingian world.[29]

Here and there, glimpses of educated Carolingian women emerge from the shadows. Gisla (ca. 757–810) and Rotrud (ca. 775–810), the sister and daughter of Charlemagne, in a very cleverly argued letter implored Alcuin to write a commentary on the Gospel of John for them because their own studies were stymied by the complexity and verbiage of Augustine.[30] Another Gisla, the wife of Count Eberhard of Friuli (d. 864), was a reader, and so were her daughters. Among the friends and relatives to whom Count Eccard of Mâcon (d. ca. 876) willed his books were several women.[31]

On a more generalized and unfortunately more anonymous level, women in religious communities engaged in intellectual pursuits. Paschasius Radbertus received his early education from the nuns at Soissons and always remembered them fondly for it. Later in life he wrote a commentary for them on Psalm 44, a wedding song, which describes a resplendent princess and her virgin companions entering the palace of the king. At their request he composed a treatise on the perpetual virginity of Mary. When he wrote to them on the Assumption of Mary, he paid tribute to their intellectual accomplishments (as well as his own!) by masking his treatise as a letter from Jerome to Paula and Eustochium, the fourth-century Roman noblewomen whose intelligent questions spurred some of Jerome's exegetical work. Perhaps at Soissons "Paula" was Abbess Theodrada, just as her cousin, Charlemagne, was known as David to his court scholars.[32]

The work of women as expert scribes at Chelles has been recognized for some time.[33] It also appears that nuns working at Corbie, Soissons, or Noirmoutiers should be credited with the almost forty surviving manuscripts copied in the well-known Corbie "a–b" script.[34] It may well be that additional evidence for scribal and intellectual activity by women remains to be discovered in medical manuscripts that deal with maladies specific to women and in the histories of the Carolingian period.[35]

One of the rare references to schooling for girls is instructive. Hincmar of Reims in his *De ecclesiis et capellis* alluded to schools for little girls *(puellulae)* but in the context of separating the educational experiences of girls from that of boys.[36] This document, of course, can be read in two ways. Obviously, boys and girls were being educated together. And just as obviously, one influential official wanted to stop the practice. Did he succeed? There is no evidence to answer that question in specific terms, but the general picture of female participation in Carolingian educational and intellectual life is quite clear. Women such as Gisla and Rotrud and the nuns who sheltered Paschasius Radbertus were educated to participate in Christian life but not to engage creatively in intellectual life. Something of the frustration intelligent women must have experienced can be sensed in a petition one master (known only as "A") carried on behalf of two nuns, one his cousin, the other the daughter of Count Baldwin of Flanders. The two women had asked "A" to intercede with his own master, an otherwise unknown but obviously highly revered teacher, "E," so that they might study with "E" and learn from him everything that pertains to salvation. "When I met with them," "A" wrote, "they pestered me to intercede with your holiness for them."[37] When women had questions, they sought out sympathetic men. While girls learned the basics and were led in the direction of sewing, embroidery, copying, and pious devotion, their brothers headed off for more intellectual pursuits.

Tutelage in the cathedral and monastic schools began at the elementary level, with instruction in reading, writing, computus, and chant. Training in one skill went hand in hand with training in another. Students began by learning to recognize the letters of the alphabet singly and then in combination. One way to help recognize letters was to copy them out. Repetitious writing practice took place on wooden tablets inlaid with wax, which could be scraped and recycled into a smooth surface, ready once again for the child's stylus. Adults continued to use these tablets for correspondence. More permanent examples of writing instruction occur on the flyleaves of manuscripts in pen trials by beginners, whose crude alphabets reveal their fledgling efforts or whose apostrophes exhort them to learn how to write: "Who knows not how to write is a living ass"; "Holy Mary, teach me how to write with a quill"; "Learn, boy, how to get money with skilled hands"; "Learn how to write, boy, so that you are not mocked." Sometimes masters would copy out passages for beginners to emulate.[38]

The student's formal exposure to the mechanics of reading and writing was continually reinforced outside the classroom. Ecclesiastical buildings were flooded with inscriptions of all kinds: incised and painted elegant display capitals, as well as more spontaneous graffiti, on walls, tombs, and even floors. Young readers could sharpen their budding skills by deciphering the more public examples of literate culture they daily encountered.[39]

In learning to read and especially to pronounce Latin, Carolingian students were taking their beginning steps in the most complex and revolutionary aspects of the Carolingian intellectual reform program. Even after years of study, accomplished scholars would still worry about their Latin pronunciation or beg indulgence for the rusticity of their prose.[40] These were no mere *topoi* or displays of false modesty. The author of the *Admonitio generalis* and the *Epistola de litteris colendis* clearly emphasized the proper use of language in reading and chanting. It was no longer sufficient, in the words of the *Epistola de litteris colendis*, for the faithful to be fortified by the appearance of monks; they had also to be instructed by what the monks said and sang. And what they said and sang were the words of God and words in praise of God, words that had to be pronounced correctly to be effective. What was new and revolutionary was the definition of what constituted correct language.

As Roger Wright has shown, inhabitants of the Romance-speaking areas of Carolingian Europe spoke and wrote the same language, "early Romance," until about the year 800. After that date those who could write continued to do so in the traditional language while spoken languages began to diverge. Everyone in the Romance-speaking lands spoke the ordinary vernacular of their regions. Children who went on to school, however, began to learn how to read in a new way, producing one sound for each written letter—precisely the way in which Anglo-Saxon and Irish "foreigners" had learned to pronounce Latin in their Germanic and Celtic cultural milieus. Alcuin and numerous other Anglo-Saxon and Irish masters applied their archaic Latin pronunciation as the norm for spoken

Latin in Carolingian Europe. The norms instituted by the reformers had a profound impact not only on Latin, which Wright calls an "invention of the Carolingian Renaissance," but also on Carolingian culture—the language of the schools was no longer the language of the people.[41]

The first major test of a student's progress in learning was mastery of the Psalter. At the very earliest stages of schooling, growth in wisdom, as Hrabanus Maurus had hoped, was to be accompanied by growth in virtue. The reading primer was also a spiritual primer. Many students, after continual drill and repetition, succeeded in committing the Psalter to memory—a prodigious task from our perspective, but not an unprecedented one in predominantly oralic societies.[42]

The Psalms remained embedded forever in the minds of Carolingian scholars and flowed from the tips of their pens into their writings more often, in most cases, than any other text. Lupus of Ferrières in his correspondence cited Augustine seventeen times, Boethius eight, Cicero twenty-one, Aulus Gellius four, Jerome twenty-four, Priscian thirteen, Servius six, and Virgil thirteen. However, the overwhelming majority of citations in his letters come from the Bible, and of these, forty-four were inspired by the Psalter.[43] John Scottus's fifteen references to the Psalms in his *Exposition on the Celestial Hierarchies* exceed the number of references to any other text, secular, sacred, or patristic, with the exception of the Gospel of John, which appears twenty-one times in the work.[44] "Beatus uir," the opening words of the First Psalm, occurs frequently among the pen trials of beginning students and even of more advanced scribes, who copied out the phrase almost instinctively when testing their quill points on the flyleaves of manuscripts.

The Psalms are songs, and while learning to read them, students learned to sing them and thus received their introduction to chant. The observation of the daily office made chant a lifelong practice. Neumic notations, the early medieval system of assigning graphic values to melody, appear as apparently random jottings in many nonmusical manuscripts, thus suggesting that students thought about or practiced their lessons away from the choir. A tenth-century manuscript of Ambrosiaster's *Commentary on the Epistle to the Romans* preserves on its back flyleaf a rare look into a master of chant's class. The teacher, an otherwise unknown Adalus, listed in the manuscript the names of his students and their responsibilities. After Geroldus sang the invitation, two groups of nine students each sang the lessons for matins.[45]

Beginning students also had to tackle the computus and thereby became skilled in arithmetical reckoning.[46] Future priests and monks would often draw on the practical skill of manipulating numbers in the perfor-

mance of their sacred and mundane duties. They had to know how to cal-
culate dates of holy days such as Easter and the equinoxes and how to use
the various tables that made that task easier. Collection of the tithe and its
distribution into fourths also required arithmetical learning, as did calculation of harvests from fields or receipts from peasants, which often fell to
clergymen. Carolingian masters were at their cleverest when attempting to
teach arithmetical reasoning. A series of "story problems" attributed to Alcuin would not be unfamiliar to modern students. "Suppose," one *propo-
sitio* suggested, "that three men are traveling together, each with his own
sister. When the six travelers came to a river, they found a boat that could
carry only two persons at a time over the river. One of the men lusted after
the sisters of his friends. How did they manage the crossing and at the
same time preserve the girls from harm?"[47]

Students who learned the elements of reading, writing, chant, and computus were ready for their own crossing into the world of the liberal arts.
Here the terrain got technical very fast. General introductions, such as
Martianus Capella's *Marriage of Philology and Mercury* and the relevant
books of Isidore of Seville's *Etymologies* helped, but these encyclopedias
needed their own commentaries. Martianus Capella's fifth-century allegory of the liberal arts especially required explanation for Carolingian students, as the many ninth-century commentaries on that text attest.[48]

Other general problems attended the study of the liberal arts. One concerned the relationship of the arts to each other and to the general concept
of Christian wisdom. Various schema were proposed, but none gained the
field. To complicate matters even further, so-called minor or mechanical
arts jostled for attention in the curriculum. These included astrology, medicine, and surprisingly, the arts of the plowman, fuller, and mason. While
the arrangement of the curriculum might seem a pedantic detail, it actually
sheds significant light on what Carolingian masters thought about wisdom, its constituent parts, and the relationships of these parts to each
other.[49] In the tenth century, Otric of Magdeburg sent a student spy into
the classroom of Gerbert of Aurillac when he heard that, in his discussion
of theoretical knowledge, Gerbert subordinated physics to mathematics.
When the student erroneously confirmed the misinformation that had
come Otric's way, the stage was set for a personal debate on the various
subdivisions of knowledge, which took place in Ravenna before no less a
personage than Emperor Otto II (r. 983–1002) of the Holy Roman
Empire.[50]

While such lofty discussions probably rarely beset Carolingian class-
rooms, nagging concerns about the appropriateness of the liberal arts in
Christian education lingered even after scholars such as Alcuin and John

Scottus "christianized" the arts by demonstrating their utility in a Christian framework.[51] But syllogistic reasoning was often suspect, and Ermanric of Ellwangen (ca. 815–74) even dreamt that Virgil had come to haunt him. One master toward the middle of the ninth century felt compelled to justify the study of pagan literature in Christian schools by citing the opinions of patristic authorities who had dealt with the same problem centuries earlier.[52]

Despite the reservations of some about the appropriateness of the arts and quarrels among masters about their definition and relationship to each other, study of the arts became the bedrock of Carolingian schooling, the foundation that some students used to mount to the highest study of all, the study of the wisdom and mysteries of Scripture.[53]

This journey began with the study of Latin grammar. Carolingian schools inherited a rich harvest of Latin and early medieval texts with which to begin the study of Latin language and literature. Anglo-Saxon and Irish scholars also brought their books to the Continent in the eighth and ninth centuries. Many of the grammars they carried in their pouches had dropped out of circulation centuries earlier and were rare on the Continent. Masters such as Alcuin and Sedulius Scottus (act. ca. 840–ca. 860) added to these resources by producing grammatical commentaries that reflected their own "Latin as a foreign language" approach to grammar and pronunciation.[54]

Grammatical studies proceeded along three tracks simultaneously. Depending on local resources, a manual such as Donatus's *Ars maior* and *Ars minor* introduced students to the parts of speech. Many of these manuals are organized in a dialogue format. Donatus's manual, for example, begins with the question, "How many parts of speech are there?" and continues with the answer, "Eight." "What are they?" "Noun, pronoun, verb, adverb, participle, conjunction, preposition, and interjection." The first chapter of the *Ars minor* introduces the student to the noun: "What is a noun?" it begins. The grammar then goes on to explore the attributes of nouns.[55] The same strategy is followed with the other parts of speech. Many grammars also discussed bad grammar—technically *barbarismus, solecismus, acrylogia, cacemphaton, pleonasmos, perissologia, macrologia, tautologia, eclipsis, tapinosis, cacosyntheton,* and *amphibolia*—and provided examples of each kind of grammatical vice.

What must have been obvious to a Latin speaker in the late Empire, when Donatus taught St. Jerome, was not so obvious to Frankish students in the ninth century. Carolingian masters had to explain the grammarians. Donatus's simple query about the number of the parts of speech and the single word reply, "Eight," elicited fifty-five lines of comment in the Corpus Christianorum edition of Sedulius Scottus's commentary on Donatus. Sedulius warned his students that the response, "Eight," did not mean that the parts of speech were something named "eight," but that there were eight parts of speech. Where Donatus's manual listed the eight parts, Sedulius's commentary briefly defined each one for learners who may have encountered the words *nomen* and *uerbum* for the first time. Sixteen lines of Sedulius's comment on the first two lines of Donatus anticipated a question about why there were not fewer or more than eight parts of speech. His answer was that the human voice articulates only eight properties such as naming, or describing actions or feelings, or interjecting.[56]

While learning the mechanics of grammar, students embarked on a second, parallel track and began to expand their Latin vocabularies by studying glossaries and specialized word lists. Glossaries were essentially dictionaries that presented simpler equivalents for Latin words. The various glossaries available are generally known to us by their first words: *Abauus, Abolita, Abrogans, Abstrusa*. The *Liber glossarum*, with its more than 500,000 entries, was one of the most useful guides to Latin vocabulary.[57] With entries culled from a vast variety of authors and works—including Jerome, Ambrose, Augustine, Isidore of Seville, Virgil, Orosius, and medical and scientific texts—all alphabetically arranged, the *Liber glossarum* was more an encyclopedia than a dictionary.

While modern critical editions of these books seem lifeless on the printed page, the actual manuscripts used in the schools are fascinating. When Carolingian masters and students entered marginal marks, underlinings, notes, and additions into their glossaries, they were also entering into the historical record impressive evidence of their creative use of these storehouses of Latin language and lore. The flyleaves of glossaries are especially interesting for the fragments of texts and odd notes they preserve from the classroom experience. The flyleaves of one copy of the *Liber glossarum* bear an extract from Bede's (672/3–735) guide to Latin pronunciation and spelling, the *De orthographia*, intended undoubtedly to be at the ready when troublesome words were encountered.[58]

Two kinds of specialized glossaries also supported grammatical studies. Bilingual glossaries helped students to bridge the gap between the vernacular and Latin.[59] This is not to suggest that the vernacular was disdained in the schools. Lupus of Ferrières sent three young monks to the monastery of Prüm precisely to learn German because it was such a useful language to know.[60] The councils of Tours in 813 and Mainz in 847 as well as the statutes of Vesoul recommended explicitly that priests be able to preach in the languages of their parishioners.[61] To earn entry to the higher wisdom defined by the arts and the Scriptures, however, students needed all the help they could get to move beyond their vernaculars to the comprehension of Latin. Surviving Greek-Latin glossaries and word lists suggest that students could even advance beyond Latin to the study of Greek. Enough Greek shows up in Carolingian poetry, exegeses, and philosophy generally and in the court of Charles the Bald specifically to prove that some Carolingian students learned Greek, as far as one was able to do so in the ninth century.[62]

A second kind of specialized glossary helped students to read specific authors. Not quite commentaries, these reading aids, often called *scholia*, explained the rare and not so rare vocabulary of authors such as Virgil and Sedulius. First-time readers of the *Aeneid* must have found it useful to learn that *Carthago* was an African city or that a *thensa* was a cart or vehicle in which likenesses of the gods were drawn.[63] Classical texts were not the only ones that inspired glossaries. Students also needed help with the Bible. A whole battery of pedagogical aids—ranging from Jerome's guides, to Hebrew personal and place names, to contemporary ninth-century glosses on obscure biblical vocabulary—helped with the task.[64]

Glossaries, of course, were not used in isolation. The third track in grammatical studies was actual study of the authoritative texts. Reading the so-called school texts, a canon of classical and late antique authors, taught students proper Latin usage and the arts.[65] The works of the Fathers and the Bible also provided bases for religious instruction. Carolingian masters and their students faced a formidable challenge when they confronted the great minds of antiquity and late antiquity and the word of God itself.

Carolingian masters proved what adept teachers they were by responding to the challenge with an outpouring of commentaries on secular and sacred writings in order to accommodate these difficult texts to their audiences. Their strategies could be as simple as using a system of marks or letters of the alphabet to rearrange the order of words in a text so that a student could untangle the sometimes tortuous periods of classical and patristic Latin.[66] Or they produced full-blown commentaries on Virgil, Boethius, Martianus Capella, and other classical and late antique authors.

The case of the Martianus Capella commentaries is especially illustrative of classroom technique. The commentaries usually begin with an *accessus*, an introduction that sets the author and the work in historical and literary context. The accessus was arranged around the seven *periochae:* an account of the author's life; the title of the work; the quality or kind of work it is; the intention of the work; the number of books it contains; the order of the books; and an explanation of the work.[67] The commentary then proceeded to explain selected words or passages in order.

The explanations generally were not profound, and one looks long and hard for flights of creative interpretation in these commentaries. The fact of the matter is that they were intended for beginners and the needs of the schoolroom. They also were never considered complete and "published" as finished works—a problem that has especially bedeviled editors of the Martianus Capella commentaries.[68] One suspects that when a student transferred a master's comments from wax tablets to parchment for later use the master's comments were "frozen." Meanwhile, the master's commentary would continue to evolve, eventually to be recorded by another student in a slightly different version.

When it came to commenting on the Fathers or on the books of the Bible, Carolingian teachers realized that they were on quite different terrain. While many of these commentaries were written on demand for ecclesiastical or secular superiors, the needs of the classroom inspired a number of them. Christian of Stablo (act. ca. 860–80) wrote a commentary on Matthew because his students, like Gisla and Rotrud earlier in the century, could not fathom the gospel even after reading it through twice and consulting Jerome's commentary. Christian adapted techniques from the study of the liberal arts in his own commentary on Matthew and began by discussing the *tempus, locus*, and *persona* of the book.[69] Ercanbert of Fulda (act. 846–65) wrote out the oral comments of his master Rudolf on the Gospel of John, "neither adding or cutting anything," because he thought the master's words would fade from memory.[70] Students and other readers placed an almost impossible burden on Carolingian biblical commentators. They wanted guides that were clear, brief, and based on as many of the Fathers as possible. This required no little ingenuity and courage on the part of the masters, who were well aware of the danger of misrepresenting the authorities or falling into doctrinal error.[71]

Grammar, understood broadly as secular and divine literature, occupied most students most of the time in Carolingian schools. One experienced reader of Priscian's *Institutiones grammaticae* neatly captured the centrality of grammatical studies when he wrote at the end of his copy of Priscian that "It's like a sea without a shore / Once you fall in, you rise no more."[72] But while grammar and grammatical thinking dominated Carolingian intellectual life, in the same way that dialectic and mathematics would provide the organizing and interpretive principles for later ages,[73] study of the other arts was pursued for its own sake and for what it could contribute to the comprehension of texts.

Rhetoric and dialectic were especially useful skills. The boundary between grammar and rhetoric is not an easy one to draw, especially since the inappropriateness of classical rhetoric for public discourse by preachers, judges, and public officials in the Carolingian world meant that rhetoric became a literary skill. Knowledge of the figures of speech as well as of the technique of constructing an argument was useful in literary exercises and treatises, but discouraged in public speech. Preachers from the time of Caesarius of Arles in the sixth century through the Carolingian period were reminded to preach in a simple, clear fashion and not to make declamations as if they were performing before scholars. In fact, Carolingian preachers were encouraged to use the vernacular, *Thiotiscam* (German) and the *rustica Romana lingua*, since German speakers could not understand Latin, and Romance speakers could not understand the new Carolingian pronunciation of Latin.[74] In their writings and their discourse among themselves, however, they emulated the style of the classical masters, whose examples were reinforced by late antique Christian authors such as Cyprian, Ambrose, Augustine, Hilary, and Pope Leo I.[75]

Students in the schools learned how to write letters of condolence with all the stock phrases, how to describe a king, how to compose a debate between winter and spring, how to write encomia, and how to draft letters announcing the election of a bishop or the death of a member of the community.[76] It was not plagiarism but schooling that led Einhard (ca. 770–840) to portray Charlemagne in terms Suetonius had used to describe Roman emperors. When biblical commentators defended their tactic of borrowing from many different authors, it naturally occurred to them to employ metaphors. Extracts from a variety of authorities in a commentary were likened to the pipes of an organ, which individually emit different sounds, but when played together bring forth a harmonious melody.[77] Or, by way of justifying the eclectic nature of their works, they suggested that the ideal beautiful woman is one composed of the different attributes of several pretty women.[78] The most sophisticated practitioners of Carolingian rhetoric knew how to use rhymed prose, parallelism, panegyric, and other rhetorical skills to good effect.[79]

It was once thought that dialectical studies in Carolingian schools were but a small peak in a yawning intellectual chasm between Augustine and Boethius on the one hand and the masters of the eleventh century on the other. Most comment has focused on the seeming Irish penchant for syllogistic analysis, on Fridugisus of Tours's (d. 834) treatises on "nothing" and "shadows," and on John Scottus's use of dialectical reasoning in his work on predestination. Interest in dialectic in Carolingian schools was both deeper and wider than these seemingly isolated examples suggest. The sources for Carolingian dialectical studies were largely Claudianus Mamertus, Augustine, and Boethius. Alcuin, as he did in so many other areas of Carolingian pedagogy, oriented dialectical studies when he compiled a manual on the subject, the *De dialectica*, which, while it derived from earlier authorities, addressed issues of particular interest to Alcuin and his circle.

Alcuin's teachings and those of Candidus Wizo, his pupil, circulated throughout the ninth century as the *Dicta Albini* and the *Dicta Candidi*. Students who studied these texts considered such thorny matters as the Trinity, God's vision, Christ's physical and spiritual body, and the existence of God. Interest in dialectic was spurred by late eighth- and ninth-century debates on images, predestination, the Trinity, and on universals. By the second half of the ninth century, a considerable set of glosses had developed on Aristotle's ten categories, especially at the school of Auxerre. Scholars such as Ratramnus (act. 844–68) and the shadowy but brilliant Hadoard at Corbie found in the categories a useful analytical tool when they tried to unravel complex matters and arrive at precise definitions.[80]

Evidence of dialectical reasoning in the *Libri Carolini* and in the writings of Alcuin, Fridugisus, John Scottus, Heiric and Remigius of Auxerre, Ratramnus and Hadoard of Corbie, and many others is incomprehensible without acknowledging dialectical studies in the schools. Some of these masters taught dialectic, and their lessons have survived in the form of glosses and the *dicta*. Students practiced formal syllogistic exercises on the flyleaves of manuscripts. They learned that God is not "anywhere," because only bodies can be contained in places, and since God does not have a body, he cannot be "anywhere."[81] Even in their grammatical studies, students were sometimes led to consider whether nouns were only names or whether they stood for creatures.[82]

Theological questions, especially questions about the Trinity, the existence of God, and God's attributes, animated dialectical studies. Alcuin praised the dialectical prowess of a nun and invited her to consider fifteen dialectical *interrogationes*. Each question focused on the relationship of Christ to the Father and drew forth a response that led to an inference and a question that was intended to refute Adoptionist heretics. Proceeding "per interrogationes et responsiones" proved that Christ was truly and fully God.[83] Another set of logical questions about God's existence began by asking "What, if God exists, do you think he is?" The interlocutor's response that God is the good of which there was none better and the mighty of which there is none mightier set off a string of such interchanges, which concluded seventeen questions later with the affirmation that God does indeed exist.[84]

The dialectical question-and-response format in which these issues were explored was undoubtedly very useful in the classroom, where students learned by repetition and memorization. The classroom format crossed over into written texts. It survives in letters scholars wrote to each other and even provided the formal structure for biblical commentaries in the ninth century.

If modern students of Carolingian education have paid less attention to the quadrivial arts—arithmetic, geometry, astronomy, and music—it has not been because these subjects were neglected in the schools. One suspects that historians, whose training is primarily humanistic and literary, find little of interest and less to understand in treatises on planetary motion, calendar reckoning, or musical theory. But there was a lively interest in these subjects in the schools, and computus was expressly required as a field of study in the *Admonitio generalis*. The practical necessity simply of telling time and charting the course of the seasons and years required that all educated persons be trained in the computistical arts of arithmetic, geometry, and astronomy.[85]

Erecting buildings, defining boundaries, calculating ratios, charting the harmony of the celestial bodies, and making accurate translations from one calendar system to another—Roman to Hebrew, for example—taxed the ingenuity of teachers and students alike. The debates over images and the Trinity in the Carolingian court had their analogue in court battles over changes in the calendar for 797 and a special meeting called in Aachen in 809 to resolve computistical problems.[86] Einhard possessed a formidable scientific mind, which has led at least one modern scholar to call him an "engineer."[87] Lupus of Ferrières was fascinated by a comet, watched it closely for several days, and described it in impressive detail before it disappeared.[88] One of the little-noticed benefits of the microscopic attention paid to the Plan of Saint Gall is what it has revealed about Carolingian draftsmanship and measurement.[89]

Medieval manuscript collections are rich in manuals and school exercises that reflect the important role scientific studies played in the Carolingian schools. The fundamental works that undergirded scientific studies in the schools were Boethius's treatises on arithmetic and geometry; Martianus Capella's liberal arts manual; Cassiodorus's *Institutes*; the works of

Isidore of Seville, Pliny, Vitruvius, and Victorius of Aquitaine; and the corpus of Roman surveyors.[90] Bede's works, especially his *De natura rerum, De temporibus liber,* and *De temporum ratione,* belong in a special category. Bede had a real genius for his subject and was an admirable synthesizer.[91] Carolingian masters added their own works to the schoolroom shelves. Dicuil, an Irish monk and palace intimate during the first quarter of the ninth century, wrote a treatise on astronomy and one on the measurement of the earth.[92] Hrabanus Maurus prepared a computus manual.[93] Helperic turned his lectures on Bede's computus into a book because his students could not remember his comments and found Bede rough going.[94]

Everywhere Carolingian masters added notes to their school texts in order to break complex material down into more elementary forms. It was no easy task to correlate the moon's phases with planetary formations or to teach students calendar systems that came in 8-, 84-, 85-, 112-, and 532-year cycles. Remembering how to find the nones, ides, and calends of each month required Frankish students to think as Romans—a virtually impossible task. But they could memorize verses similar to our "Thirty days has September" to help them: "Nonae aprilis norunt quinos. . . ." One ninth-century master when teaching Bede's *De temporum ratione* gave examples, recorded in the margins of his manuscript, based on the current year, 873, so his students could more easily comprehend Bede's lesson.[95]

This essentially pedagogical concern encouraged masters to try to make scientific principles visual in the form of graphs and charts. Most of these illustrations have to do with planetary configurations, but graphic depictions of all kinds of subjects, from *Sapientia* itself and its constituent parts to musical tropes to the morbidity of diseases, were represented by diagrams. These illustrations often are quite complex. Teachers used them to convey verbal doctrine in images of high visual impact and thus moved between two kinds of cognition. A diagram in a Fleury manuscript depicts the relationships among the four elements, the four seasons, the four humors, and the four ages of man all in one image.[96] Michael Evans has studied the implications of this kind of thinking, or what Bruce Eastwood has called the "submerged assumptions" of visual images, for the high Middle Ages.[97] The inquiry ought also to be extended to the drawings that accompanied school texts of the Carolingian period, for while texts may have inspired the images, the images pushed thought beyond the limits imposed by words.

The most wide-ranging of all the liberal arts studied in the schools was music, or harmonics as it was sometimes called. Musical intervals could be correlated with the distances between planets as Pliny the Elder taught. Or as Aurelian of Réôme, mid-ninth-century author of a *De musica*, taught, music is superior to all arts because it is the art of the angels, and its power moves even the beasts of the earth, the serpents, dolphins, and vultures.[98] Between these celestial and terrestrial extremes toiled Carolingian students, who needed to know both the theory and practice of music.

A basic knowledge of chant learned at an early age no doubt sufficed for those for whom the daily office was no more than a routine chore to be fulfilled as rapidly as possible.[99] Masters, however, had to work hard to keep up with the changes in Carolingian musical theory and practice. For one thing, the different practices in the Carolingian lands, where uniformity in the praise of the Lord was the goal, made the choir a potential battlefield. Charlemagne himself entered upon that contested ground at least five times, according to Notker of Saint Gall's rendition of the great emperor's life.[100] Whether or not the incidents Notker reported actually took place is beside the point. What is clear is that Notker knew implicitly that his audience would understand the pressure to perform perfectly the public praise of God and thus would appreciate and find plausible stories about monks who could not sing or who sang incorrectly.

Recognizing incorrect chant and reforming it were two different things. In the generation after Charlemagne, Helisachar, Louis the Pious's chancellor from 814 to 819 and abbot of Saint-Aubin in Angers and later of Saint-Riquier, recalled to Bishop Nidibrius of Narbonne (r. ca. 799–ca. 822), a fellow palace intimate, how discordant the admixture of Roman and Frankish usages had become. In the preface to his new antiphonary, which he sent to Nidibrius, Helisachar was sensitive to the potential for tension between tradition embodied in sacred verse and the demands of art, but in the end his antiphonary endorsed modifications made by "melodiae artis magistros."[101]

On the theoretical side, the traditional curriculum based on Augustine, Cassiodorus, Isidore of Seville, and the ninth book of Martianus Capella was transformed forever by the assimilation into the curriculum of Boethius's *De musica* in the ninth century. The integration of Boethius's Platonic and Pythagorean musical theories into the Carolingian schoolroom apparently was first attempted by John Scottus Eriugena in his commentary on Martianus Capella.[102] At least one music teacher confessed that Boethius's theories were beyond his comprehension. By the end of the ninth century, however, Remigius of Auxerre was using Boethian theory with confidence and two anonymous ninth-century schoolbooks, the *Alia musica* and the *Musica enchiriadis,* borrowed extensively from it.[103]

No tour of the Carolingian schoolroom and its curriculum would be complete without at least mentioning some of the many other studies that occupied students and masters. Specialized studies of script, Tironian notes, law, medicine, the sacraments, and the skills of the chancery and, especially, the liturgy were all pursued in Carolingian schools.[104] But no school ever offered the full range of theoretical and practical studies that was possible in the Carolingian realms. Everything depended on local resources, interests, and talents. Indeed, the unevenness of the curriculum fostered interdependence among centers and stimulated masters and students to create networks that linked schools, libraries, and, of course, people. The studies of three students who became masters in their own turn offer a more local and personal perspective on schooling in the Carolingian world.

❖

Walahfrid Strabo was born in 808 or 809 and as a young boy entered the monastery of Reichenau. He studied at Fulda under Hrabanus Maurus, but returned to Reichenau where he eventually became abbot. His active political and scholarly life was cut short when he drowned in the Loire River during the summer of 849. If Walahfrid can no longer be credited as author of the *Glossa ordinaria*, he still did manage to edit the histories of Einhard and Thegan and to produce a body of poetry and saints' lives that have earned him a secure place among second-generation Carolingian scholars.[105]

In 1950 Bernhard Bischoff announced his discovery of Walahfrid's personal notebook, a manuscript preserved today at Saint Gall.[106] Walahfrid Strabo began his notebook at Reichenau in 825, when he was about sixteen years old, and took it with him when he went to Fulda for further schooling. It continued to serve him when he became a teacher. The earliest parts of the manuscript contain Hrabanus Maurus's computus. The student's interest in reckoning remained with him throughout his short life. Hands W III and W IV, which Bischoff identified as Walahfrid's mature script, copied the portions of the manuscript containing extracts from Bede's *De temporibus* and various chronicles and calendars. Walahfrid was interested in other subjects as well. One hundred and sixty-nine pages of the 394-page manuscript contain a variety of grammatical texts including Donatus, Priscian, Bede's *De arte metrica* and *De schematibus et tropis*. A third interest is represented by a series of medical texts and extracts from Palladius's *De agricultura* and Bede's *De natura rerum*.

Some of the texts Walahfrid copied into his personal manuscript reveal preoccupations that are reflected in his own literary works such as the poem on his garden, *De cultura hortorum*. But to see the Saint Gall manuscript only as a window into Walahfrid's work would be to miss its significance. His notebook's broad-gauged eclecticism mirrors his schooling and the lifelong appeal that grammar and the computus had for the poet and hagiographer.

The career of Heiric of Auxerre outwardly mirrored that of Walahfrid Strabo.[107] Born in 841, Heiric also kept a personal notebook. In the margins alongside the calendar in his book he recorded the significant events of his life, including his tonsuring in 850 at age nine, the beginning of his subdiaconate in 859 at age eighteen, and his ordination as a priest in 865 when he was twenty-four years old. Although he began his schooling at Auxerre, Heiric traveled to Ferrières and then to Soissons to complete his education. He left a partial record of his early education in the *Collectanea*, a compilation of notes he put together from the time he studied first with Haimo of Auxerre (d. ca. 875) and then with Lupus of Ferrières.[108] These *ludicra pulchra*, as Heiric called them, consisted of two sorts: secular learning picked up in Lupus's school and divine wisdom learned at the feet of Haimo.

Lupus taught Heiric to rifle classical authors for pithy sayings that could adorn his own writings. This part of the *Collectanea* presents a fine example of grammatical and rhetorical studies in the Carolingian schools. Most of the extracts Heiric copied at Ferrières were plucked from Valerius Maximus's book of memorable sayings and deeds compiled originally in the first century A.D. This treasure trove of lore about famous Greeks and Romans and historical events in the ancient world could be plundered to elevate the tone and style of one's own work. A section on prodigies records the story about the bees who deposited honey on the lips of sleeping Plato when he was a babe in the cradle as a prediction of the future sweetness of his thought. Lupus's student had at the ready pithy sayings on dreams, miracles, military discipline, patience, abstinence, continence, poverty (the story of Cornelia and her sons, her true "jewels"), conjugal love, old age, and reverence toward parents. Lupus also provided his students with short portraits of the Roman emperors based on Suetonius.[109]

The tone of the second section of the *Collectanea* changes dramatically. Not only was the tuition Heiric received from Haimo different in content—it focused on the Bible—its format was also different. Haimo taught by posing contrary questions, and thus Heiric's *Scholia quaestionum* preserves puzzles such as this: How is it possible that Christ in Luke 18:19 says that "No one is good but God alone," while earlier in the same book

(Luke 7:45) we find the statement, "A good man draws what is good from the store of goodness in his heart?"[110] Again, if avarice is the root of all evil, how is it that all sin begins with pride?[111] Heiric's record of his education with Haimo reveals a more active, controversial strain than is suggested by the essentially passive mastery of rhetorical embellishments he imbibed from Lupus of Ferrières.

No information survives about the early education of Martin Hiberniensis, or Martin the Irishman.[112] In the margins of his calendar Martin recorded his birth date, 819. A colleague recorded his death in 875 in the same calendar. Martin probably received his first schooling in Ireland or England and came to the Continent as an adult, much like his Irish contemporaries, John Scottus Eriugena and Sedulius Scottus.[113] Martin taught the arts and Greek and put together an impressive collection of books, most of which passed to masters who succeeded him at the cathedral school of Laon.

One of the books Martin used, MS Laon, Bibliothèque Municipale, 265, has not attracted much attention, but it was carefully put together by him and reflects his interest in pastoral and dogmatic teaching. At first glance, the manual he used to teach his students what they had to know as priests appears paleographically as a miscellaneous hodgepodge of texts from at least seven different manuscripts. If Martin had not written a table of contents for the entire collection on the first folio of his manuscript, one might easily surmise that it had been put together much later by some librarian interested in preserving fragments from various manuscripts.

The 191 leaves of Martin's collection contain some twenty-six separate texts. Many of them can be classified as broadly doctrinal. Excerpts from two sermons of Gregory the Great treat the resurrection of the body and the virtue of charity. A passage from Gregory's *Moralia* conveys a handy précis on the seven principal vices. Jerome's letter to Rusticus on penance drew special attention from Martin since he marked it with his characteristic asterisk several times. Important summaries of basic Christian belief appear in the manuscript in the form of Augustine's sermon on the Symbol, Gennadius of Marseilles's *De ecclesiasticis dogmatibus*, and the second book of Isidore of Seville's *Differences*.

Several of the texts concern christological themes. The *Acta Pilati*, an apocryphal work, recounts the trial of Christ. An excerpt from Jerome's commentary on Daniel describes the Antichrist. Two texts from the pen of Fulgentius of Ruspe, the *Liber ad Donatum* and the *De fide*, address a burning issue in the ninth century, the Trinity. Not all the texts deal with doctrinal or theological matters. Many of them center on the practice of

Christian life and have as their focus the Carolingian laity. These texts concern baptism, marriage, blessings for the people, the Mass, and the Mass for the Dead. Eight sermons, including one that warns against idolatry and other pagan practices, appear primarily pastoral in intent. Martin's manuscript also contains an unpublished Carolingian commentary on the Lord's Prayer.[114]

Martin's manuscript brings this essay full circle again to the text with which this exploration into the schools of the Carolingian world began— the *Admonitio generalis*. When it ordained the establishment of schools, the *Admonitio* also provided for checking the competency of parish priests. Subsequent Carolingian legislation and episcopal statutes throughout the ninth century elaborated a system of what might be called clerical quality control. The subjects parish priests had to know and to be able to communicate to the Carolingian people are mirrored almost perfectly by the texts in Martin's manuscript.[115]

These cameos of Walahfrid Strabo, Heiric of Auxerre, and Martin Hiberniensis as students and masters only begin to illustrate the richness and variety of Carolingian schooling.[116] Multiplied many times over, the studies and work of Carolingian masters and students testify eloquently to the creative talents that were unleashed in the schools in the attempt, as McKitterick has noted, "to put a social ideal into practice, and to create a society with a future."[117]

Notes

1. "O quam dulcis uita fuit, dum sedebamus quieti inter sapientis scrinia, inter librorum copias, inter uenerandos patrum sensus; quibus nihil defuit, quod relegiosae uitae et studio scientiae deposcebat." *Alcvini sive Albini Epistolae*, no. 281, ed. Ernst Dümmler, MGH, Epp. 4 (Berlin, 1895), p. 439, lines 23–26. For this theme and other Carolingian reflections on school life, see John J. Contreni, "The Carolingian School: Letters from the Classroom." For Alcuin, see the masterful essay by Donald A. Bullough, "Alcuin and the Kingdom of Heaven: Liturgy, Theology, and the Carolingian Age."

2. For the *Admonitio generalis*, see MGH, Capit., no. 22, ed. Alfred Boretius, vol. 1 (Hannover, 1883), pp. 52–62 (trans. in P. D. King, *Charlemagne: Translated Sources*, pp. 209–20); also, Friedrich-Carl Scheibe, "Alcuin und die Admonitio Generalis." The circular letter known as the *Epistola de litteris colendis* survives in the copy directed to Abbot Baugulf of Fulda (780–802); see MGH, Capit., no. 29, ed. Boretius, 1:79 (trans. in H. R. Loyn and John Percival, *The Reign of Charlemagne: Documents on Carolingian Government and Administration*, pp. 63–64); see also Luitpold Wallach, "Charlemagne's *De litteris colendis* and Alcuin," in Wallach, *Alcuin*

and Charlemagne: Studies in Carolingian History and Literature, pp. 198–226.

3. "Optamus enim uos, sicut decet ecclesiae milites, et interius deuotos et exterius doctos castosque bene uiuendo et scholasticos bene loquendo, ut, quicunque uos propter nomen Domini et sanctae conuersationis nobilitatem ad uidendum expetierit, sicut de aspectu uestro aedificatur uisus, ita quoque de sapientia uestra, quam in legendo seu cantando perceperit, instructus omnipotenti Domino gratias agendo gaudens redeat." MGH, Capit., no. 29, ed. Boretius, 1:79, lines 37–42 (Loyn and Percival trans., p. 64).

4. The portrait appears in the "Psalter of Charles the Bald" (MS Paris, B.N., lat. 1152, fol. 3v) and is dated to sometime before 869; for a copy, see Jean Hubert, Jean Porcher, and Wolfgang Fritz Volbach, *L'Empire carolingien*, p. 147 (fig. 135) (p. 147 [fig. 135] in the English trans.).

5. "Ne aliquis, quaeso, huius pietatis ammonitionem esse praesumtiosam iudicet, qua nos errata corrigere, superflua abscidere, recta cohartare studemus, sed magis beniuolo caritatis animo suscipiat." MGH, Capit., no. 22, ed. Boretius, 1:53, line 43, to 1:54, line 2 (King trans., p. 209).

6. "Obsecramus, ut bonam et probabilem habeant conversationem, sicut ipse Dominus in evangelio [Matt. 5:16] praecipit: 'sic luceat lux uestra coram hominibus, ut uideant opera uestra bona et glorificent patrem uestrum qui in celis est,' ut eorum bona conuersatione multi protrahantur ad seruitium Dei, et non solum seruilis conditionis infantes, sed etiam ingenuorum filios adgregent sibique socient. Et ut scolae legentium puerorum fiant. Psalmos, notas, cantus, compotum, grammaticam per singula monasteria uel episcopia et libros catholicos bene emendate; quia saepe, dum bene aliqui Deum rogare cupiunt, sed per inemendatos libros male rogant. Et pueros uestros non sinite eos uel legendo uel scribendo corrumpere; et si opus est evangelium, psalterium et missale scribere, perfectae aetatis homines scribant cum omni diligentis." Ibid., 1:59, line 42, to 1:60, line 7 (King trans., p. 217; however, where King has "musical notation" for *nota*, I have retained the original. The reference is to the medieval form of shorthand, Tironian notes).

7. For these earlier programs, see Pierre Riché, *Education and Culture in the Barbarian West, Sixth through the Eighth Centuries*, trans. John J. Contreni. For a handy précis of ninth-century educational legislation, see Riché, *Ecoles et enseignement dans le haut moyen âge: Fin du Ve siècle–milieu du XIe siècle*, pp. 354–55. For a more detailed analysis, see Rosamond McKitterick, *The Frankish Church and the Carolingian Reforms, 789–895*.

8. See Contreni, "The Carolingian Renaissance"; Riché, *Ecoles et enseignement*, pp. 103–10; Janet L. Nelson, "On the Limits of the Carolingian Renaissance"; and Giles Brown, "Introduction: The Carolingian Renaissance."

9. See *Rabani Mauri De institutione clericorum libri tres*, ed. Aloisius Knoepfler, Veröffentlichungen aus dem Kirchenhistorischen Seminar München 5 (Munich, 1900). For Hrabanus's life, the best sketch is now John M. McCulloh, introduction to *Rabani Mauri Martyrologium*.

10. See the edition prepared by Erwin Rauner, "Notkers des Stammlers 'Notatio de illustribus uiris,' I: Kritische Edition," *Mittellateinisches Jahrbuch* 21 (1986): 34–69.

11. On this theme, see McKitterick's chapter on the organization of written knowledge in *The Carolingians and the Written Word*, pp. 165–210; and Silvia Cantelli, "L'Esegesi al tempo di Ludovico il Pio e Carlo il Calvo."

12. For these themes, see Claudio Leonardi, "Alcuino e la scuola palatina: Le ambizioni di una cultura unitaria"; Leonardi, "Martianus Capella et Jean Scot: Nouvelle présentation d'un vieux problème"; Roberto Giacone, "Giustificazione degli 'Studia liberalia' dalla sacralizzazione alcuiniana all'immanentismo di Giovanni Scoto Eriugena"; Contreni, "Inharmonious Harmony: Education in the Carolingian World."

13. See Dieter von der Nahmer, "*Dominici scola seruitii*: Über Schultermini in Klosterregeln."

14. See Walter Horn and Ernest Born, *The Plan of St. Gall: A Study of the Architecture and Economy of, and Life in a Paradigmatic Carolingian Monastery*, 2:168–75. For the "external school," see M. M. Hildebrandt, *The External School in Carolingian Society*.

15. See Horn and Born, *The Plan of St. Gall*, 1:311–13; Riché, *Ecoles et enseignement*, pp. 190–91.

16. See Bullough, *The Age of Charlemagne*, pp. 99–128; Bullough, "*Aula Renovata*: The Carolingian Court before the Aachen Palace"; McKitterick, "The Palace School of Charles the Bald."

17. For a rapid survey of these schools, see Riché, *Ecoles et enseignement*, pp. 99–110.

18. See McKitterick, *The Frankish Church and the Carolingian Reforms*, pp. 45–79.

19. See the *Capitula Herardi*, chap. 17, PL 121:765c: "Ut scholas presbyteri pro posse habeant et libros emendatos."

20. Theodulf of Orléans, *Erstes Kapitular*, chap. 2, ed. Peter Brommer, MGH, Capitula Episcoporum, pt. 1 (Hannover, 1984): "Haec sunt enim arma, lectio videlicet et oratio, quibus diabolus expugnatur. Haec sunt instrumenta, quibus aeterna beatitudo acquiritur. His armis vitia comprimuntur; his alimentis virtutes nutriuntur" (p. 105); ibid., chap. 20: "Presbyteri per villas et vicos scolas habeant. Et si quilibet fidelium suos parvulos ad discendas litteras eis commendare vult, eos suscipere et docere non rennuant, sed cum summa caritate eos doceant. . . . Cum ergo eos docent, nihil ab eis pretii pro hac re exigant nec aliquid ab eis accipiant excepto, quod eis parentes caritatis studio sua voluntate obtulerint" (p. 116).

21. Flodoard, *Historia Remensis ecclesiae*, bk. 4, chap. 9, ed. Ioh. Heller and G. Waitz, MGH, SS 13 (Hannover, 1881):

> Folco, sollicitus circa Dei cultum et ordinem ecclesiasticum, amore quoque sapientiae feruens, duas scolas Remis, canonicorum scilicet loci atque ruralium clericorum, iam pene delapsas, restituit, et euocato Remigio Autisiodorense magistro, liberalium artium studiis adolescentes clericos

exerceri fecit; ipseque cum eis lectioni ac meditationi sapientiae operam dedit. Sed et Hucbaldum Sancti Amandi monachum, uirum quoque disciplinis sophicis nobiliter eruditum, accersiuit et ecclesiam Remensem preclaris illustrauit doctrinis. (P. 574, lines 39–45)

For Fulco, see Gerhard Schneider, *Erzbischof Fulco von Reims (883–900) und das Frankenreich*, esp. pp. 239–44; and Michel Sot, *Un Historien et son Eglise: Flodoard de Reims*, pp. 112–213. Fulco was killed in June 900 by Baldwin of Flanders and his men.

22. See Carl I. Hammer, Jr., "Country Churches, Clerical Inventories and the Carolingian Renaissance in Bavaria."

23. See McKitterick, *The Carolingians and the Written Word*, pp. 77–134.

24. *Institutio de diuersitate officiorum*, IX, ed. Kassius Hallinger, Corpus consuetudinum monasticarum, 10 vols. (Siegburg, 1963–80): "Tunc sequatur scola laicorum puerorum cum flammulis septem. Quos statim subsequantur nobiles uiri septeni et septeni a preposito uel decano electi. Feminae uero nobiliores similiter obseruent. Tunc iterum procedant septem iam dictae forinsicae cruces; ipsas sequantur pueri et puellae, quae canere sciunt orationem dominicam et fidem, uel cetera, quae eis auxiliante domini insinuare precepimus" (1:297). Carolingian religious houses began to use church bells to encourage popular attendance at and participation in the liturgy; see the references cited by Donald A. Bullough and Alice L. H. Corrêa, "Texts, Chant, and the Chapel of Louis the Pious," p. 490 (repr. with revisions in Bullough, *Carolingian Renewal*, p. 242).

25. Theodulf of Orléans, *Erstes Kapitular*, chap. 19, ed. Brommer, MGH, Capitula Episcoporum: "Si quis ex presbyteris voluerit nepotem suum aut aliquem consanguineum, ad scolam mittere, in ecclesia sanctae Crucis aut in monasterio sancti Aniani aut sancti Benedicti aut sancti Lifardi aut in ceteris de his coenobiis, quae nobis ad regendum concessa sunt, ei licentiam id faciendi concedimus" (1:115–16).

26. See Peter R. McKeon, *Hincmar of Laon and Carolingian Politics*, p. 14.

27. MGH, Capit., no. 22, ed. Boretius: " . . . et non solum seruilis conditionis infantes, sed etiam ingenuorum filios adgregent sibique socient" (1:60, lines 1–2).

28. See Suzanne F. Wemple, *Women in Frankish Society: Marriage and the Cloister, 500 to 900*, pp. 175–88; also Karl F. Morrison, "Incentives for Studying the Liberal Arts," pp. 50–52, for the patristic background.

29. For Dhuoda, see *Dhuoda, Manuel pour mon fils: Introduction, texte critique, notes*, ed. Pierre Riché, Sources Chrétiennes 225 (Paris, 1975); and Dhuoda, *Handbook for William: A Carolingian Woman's Counsel for Her Son*, trans. Carol Neel (Lincoln, Nebr., and London, 1991).

30. See *Alcvini Epistolae*, no. 196, ed. Dümmler, MGH, Epp. 4:323–25. It was not because they were women that Gisla and Rodtrud had a difficult time with Augustine. Bishops, abbots, monks, and kings also complained about the wordiness and difficulty of the Fathers when they asked their favorite Carolingian masters to write clearer, more literal biblical commentaries for them; see Contreni, "Carolingian Biblical Studies," pp. 90–93.

31. For the libraries and wills of Eberhard and Eccard, see Riché, "Les Bibliothèques de trois aristocrates laïcs carolingiens"; and McKitterick, *The Carolingians and the Written Word*, pp. 245–50.

32. See *Pascasii Radberti Expositio in Psalmum XLIV*, ed. Bede Paulus, CC cont. med. 94 (Turnhout, 1991); *De partu Virginis*, ed. E. Ann Matter, CC cont. med. 56c (Turnhout, 1985), pp. 9–89 (text, pp. 47–89); *De assumptione sanctae Mariae uirginis*, ed. Albert Ripberger, ibid., pp. 99–162 (text, pp. 109–62). For Paschasius's career, see Franz Brunhölzl, *Geschichte der lateinischen Literatur des Mittelalters*, 1:369–79; and David Ganz, *Corbie in the Carolingian Renaissance*.

33. See Bernhard Bischoff, "Die Kölner Nonnenhandschriften und das Skriptorium von Chelles."

34. See T. A. M. Bishop, "The Scribes of the Corbie a–b"; and Ganz, *Corbie*, pp. 48–56, who reserves judgment on the matter. See also the important study by McKitterick, "Frauen und Schriftlichkeit im Frühmittelalter."

35. See, e.g., Ernest Wickersheimer's description of MS Paris, B.N., lat. 11218, in his *Les Manuscrits latins de médecine du haut moyen âge dans les bibliothèques de France*, pp. 100–112; and Nelson, "Perceptions du pouvoir chez les historiennes du haut moyen âge."

36. See *Collectio de ecclesiis et capellis*, ed. Martina Stratmann, MGH, Fontes iuris Germanici antiqui in usum scholarum separatim editi 14 (Hannover, 1990): "Ut diuinum officium non dimittant et scolarios suos modeste distringant, caste nutriant et sic litteris imbuant, ut mala conuersatione non destruant, et puellas [*sic*] ad discendum cum scholariis suis in scola nequaquam recipiant" (p. 100, lines 6–9). *Puellulas* is the corrected reading of Hincmar's manuscript.

37. "In quo primo colloquio obnixe me rogauerunt, ut apud uestram sanctitatem pro illis intercederem." *Epistolae variorum inde a saeculo nono medio usque ad mortem Karoli II (Calvi) imperatoris collectae*, no. 26, ii, ed. Ernst Dümmler, MGH, Epp. 6 (Berlin, 1925), p. 186, lines 15–30, at lines 17–18. The nuns were members of the monastery of Saint Mary, possibly the one at Soissons.

38. See Bischoff, "Elementarunterricht und Probationes Pennae in der ersten Hälfte des Mittelalters"; and Ganz, "The Preconditions for Caroline Minuscule," esp. pp. 34–35. For an eleventh-century sketch of students with their writing instruments, see pl. 4 in Colette Jeudy, "Le *Scalprum Prisciani* et sa tradition manuscrite."

39. See John Mitchell, "Literacy Displayed: The Use of Inscriptions at the Monastery of San Vincenzo al Volturno in the Early Ninth Century"; and J. Marilier and J. Roumailhac, "Mille ans d'épigraphie dans les cryptes de Saint-Germain d'Auxerre (857–1857)."

40. See the references in Contreni, "The Carolingian School," pp. 95–96; and Contreni, "Carolingian Biblical Studies," pp. 91–92.

41. Roger Wright, *Late Latin and Early Romance in Spain and Carolingian France*: "'Latin,' as we have known it for the last thousand years, is an invention of the Carolingian Renaissance" (p. ix). See also Wright, "On Editing 'Latin' Texts Written by Romance Speakers."

42. See Riché, *Education and Culture*, pp. 464–66.

43. See *Servati Lupi Epistulae*, ed. Peter K. Marshall, Bibliotheca Scriptorum Graecorum et Romanorum Teubneriana (Leipzig, 1984), pp. 133–42.

44. See *Iohannis Scoti Eriugenae Expositiones in Ierarchiam Coelestem*, ed. Jeanne Barbet, CC cont. med. 31 (Turnhout, 1975), pp. 222–24.

45. MS Laon, Bibliothèque Municipale, 107, fol. 119r. For a plate of this leaf, see Giuseppe Billanovich, "Dall'antica Ravenna alle biblioteche umanistiche," pp. 89–90; see also Contreni, *The Cathedral School of Laon from 850 to 930: Its Manuscripts and Masters*, pp. 146–47.

46. Valuable insights on this subject are provided by editors' comments prepared as introductions to their editions of the basic texts. See Charles W. Jones, introduction to *Bedae Opera de temporibus*, pp. 3–172; and Wesley M. Stevens, introduction to *Rabani Mogontiacensis episcopi De computo*, pp. 165–89.

47. See the *Propositiones Alcuini doctoris Caroli Magni imperatoris ad acuendos iuvenes*, PL 101:1149b–c. The *solutio* to the puzzle recommended that a brother and sister make the first crossing. The sister should remain alone on the other side while her brother returns the boat to their companions. Next, the other two sisters row the boat across the river where the first girl is waiting. One of them returns the boat to the three brothers on the other shore, and so on.

48. See Leonardi, "I codici di Marziano Capella"; see also Leonardi, "Martianus Capella et Jean Scot: Nouvelle présentation d'un vieux problème."

49. On these themes, see Contreni, "John Scottus, Martin Hiberniensis, the Liberal Arts, and Teaching."

50. The source for this debate is bk. 3, chaps. 55–65, of the *Historia* of Richer of Reims; see Richer, *Histoire de France (888–995)*, ed. Robert Latouche, 2nd ed., 2 vols., Les classiques de l'histoire de France au moyen âge 12, 17 (Paris, 1964–67), 2:66–80. The controversy is retold by Riché, *Gerbert d'Aurillac, le pape de l'an mil*, pp. 58–63.

51. See Leonardi, "Alcuino e la scuola palatina"; Giacone, "Giustificazione degli 'Studia liberalia' dalla sacralizzazione alcuiniana all'immanentismo di Giovanni Scoto Eriugena." See also Morrison, "Incentives for Studying the Liberal Arts."

52. See the poem edited by Bischoff, "Theodulf und der Ire Cadac-Andreas." Ermanric's dream is recorded in a letter he wrote to the abbot of Saint Gall; see *Ermenrici Elwangensis Epistola ad Grimaldum abbatem*, ed. Ernst Dümmler, MGH, Epp. 5 (Berlin, 1899), pp. 561–62. For an apparently original ninth-century reflection on the tension between Christian and pagan learning preserved in MS Paris, B.N., lat. 5600; see Contreni, "Learning in the Early Middle Ages," n. 37.

53. See Contreni, "Carolingian Biblical Studies"; and chap. 5 in this volume, by Bernice M. Kaczynski.

54. See Louis Holtz, *Donat et la tradition de l'enseignement grammatical: Etude sur l'"Ars Donati" et sa diffusion (IVe–IXe siècle) et édition critique*; Vivien Law, *The Insular Latin Grammarians*; Law, "The Study of Grammar";

Grammatici Hibernici Carolini aevi, ed. Louis Holtz and Bengt Löfstedt, CC cont. med. 40, 40A, 40B, 40C (Turnhout, 1977); and Alcuin, *Grammatica: Disputatio de uera philosophia*, PL 101:847–902.

55. See Donatus, *Ars Minor*, chaps. 1–2, in Holtz, *Donat et la tradition*, pp. 585–87.

56. See Sedulius Scottus, *In Donati artem minorem*, ed. Bengt Löfstedt, *Grammatici Hibernici Carolini Aevi*, III, 2, CC cont. med. 40C, pp. 6–7.

57. See Gernot Wieland, "Latin Lemma—Latin Gloss: The Stepchild of Glossologists"; and *La Lexicographie du latin médiévale et ses rapports avec les recherches actuelles sur la civilisation du moyen âge*. For editions of glossaries, see Georg Goetz, ed., *Corpus glossariorum latinorum*, 7 vols. (Leipzig and Berlin, 1888–1923; repr., Amsterdam, 1965); and Wallace M. Lindsay, J. F. Mountford, and J. Whatmough, eds., *Glossaria latina iussu Academiae Britannicae edita*, 5 vols. (Paris, 1926–31; repr., Hildesheim, 1965). For the *Liber glossarum*, see Ganz, *Corbie*, pp. 53–54; Ganz, "Heiric d'Auxerre: Glossateur du *Liber glossarum*"; and Ganz, "The 'Liber Glossarum': A Carolingian Encyclopedia."

58. MS Laon, Bibliothèque Municipale, 445; see Contreni, *Cathedral School of Laon*, p. 69.

59. See, e.g., Elias Steinmeyer and Eduard Sievers, eds., *Die althochdeutschen Glossen*, 5 vols. (Berlin, 1879–1922). In *The Carolingians and the Written Word*, pp. 7–22, McKitterick argues that Latin was the vernacular in the Romance regions of the Carolingian realms and that it served as a second language for administrative and religious purposes in the Germanic regions.

60. *Servati Lupi epistolae*, no. 70, para. 2 ("cuius usum hoc tempore pernecessarium nemo nisi nimis tardus ignorat"), and no. 91, para. 5, ed. Marshall, pp. 73–74, 89.

61. For these statutes and other evidence bearing on the significance of vernacular instruction, see McKitterick, *The Frankish Church*, pp. 184–205.

62. See Edouard Jeauneau, "Jean Scot Erigène et le grec"; A. C. Dionisotti, "Greek Grammars and Dictionaries in Carolingian Europe"; Walter Berschin, *Greek Letters and the Latin Middle Ages: From Jerome to Nicholas of Cusa*; and Kaczynski, *Greek in the Carolingian Age: The St. Gall Manuscripts*.

63. For an example, see the unpublished *Glossae super Virgilium epithetis suis conuenientes*, in MS Laon, Bibliothèque Municipale, 468, fol. 36ra, in the facsimile edition, *Codex Laudunensis 468: A Ninth-Century Guide to Virgil, Sedulius, and the Liberal Arts*, ed. Contreni.

64. See Contreni, "Carolingian Biblical Studies," pp. 79, 96–98.

65. See Günter Glauche, *Schullektüre im Mittelalter: Entstehung und Wandlungen des Lektürekanons bis 1200 nach den Quellen dargestellt*.

66. See Maartje Draak, "Construe Marks in Hiberno-Latin Manuscripts"; Draak, "The Higher Teaching of Latin Grammar in Ireland during the Ninth Century"; and Fred C. Robinson, "Syntactical Glosses in Latin Manuscripts of Anglo-Saxon Provenance." Continental masters also made use of syntactical glossing; see MS Paris, B.N., lat. 10307, a schoolbook

from the last quarter of the ninth century with texts of Virgil, Servius, and Sedulius.

67. See, e.g., John Scottus, *Glosae Martiani*, 3:1–4, ed. Jeauneau, "Commentaire érigénien sur Martianus Capella," in Jeauneau, *Quatre thèmes érigéniens*, pp. 101–2; the numbers cited by Jeauneau in his edition refer to the page and line numbers in *Martianus Capella*, ed. Adolfus Dick, rev. ed., Bibliotheca Scriptorum Graecorum et Romanorum Teubneriana (Stuttgart, 1969). For this pedagogical genre, see R. B. C. Huygens, *Accessus ad auctores*.

68. On this general textual problem, see Gangolf Schrimpf, "Zur Frage der Authentizität unserer Texte von Johannes Scottus' 'Annotationes in Martianum.'"

69. See *Expositio in Matthaeum evangelistam*: "In omnium principiis librorum tria quaerenda sunt, tempus, locus, persona. Similiter de isto Evangelio, haec tria tenenda sunt" (PL 106:1264b).

70. See *Epistolae variorum inde a morte Caroli Magni usque ad divisionem imperii collectae*, no. 34, ed. Dümmler, MGH, Epp. 5:358–59: "Scripsi autem, ut ab ore uestro accepi, nihil addendo uel minuendo, in quantum me emula non retardauit obliuio" (p. 359, lines 1–2).

71. See Contreni, "Carolingian Biblical Studies," pp. 85–93; Cantelli, "L'Esegesi al tempo di Ludovico il Pio e Carlo il Calvo"; and Cantelli, *Angelomo e la scuolo esegetica di Luxeuil*.

72. See Margaret T. Gibson, "RAG Reads Priscian."

73. On this fundamental point, see Jean Jolivet, *Godescalc d'Orbais et la Trinité: La Méthode de la théologie à l'époque carolingienne*; and Brunhölzl, "Der Bildungsauftrag der Hofschule," for the programmatic nature of Alcuin's *Grammatica: Disputatio de uera philosophia*, which is suggested in the complete title of his work.

74. See Wright, *Late Latin and Early Romance*, pp. 118–22, for the pertinent text from the Council of Tours in 813 and for this interpretation of it.

75. See Alcuin, *De rhetorica*, lines 1000–1010, in *The Rhetoric of Alcuin and Charlemagne: A Translation with an Introduction, the Latin Text, and Notes*, ed. Wilbur Samuel Howell, Princeton Studies in English 23 (Princeton, N.J., 1941), p. 132; also Elisabeth Dahlhaus-Berg, *Nova Antiquitas et Antiqua Novitas: Typologische Exegese und isidorianisches Geschichtsbild bei Theodulf von Orléans*, pp. 116–37, 146–60.

76. For collections of formularies, see *Formulae Merowingici et Karolini aeui*, ed. Karl Zeumer, MGH, Leges (Hannover, 1886); also, James J. Murphy, *Rhetoric in the Middle Ages: A History of Rhetorical Theory from Saint Augustine to the Renaissance*, pp. 194–202.

77. See, e.g., Angelomus of Luxeuil in the preface to his commentary on the Canticle of Canticles, MGH, Epp. 5:627, where he also describes his work in these terms: "ut quod ego more medicorum ac pigmentariorum, qui ut diuersa unguenta et antidota temperatim possint componere" (lines 27–28).

78. See the prologue to Paschasius Radbertus's commentary on Matthew, in *Epistolae variorum inde a saeculo nono medio usque ad mortem Karoli II*

(Calvi) imperatoris collectae, no. 6, ed. Dümmler, MGH, Epp. 6:141 (a later edition in *Pascasii Radberti Expositio in Matheo Libri XII*, ed. Bede Paulus, CC cont. med. 56, 56A, 56B [Turnhout, 1984], 56:6); and Bishop's comment on this passage, "The Scribes of the Corbie a–b," pp. 523–24.

79. See Dahlhaus-Berg, *Nova Antiquitas et Antiqua Novitas*, pp. 116–37, 146–60; and Claude Carozzi's introduction to *Adalbéron de Laon: Poème au roi Robert*, pp. ix–cxl.

80. See John Marenbon, *From the Circle of Alcuin to the School of Auxerre: Logic, Theology, and Philosophy in the Early Middle Ages*, the fundamental work on Carolingian dialectic; Ganz, *Corbie*, pp. 81–102; and Marcia L. Colish, "Carolingian Debates over *Nihil* and *Tenebrae*: A Study in Theological Method."

81. "De loco Dei," in Marenbon, *From the Circle of Alcuin to the School of Auxerre*, p. 158.

82. Jeudy, "Le Florilège grammatical inédit du manuscrit 8° 8 de la bibliothèque d'Erfurt," p. 99.

83. See *Alcvini Epistolae*, no. 204, ed. Dümmler, MGH, Epp. 4:337–49: "Interrogandum est, si aliquid adorandum nobis sit aut colendum, nisi uerus Deus. Si dicit non esse, inferendum est: quomodo adorabis filium uirginis, si non est uerus Deus? . . . His ita confirmatis per interrogationes et responsiones, quid superest, nisi Christus Iesus uerus credatur Deus? uerus et plenus et unus credatur filius? proprius et perfectus adoretur et laudetur ab omni creatura?" (p. 339, lines 30–32; p. 340, lines 4–6).

84. For this text, see Marenbon, *From the Circle of Alcuin to the School of Auxerre*, pp. 154–57.

85. Helperic, in the preface to his computus manual, argued that no one, lay or cleric, should remain ignorant of computus; see *Lupi abbatis Ferrariensis epistolarum additamentum*, no. 8, ed. Dümmler, MGH, Epp. 6:120: "Cottidiana igitur annuaque compoti argumenta uulgatiora et quae ne laicus quidem, nedum clericus, inpune ignorauerit" (lines 4–6). For arithmetic, geometry, and astronomy, see the essays in Paul Leo Butzer and Dietrich Lohrmann, eds., *Science in Western and Eastern Civilization in Carolingian Times*.

86. See Alcuin's letter, among several on this subject, to Charlemagne in *Alcvini Epistolae*, no. 145, ed. Dümmler, MGH, Epp. 4:231–32; also, *Capitula de quibus conuocati compotistae interrogati fuerint*, in *Epistolae variorum Carlo Magno regnante scriptae*, no. 42, ed. Dümmler, MGH, Epp. 4:565–67. For additional references to early ninth-century computistical literature, see Stevens, introduction to *Rabani Mogontiacensis episcopi De computo*, pp. 171–75; Patrick McGurk, "Carolingian Astrological Manuscripts," with pls.; Arno Borst, "Alkuin und die Enzyklopädie von 809"; and Lohrmann, "Alcuins Korrespondenz mit Karl dem Grossen über Kalender und Astronomie."

87. See Wesley M. Stevens, "Compotistica et Astronomica in the Fulda School," p. 39.

88. See his *Epistola ad Altuinum*, para. 13, in *Servati Lupi epistolae*, no. 20, ed. Marshall: "quam rem aliquot dies scrupulose obseruans" (p. 28).

89. See "Method of Rendering," in Horn and Born, *The Plan of St. Gall*, 1:53–63; and A. Hunter Dupree, "The Significance of the Plan of St. Gall to the History of Measurement: A Link between Roman, and English and American Systems of Measurement."

90. See Wesley Stevens, "Compotistica et astronomica," pp. 36–43. These pages are fundamental for understanding the place of geometry—all but ignored by modern scholars—in Carolingian learning.

91. See *Bedae Opera de temporibus*, ed. Charles W. Jones, Mediaeval Academy of America, Publications 41 (Cambridge, Mass., 1943); and *Bedae Venerabilis opera*, pt. 6, *Opera didascalica*, ed. Jones, 3 vols., CCSL 123A–C (Turnhout, 1975–80).

92. See Mario Esposito, "An Unpublished Astronomical Treatise by the Irish Monk Dicuil"; and *Dicuili Liber de mensura orbis terrae*, ed. John J. Tierney, Scriptores Latini Hiberniae 6 (Dublin, 1967). For Dicuil, see also James F. Kenney, *The Sources for the Early History of Ireland, Ecclesiastical: An Introduction and Guide*, pp. 545–48; Michael Lapidge and Richard Sharpe, *A Bibliography of Celtic-Latin Literature, 400–1200*, pp. 174–75; and Werner Bergmann, "Dicuils *De mensura orbis terrae*." For additional evidence, see Bruce S. Eastwood, "The Astronomy of Macrobius in Carolingian Europe: Dungal's Letter of 811 to Charles the Great."

93. Wesley Stevens, introduction to *Rabani Mogontiacensis episcopi De computo*, pp. 165–97.

94. See *Lupi abbatis Ferrariensis epistolarum additamentum*, no. 8, ed. Dümmler, MGH, Epp. 6:119–20, for the preface. This computus, also known as the *Ars calculatoria*, has sometimes been attributed to Heiric of Auxerre; see Stevens's introduction to *Rabani Mogontiacensis episcopi De computo*, p. 172, n. 30.

95. See the marginal notes to *De temporum ratione*, xlvii ("De annis dominicae incarnationis"), in MS Berlin, Deutsche Staatsbibliothek, Phillipps 1832, published in *Bedae Venerabilis Opera*, pt. 6, *Opera didascalica*, ed. Jones, vol. 2, CCSL 123B:429–30. For the master responsible for the Bede glosses, see Jones's introduction to *De temporum ratione Liber*, ibid., pp. 257–61; and Contreni, *Cathedral School of Laon*, pp. 124–29.

96. See the sketch published by Jeudy, "Le *Scalprum Prisciani*," pl. 4; also, Ganz, "A Tenth-Century Drawing of Philosophy Visiting Boethius"; Marie-Elisabeth Duchez, "Jean Scot Erigène, premier lecteur du De institutione musica de Boèce?" esp. pls. 2–4; and Wickersheimer, *Les Manuscrits latins de médecine*, pls. 1–10 (pl. 1 for the Fleury drawing in MS Chartres, Bibliothèque Municipale, 62).

97. Michael Evans, "The Geometry of the Mind"; Bruce S. Eastwood, "Medieval Science Illustrated," p. 203; see also Eastwood, "Plinian Astronomical Diagrams in the Early Middle Ages" (with pls.).

98. *Epistolae variorum inde a saeculo nono medio usque ad mortem Karoli II (Calvi) imperatoris collectae*, no. 1, ed. Dümmler, MGH, Epp. 6:130: "Bestias quoque, serpentes, uolucres ac delfines suum ad auditum prouocat, sicut et supra in laude musicae disciplinae, prout potuimus diximus. Et quid plura? musica ars omnes exsuperat artes. Angeli quoque quod Deo

laudes more huiusce disciplinae in arcae referunt siderea, lecta Apocalipsi
nemo qui dubitet" (lines 4–7). See *Aurelian: Musica disciplina*, ed.
Lawrence A. Gushee, Corpus scriptorum de musica 21 (n.p., 1975).

99. An anonymous monk blasted contemporary negligence of the praise of
God in the dedication of his own treatise on the Psalms to Bishop Batheric
of Ratisbon (817–847); see *Epistolae variorum inde a morte Caroli Magni
usque ad divisionem imperii collectae*, no. 35, ed. Dümmler, MGH, Epp.
5:359–60: "Sunt namque nonnulli, qui tantum ob uerecundiam hominum,
ne forte ignaui ab ipsis iudicentur, intrantes ecclesiam sine antiphonis
cursim et omni cum uelocitate, ut citius ad curam carnis exeant peragen-
dam, diuinis negligenter assistunt laudibus, cum in mundanis studiosi
habeantur operibus" (p. 359, lines 33–36).

100. *Notkeri Balbvli Gesta Karoli Magni Imperatoris*, bk. l, chaps. 7, 8, 10, 19;
bk. 2, chap. 7, ed. Hans F. Haefele, MGH, SS rer. Germ., new ser., 12
(Berlin, 1959; repr., Munich, 1980), pp. 9–11, 12–13, 25, 58. See also
Susan Rankin, "Carolingian Music"; Bullough and Corrêa, "Texts, Chant,
and the Chapel of Louis the Pious"; and Cyrille Vogel, "Les Motifs de la
romanisation du culte sous Pépin le Bref (751–768) et Charlemagne (774–
814)." For more on the development of music performance in the
Carolingian age, see chap. 4 in this volume, by Richard L. Crocker.

101. See *Epistolae variorum inde a morte Caroli Magni usque ad divisionem imperii
collectae*, no. 6, ed. Dümmler, MGH, Epp. 5:307–9; and Michel Huglo,
"Les Remaniements de l'Antiphonaire grégorien au IXe siècle: Hélisachar,
Agobard, Amalaire."

102. Duchez, "Jean Scot Erigène, premier lecteur du De institutione musica de
Boèce?"

103. See the *Musica enchiriadis* in Hans Schmid, ed., *Musica et scolica enchiriadis
una cum aliquibus tractatulis adiunctis*, Veröffentlichungen der Musik-
historischen Kommission (Munich, 1981), and Leonie Rosenstiel, trans.,
Music Handbook = Musica enchiriadis, Colorado College Music Press
Translations 7 (Colorado Springs, 1976); the *Alia musica*, ed. Jacques
Chailley (*Alia Musica [Traité de musique du IXe siècle]*, Publications de
l'Institut de Musicologie de l'Université de Paris 6 [Paris, 1965]); and
Marcel Pérès, "Rémi et la musique." Edmund Brooks Heard has observed
that Latin *alia* is the medieval spelling of Greek *halia* and that, therefore,
the correct English title of this work is *A Musical Compendium*; see Heard's
"Alia Musica: A Chapter in the History of Medieval Music Theory," p. 19.

104. For a brief survey of these subjects, see Riché, *Ecoles et enseignement*,
pp. 221–45, 276–80.

105. See Brunhölzl, *Geschichte der lateinische Literatur* 1:345–58, 557–59;
Eleanor Shipley Duckett, *Carolingian Portraits: A Study in the Ninth
Century*, pp. 121–60; Wesley M. Stevens, "Walahfrid Strabo—a Student at
Fulda"; Stevens, "Compotistica et astronomica," 1:31–63; Peter Godman,
Poetry of the Carolingian Renaissance, pp. 34–40; and Godman, *Poets and
Emperors: Frankish Politics and Carolingian Poetry*, pp. 133–47.

106. Bischoff, "Eine Sammelhandschrift Walahfrid Strabos (Cod. Sangall.
878)," with pls.; an earlier version was published in *Aus der Welt des Buches:
Festgabe zum 70. Geburtstag von Georg Leyh*, pp. 30–48.

107. See Brunhölzl, *Geschichte der lateinische Literatur* 1:481–85, 571–72; Riccardo Quadri, introduction to *I Collectanea di Eirico di Auxerre*, ed. Quadri, pp. 3–28; Joachim Wollasch, "Zu den persönlichen Notizen des Heiricus von S. Germain d'Auxerre"; and Eckhard Freise, "Kalendarische und annalistische Grundformen der Memoria."

108. Heiric's *Collectanea* was edited and published by Quadri, *I Collectanea di Eirico di Auxerre*, pp. 77–161.

109. Ibid., pp. 78–113.

110. Ibid., p. 115.

111. Ibid., p. 127.

112. See Contreni, *Cathedral School of Laon*.

113. See John J. O'Meara, *Eriugena* (Oxford, 1988); and the sketch of Sedulius Scottus's life provided by Edward Gerard Doyle in his introduction to *Sedulius Scottus: On Christian Rulers and the Poems*, trans. Doyle, pp. 9–48.

114. See Contreni, *Cathedral School of Laon*, pp. 130–33, for details on these texts.

115. See McKitterick, *The Frankish Church and the Carolingian Reforms*, pp. 45–79; and E. Vykoukal, "Les Examens du clergé paroissial à l'époque carolingienne."

116. See, e.g., Gottschalk, *Oeuvres théologiques et grammaticales de Godescalc d'Orbais*, ed. Cyrille Lambot; *Sedulii Scotti collectaneum miscellaneum*, ed. Dean Simpson, CC cont. med. 67 (Turnhout, 1988); and Morrison, "Unum ex multis: Hincmar of Rheims' Medical and Aesthetic Rationales for Unification."

117. McKitterick, *The Frankish Church and the Carolingian Reforms*, p. 209.

4

Carolingian Chant:
Roman, Frankish-Roman, Frankish

R I C H A R D   L .   C R O C K E R

As the Carolingian Franks picked their way—figuratively and literally—among the Roman ruins, they encountered many strange and wonderful things. But it is a mistake to think that they learned about these in a systematic fashion, starting from a core of well-defined principles and procedures. Instead, they encountered these things in a state where the cultural system had disappeared. The Franks had to deal with items individually, out of context, without relationship to each other. They extrapolated from single, isolated items, combining these with other items not according to a tradition of cultural coherence but only according to Frankish imagination and resourcefulness.

Learning about the music of the Roman world involved several different—indeed disparate—matters. Closest to hand was the repertory of Christian Latin chant sung in Rome, especially by the papal choir. Then there was a corpus of theoretical writings about the music of secular Latin culture.[1] These theoretical writings were accessible in comprehensive summaries by Boethius (d. ca. 524) and Martianus Capella (fourth or fifth century); the musical practice, however, on which these writings were based was almost certainly no longer available to the Franks. And the Roman musical practice that they could and did learn had no direct connection to the theoretical writings. The Franks learned both the theory and the practice, and eventually made them go together, but with results that were completely new as far as the Latin West was concerned.[2] This same

142

process went on in more detailed ways in a number of different contexts and affected the ways the Franks learned and used all aspects of music—indeed, the very nature of music as they conceived it.

In this chapter I will be concerned only with the Franks' learning of the Roman chant, the chant they found sung in the city of Rome, at Mass and in the Divine Office.[3] The process of learning was begun in earnest under Pepin III, right after 750 and carried out under Charlemagne as a function of his political program; leadership was provided especially by Chrodegang, bishop of Metz, along with others. The activity took place first and foremost in the environment of the Carolingian homeland, the broad triangle between the Seine and the Rhine rivers.[4] The program involved the highest levels of episcopal and monastic organization, although the work itself devolved mainly on the monastic cantors. In contrast, the learning of theory was without either official backing or any defined goal and was completely a function of individual, isolated monastic scholars; it was slow to produce results. But the Franks worked hard at learning the Roman chant, and by 850 there was in place in the north a repertory of chant that had not been there before. The important historical question is, exactly what came from Rome? We can see precisely what was the state of things "after," because one of the steps the Franks took was to develop written records of the melodies; but we have no such records from Rome and are at a loss to say just what the Roman melodies were. Much of modern chant scholarship is devoted to reconstructing the melodies as sung in Rome.[5]

The situation is complicated by the fact that the Franks edited the chant they received from Rome. In fact, their editions are the only ones we have. So even when we have a chant or group of chants that we are reasonably sure came from Rome (usually on the grounds of liturgical use), there is a further question of what the chant sounded like in Rome and how much the Franks changed it. For repertorial purposes we can call a chant Roman if liturgical evidence warrants it; but in order to reflect accurately the sources in which the chant comes to us, we should have to call it Frankish-Roman. The situation is complicated even more by the fact that the Franks became very skilled at imitating Roman chant. We can tell which the imitations are, and how good they are, by various technical aspects of liturgy and documentation. Hence we can distinguish with moderate reliability among chant imported from Rome (even if edited), chant made in the land of the Franks in imitation of Roman chant, and Frankish chant developed from a Roman model but significantly modified.[6]

Over against those kinds of musical activity stands the development of new, different musical styles and repertories. These are represented most clearly by the genres of hymn, trope, and sequence. In their extreme examples they are very different from Roman chant. These genres are represented —first only by small numbers of instances—in the north from around 800 on; therefore they qualify as specifically "Carolingian" musical productions.[7]

Thus, there are several moments in the Carolingian learning of Roman musical practice: (1) the maintenance of the chant repertory from Rome; (2) the extension of the chant repertory from Rome (especially in the Office); and (3) the development of new forms and styles by the Franks.

All these developments were, in the north, in the hands of a Frankish cantor, who was the director of music either in a monastery or at a cathedral.[8] His job was to maintain the repertory of chant sung at Mass and in the Office in that place. His regular duties included learning and singing the newly imported Roman chant; training and leading a choir and—in a monastery—the whole community in certain portions of the Office; teaching everyone, but especially young boys in the school, their Latin; copying, or having copied, chant books and maintaining them in the library; keeping track of the calendar, or computus. As further extensions of these activities, the cantor, if he was musically gifted and motivated, might provide new chants, either for traditional occasions or new ones (such as a new saint's day), and either in the traditional Roman style (as the cantor understood it or modified it) or in the new Frankish style.

❖

The first type of musical activity to be illustrated is the maintenance of the Roman repertory. (I use the term "maintenance" to avoid the term "tradition," the application of which is problematic within the context of contemporary discussions of "oral tradition.") The principal example of Roman chant as maintained by the Franks can well be the most elaborate kind of piece, called a *Responsorium graduale*, or Gradual. There are about 115 such chants in the Frankish-Roman repertory in a total of about 500 Frankish-Roman chants for Mass.[9] The Gradual "Constitues eos principes" was sung at Mass on feasts of the apostles, especially Peter, between the Epistle and Gospel.

Responsorium graduale, for Apostles (Roman)

Constitues eos principes super omnem terram;
memores erunt nominis tui, Domine.
V. Pro patribus tuis nati sunt tibi filii:
propterea populi confitebuntur tibi.
Constitues . . . [10]

EXAMPLE 1

This elaborate style of Roman chant is called melismatic because it occasionally sets many pitches to a single syllable, in a melisma; this is only the most obvious manifestation of a melodic effusiveness that is at the same time carefully worked out and so varied as to sound spontaneous. This style is so impressive that there does not seem to be much one can do except admire it; and that was what the Franks did. Not much new musical activity appears to have been inspired by this particular kind of Roman chant. How much they admired it, however, can be gauged by the care with which they preserved it.[11]

Frankish cantors learned such chants in the first place by memory from a Roman cantor. At one time memorization of the chant repertory was considered not believable; but with the realization that memorization was a standard—if not the standard—method of learning in earlier times (as well as a more accurate assessment of the extensive use of memorization by modern musicians) this no longer seems a problem. Some Carolingian scholars must have memorized thousands of lines of Virgil, and monastics memorized the Psalter as a matter of course. But then the Franks developed a system of musical notation to record all these chants, to supplement their memories and stabilize the repertory. This notation, which resulted in complete chant books in standardized format by 900, is remarkable in showing great care to record subtle nuance of performance. The notation does not, however, include much pitch content. Clearly the pitch content of these melodies is the easiest element to remember; what the notation was designed to do was to preserve not the pitch content, but rather the subtle, intricate nuance of rhythm and phrasing.[12]

Different systems of notation were developed in different localities, and comparison among the earliest completed chant books (a major activity of chant scholars, especially in recent years) shows on one hand an overwhelming agreement among the sources, perhaps on the order of eighty or ninety percent, and on the other hand slight but persistent variation in detail, both in pitch and nuance. Such variation has the principal effect of alerting us to the importance the scribe and cantor (often the same person) must have attached to nuance as an essential feature of the excellence of Roman chant. An illustration of the function of memorization is given by the way the melisma at the end of example 1 is notated in two earliest sources, one from Laon, the other from Saint Gall. The two notations diverge decisively at this melisma, and the notation from Laon is incomplete, which we can tell from collation and also from the use of a melodic formula for the terminal melisma.

St. Gall

Laon

The signs given above for the Laon manuscript mean something quite different from those of the Saint Gall manuscript, and the last sign given for Laon is that scribe's "etc."[13] The continuation and meaning of the whole, which is formulaic, have been supplied from a parallel passage. This is, in all respects, a common and oft-commented situation in such Graduals. It merely shows that things that were exactly the same could be memorized rather than recorded; the record, then, had the purpose of keeping track of individual differences. Such a difference can be detected on the last syllable of "memores" in the notation below, which has one pitch, A, in Saint Gall, two pitches, B-flat, A, in Laon; also "-mor-" has an *a*, for "augment," in Laon, with no equivalent sign in Saint Gall (whereas Laon's *a* over "me-" has an equivalent in Saint Gall).[14]

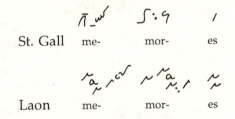

St. Gall   me-   mor-   es

Laon   me-   mor-   es

A slight difference; and the fact that it is clearly preserved shows the care with which this segment of the repertory was maintained. Difference in nuance is found over the word "super," below, where Laon has a *t* for "tenete" over "su-."[15]

St. Gall   su- per

Laon   su- per

And again, over the word "tuis," below: Saint Gall indicates *c* for "celeriter," while Laon has an *a* for "augment."[16]

St. Gall   tu- is

Laon   tu- is

It may be that neither version is wrong, that is, not "authentic"; it may be that such differences merely represent the different ways the chant was sung in two localities. Nonetheless, the cumulative effect of the nuances could make a substantial difference between local practices.

The Franks' learning of these chants was carried out by direct imitation of the model through memorization, supported by the resourceful development of a whole new method of written documentation. The result was a remarkably systematic and permanent preservation of these elaborate chants for Mass. As it turned out, the Franks composed relatively little new chant in this Roman style. The immediate significance of these Roman Mass chants was that the Franks learned them and sang them daily. The eventual significance was that these chants were the "classics" of their musical literature, providing standards of taste and excellence even though not models for new styles or structures.

With other types of chant we find other conditions, and with the repertory of antiphons for the Divine Office we move into the second phase, that of development of the repertory past simple maintenance.[17] Antiphons are—generically at least—much shorter, simpler pieces used in conjunction with psalms. The antiphon "Astiterunt iusti" for Ss. John and Paul (example 2) can illustrate a Roman antiphon of moderate length.[18]

Antiphon at the Magnificat, for Ss. John and Paul (26 June) (Roman)

Astiterunt iusti ante dominum
et ab invicem non separati sunt:
calicem Domini biberunt
et amici Dei appellati sunt.[19]

Deceptively simple, such antiphons conceal a wealth of very refined choices in the succession of pitches—and this is true even though this an-

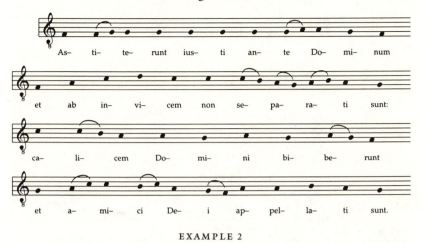

As– ti– te– runt ius– ti an– te Do– mi– num

et ab in– vi– cem non se– pa– ra– ti sunt:

ca– li– cem Do– mi– ni bi– be– runt

et a– mi– ci De– i ap– pel– la– ti sunt.

EXAMPLE 2

tiphon belongs to a large group of two or three hundred that share a relatively small stock of idioms. The Divine Office, unlike the Mass, offered abundant opportunity for new occasions and new chants, and the Franks enthusiastically embarked on a program of massive development, which included at least doubling the size of the antiphon repertory, from less than one thousand brought north from Rome to more than two thousand by the high Middle Ages. These repertories are the subject of current research. The antiphon "Egregius dei martir Vincentius" seems to be Frankish antiphon and has a good chance of being early enough to be Carolingian.[20]

Antiphon at the Benedictus, for St. Vincent (22 January) (Frankish)

Egregius dei martir Vincentius
diri tormentorum suppliciis
pro Christo alacriter superatis
ac felicis pugne agone constanter expleto
tandem pretiosa resolutus
in morte celo triumphans spiritum redidit.[21]

This example (example 3) can represent hundreds of antiphons produced in the north, using the idioms of the Roman repertory of Office antiphons while expanding the dimensions of the typical antiphon and—in ways too intricate to discuss here—modifying and developing both the

E- gre- gi- us de- i mar- tir Vin- cen- ti- us

di- ri tor- men- to- rum sup- pli- ci- is

pro Chri- sto a- la- cri- ter su- pe- ra- tis

ac fe- li- cis pug- ne a- go- ne con- stan- ter ex- ple- to

tan- dem pre- ti- o- sa re- so- lu- tus

in mor- te ce- lo tri- um- phans

spi- ri- tum red- di- dit.

EXAMPLE 3

idioms and the pitch context in which they appear.[22] In individual cases the modification is perhaps not such as to produce a noticeable difference compared to Roman antiphons; indeed, the intent of the Frankish cantor seems to have been to reproduce the style of the Roman antiphon.

The feature of the Roman chant that I feel the Franks most admired and most carefully re-created was the perpetual variety in the melodic and rhythmic flow at the lowest level, the level of single syllables and the pitches that went with them. Roman antiphon style avoided a series of two-note groups over successive syllables, for example, or a series of three-note groups; such groups were usually alternated with each other and with single notes to produce a varied, seemingly casual succession. Similarly with melodic direction: continuous ascents or descents were avoided, and instead these simple melodies turned and twisted up and down in un-predictable ways. The Roman cantors clearly had word accents in mind but treated them in a bewildering variety of ways. Modern attempts to find system in all of this have not, I feel, been convincing and, more important, seem to miss the musical point, which is the variety in succession.[23] The Franks, in any case, admired this variety—so much so that even though they systematized and regularized many other aspects of music, the variety persisted until the end of the Middle Ages. The style itself, as used by the Romans, is peculiarly analogous to and appropriate for prose texts (as from the Latin Psalter); but the Franks used it even for verse texts, as we shall see.

There was, however, a difference between the way a Frankish cantor used this style and the way it had been used by the Romans—a difference I feel reflects a basic attitude of the Franks toward the antiquity they were assimilating. Eventually, by the end of the Middle Ages, this resulted in a very different style of chant; but even during the ninth century such an effect may be perceptible. While the Frankish cantor made full use of families of Roman idioms in composing new chants, he did not necessarily use the Roman melody types—that is, he did not necessarily follow exactly a Roman melody. In many antiphons he tended to move in Roman style freely throughout an appropriate pitch set, filling it systematically with movement up and down. The resulting melodic movement had something abstract about it—going through the precise Roman idiom, it seemed detached from specific Roman melodies. While the end result has a weakened relationship to Roman melodic style, it greatly strengthened the pitch set as it occupied the interval of a fifth or an octave—and this led directly to the kinds of pitch sets and melodies characteristic of European music for the next several centuries.[24]

In connection with the melismatic chants for Mass (as in example 1), we saw the kind of elaborate notation the Franks developed to assist the maintenance of that repertory. Such notation was less important for the large and growing repertory of antiphons; but for this repertory the Franks developed another system, that of modal classification. To summarize an extensive topic as briefly as possible, an antiphon was sung before and after (sometimes also within) a psalm as a frame; the psalm was sung to a "psalm tone" or simple formula, which had to be compatible in its selection of pitches and with the melody of the antiphon.

All of this came from Roman practice, but what did not come north with the Roman chant was any systematic way of insuring tonal compatibility. The Frankish cantors early on developed such a system, drawing, apparently, upon a Byzantine model (concerning which we have no knowledge that can be documented earlier than the Franks themselves). First, the Franks stabilized the psalm tones themselves into a set of eight standard ones; then they devised ways of classifying antiphons into eight classes so as to be directly matched up with the eight psalm tones. This development took place some time between 750 and 850. The documentation after 850 gives abundant evidence that the working out of the system involved much resourcefulness and individual—sometimes eccentric—solutions; but the end result was clear and orderly and was one of the first manifestations of an indigenous Western theory of music. It is also a manifestation of what seems an overriding need on the part of the Franks to learn something by systematizing it, a need that is surely one of our main concerns here.[25]

Once having developed a system, the Franks seem to have had a consequent need—less evident, perhaps—to use it to create something new. This happened, at any rate, with the modal classification of antiphons. In order to explain the result, I need to describe briefly the plan of the Roman Night Office. On feasts and saints' days the Night Office consisted of a succession of three psalms, each with its antiphon, then three lessons, each followed by a responsory; all of this was repeated three times, each time with different material. So in the Night Office as a whole, for any given feast or saint's office, there were nine antiphons (and also nine responsories, but these are not our concern here). In Roman practice there was no apparent plan to the use of antiphon melodies and psalm tones in the Night Office. On some occasions a single antiphon melody might have been used for many of the antiphon texts; on other occasions there might have been more variety.

Some time during the ninth century the Frankish cantors had the idea of applying the newly forged modal classification directly to the production of new antiphons for new Offices. They put the first antiphon in the first class or mode, the second antiphon in the second mode, and so on throughout the Night Office. At the eighth antiphon, of course, they ran out of modes, and the most frequent solution (but not the only one) was to begin again with mode one for the ninth antiphon. Such a "numerical" set of antiphons is ascribed to Hucbald (ca. 850–930), the Frankish cantor best known to us. The same principle was extended over the whole Office, that is, a single twenty-four hour cycle of services, by Bishop Stephen of Liège in three Offices he composed in the years around 900.[26] This method of composing eventually became very popular, resulting in hundreds of numerical Offices by the end of the Middle Ages. Why the Frankish cantors did this and what the musical result was are subjects too far-reaching to go into here; but the phenomenon surely shows the Franks making their pedagogical systems bear fruit in musical practice.

In example 4 the Frankish chant is a little more clearly distinct from its

EXAMPLE 4

Roman model than in the case of the two antiphons in examples 2 and 3—perhaps not on first hearing, but after a more extended acquaintance the differences would emerge.[27] Of the proper chants for Mass in the Roman repertory (Introit, Gradual, Alleluia, Tract, Offertory, Communion), the Alleluia was the least numerous, and perhaps for that reason was the most cultivated by the Franks; as I mentioned, they scarcely added to the other Mass genres at all. A scholarly edition of the earlier Alleluia melodies runs to some four hundred items, of which many if not most are Frankish.[28] These Alleluias were used regularly at Mass and so appear to the casual modern observer to be part of the Roman repertory. In this case the Frankish cantors followed the Roman musical format of the Alleluia, and only a study of the inner workings of the melodies reveals the differences from the Roman style. Example 4 shows the Alleluia for the Fourth Sunday after Easter—by consensus of specialists it is Frankish not Roman—and by the happy instance of a datable document we are assured that it existed by the second quarter of the ninth century, almost within Charlemagne's lifetime.[29]

Alleluia, for Paschaltide (Frankish)

Alleluia. V. Christus resurgens ex mortuis, iam non moritur: mors illi ultra non dominabitur. Alleluia.[30]

Frankish features to be studied here include the systematic use of the melodic material on the word "alleluia" in the verse "Christus resurgens," with both literal repetition and motific extension; the inner structure of the mighty melisma on "mors"; and the very firm way the whole melody sits in its framework of pitches—so firmly that the modern observer is apt to exclaim, "True Dorian!" But in fact the melody makes little if any use of the idioms found in Roman Graduals in this mode, and there seems to be no Roman Alleluia model. The conclusion I draw from this and many other such cases is that our modern understanding of "true Dorian," and more generally of "true Gregorian," is one based largely on the Frankish development.

⚜

The examples so far have been taken from a stylistic continuum that leads from Roman to Frankish chant. As long as we look at types of chant cultivated by the Romans, the differentiation of the Frankish chants depends on stylistic considerations. All of the following examples, however, involve types of chant not cultivated by Romans, as far as we can tell, and the differentiation is in the first place one of documentation and repertory. Here, the stylistic differentiation may at first be slight but becomes increasingly obvious.

The hymn of praise, "Gloria in excelsis," was sung at Mass by the Romans in the eighth century, but we cannot be sure what melodies were used; all the melodies we have are from Frankish documents. And these melodies do not appear in the Frankish documents that purport to represent the Roman repertory, documents that contain the Roman proper chants for the Mass. Repertorial studies and collation present as "Gloria A" the melody that seems to be the earliest Frankish one we have for this text; it would be a Frankish supplement to the Roman chants to be sung at Mass. The melody might be "Gallican," that is, northern and pre-Carolingian; more likely it is early Carolingian.[31] The beginning of the text includes the quotation from Luke's Gospel and four acclamations.

Gloria in excelsis (Frankish)

Gloria in excelsis deo: et in terra pax hominibus bonae voluntatis.
Laudamus te.
Benedicimus te.
Adoramus te.
Glorificamus te. (etc.)

This is one of the most elaborate, most melismatic, settings of the text we have, among the fifty or so preserved in medieval sources.[32] It seems to be the principal melody the Carolingians used for festal occasions, to replace whatever very simple, congregational recitations of the text they might have got from Roman practice. (Most of the melodies in modern chant books are of demonstrably northern origin, some late in the Middle Ages.)

The text of the "Gloria in excelsis" as used in Christian worship goes back to the fourth or fifth century, but its position at Mass was not stabilized until later—the sixth or seventh century in the West.[33] The text is of a type that can be called stichic, consisting of *stichs,* or one-line elements that are combined in an aggregate. The sources that preserve the melody of example 5 also preserve further stichs of Carolingian origin to be added ad libitum to the Gloria. The Carolingian term *trope,* which means essentially the same thing as the term *versus* (verse) in the sense of "stich," can have the specific meaning here of a stich added after the base text has been

EXAMPLE 5

canonized. The point is, there is nothing new about stichic combination; it is a very old and widespread habit, seemingly indigenous to ritual song in any form. Many of the Psalms, in particular, can be understood as stichic aggregates, and the Roman practice of combining psalms with antiphons can be understood as an extension of stichic practice.[34] The Carolingians' use of tropes goes hand in hand with their concern to use base texts already canonized, or to canonize such texts themselves. Here is a favorite stich or trope added to the end of the Gloria, just before "Cum sancto spiritu . . ."

Trope to the end of Gloria (Frankish)

Regnum tuum solidum per———manebit in eternum.[35]

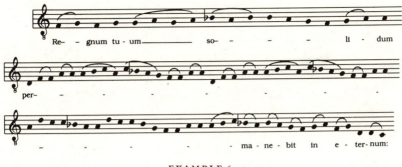

EXAMPLE 6

The trope in example 6 includes a Frankish melisma, with the same kind of internal melodic repetition as in "Alleluia Christus resurgens." This melisma could also be underlaid with words, one syllable per note, and we refer to that phenomenon by the Carolingian term *prosula,* although none of these terms was used by the Carolingians as systematically as by us.

Much more elaborate sets of tropes were provided for the "Gloria in excelsis," and these represent another new category of chant developed by the Franks. Example 7 shows a set of four lines beginning "Laus tua"; these are to be inserted line by line before the first four acclamations in the Gloria text, as indicated. Trope and base text could be sung in alternation between different singers or groups of singers—the practice referred to in Greek by *antiphona,* in Latin by *alternis vicibus,* or some similar expression.

Tropes to the beginning of Gloria in excelsis (Frankish)

Laus tua deus resonet coram te rex: LAUDAMUS TE
Qui venisti propter nos rex angelorum deus: BENEDICIMUS TE
In sede maiestatis tuae: ADORAMUS TE
Gloriosus es rex Israel in throno patris tui: GLORIFICAMUS TE
(etc.)[36]

This is only the beginning of this set of tropes; it continues to the end of the Gloria, approximately doubling its length. Like a few of the other early sets, this one is moderately unstable: lines can be used separately, or other lines can be substituted. Soon the sets became more stabilized, taking on the aspect of a fixed composition. Some sets, like this one, are in prose, but some are in verse, and for the Carolingians this often involved

1. Laus tu- a de- us re- so- net co- ram te———— rex:——
                                                    LAUDAMUS TE

2. Qui ve— — — — — ni- sti pro- pter nos rex

an- ge- lo- rum de— us:
                                    BENEDICIMUS TE

3. In se- de——————— ma- ie- sta- tis tu- ae:——

                                    ADORAMUS TE

4. Glo- ri- o- sus es rex Is- ra- el in thro- no pa- tris

tu- i———————————————
                                    GLORIFICAMUS TE

EXAMPLE 7

imitations of classical verse models in quantitative meters—another antiquity, represented by Virgil and Horace, as well as other Latin poets. What is fascinating in the musical application of this antiquity is to see it peacefully coexisting with other unrelated antiquities or with novelties. Example 8 shows a fixed set of tropes by Hucbald, written around 900, in dactylic hexameters.[37]

Tropes for the "Gloria in excelsis," by Hucbald (ca. 900)

Quem vere pia laus quem solum condecet hymnus:
    LAUDAMUS TE
Cuncta super quia tu deus es benedictus in evum:
    BENEDICIMUS TE
Qui dominator ades celi terreque marisque:
    ADORAMUS TE
Gloria quem perpes manet imperiumque perhenne:
    GLORIFICAMUS TE (etc.)[38]

1. Quem ve— re pi— a laus quem so— lum
con— de— cet hym— nus: LAUDAMUS TE

2. Cun— — cta su— per qui— a tu——— de— us es
be— ne— di— ctus——— in e— vum: BENEDICIMUS TE

3. Qui do— mi— na— tor ad— es ce— li ter— re— que
ma— — — ris— que: ADORAMUS TE

4. Glo— ri— a quem per— pes ma— — — — net im— — pe— ri— um
que per— hen— ne: GLORIFICAMUS TE

EXAMPLE 8

The Carolingians composed thousands of hexameters and frequently set them to chant, especially as tropes. They used the Roman antiphon style as they had learned it in connection with prose texts; they set the hexameter syllable by syllable, as if it were prose, with single notes or groups of notes in the free variety of the Roman style, observing only the caesura and the number of syllables in each hexameter verse. For these purposes they simply ignored the classical quantities. The syllable count, already identified by the Venerable Bede as the "number of syllables," became the single most important factor—and often the only one—taken into consideration in verse, especially as it related to musical setting. Throughout the trope repertory (which eventually became large) the favored style of musical composition was that of the antiphons the Franks provided for the Office, such as in example 3, "Egregius dei martir Vincentius." Much more numerous than Gloria tropes were tropes for the Gregorian Introit; these were developed into large repertories in the tenth century, recorded in chant books in the order of the liturgical calendar on the model of the Gregorian chant books.

The Frankish interest in verse found a much more productive category in the hymn, and for this they turned to yet another antiquity, the hymns of Ambrose, bishop of Milan (d. 397). Ambrose had developed a type of stanza for hymns, with a fixed number of syllables and verses; he provided a small number of texts in this form.[39] They found their way into the Benedictine Office, but not into the Office as sung in Rome, since the Romans had an abiding mistrust of text other than those from canonical Scripture.[40]

The rest of the world, however, sang and composed new texts, and those by Ambrose provided what became the most popular model. Other models were provided by Prudentius (348–413) and Venantius Fortunatus (d. after 600).[41] All of these were enthusiastically taken up by the Franks, resulting in something like ten thousand items by the end of the Middle Ages (as collected in the *Analecta hymnica medii aevi*). I believe this to be an extremely important development; medieval texts set to music are—except for the Gregorian—largely in verse (as are texts set to music since the Middle Ages); and much of it is in stanzaic form. The Ambrosian type of hymn represents an extensive corpus of verse in stanzaic form set to music centuries before the later medieval repertories of song; it precedes those later repertories diachronically and, I believe, is their morphological basis.

Even though the text "Veni creator" is no longer attributed to Hrabanus Maurus, it can still be dated to the ninth century. We cannot be sure the melody is Carolingian, but it may fairly represent the style first used by the Franks for hymns.[42] This is, again, the melodic style of their Office antiphons. The Ambrosian stanza consists of four lines of eight syllables each, and the lines are grouped two plus two; the caesura at the end of the second line is almost always observed, while the first and third lines may run on. The melodic settings reflect this systematically but set individual syllables with the same variety of single notes and groups of two or three notes observed in antiphon style. There the rhythmic variety coexisted easily with the prose of the texts, while with the exact and regular syllable count of hymns it seems anomalous. It may be that in their rendition they equalized the duration of each syllable, singing two or three notes in the time of one as needed. For Frankish purposes the original quantitative meter—iambic dimeter—was again ignored.

Hymn (Frankish)

Veni creator spiritus, mentes tuorum visita,
imple superna gratia, quae tu creasti pectora.

Qui diceris Paraclitus, altissimi donum dei,
Fons vivus, ignis, caritas, et spiritalis unctio.
(etc.)[43]

Example 9 includes the first two stanzas; Ambrose's own hymns had
eight stanzas. Later medieval hymns could have up to twenty or thirty
stanzas. Other stanzas favored by the Carolingians were the sapphic, on
the model of Horace and used especially for saints' offices; and the "Pange
lingua" model of Fortunatus.[44]

Of all the new types of chant discussed here, the Carolingian sequence
illustrates best the ambitions and achievements of the Frankish cantors.[45]
In music as well as words it is clearly distinct from anything that came
north from Rome. It often assumes large dimensions and, through extensive pitch range and brilliant use of the upper register, can present an impressive melodic display. Individual sequences show strong tendencies
toward carefully worked out plans and details, resulting in fully integrated,
independent compositions. The melodic style is forceful and direct—and
unmistakably different from Mass chants of the Frankish-Roman "Gregorian" archetype. And as a sign of the success of the sequence and the
importance the Franks attached to it, they inserted the sequence into
the liturgy of the Mass, right after the most important Gregorian chants,

EXAMPLE 9

the Gradual and Alleluia; the Alleluia, as we saw, was the only Mass proper extensively cultivated by the Franks.

The Carolingian sequence also illustrates well the Frankish tendency to appropriate single artistic elements of words and melody from wherever, then to combine them to produce new styles and forms. Antecedents can be found for almost all elements of the ninth-century sequence, but the resulting combination seems new as of around 850; at any rate, no well-documented example has come to light from an earlier date.

The words of a sequence are in prose, not verse—hence the technical term *prosa* regularly used in the Middle Ages. It is not the prose of the Psalter nor of the Gospel narrative (used frequently for the larger antiphons, Frankish as well as Roman, of the Office). Rather, it is the prose of ceremonial and festal commemoration, often acclamatory, used by the Franks for a number of purposes, such as (for instance) their new antiphons for saints. This kind of prose tends to be highly structured; indeed, the prose style of sequences has long been identified with so-called art prose, derived by the Carolingians from the elaborate style of the later Roman empire.[46]

So, being in prose, the lines of a sequence are frequently much longer than the nominal maximum of sixteen syllables for a line of verse. Nevertheless the lines of an early sequence are usually arranged in pairs, like couplets, based on the number of syllables. Each line of a pair has the same number of syllables so each can be sung to the same melody; then the next pair has a different number of syllables and is sung to a different melody. The arrangement of the whole sequence is progressive and open-ended, moving through a succession of couplets of varying length, each with its own phrase of melody. The words, then, do not lack structure, but only the systematically regular repetition of verse; similarly the melody does not lack structure, only the stanzaic repetition of an Ambrosian hymn melody. In the case of both words and melody, antecedents for the structures can be found, but they are not combined and integrated with each other in the imposing dimensions of the early Carolingian sequence.

The melodies make little or no use of the ornamental antiphon style the Franks used for Office antiphons and for tropes; rather, the sequence melodies are set with one note per syllable in a lean, highly directed style. There is nothing new about "syllabic" setting of text (it is used extensively, for instance, in the psalmody of the Office), but there are no models for syllabic settings with melodies as wide-ranging and highly inflected as the early sequences. These do seem to represent a new kind of music on the Carolingian scene.

The sequence in example 10 is not one of those for which Notker the Poet of Saint Gall provided a text, and hence is not one of those discussed in my study of the early medieval sequence.[47] It is nonetheless a ninth-century sequence and Carolingian, and Wolfram von den Steinen suggested for it a place of honor among the first generation sequences.[48]

Sequence (Prose) (Frankish)

1. Nostra tuba
2a. nunc tua clementia Christe regatur iam iamque pia.
b. Exaudi precamina te laudantia mente devota.
3a. Ita nam laus est tibi grata vox si quod nostra sonat conscientia canat.
b. Quod ut omnibus praeveniat indefesse divina precentur auxilia.
4a. Nam quicumque digne merentur ea
b. Omnia semper ei salubria;
5a. Quibus sine humana cogitata non utilia.
b. Relinquentes igitur itinera nimium lata,
6a. Angustam viam gradiamur que nos patriam ducat ad almam,
b. Haec enim sacra vestigia redemptori pio placita.
7. Qui nostra tempora pie disponat semper nosque protegat;
8. Canticaque ei nostra placeant per cuncta seculorum secula.[49]

A previous example (example 5) was a setting of "Gloria in excelsis," one of the chants at Mass whose text does not change from one occasion to the next. Late medieval and modern usage groups such chants together under the name "Ordinary of the Mass"; but in the ninth century the Franks were providing special melodies for such texts one by one, with no consideration of them as a group. By the end of the ninth century there might have been half a dozen festal settings of "Gloria" and perhaps the same number of settings of "Kyrie eleison," to be sung just before "Gloria" at the start of Mass.[50] The Kyrie in example 11 is perhaps one of the earliest of the Frankish settings and certainly the most elaborate and brilliant of the early ones.[51]

Carolingian settings of the Kyrie to be sung at Mass included relatively extensive Latin acclamations to expand and enhance the bare Greek expressions. These come in sets of nine, because simultaneously the Franks stabilized the Kyrie into thrice "Kyrie eleison," thrice "Christe eleison," and again thrice "Kyrie eleison." The language of the Latin acclamations is prose—the kind of prose found in sequences—and sometimes these

EXAMPLE 10

Kyries were called *prosae* for that reason. But the language seems closer to verse, perhaps because the lines tend to be shorter than those of the sequence and because the thrice three grouping of lines has something of the regularity of verse forms. At any rate, such Kyries were sometimes called *versus*. The melodic settings show the same syllabic style found in the sequence and sometimes the same tendency to rise toward a climax at the end, with steadily expanding, and eventually subdivided, phrases.

EXAMPLE 11

6. O the— os a— gi— e sal— va vi— vi— fi— ca
re— dem— ptor no— ster e— lei— son.
7. Cla—mat in— ces— san— ter nunc quo— que con— ci— o et di— cit e— lei— son.
8. Mi— se— re— re fi— li De— i vi— vi no— bis tu e— lei— son.
9. In ex— cel— sis De— o ma— gna sit glo— ri— a e— ter— no Pa— tri
Qui nos nu— mi— ne gu— ber— nat pro— pri— o re— si— dens
in ar— ce su— per— na
Di— ca— mus in— ces— san— ter om— nes u— na vo— ce e— lei— son.

EXAMPLE 11 continued

Kyrie eleison (Frankish)

1. Tibi Christe supplices exoramus cunctipotens, ut nostri digneris eleison.
2. Tibi laus decet cum tripudio iugiter atque tibi petimus dona eleison.
3. O bone Rex qui super astra sedes et Domine qui cuncta gubernas eleison.
4. Tua devota plebs implorat iugitur ut illi digneris eleison.
5. Qui canunt ante te precibus adnue et tu nobis semper eleison.
6. O theos agie salva vivifica redemptor noster eleison.
7. Clamat incessanter nunc quoque concio et dicit eleison.
8. Miserere fili Dei vivi nobis tu eleison.

9. In excelsis Deo magna sit gloria eterno Patri,
    Qui nos numine gubernat proprio residens in arce superna
    Dicamus incessanter omnes una voce eleison.[52]

Example 1, the Roman Gradual, while no less impressive than this Kyrie, was a much less obvious, perhaps more sophisticated piece of music. As I tried to suggest, the Franks were in intimate contact with the Roman art of singing, were responsible for preserving it for us, and indeed may have had much to do with the final edited form in which it comes to us. My examples have been selected to show the Frankish cantors moving, in a few short decades, from learning that Roman art, passing through imitation and subtle modification, to the development of new styles and forms. This development surely is a demonstration of education bearing fruit in experience.

Notes

1. See the survey of sources in Nancy Phillips, "Classical and Late Latin Sources for Ninth-Century Treatises on Music."
2. General discussions in Joseph Smits van Waesberghe, *Musikerziehung: Lehre und Theorie der Musik im Mittelalter*; and Lawrence A. Gushee, "Questions of Genre in Medieval Treatises on Music."
3. Introduction to these repertories, with tools and material, in Richard L. Crocker, "Liturgical Materials of Roman Chant"; see also David Hiley, "Recent Research on the Origins of Western Chant"; and Richard Pfaff, *Medieval Latin Liturgy: A Select Bibliography*. The standard reference work is now Hiley, *Western Plainchant: A Handbook*.
4. See the account in Bruno Stäblein, "Einführung"; see also Rosamond McKitterick, *The Frankish Church and the Carolingian Reforms, 789–895*.
5. See Helmut Hucke, "Karolingische Renaissance und gregorianische Gesang"; Hucke, "Gregorianische Fragen"; Kenneth Levy, "Charlemagne's Archetype of Gregorian Chant"; Levy, "On Gregorian Orality"; David Hughes, "Evidence for the Traditional View of the Transmission of Gregorian Chant"; Leo Treitler, Levy, and Hughes, "Communications"; Crocker, "Liturgical Materials of Roman Chant"; Hiley, "Recent Research on the Origins of Western Chant"; James McKinnon, "Christian Antiquity"; McKinnon, "Emergence of Gregorian Chant in the Carolingian Era"; and Peter Jeffrey, *Re-Envisioning Past Musical Cultures: Ethnomusicology in the Study of Gregorian Chant*.
6. Exploration in connection with antiphons in Crocker, "Matins Antiphons at St. Denis."
7. Survey in Crocker, "Medieval Chant."
8. Introduction in Margot E. Fassler, "The Office of Cantor in Early Western Monastic Rules and Customaries: A Preliminary Investigation."

9. A synoptic display of the words of the chants in the eighth- and ninth-century Frankish-Roman repertory is in René Jean Hesbert, *Antiphonale missarum sextuplex*. A modern edition of words and melodies is in *Graduale Triplex, seu Graduale Romanum Pauli PP.VI cara recognitum et rhythmicis signis a Solesmensibus monachis ornatum, Neumis Laudunensibus (Cod. 239) et Sangallensibus (Codicum San Gallensis 359 et Einsidlensis 121) nunc auctum* (Solesmes, 1979) (cited hereafter as *Graduale Triplex*), a Roman Catholic Gregorian chant book. Discussion of the repertory of Gradual responsories is in Willi Apel, *Gregorian Chant*, pp. 344–63; and Crocker, "Chants of the Roman Mass."

10. Hesbert, *Antiphonale missarum sextuplex*, Mass formulary 122.

11. *Graduale triplex*, p. 426.

12. See Hiley, "Recent Research on the Origins of Western Chant"; Solange Corbin, *Die Neumen*; Eugene Cardine, *Gregorian Semiology*; Treitler, "The Early History of Music Writing in the West"; Treitler, "Reading and Singing: On the Genesis of Occidental Music-Writing"; Johann B. Göschl, "Der gegenwärtige Stand der semiologischen Forschung"; and Levy, "On the Origin of the Neumes." The best summary discussion is in Hiley, *Western Plainchant*, chap. 4.

13. *Graduale triplex*, p. 426; Saint Gall MS 359 in *Cantatorium (IXe siècle): No. 359 de la Bibliothèque de Saint-Gall*, Paléographie musicale, 2nd ser., 2 (Tournai, 1924), p. 103 of the fasc. = p. 123 of the manuscript; Laon MS 239 in *Antiphonale missarum Sancti Gregorii (IXe–X siècle): Codex 239 de la Bibliothèque de Laon*, Paléographie musicale 10 (Tournai, 1909), p. 135 of the fasc. = fol. 68 of the manuscript. The abbreviation in the Laon manuscript is expanded using RG Convertere, at "tuos"; *Graduale triplex*, p. 295 = Laon, p. 151.

14. As cited in n. 13, above.

15. As cited in n. 13, above.

16. As cited in n. 13, above.

17. See Roger Reynolds, "Divine Office," for an outline of the Divine Office. An introduction to the chant of the Office can be found in Crocker, "Chants of the Roman Office." Basic inventories and catalogues of chants can be found in Hesbert, *Corpus antiphonalium officii*.

18. Antiphonale of Saint-Denis, ca. 1140–50: Paris, B.N., lat. MS 17296, fol. 174.

19. Hesbert, *Corpus antiphonalium officii*, vol. 2, Office formulary no. 100; vol. 3, no. 1505.

20. See, in general, Hucke, "Musikalische Formen der Officiumsantiphonen"; Michel Huglo, "Antiphon"; and Crocker, "Matins Antiphons at St. Denis."

21. Hesbert, *Corpus antiphonalium officii*, vol. 2, Office formulary no. 46; vol. 3, no. 2618.

22. Antiphonale of Saint-Denis: Paris, B.N., lat. 17296, fol. 65.

23. The best summary of the problem of the relationship of words and melody is John Stevens, *Words and Music: Song, Narrative, Dance, and Drama, 1050–1350*.

24. Compare the observations in Jeremy Yudkin, *Music in Medieval Europe*, p. 204.

25. General discussions in Harold Powers, "Mode"; Charles Atkinson, "The *Parapteres: Nothi* or Not?"; Terence Bailey, "Accented and Cursive Cadences in Gregorian Psalmody"; Michel Huglo, *Les Tonaires: Inventaire, analyse, comparaison*; Crocker, "Chants of the Roman Office," pp. 165–69; and Crocker, "Medieval Chant," pp. 278–83.
26. Antoine Auda, *L'Ecole musicale liègeoise au Xe siècle: Etienne de Liège*; and Crocker, "Matins Antiphons at St. Denis," p. 445.
27. *Graduale Triplex*, p. 226.
28. Karlheinz Schlager, *Alleluia-Melodien I (bis 1000)*; also Schlager, *Thematischer Katalog der ältesten Alleluia-Melodien aus Handschriften des 10. und 11. Jahrhunderts*; and Schlager, "Alleluia I: Latin Rite."
29. Smits van Waesberghe, "Zur ursprünglichen Vortragsweise der Prosulen, Sequenzen, und Organa" (with facsimile); and Smits van Waesberghe, "Notation" (facsimile).
30. Not in Hesbert, *Antiphonale missarum sextuplex*.
31. Bruno Stäblein, "Gloria in excelsis Deo"; Crocker, "Gloria in excelsis"; Crocker, "Medieval Chant," p. 230; Detlov Bosse, *Untersuchungen einstimmiger mittelalterlicher Melodien zum Gloria in excelsis*; but better in Klaus Rönnau, *Die Tropen zum Gloria in excelsis Deo*, p. 206; Paul Evans, *The Early Trope Repertory of Saint Martial de Limoges*, p. 254; and Ruth Steiner, "Trope (i) 3: Introit Tropes."
32. Rönnau, *Die Tropen zum Gloria in excelsis Deo*, p. 206; Evans, *The Early Trope Repertory of Saint Martial de Limoges*, pp. 254ff.
33. Klaus Gamber, "Die Textgestalt des Gloria in excelsis."
34. See Crocker, "Medieval Chant," pp. 246ff, 264ff. The standard edition of trope texts is now *Corpus troporum*, ed. R. Jonsson et al., vol. 1–, Studia Latina Stockholmiensa (Stockholm, 1975–). Melodies for Introit tropes can be found in Günter Weiss, *Introitus-Tropen*, Monumenta Musica Medii Aevi 3 (Kassel, 1970).
35. Rönnau, *Die Tropen zum Gloria in excelsis Deo*, pp. 179–87.
36. Ibid., pp. 140, 211ff.
37. Rembert Weakland, "Hucbald as Musician and Theorist"; Weakland, "The Compositions of Hucbald"; and Crocker, "Hucbald." Musical notation of example 8: Rönnau, *Die Tropen zum Goria in excelsis Deo*, pp. 159, 240.
38. Rönnau, *Die Tropen zum Gloria in excelsis Deo*, p. 152.
39. Texts in Guido Maria Dreves, *Lateinische Hymnendichter des Mittelalters*, pp. 10–21.
40. See summaries in Steiner, "Hymn"; H. Gneuss, *Hymnar und Hymnen im englischen Mittelalter*; and Joseph Szövérffy, *Die Annalen der lateinischen Hymnendichtung: Ein Handbuch*, vol. 1: *Die lateinischen Hymnen bis zum Ende des XI. Jahrhunderts*.
41. Texts in Dreves, *Lateinische Hymnendichter des Mittelalters*, pp. 22–46, 70–88.
42. Stäblein, *Hymnen I: Die mittelalterlichen Hymnenmelodien des Abendlandes*, is the first and only comprehensive scholarly edition of melodies for medieval hymns.
43. Ibid., p. 260, from the "Hymnar von Kempten," Zurich, Zentralbibliothek, MS Rh 83 (ca. 1000).

44. Text in Dreves, *Lateinische Hymnendichter des Mittelalters*, p. 71.

45. General discussion in Crocker, "The Sequence"; and Crocker, *The Early Medieval Sequence*.

46. Originally discussed by Eduard Norden, *Die antike Kunstprosa vom VI. Jahrhundert vor Christus bis in die Zeit der Renaissance*.

47. Crocker, *The Early Medieval Sequence*.

48. Wolfram von den Steinen, "Die Anfänge der Sequenzendichtung," 41:21–22, 46–48.

49. Crocker, "The Sequence," p. 279.

50. The difficult early history of "Kyrie eleison" is reviewed by John Baldovin, *The Urban Character of Christian Worship: The Origins, Development, and Meaning of Stational Liturgy*, pp. 242–47.

51. Summaries of Frankish melodies of "Kyrie eleison" in Crocker, "Kyrie eleison"; and Crocker, "Medieval Chant," pp. 271–78. Medieval melodies are catalogued in Margareta Landwehr-Melnicki, *Das einstimmige Kyrie des lateinischen Mittelalters*; a study of an early repertory is in David Bjork, "The Kyrie Repertory in Aquitanian Manuscripts of the Tenth and Eleventh Centuries."

52. Landwehr-Melnicki, *Das einstimmige Kyrie des lateinischen Mittelalters*, no. 55; Bjork, "The Kyrie Repertory in Aquitanian Manuscripts of the Tenth and Eleventh Centuries," vol. 1, chap. 6, pp. 219–59; cf. Evans, *The Early Trope Repertory of Saint Martial de Limoges*, pp. 266ff.

5

Edition, Translation, and Exegesis:
The Carolingians and the Bible

B E R N I C E   M .   K A C Z Y N S K I

arolingian society, as we have become increasingly aware, valued books, and of the books it had it valued the Bible most. Scripture was a central preoccupation of the literate classes; it formed, certainly, the main reading of scholars in monasteries and courts. Rulers, too, whether literate or not, wished to know what it said, and literate laymen and women were interested in scriptural matters.[1]

What is striking about the reading of the Bible in the ninth century is not simply that people in many different walks of life wished to do it. It is also that they gave attention to the biblical text. They shared a realization that it was necessary to establish its history—to know how it had been edited and translated into Latin—before attempting to undertake its exegesis. Because they were members of a society so concerned with the supply of books, they were conscious of the tasks of edition and revision; because they read them in a language they did not normally speak, they were familiar with the exercise of translation. The recognition of the importance of these acts was a distinctive feature of Carolingian scholarship. In their attention to philological procedures and details, to the work of editing, revising, and translating, ninth-century scholars made a lasting contribution to the ways in which Europeans would think about the Bible.

Their first effort was to secure an accurate Latin text. Alcuin's Bible is perhaps the best known of these works; he presented it to Charlemagne on the occasion of his coronation as emperor, and thereafter Alcuin's scriptorium at Tours made many copies.[2] At least four other editions survive from the late eighth and early ninth centuries, testifying to a great concern for the revision of the Latin Bible.[3] A second effort was directed toward the production and distribution of manuscripts. There is evidence for the intention in contemporary legislation: public authority emphasized education and made explicit the need to learn from Scripture.[4] Indeed, the scriptoria produced biblical manuscripts in large quantities, and the compilers of library catalogues put these books first in lists of their holdings.[5] Despite the many copies of scriptural texts in circulation, however, not all monastic or episcopal centers could be expected to have the pandect, a manuscript copy of the whole Bible.[6] This is an interesting fact, and it suggests that much book production was intended merely to supply basic classroom requirements. A third task was to interpret Scripture. For the Carolingian commentators, this meant turning to the fathers of the church. "The first necessity," writes Beryl Smalley, "was to make the patristic tradition available and intelligible."[7]

The eighth and ninth centuries marked a period of heightened interest in Christian antiquity. Much attention was given to the church fathers, especially in the monasteries, where the culture was based on the Bible and its interpretation.[8] The Rule of St. Benedict itself was a patristic document. And the thoughts of the early teachers—the "fathers," the "doctors," the "defenders of the faith"—suffused monastic life.[9]

The process by which their work was gathered up in the monasteries of northern Europe is often seen, as Smalley's remark implies, as the reception of a tradition. I should like to argue here that it was that and something more: that when patristic texts were passed through the hands of Carolingian scholars they were configured and reconfigured as much as they were read. Carolingians turned to the Fathers for guidance, certainly; but it is just as certainly true that, to quite a considerable extent, it was the work of the Carolingians that helped to define the tradition and to establish it.[10]

Let us examine this proposition against the background of the reading of Scripture. Here the dominant figure was St. Jerome (ca. 340–420). In the ninth century, Jerome's edition of the Bible, familiar to us today as the Vulgate, or *Vulgata editio*, was coming to be adopted generally throughout the empire.[11] The Vulgate was in part a revision of older Latin versions of Scripture, in part a new translation from Greek and Hebrew sources. Jerome's contribution was manifold: he edited, translated, and commented. His works formed the basis of Carolingian biblical scholarship. "Be mindful," wrote Alcuin, "of the most blessed Jerome, the most celebrated teacher of divine Scripture in the holy Church."[12]

Before considering the ways in which Frankish scholars responded to Jerome, it might be useful to review his writings. The early history of the Vulgate Bible is complicated, to some extent because Jerome did not set about his task in an orderly fashion. He moved from book to book, often retracing his steps and correcting earlier work. In 384 he gave Pope Damasus a revision of the Four Gospels—the first in what would become a very long series of revisions and translations that occupied him until his death.[13]

Jerome did not approve of the Old Latin translations current in his own time; he insisted that the Latin Scriptures must be based on a knowledge of the original texts. In a famous letter on the translation of the Psalms, he wrote:

> When the Latins face a problem caused by variant readings in different copies of the New Testament, they return to the Greek, the language in which the New Testament was written; in the same way, we must consult the Hebrew original when Greeks and Latins disagree about an Old Testament text. Only in this way will the little streams that flow from the original spring retain their purity.[14]

One example will serve to illustrate his method. Jerome was especially fascinated by the Psalter, and he returned to it again and again. Between 382 and 384 he began revising the Old Latin Psalter used in Rome; the text now known as the Roman Psalter was once thought to represent that revision. (It now appears, however, that Jerome's work has been lost and that the text as we have it represents the unrevised Old Latin prototype.) Shortly thereafter, in 386 and 387, Jerome prepared a new Latin version on the basis of the Greek columns in Origen's *Hexapla*. It was this version, later known as the Gallican Psalter, that found its way into the Vulgate edition. The third of Jerome's translations, the Hebrew Psalter, was made directly from the Hebrew some time before 392.[15]

Jerome's attention to textual matters made him a rarity among Latin scholars of his day. The philological approach to Scripture—as opposed, for instance, to the allegoresis of Ambrose and Augustine—was little understood. Indeed, most of his contemporaries saw his work as meddlesome tampering with texts that had been hallowed by tradition; they preferred the Old Latin translations. Augustine even wrote to discourage

him from translating directly from the Hebrew. It was sufficient to use the
Greek of the Septuagint, he said, for that translation had been divinely inspired.[16] Jerome defended his position in the prefaces to his new revisions
and translations and developed it further in numerous scriptural commentaries and handbooks.[17]

In addition to his writings on the Bible, Jerome translated works by
Origen, Eusebius, and Didymus. He wrote books on church history and
controversy, including *On Famous Men, Dialogue with a Luciferian,* and
Lives of the Hermits. He was the author of a remarkable collection of letters.
Jerome's literary activity was, in the words of his recent biographer J. N.
D. Kelly, "prodigious, sometimes feverish."[18]

The Franks, however, valued him most for his gift of the Latin Bible.
Ratramnus of Corbie called him the "translator of the Divine Law, most
skilled in all the sciences," and "most learned in the Latin, Greek, and
Hebrew languages."[19] Hincmar of Reims described Jerome as "most expert in the Hebrew, Greek, and Latin tongues." And, he added, "carrying
on his inquiry with the Lord's inspiration, he was rewarded by penetrating
to the marrow and very vitals of Sacred Scripture."[20] Ninth-century
scholars have left behind many such expressions of praise.[21] They show
both the veneration in which Jerome was held and the reasons for it: he
was the translator of the Bible, knew the original languages, and was very
learned. What had been, in Jerome's own lifetime, an exceedingly controversial approach to Scripture by this time was regarded as authoritative.

How had it happened? I think some explanations are to be sought in
the particular circumstances of Frankish society, where the impetus to provide books led scholars to respect editing, and where the use of multiple
languages by the learned led them to think about translating. They read
the Bible in a Latin they did not normally speak. They were accustomed,
therefore, to move quickly from one form of Latin to another or from
Latin to the vernacular.[22] They were aware of the process of translation in
their own lives and knew its difficulty, its compromises, and its necessity.

Jerome had traveled freely in the Mediterranean world of late antiquity,
studying Latin in Rome with Aelius Donatus, perfecting his Greek in Antioch and Constantinople, and learning Hebrew with a converted Jew in
the Syrian desert. Four hundred years later, in the more restricted universe
of the Frankish kingdoms, the same possibilities did not exist. Few
scholars learned Hebrew or Greek; we do not know of any who learned
both.[23] Yet they continued to have before them the admonitions of writers
like Isidore of Seville, who said: "There are three sacred languages,
Hebrew, Greek, and Latin, and they are supreme through all the world."[24]

Jerome's knowledge of the biblical languages was a fact that impressed itself vividly upon the Franks. They referred to it often, not only in their written texts but also in the visual arts. Portraits of Jerome in biblical manuscripts, common through the period, illustrate his philological activities.[25] Their iconography marks a departure from late-antique precedents. Let us consider three examples.

Perhaps the earliest such reference comes from the court of Charlemagne. The ivory covers of the Dagulf Psalter (Paris, Musée du Louvre, Ivories 9 and 10) were made sometime between 783 and 795. They originally contained the corrected text of a Psalter Charlemagne had prepared as a gift for Pope Hadrian I (r. 772–95).[26] A dedicatory verse by the scribe Dagulf connects the covers to the manuscript and to Jerome's revision: "The thorns were drawn from the Psalter by the studies of a man who kept vigil through the night."[27]

On the upper panel of the front cover (see fig. 5 in chap. 6), a youthful King David is shown composing the Psalms and dictating to scribes; on the lower panel, David sits on a throne and plays his harp, surrounded by musicians and attendants. The back cover portrays Jerome. He is an elderly figure with a bald head and short beard. The upper panel shows the presbyter Boniface handing a scroll to Jerome, who rushes to meet him. The scroll contains, presumably, a message from Pope Damasus asking him to revise the Psalter.[28] In the background are some buildings representing Jerusalem. On the lower panel, Jerome is shown holding the Psalter in his hand and dictating his revision to scribes.

Anton von Euw has shown that the scenes from Jerome's life are compilations based on prefatory texts in the manuscript. They do not seem to have any iconographical precedent. The Jerome panels, he suggests, were made up at the Carolingian court to provide a match for the David panels.[29] The pairing was new. It drew attention to Jerome's work of revision and translation by setting it beside David's work of composition. Jerome's cover was not, as it might have been, simply the reinterpretation of a late-antique author portrait. Rather, the two covers were to be read together, and together they honored the men to whom the Carolingians owed their Psalter.

Later illustrations made more pointed reference to Jerome's role as translator. An important example is the frontispiece to the prefaces of St. Jerome in the Vivian Bible, the so-called First Bible of Charles the Bald (Paris, Bibliothèque Nationale, MS lat. 1, fol. 3v; reproduced as the frontispiece to this volume). The manuscript was copied at Tours about 845 and dedicated to the king by the lay-abbot Count Vivian and the monks of

St. Martin. Like its companion, the Jerome frontispiece in the San Paolo Bible (Rome, San Paolo fuori le mura, Bible, fol. 3v), it has as its theme Jerome as translator of the Bible.[30]

In the Vivian Bible, scenes from the life of Jerome are arranged in three panels, with inscriptions on purple bands below that explain the episodes.[31] Above and to the left, Jerome, wearing Carolingian garments, leaves the city of Rome (personified by a female figure holding a lance and shield). A ship sets sail for the East. In Jerusalem, to the right, Jerome gives coins to his Hebrew teacher. The second panel shows Jerome interpreting Scripture for Paula, her daughter Eustochium, and two other women. To the right, a monk takes down Jerome's words, while behind him, two men begin to multiply the text (one reads, the other takes dictation). In the bottom panel, Jerome gives copies of his completed Latin Bible to six monks, who carry them off to buildings on the left and right.

The sources of the Jerome frontispieces are unknown.[32] No late-antique narrative scenes of Jerome's life survive, although scholars have proposed a fifth-century model. It seems likely that, whatever his visual models, the artist also consulted some biographical source. It too is unknown. The frontispieces present an oversimplified chronology of Jerome's travels that was first given in the sixth-century *Chronicle* of Marcellinus Comes. By the ninth century, however, the chronology had become familiar; it circulated in two anonymous biographies of the saint.[33]

Motifs and devices borrowed from other contexts seem to have been adapted to a new theme.[34] Here again, Carolingian artists illustrated their debt to Jerome. And they did it quite literally, in a narrative beginning with Jerome's travels to the places where he studied Latin, Hebrew, and Greek, and ending with his distribution of Bibles to monks, who returned with them to their monasteries.

It was probably not a coincidence that so graphic an account of the preparation of the Bible came from the scriptorium at Tours. Tours had been Alcuin's home at the end of his life, and the monks of St. Martin had made many copies of his text. They had an appreciation for the work of revision. Nor was it likely to be a coincidence that the emphasis on Jerome's work of translation was to be found in a Bible addressed to Charles the Bald, as there was considerable interest in Greek at his West Frankish court. The scholar John Scottus Eriugena (ca. 810–ca. 877) was director of the court school and author of a remarkable series of translations of Pseudo-Dionysius, Gregory of Nyssa, and Maximus the Confessor. Indeed, John Scottus compared himself to Jerome in the introduction to his translation of Pseudo-Dionysius.[35] Others at the court, who knew less

Greek, played at translation by writing macaronic verse with Greek words gleaned from glossaries.[36]

Liuthard, principal painter at the court school of Charles the Bald, gives us an author portrait of Jerome. It was done about 860, in a Psalter executed for the king's personal use (Paris, Bibliothèque Nationale, MS lat. 1152, fol. 4r; see fig. 1).[37] The miniature follows the familiar stylistic model of an evangelist portrait, that is, a representation of Matthew, Mark, Luke, or John. Jerome is shown at work on his translation. As in the Vivian Bible, it is a youthful Jerome—beardless, tonsured, and haloed. He is seated on a cushioned throne under a canopied arcade. His left hand touches a lectern holding an open book; with his right hand he dips a pen into a pot of ink. The richness of the clothing, the throne, and the elaborate setting suggest that the painter wished to stress the importance of his subject. Jerome is identified by an inscription: "Jerome, noble translator and mighty priest, nobly translates the Psalms of David."[38]

These few examples point to the development of a new iconography of Jerome in the Frankish kingdoms. Both the portraits and their inscriptions attest to his scholarship. Jerome's work on the Psalter came increasingly to be compared with David's, because the Franks relied upon Jerome's texts. He had labored through many nights, as Dagulf put it in his dedicatory verse, to draw the thorns from the Psalter. Jerome's work of translation was increasingly valued in a society that experienced firsthand the complicating factor of linguistic diversity. It was a society, moreover, aware that knowledge of the biblical languages was becoming a precarious achievement.

The Carolingians, then, found their own reasons to appreciate Jerome. His contemporaries had often disagreed with him; Augustine and others were satisfied with the Old Latin Bible and saw no need for further revision and translation. By the end of the eighth century, however, circumstances had changed. The Carolingians knew that such activities were important, for they would not have had their Bible without them.

Jerome's work represented an approach to Scripture that had great appeal for many Carolingian scholars. His writings often formed part of the apparatus in Carolingian biblical manuscripts. His famous Letter 53, to Paulinus on the study of the Bible, preceded copies of Alcuin's text; Letter 106, to Sunnia and Fretela on the translation of the Psalms, introduced scholarly editions of the Psalter; and the biblical prefaces frequently appeared in editions of Scripture.

Jerome's scriptural commentaries were extremely popular.[39] As a rule, he began a commentary with an analysis of the Latin text of the relevant

FIGURE 1. Court school of Charles the Bald: St. Jerome translating the Psalms. Paris, Bibliothèque Nationale, MS lat. 1152, fol. 4r. Photo: Paris, Bibliothèque Nationale.

passage. He discussed the translation and compared it with other translations, and he compared the Latin with the original Greek or Hebrew. Next he explained the literal meaning of the text, what he called the historical verity (*historiae veritas* or simply *historia*); and, finally, he probed its figurative and allegorical meaning in order to come to the "secrets of spiritual understanding" *(spiritualis intelligentiae sacramenta)*.[40] Jerome made linguistic problems the basis of his exegesis.

There were those, of course, for whom such detail seemed superfluous. Teachers simplified his narratives, removing philological discussions they thought were above the heads of their pupils.[41] Josephus Scottus shortened Jerome's commentary on Isaiah by removing the references to variant Greek readings.[42] Christian of Stablo defended his writing of a new commentary on Matthew by saying that his readers would not understand Jerome's commentary without the help of a commentary on Jerome.[43]

But for many, Jerome was an inspiration. Perhaps it was his work on the Psalter that made the most lasting impression. It had been Jerome's favorite biblical book, and it was the favorite, too, of readers in the Middle Ages. Jerome had left three recensions: the Roman Psalter, the Gallican Psalter, and the Hebrew Psalter. Ludwig Traube wrote:

> Scarcely any facts of textual tradition which confronted the Western Middle Ages contributed as much to the awakening of critical thought and widening of the intellectual horizon as the existence of Jerome's three Psalters, their deviations from each other, their relationship to the Hebrew original and to the Septuagint translation, Jerome's extensive commentary on specific passages, with reference to still other Greek translations, and the concise but eloquent style which his critical notations incorporate into the text of the Gallican Psalter.[44]

In order to compare the texts, Carolingian scholars devised what was to become one of their characteristic study instruments: the triple, or tripartite, Psalter *(Psalterium triplex, Psalterium tripartitum)*. In these books, the three Latin texts were presented in parallel columns, so that readers could make line-by-line comparisons.[45]

Another type of study book was the bilingual Psalter. The form of the Greek-Latin codex had been inherited from late antiquity. The Franks used it for the study of Scripture *(Psalterium duplex)*. The double Psalters gave a Greek version (usually the Septuagint) in one column and one of Jerome's Latin versions in another. Irish scribes on the Continent preferred an interlinear arrangement, with the Latin translation written above the Greek original.[46]

Still more careful textual study was made possible by the introduction of the quadripartite Psalter *(Psalterium quadruplex, Psalterium quadrupartitum)*. In A.D. 909 Salomon III, bishop of Constance and abbot of Saint

Gall, commissioned the first such work from the scriptorium of the abbey. (It is now Bamberg, Staatsbibliothek, Msc. Bibl. 44 [A.I.14]).[47] The Psalter presented, in four parallel columns, Jerome's Gallican, Roman, and Hebrew Psalters, and the Greek text of the Septuagint, given in Latin transliteration (see fig. 2). A dedicatory verse of forty-four dactylic hexameters explained the history of Jerome's translations from the Greek and Hebrew sources. The purpose of the four texts in the edition, it said, was

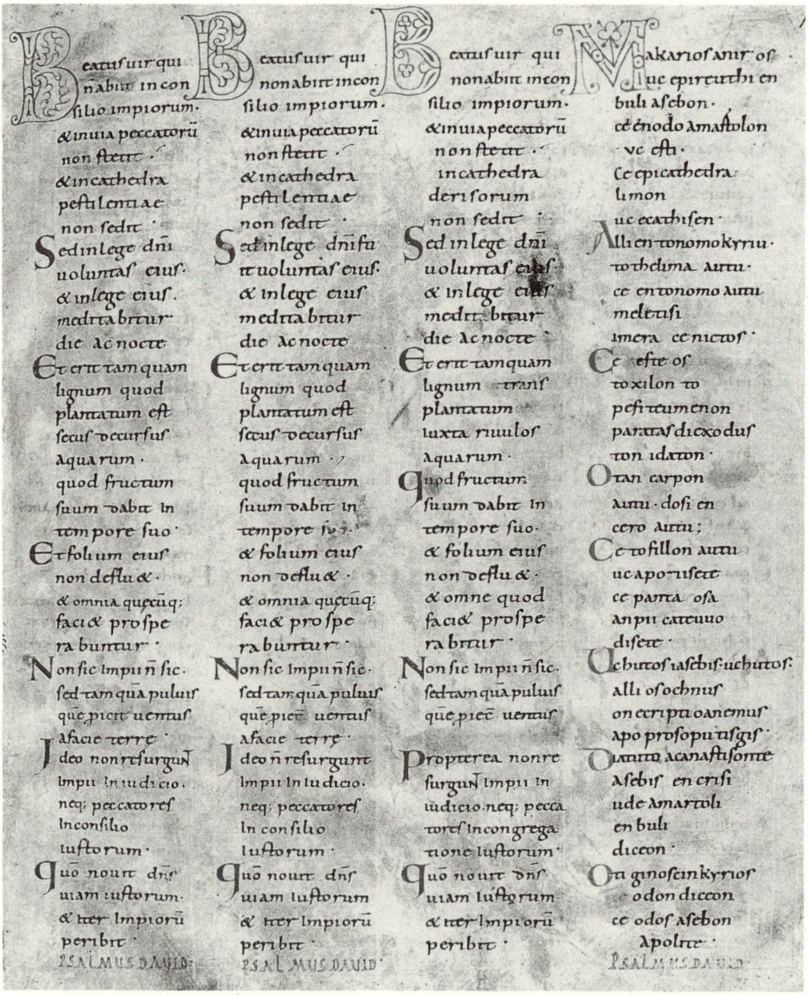

FIGURE 2. Scriptorium of Saint Gall: The quadripartite Psalter of Bishop Salomon III. Bamberg, Staatsbibliothek, Msc. Bibl. 44 (A.I.14), fol. 12r. Photo: Bamberg, Staatsbibliothek.

to enable learned men to follow four routes to the hidden meaning of Scripture.[48]

These manuscripts were books for scholars. They were used by men who were highly trained and who, like Jerome, assigned priority to linguistic problems. Scholars did not need to know the original languages of Scripture to recognize differences in the Latin texts. They could—and did—consult Jerome's Letter 106 on the translation of the Psalms to learn the reasons for the different renderings of Greek and Hebrew.[49] Jerome in all his work had pointed to the connection between translation and exegesis. The multiple Psalters permitted Frankish scholars to explore it.

Jerome had been a conspicuous figure in his lifetime—as translator and expositor of Scripture, as a satirist and Latin stylist, and as a hermit in the desert. His work had often been controversial. After his death the hostility seemed to fade, and "for the next thousand years and more," remarks Kelly, "a crescendo of adulation was to surround him."[50]

The Carolingians were among the first to recognize his achievement. He had given them the Latin Bible. Their debt was immediate. They sought to define it. In the art of their manuscripts they called attention to Jerome's textual scholarship, and in a novel series of editions they carried his work forward. They sought, too, to interpret his life. Two anonymous writers of the mid-ninth century composed biographies of him; in one, Jerome was assigned his earliest, and for many centuries his only, miracle.[51] Indeed, they venerated him as a saint: Florus of Lyons, Hrabanus Maurus, Wandelbert of Prüm, Ado of Vienne, and Usuard were among those who listed his name in the martyrologies.[52]

The Franks greeted Jerome with a new spirit of welcome and, in doing so, distinguished themselves from many of his Christian contemporaries. What brought about the change? It had to do, surely, with the nature of Carolingian society, and with its urgent need for books. The men of late antiquity might take for granted a supply of learned texts, but those of the eighth and ninth centuries could not. Carolingian scholars were vitally concerned to establish the text of the Latin Bible, to make copies and distribute them, and to understand the text itself. In all of these activities they relied upon the example of Jerome. Their own efforts, moreover, had given them a particular understanding of his. More than people in other times, perhaps, they knew the importance of editions, revisions, and translations. That is why their actions cannot simply be described as the reception of texts from late antiquity. In their adoption of Jerome's philological methods and in their invention of new images of him and assertion of new roles for him, the Carolingians defined and established a tradition.

ꟿotes

1. Annotations in a ninth-century library catalogue from the abbey of Saint Gall give evidence for the lay interest in Scripture. Among the borrowers of books were Emperor Charles the Fat (839–88) and his wife, Richardis. Charles had borrowed a volume of homilies on the Gospels by Gregory the Great; Richardis had taken a volume of Gregory's homilies on Ezekiel and another volume of Jerome on the prophets: Saint Gall, Stiftsbibliothek, MS 728, p. 6; printed in Paul Lehmann, *Mittelalterliche Bibliothekskataloge Deutschlands und der Schweiz*, 1:72–73. For prompting my interest in the complex nature of early medieval literacy, I am indebted to Rosamond McKitterick's book *The Carolingians and the Written Word*. I thank the Arts Research Board of McMaster University for assistance in obtaining the photographs reproduced here.
2. Bonifatius Fischer, *Die Alkuin-Bibel*.
3. For these editions, see Fischer, "Bibeltext und Bibelreform unter Karl dem Grossen." See also Laura Light, "Versions et révisions du texte biblique." The bibliography on the subject is vast. For a critical review of scholarship to date, see John J. Contreni, "Carolingian Biblical Studies."
4. The point is made by Contreni, "Carolingian Biblical Studies," pp. 74–77.
5. On the priority of Bibles in the library catalogues, see McKitterick, *The Carolingians and the Written Word*, p. 197.
6. There was a copy at Saint Gall: Saint Gall, Stiftsbibliothek, MS 728, p. 5; printed in Lehmann, *Mittelalterliche Bibliothekskataloge*, 1:71: "Bibliotheca una." The pandect is listed first in the catalogue, followed by individual books of the Old and New Testaments.
7. Beryl Smalley, *The Study of the Bible in the Middle Ages*, p. 37.
8. See Jean Leclercq, *The Love of Learning and the Desire for God: A Study of Monastic Culture*, pp. 89–111.
9. On the early history of the terminology used to describe church teachers, see Berthold Altaner and Alfred Stuiber, *Patrologie: Leben, Schriften und Lehre der Kirchenväter*, pp. 3–5. (An English trans. of the book is available, but it is based on an earlier edition: Altaner, *Patrology*, trans. Hilda C. Graef [Freiburg, 1960], pp. 3–5.)
10. This is a large theme to which I shall return in other studies.
11. The term *Vulgata editio* became customary in the thirteenth century: see Altaner and Stuiber, *Patrologie*, p. 398. For an overview, see Raphael Loewe, "The Medieval History of the Latin Vulgate."
12. *Commentaria in s. Joannis evangelium*, in PL 100:740: "Memento clarissimum in sancta Ecclesia divinae Scripturae doctorem, beatissimum siquidem Hieronymum." See also PL 101:279, 742, 774.
13. On Jerome's complex pattern of work, see Jean Gribomont, "The Translations: Jerome and Rufinus."
14. *Epistula 106, Ad Sunniam et Fretelam, de psalterio, quae de LXX interpretum editione corrupta sint*, in *Saint Jérôme: Lettres*, ed. and trans. Jérôme Labourt, 8 vols. (Paris, 1949–63): "Sicut autem in nouo testamento, si quando apud Latinos quaestio exoritur, et est inter exemplaria uarietas, recurrimus ad

fontem Graeci sermonis, quo nouum scriptum est instrumentum, ita et in ueteri testamento, si quando inter Graecos Latinosque diuersitas est, ad Hebraicam confugimus ueritatem; ut quicquid de fonte proficiscitur, hoc quaeramus in riuulis" (5:105) (English trans. in Eugene F. Rice, Jr., *Saint Jerome in the Renaissance* [Baltimore, 1985], p. 17). On the reception of the letter in the early Middle Ages, see Bernice M. Kaczynski, "Greek Glosses on Jerome's *Ep. CVI, Ad Sunniam et Fretelam,* in MS Berlin (East), Deutsche Staatsbibliothek, Phillipps 1674." Much has been written about Jerome's view of translation. For a recent account, see Rita Copeland, *Rhetoric, Hermeneutics, and Translation in the Middle Ages: Academic Traditions and Vernacular Texts,* pp. 45–55.

15. See Gribomont, "The Translations," pp. 223–26; and Colette Estin, "Les Traductions du Psautier." See Adam Kamesar, *Jerome, Greek Scholarship, and the Hebrew Bible: A Study of the "Quaestiones Hebraicae in Genesim,"* for an analysis of his approach to the biblical languages.

16. On the correspondence of Jerome and Augustine, see J. N. D. Kelly, *Jerome: His Life, Writings, and Controversies,* pp. 217–20.

17. For Jerome's defense against "the howling dogs who rage savagely against me," see Kelly, *Jerome,* pp. 168–70.

18. Ibid., p. 141. For a survey of Jerome's work, see Altaner and Stuiber, *Patrologie,* pp. 394–404, 632–34; and Gribomont, "The Translations," pp. 212–46. Jerome reviewed his own writings in *De viris illustribus* 135, ed. Wilhelm Herding (Leipzig, 1924), pp. 65–66.

19. Ratramnus of Corbie, *De partu sanctae Mariae* 28, ed. J. M. Canal, *Marianum* 30 (1968): 105: "Hieronymus, sacrae legis interpres; omnium peritissimus disciplinarum, fidei turris inconcussa, sapientiae lampade splendissimus, eloquio facundissimus, latini, graeci, hebraeique sermonis doctissimus."

20. *De praedestinatione Dei,* in PL 125:246: "Et sanctus Hieronymus, Hebraicae, Graecae, et Latinae linguae peritissimus, qui dicitur ut nucem juxta nucleum frangens, medullas et ipsa viscera Scripturae sanctae investigando, Domino inspirante, penetrare promeruit."

21. More *testimonia* are collected in PL 22:213–36. For a discussion, see M. L. W. Laistner, "The Study of St. Jerome in the Early Middle Ages," p. 237.

22. Much remains to be learned about the complex linguistic relationships of early medieval Europe. For a provocative reassessment, see McKitterick, *The Carolingians and the Written Word,* pp. 1–22.

23. See Bernhard Bischoff, "The Study of Foreign Languages in the Middle Ages." On Hebrew, see Matthias Thiel, *Grundlagen und Gestalt der Hebräischkenntnisse des frühen Mittelalters.* On Greek, see Walter Berschin, *Greek Letters and the Latin Middle Ages: From Jerome to Nicholas of Cusa;* and Kaczynski, *Greek in the Carolingian Age: The St. Gall Manuscripts.* On the process of translation, see Kaczynski, "Medieval Translations: Latin and Greek."

24. Isidore of Seville, *Etymologies* 9.1.3–4.

25. For general surveys of the iconography of Jerome, see Bernard Lambert,

Bibliotheca Hieronymiana Manuscripta: La Tradition manuscrite des oeuvres de saint Jérôme, 4:A:53–76 and pls.; Renate Jungblut, *Hieronymus: Darstellung und Verehrung eines Kirchenvaters*; and Peter Bloch and Hermann Schnitzler, *Die ottonische Kölner Malerschule*, 2:144–52 and pls. 630–48.

26. The ivory covers and the manuscript are now separated. The Psalter is in Vienna, Österreichische Nationalbibliothek, MS 1861. See Kurt Holter, ed., *Der Goldene Psalter "Dagulf-Psalter": Vollständige Faksimile-Ausgabe im Originalformat von Codex 1861 der Österreichischen Nationalbibliothek*, 2:58–65.

27. Printed in Holter, *Der Goldene Psalter "Dagulf-Psalter"*, 2:47:

> Illic psalterii prima ostentatur origo,
> Et rex doctiloquax ipse canere choro,
> Utque decus rediit sublatis sentibus olim,
> Quod fuerat studio pervigilante viri.

28. The role of the pope has frequently been exaggerated. In the preface to his revision of the Gospels, Jerome attributes the initiative for the work to him, but this may simply be a literary convention. In fact, it is not certain at whose initiative Jerome undertook the early Roman revisions of the Gospels and the Psalter. See Gribomont, "The Translations," pp. 220–23.

29. Anton von Euw, "Studien zu den Elfenbeinarbeiten der Hofschule Karls des Grossen," pp. 54–56.

30. On the two frontispieces, see Wilhelm Koehler, *Die karolingischen Miniaturen*, vol. 1: *Die Schule von Tours*, pt. 2, *Die Bilder*, pp. 50–53, 314–17; Joachim E. Gaehde, "The Turonian Sources of the Bible of San Paolo Fuori Le Mura in Rome," pp. 361–65; and Herbert L. Kessler, *The Illustrated Bibles from Tours*, pp. 6–7, 84–95.

31. See MGH, Poetae 3:248:

> Exit Hieronimus Roma condiscere verba
> Hierusalem Hebraeae legis honorificae.
> Eustochio nec non Paulae divina salutis
> Iura dat altithrono fultus ubique deo.
> Hieronimus, translata sibi quae transtulit almus,
> Ollis hic tribuit, quis ea composuit.

For the *tituli* of the San Paolo Bible, see MGH, Poetae 3:259–60.

32. Kessler, in *The Illustrated Bibles*, observes that "these are among the most enigmatic ninth-century paintings. The subjects of the episodes in them have not been precisely identified; their relationship to one another has not been fully established; and their textual and pictorial sources remain unknown" (p. 84).

33. See Rice, *Saint Jerome in the Renaissance*, p. 25.

34. Florentine Mütherich and Joachim E. Gaehde, *Carolingian Painting*, p. 77.

35. On John Scottus Eriugena, the greatest translator of the early Middle Ages, see Edouard Jeauneau, "Jean Scot Erigène et le grec"; and Jeauneau, "Jean Scot Erigène: Grandeur et misère du métier de traducteur." For the comparison to Jerome, see MGH, Poetae 3:547: "Quod si quorumdam mordetur dente feroci / Hoc leue: namque meo contigit Hieronimo."

36. The "Carmina Scottorum" appear in MGH, Poetae 3:685–701.

37. Wilhelm Koehler, *Die karolingischen Miniaturen*, vol. 5: *Die Hofschule Karls des Kahlen* (with Florentine Mütherich), p. 138.

38. See MGH, Poetae 3:243: "Nobilis interpres Hieronimus atque sacerdos / Nobiliter pollens transscripsit iura Davidis."

39. For a list of the commentaries, see Friedrich Stegmüller, *Repertorium Biblicum Medii Aevi*, 3:51–74. For a discussion of their popularity in the eighth and ninth centuries, see Laistner, "The Study of St. Jerome," pp. 239–45.

40. *Commentariorum in Hiezechielem Libri XIV* 13.42.13, in *S. Hieronymi presbyteri opera*, pt. 1, *Opera exegetica*, vol. 4, ed. Franciscus Glorie, CCSL 75 (Turnhout, 1964), pp. 615–16.

41. See Contreni, "Carolingian Biblical Studies," pp. 79–80, for a discussion of pedagogical concerns as a stimulus for exegesis.

42. *Appendix ad Alcvini Epistolas*, no. 1, ed. Ernst Dümmler, MGH, Epp. 4 (Berlin, 1895), p. 483.

43. *Epistolae variorum inde a saeculo nono medio usque ad mortem Karoli II (Calvi) imperatoris collectae*, no. 24, ed. Dümmler, MGH, Epp. 6 (Berlin, 1925), pp. 177–78.

44. *Deutsche Literaturzeitung* 25 (1904): 134–35, quoted by Berschin, *Greek Letters and the Latin Middle Ages*, p. 50.

45. Berno of Reichenau, in the early eleventh century, mistakenly thought the arrangement itself came from Jerome; see Berschin, *Greek Letters and the Latin Middle Ages*, pp. 50–51.

46. On all of these biblical manuscripts, see Kaczynski, *Greek in the Carolingian Age*, pp. 75–98 (with bibliog. and pls.).

47. On the Psalter, see Kaczynski, *Greek in the Carolingian Age*, p. 78; and Berschin, "Salomons III. Psalterium quadrupartitum in Köln und Heidelberg."

48. The poem is printed by Arthur Allgeier, "Das Psalmenbuch des Konstanzer Bischofs Salomon III. in Bamberg: Eine Untersuchung zur Frage der mehrspaltigen Psalterien." Photographs of the two manuscript pages containing the poem are published in Berschin, "Salomons III. Psalterium quadrupartitum," p. 328.

49. See above, n. 14.

50. Kelly, *Jerome*, p. 333. On Jerome's posthumous reputation, see also Laistner, "The Study of St. Jerome," pp. 253–55; and Rice, *Saint Jerome in the Renaissance*.

51. For the two biographies, *Vita (I) S. Hieronymi (Inc. "Hieronimus noster")* and *Vita (II) S. Hieronymi (Inc. "Plerosque nimirum")*, see PL 22:175–84, 201–14. See also *Clavis Patrum Latinorum*, ed. E. Dekkers, no. 623, p. 142, and no. 622, p. 141. Jerome's miracle (the extraction of a thorn from a lion's paw) is given in the *Vita (II)*. For a discussion, see Rice, *Saint Jerome in the Renaissance*, pp. 37–45; and Berschin, *Biographie und Epochenstil im lateinischen Mittelalter*, 3:68–69.

52. On Jerome's place in the martyrologies, see René Aigrain, *L'Hagiographie: Ses sources, ses méthodes, son histoire*, pp. 51–68.

6

Carolingian Art and Politics

L A W R E N C E   N E E S

F ew works of medieval art are so often reproduced as the famous portrait coins of Charlemagne (fig. 3). The proud motto *Karolus Imperator Augustus* (Charles Emperor Augustus) written in classicizing
epigraphic capital letters, combines with the handsome profile view of the
ruler wearing diadem and chlamys to evoke the heritage of ancient Rome
and thus to represent the Carolingian "renaissance."[1] Hence the renown
of the image, which seems to embody the modern historiographical conception that the essential character and indeed the intention of the Carolingian court was, at least in cultural terms, a revival of ancient Rome.[2]
Since we know that Charlemagne received the Roman imperial title only
on Christmas Day 800, and that the surviving coins of this portrait type all
postdate that event, in fact postdate 804, this coin series has plausibly been
said to reflect the imperial coronation, especially as all three of Charlemagne's earlier coin series were of an entirely different aniconic type.[3]

In the case of the Charlemagne portrait coin, nearly all scholars seem
happily prepared to grant the relationship between a political event and its
reflection shortly thereafter in a work of pictorial art,[4] as most scholars are
prepared to grant the connection between art and contemporary political
events in other historical periods. However, in the Carolingian period the
Charlemagne portrait coins are commonly held to have been a special
case.[5] If one asks the question in broader terms, "How did the imperial
coronation affect the development of Carolingian art?" it proves very diffi-

FIGURE 3. Portrait coin of Charlemagne (obverse). Staatliche Museen zu Berlin. Reproduced by permission of the Staatliche Museen zu Berlin.

cult to move beyond this single coin type, since other apparently classicizing or Romanizing works are as likely to predate as to postdate 800.[6] Thus, insofar as the development and interpretation of the so-called Court School manuscripts and related works of art are concerned, the imperial coronation appears to be at most a minor issue, and perhaps altogether irrelevant.

It is a view still held by some that specific contemporary relevance of Carolingian art is all but impossible to determine in light of the Carolingian artist's tendency to rely upon earlier models, and that we bootlessly spend our time in looking for such specific connections and significance. Rosamond McKitterick recently observed that "it is unfashionable to link manuscript images with anything the artist has seen in real life," before proceeding to suggest, I think rightly, that a miniature in the Utrecht Psalter (fig. 4) reflects the artist's familiarity with a contemporary Frankish synod or assembly, which he intended to recall in this new context.[7] Her criticism of the long prevailing tendency among art historians is both painful and justified, and by no means a dead issue. Indeed, in an article published in 1988, a well-known scholar of Carolingian and other early medieval art, Herbert Kessler, has argued that in the early Middle Ages the artists' "goal was generally to come as close as possible to reproducing the model," and that such a goal all but precludes important contemporary references that we might term political.[8]

Perhaps I should say that in the view succinctly articulated by Kessler, which emphasizes the role of prior pictorial models, only specific contemporary political references are excluded, for in fact in the same article he argues that the choice of models is itself a highly charged political statement in a general sense, that "the implications of origin connoted by style were exploited by patrons and artists, as when Charlemagne set about to attach his court to the age of Constantine by rehabilitating classical

PICCATORVM ·CARNIS   RISURRECTIONEM·   UITAMAETERNAM·AMEN

INCIPITFIDESCATHO   LICAM
CICACIACEUULT   M   UNAESTDIUINITASAE   SIMILITEROMNIPOTENS
SALUUSESSEANTEOMNIA   QUALISGLORIACOAET   PATER · OMNIPOTENSEL·
OPUSESTUTTENEATCATHO   NAMALESIAS   LIUSOMNIPOTENSETSPSSCS
LICAMFIDEM   QUALISPATERTALISFILIUS   ETTAMENNONTRESOMNI

FIGURE 4. Utrecht Psalter: a church council. Utrecht, Universiteitsbibliotheek, MS 32, fol. 90v. Reproduced by permission of the University Library, Utrecht.

forms."[9] If this interpretation of Charlemagne's artistic patronage is correct, then clearly Carolingian art is profoundly political. However, this view makes the Carolingian artists appear almost as precocious post-modernists, since the presence of systems of references to earlier works of art is alleged to have been the central significance of their art. Such a view is of ancient and, one might say, august historiographical tradition, since already in the early nineteenth century Hegel wrote that the essential feature of Germanic history was its initial reference to the Roman heritage: "The process of culture they [the Germans] underwent consisted in taking up foreign elements and reductively amalgamating them with their own national life."[10]

I do not by any means doubt that Carolingian artists often, perhaps even normally, followed models in both style and iconography, but I am very much disposed to doubt that their own aims and understanding went no further than this, even if we today from our distant perspective choose to regard their aims and understanding as less interesting and significant than their contributions to a grand Hegelian historical development. Indeed, it seems to me not only that Carolingian artists invented images quite without any pictorial models when the occasion demanded,[11] but also that, in at least some instances, they chose and adopted models in such a way that the works of art they produced bear directly upon contemporary Carolingian circumstances and issues. It is not my intention here to provide a survey of all previous attempts to link Carolingian works of art with a political context.[12] Instead, I hope to do no more than point toward a few particular works of art that appear to me to shed light upon this general question, and if I can persuade readers that Carolingian works of art ought to be investigated with the possibility in mind that they might have some connection with contemporary issues, then I will be well contented.

❅

In some cases, the specific political significance of Carolingian artistic works can scarcely be doubted. A good example is the Dagulf Psalter, produced at Charlemagne's orders as a gift for Pope Hadrian I, as the verses at the beginning of the volume itself attest, and datable, at least in my view, to 794–95. The volume opens not with the Psalms themselves, but with a nearly unprecedented collection of creeds and other prefaces that occupy a full twenty-three folios. The inclusion of the credal collection conveys a message to the pope that Charlemagne and his court know and follow the venerable orthodox traditions of the church, and Donald Bullough has shown how this statement and the specific texts of some of the creeds relate to positions taken in the *Libri Carolini* written at the court in about 793.[13] No one doubts that at least one significant aspect of the *Libri Carolini*—the great treatise that attempted to rebut the actions of the Seventh Ecumenical Council at Nicaea in 787, in which the Byzantine church accepted the legitimacy of venerating religious images—is its polemical and political purpose.[14] I therefore think I am on firm ground when I claim the credal collections included in the contemporary Dagulf Psalter as a pointed political statement. What then of the artistic decoration of the manuscript in which that political message was intended to reach the pope?

The theme of authoritative transmission of orthodox texts and doctrines is a central political message of the Dagulf Psalter, as well as of many Carolingian legal and administrative pronouncements, and is underscored by visual images, for instance by the two ivory panels that formed the original covers of the book (fig. 5). These show four scenes, two on each panel, of which the first, David playing his lyre, is a traditional element of Psalter decoration—as, for example, in the slightly earlier but also eighth-century Vespasian Psalter from Canterbury—and clearly follows some sort of model.[15] The artist or patron of this iconographic program was here perfectly well served by an existing pictorial composition that must have been

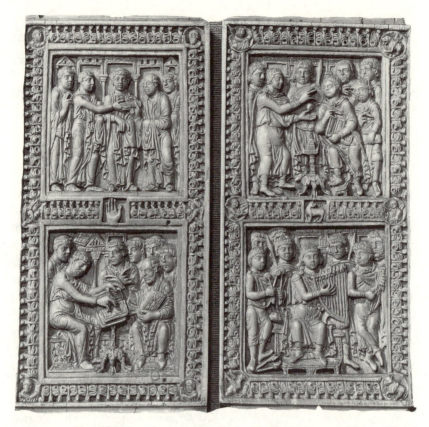

FIGURE 5. Dagulf Psalter: ivory covers. Paris, Musée du Louvre. Photo: Cliché des Musées Nationaux.

in common circulation and accessible to the workshop, and thus felt no need to, as it were, reinvent the wheel. However, it is either very difficult or altogether impossible to find good parallels for the other scenes of the Dagulf Psalter cover, for which close pictorial models in earlier art cannot be adduced.[16]

The other three scenes of the ivories show David selecting the scribes who will write down the Psalms, Jerome receiving from Pope Damasus a commission to translate the Psalms into Latin, and Jerome dictating his new translation to a secretary. Clearly these unprecedented scenes bear upon a general issue of ecclesiastical authority, specifically papal authority. This general issue is, however, specifically linked to a contemporary political situation, not only the Iconoclastic controversy but also the emerging dispute over Adoptionism, in regard to which Carolingian policy sought to invoke papal authority as support for views of the Carolingian court.[17] As already noted, the texts in the book covered by the ivory panels directly relate to these controversies, and it is, in fact, these prefatory texts, rather than the Psalms themselves, that explain the unique iconography of the covers of the Dagulf Psalter, as has long been noted by scholars. These surely qualify as "political" images, and it seems to me perverse to argue that their special features are the product of mere coincidence. They share with the portrait coins of Charlemagne of about a decade later very close dating and unusual form and subject matter, and are thus relatively easy to interpret in specific terms. They should at the very least indicate that such interpretations were not beyond the grasp or interest of Carolingian artists and patrons.

❖

The really difficult hermeneutical problems arise when dealing with works that are part of a series, a pictorial tradition, and thus are not manifest inventions or else are not so closely dated. Let me take up first a work that forms part of a series and ask whether it might nonetheless carry specific political relevance to contemporary beholders.

The manuscript commonly known as the Gundohinus Gospels was written by a single scribe working in an unknown Frankish monastery and is dated to the "third year of King Pepin," probably 754. It is, then, the earliest securely dated illustrated manuscript from Carolingian Francia. It has long been recognized that the manuscript draws upon early Mediterranean sources for its texts and decoration. Indeed, I have myself argued elsewhere at length that the book probably closely follows in most respects a Gospel book written in northern Italy in roughly the middle of the sixth century, finding, for example, that the closest parallel for the enthroned beardless Christ with pearled cross nimbus between angels seen in the Gundohinus image of Christ in Majesty (fig. 6) is the apse mosaic of San Vitale in Ravenna, datable 546–48.[18]

Jean Porcher and some other scholars have taken the coincidence of a book with primarily Mediterranean sources dating from the first years of the new Carolingian dynasty as an announcement of a new "classicizing" direction of Carolingian art, the beginning of the Carolingian renaissance in art, albeit a humble and, some have even said, a crude beginning.[19] In this sense, Porcher's interpretation belongs to the historiographical tradition continued also by Kessler, a tradition that sees a general programmatic statement expressed through the style or through the models or references evoked by Carolingian artists. The model is the message, in

FIGURE 6. Gospel Book of Gundohinus: Christ in Majesty. Autun, Bibliothèque Municipale, MS 3, fol. 12v.

other words. Thus here, the Mediterranean sources of the book, even in the absence of compelling evidence of Mediterranean classicizing style, are said to suggest a latent political program, namely, the revival of the Roman Empire.[20]

If the meaning of the art of the Gundohinus Gospels is exhausted when we say that it evokes the Roman past, then what can we say of the meaning of such a book as the Lorsch Gospels, produced in the orbit of Pepin's son Charlemagne close to the imperial coronation in 800?[21] Both sets of Evangelist portraits—for example, the portraits of John from the Gundohinus and Lorsch Gospels,[22] with the figures displayed under arches on columns and with their respective eagle symbols in the lunettes above—do, after all, stem ultimately from Mediterranean traditions.[23] Surely art historical distinctions are limned with a very broad brush if we can only say that such sharply differing images in fact mean the same thing.

Obviously the Lorsch artist's work has more fully evoked the classical heritage in terms of style, and very likely directly followed some late Roman work, such as the so-called Calendar of 354, at least for salient details like the medallion-decorated mantle.[24] Florentine Mütherich has interpreted the relationship between such works as the Gundohinus and Lorsch Gospels by saying that both reflect the official goal of a Romanization of culture and society, but that the Carolingian program was both "developed" and "perfected" in the later works.[25] Such a view implies that the scribe Gundohinus aimed to make a work like the Lorsch Gospels, but failed to do so because of lack of experience or skill and lack of access to the right kind of model. In fact the evidence of the book as a whole contradicts this interpretation.

The Christ in Majesty miniature of the Gundohinus Gospels shows this artist and the intended meaning of his work in a very different and more ambitious light, suggesting a sophisticated and specific political context for his work. The two angelic beings flanking Christ are absent from the vast majority of the seemingly countless later Majesty images, such as that in the already cited Lorsch Gospels, but occur in the earlier tradition as a heritage from Roman imperial iconography, the angels of the Majesty substituting for the original soldiers.[26] Suddenly a problem begins to emerge here: if the Lorsch Gospels "develops and perfects" the imitation of Roman art crudely begun in such works as the Gundohinus Gospels, why is it that Gundohinus is in fact closer to the ancient iconography, which all the "developed and perfected" later works spurn?

Notice here two features of the Gundohinus angels. They are inscribed *cyrubin* (cherubim) and their wings are raised together so that they meet over the head of Christ. These features are unparalleled in other Majesty images whether earlier or later, yet both occur together in a different series of images, those depicting the tabernacle of the Ark of the Covenant as described in the Old Testament books of Exodus (37:7–9) and 1 Kings (6:23–28). Both descriptions specify that above the ark were two golden cherubim facing each other, with their extended wings touching, exactly as visualized in the Gundohinus Gospels miniature and in depictions of the ark, as for example in a miniature of the Ashburnham Pentateuch, a Latin manuscript most probably from the seventh century and known to have been at Tours in the Carolingian period.[27] Did Gundohinus simply confuse different models, or can we look for a sensible contemporary explanation?

The Gundohinus Gospels miniature is obviously not an image of the Ark of the Covenant, and thus the cherubim seem quite out of place here. Considering the image in relation to the contemporary political context can, however, suggest a plausible motive for this anomalous feature. The cherubim of the ark and sanctuary had been involved with the debate over images almost from the beginning of the Iconoclastic controversy in the early eighth century, since they offered the preeminent example of figural images specifically authorized by God. Both Byzantine and Carolingian authors used the image of the cherubim of the ark and sanctuary as a central element in the debate over images, the later eighth-century *Libri Carolini* discussing the cherubim at length in several places.[28] Theodulf of Orléans, the *Libri Carolini*'s author, also made use of a visual image of the cherubim in order to state his understanding of the proper interpretation of scripture and the proper attitude toward images: the justly celebrated image of the cherubim erected in his chapel at Germigny-des-Prés. There, as in the *Libri Carolini*, the image served not to justify, but rather to restrict the use of holy images in the Christian church.[29]

Clearly the imagery of the cherubim in the Gundohinus Gospels suggests some connection with one of the more important theological and political controversies of the eighth century, the Iconoclastic controversy. While it is true that the manuscript's image of Christ in Majesty belongs to a long series of images that signify in a general sense the Harmony of the Gospels and related themes, and that this generic significance was retained in the Gundohinus Gospels, a new level of specific meaning was added to the theme in that manuscript, not only through its inclusion of the cherubim but also through its direct juxtaposition of the Majesty miniature with a Trinitarian text by Jerome (or more likely Rufinus of Aquileia).[30] In the manuscript the text was, very peculiarly, written in two separate locations, the first excerpt on folios 1r–1v and the second on folio 13r, directly facing the Majesty miniature. In the absence of any codicological or historical explanation for the division of the text into two parts, one is at least entitled to investigate the possibility that this juxtaposition of image and text was no completely unmotivated accident, and that the image and text face each other because they must have been intended to be seen together.

I shall not attempt here even a summary of my argument, advanced elsewhere, that we see here no coincidence but a deliberate reaction to a contemporary historical situation; that Gundohinus became aware of the Iconoclastic arguments and rearranged the position of his texts and the details of his miniature with the deliberate intention of proclaiming his own orthodoxy and, in a broader sense, that of the Latin and Frankish church in the face of a Byzantine "innovation."[31] It may be enough here to recall that, from the very beginning of Carolingian art, we have a startlingly complex and immediate reaction to a contemporary political issue. The instance is particularly interesting and to some degree not unusual in what I take to be its political reference and content, even though no evidence suggests a close connection of the Gundohinus Gospels with patronage of the Carolingian court circle. Surely no one would call the manuscript courtly in the style or luxury of its decoration!

❧

Most of the examples to follow are, in contrast, closely connected to the court, but it is well to bear in mind that our ability to relate these works of art to a political context is more likely to be the accidental product of our sources of knowledge than of any essential apoliticism in the provinces. The courtly works of art are much better known and have been more thoroughly studied, and our documentary sources are very scanty when we leave the activities of the court circles.

An image from the court of Charlemagne whose possible relevance to contemporary political concerns has never been suggested is the front cover of MS Douce 176 in the Bodleian Library at Oxford, which bears a small ivory carving universally associated with Charlemagne's so-called Court School (fig. 7).[32] It depicts in the large central panel Christ trampling on the asp, basilisk, lion, and dragon, an image inspired by Psalm 90. That image was also the central subject in two closely related Carolingian ivory carvings: one of the two Genoels-Elderen ivories in Brussels, apparently the earliest of the three versions of the subject,[33] and one of the two famous Lorsch Gospels covers, now in the Vatican (fig. 8).[34]

Like the Lorsch panel, the Bodleian ivory is in a five-part form, but

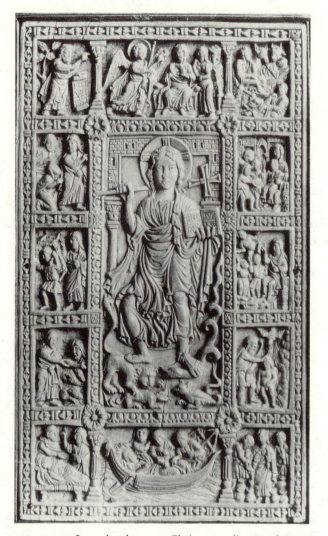

FIGURE 7. Ivory book cover: Christ trampling on the asp, basilisk, lion, and dragon. Oxford, Bodleian Library, MS Douce 176. Reproduced by permission of the Bodleian Library.

whereas the Lorsch composition is in fact five separate pieces of ivory joined together and measuring thirty-nine by twenty-eight centimeters overall, the Bodleian cover is a single ivory plaque measuring but twenty-one by twenty-one centimeters. Also differing from the Lorsch example is the iconography of the smaller satellite images of the Bodleian ivory,

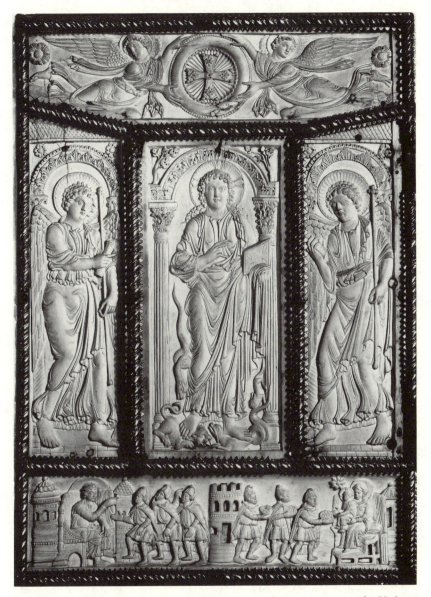

FIGURE 8. Ivory book cover from Lorsch: Christ between two angels. Vatican, Museo Sacro, Biblioteca Apostolica. Reproduced by permission of the Biblioteca Apostolica Vaticana.

which show not large angels but small narrative scenes concentrating upon the infancy and the miracles of Christ. Six of these scenes are directly copied from two fifth-century Early Christian panels in Paris and Berlin (figs. 9 and 10, respectively), presumably once part of a large five-part composition such as we see in the Lorsch Gospels cover.[35] For once we can actually compare a Carolingian work of art with its surviving model!

At first the comparison seems to suggest that the Carolingian artist was indeed a slavish copyist, but one should be wary of jumping to conclusions along this line. Note that for the scene of the marriage of Cana the Early Christian carver has provided four water jugs, but the Carolingian artist six, and it is the latter that agrees with the specific evidence of John 2:6, as was recently pointed out to me by a perceptive student, Jack Becker.[36] The Carolingian artist has in fact "corrected" his late antique pictorial model by recourse to the appropriate textual source, hardly an indication of an automaton-like slavish imitator. Of course, one must also say that the Carolingian artist has condensed the images and, we might say, removed their relatively naturalistic spaciousness, although one should remember that each of the Early Christian panels measures roughly twenty by nine centimeters and is thus nearly as large as the entire Bodleian plaque, so that the Carolingian artist faced a significant alteration of scale, and some alterations would perforce need to be made in adapting the model.

One important change vis-à-vis his model would not have been forced upon the artist of the Bodleian plaque by reduced space, however. Note that the three scenes at the left of the Bodleian ivory correspond, albeit not in the same order, to the placement of the three scenes on the Paris Early Christian panel, which would have occupied the left position in the original five-part diptych. Yet, on the other side of the Bodleian plaque, the three scenes that correspond to the Early Christian source are not all beside the central panel but have been pushed down, so that the lowest, the miracle at Cana, appears on what, in an Early Christian five-part model, would have been a different panel, the bottom rather than the side.[37] Why make this change? Presumably it was made so as to insert something at the top of the panel that was not in any model. There is indeed an obvious interpolation at the top of the panel: the figure of the prophet Isaiah holding a scroll at the upper left corner.

In his study of the Court School ivories, Thomas Hoving could find neither precedent nor parallel for linking a figure of the prophet Isaiah with the Annunciation,[38] as we see on the Bodleian plaque. Hoving proposed that the figure was copied from a lost Syrian model containing images of prophets holding scrolls, something like the famous Rossano

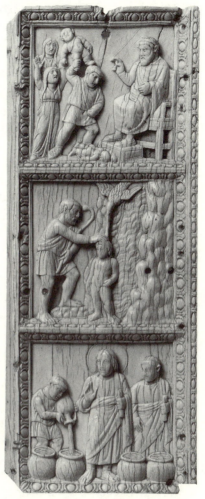

FIGURE 9. Early Christian ivory diptych panel. Paris, Musée du Louvre. Photo: copyright R.M.N.

FIGURE 10. Early Christian ivory diptych panel. Berlin, Dahlem Museum. Reproduced by permission of the Staatliche Museen Preussischer Kulturbesitz.

Gospels, where quite different half-length prophets hold scrolls beneath a series of Gospel scenes.[39] Even if this comparison is at all germane, which I doubt, Hoving suggested no motive whatsoever for the copying of such a figure. Isaiah holds an open scroll clearly inscribed *ECCE VIRGO CONCIPIET*, "Behold a virgin shall conceive," a well known and often used quotation from Isaiah 7:14. That prophetic text is quoted in Matthew

1:23 along with its continuation, "Behold a virgin shall be with child, and bring forth a son, and they shall call his name Emmanuel, which being interpreted is, God with us." The Matthew text is the lection for the vigil of the Nativity, the first Gospel reading in the famous Godescalc Gospel lectionary, written for Charlemagne in 781–83 and apparently kept at court throughout his reign.[40] Hence the inclusion of a figure of Isaiah displaying this text, which opens the roughly contemporary lectionary from the same milieu, might be explained on the basis of the ancient and understandable tendency to illustrate the first words that follow it.[41] Yet such an interpretation entails serious difficulties, as we shall see. In any event, in an ivory closely associated with Charlemagne's court, it is not at all surprising to see the reference to specific contemporary liturgical sources. But where is the indication of a singular contemporary political context or inspiration?

Bodleian MS Douce 176, the manuscript to which our ivory is now and, as far as anyone knows, always has been attached, is itself a Gospel lectionary. It is a handsomely decorated manuscript, with fine script and illumination in what has come to be called the Merovingian style, emphasizing zoomorphic letters dominated by fish and birds. No doubt because of the contrast between this style and the classicizing style of the ivory, the manuscript and its cover have often been thought to have been brought together at some late date; their mutual close connection with Charlemagne's court and almost exactly contemporary dates have been regarded as coincidental.[42] In fact, as Adolph Goldschmidt observed, although the leather-covered seventeenth-century binding into which the ivory is set cannot be the original, the ivory fits the manuscript very well in size and proportion, making it likely that the two always went together.[43] The manuscript was written in approximately the first decade of the ninth century at Chelles, the female monastery whose abbess was Gisla, Charlemagne's sister.[44] Gisla was an important figure in her own right, and during the late 790s and early years of the ninth century she was a regular correspondent of Alcuin, several of whose letters to her survive.[45] Alcuin also dedicated to Gisla his long commentary on the Gospel according to John, which was begun by 800 and completed in about 802.[46]

Alcuin is, it seems to me, a very likely sponsor of the manufacture of the ivory cover intended for a new lectionary manuscript to be written in Gisla's own monastery. Chelles had a very accomplished and active scriptorium, working in a distinctly un-Roman Frankish ornamental style.[47] Chelles surely did not have its own ivory carver, and the cover must have been executed elsewhere, presumably at or near Charlemagne's court.

Other evidence supports the view that the ivory cover was not made at Chelles for the lectionary written there and now preserved as MS Douce 176. I have already mentioned that Isaiah's prophecy as repeated in Matthew is the first lection or pericope in the Godescalc lectionary. It was also the first lection in Alcuin's lectionary as edited by Wilmart, and certainly would have been the basis for a lectionary cover produced at the court.[48] However, MS Douce 176 begins its series not with the vigil for Christmas but with the Christmas feast itself; not, therefore, with the rubric *In Vigilia Natalis Dni.* but with *In Natale Dni. ad s. Mariam*, for which the text is Luke 2:1–14. MS Douce 176 shares this opening pericope with the earlier calendar preserved in Würzburg, Universitätsbibliothek cod. M.P. th. fol. 62,[49] and therefore represents a liturgical family distinct from that employed at Charlemagne's court by Alcuin and others.

One might see the emphasis given in the Bodleian ivory to Isaiah's prophecy and to the large figure of the enthroned Virgin, who sits at the top center of the panel directly above Christ, as nothing more than a rather simple complimentary reference to the special virtue of female virginity, which Gisla and her nuns shared with Christ's mother. Such a compliment may well have been intended, and may be part of the explanation for the unusual iconography of the plaque. However, the emphasis upon the virginity of Mary, upon the angelic salutation to the Annunciation, and indeed upon Isaiah's prophecy may also have a more distinctly political implication in the late 790s or the first years of the ninth century, as can be seen through an examination of works by Alcuin and others of Charlemagne's scholars written against the Adoptionist heresy in Spain.

Donald Bullough has written that, in his *Seven Books against Felix of Urgel* written in 799 (PL 101:119–230), Alcuin "is most clearly innovatory in his treatment of Mary as the Mother of God and of her relationship both with fallen man and with the Incarnate word."[50] Indeed, the exalted position of the Virgin figures prominently throughout the treatise as a central argument against the Adoptionists. Following the fifth-century writer Arnobius, Alcuin in the same treatise also links the imperial purple wool that Mary was spinning at the moment of the Annunciation with the divinity of Christ from before his human conception (PL 101:210C). If Hoving was correct in linking the woman beside Mary in the Bodleian plaque with one of the seven daughters of Israel who were Mary's spinning companions,[51] then Alcuin's anti-Adoptionist work may help to explain another iconographic motif in the work. At the same time, it is noteworthy that Alcuin directly links this discussion of the Virgin's spinning with the angelic salutation and the conception of Christ by the

Adoptionists

Theotokos, writing "Virgo Concepit" (PL 101:211A), paraphrasing and perhaps alluding to the prophecy of Isaiah. Elsewhere in his treatise *De Incarnatione* of about the same date (PL 101:271–300), also written against the Adoptionists, Alcuin explicitly cites the prophecy of Isaiah 7:14, and approvingly notes its reappearance in Matthew 1:23, with the addition that "Emmanuel" signifies "God with us" (PL 101:276D). Alcuin is, in fact, not alone in using the Isaiah text against the Adoptionists, since Paulinus of Aquileia's *Contra Felicem* of 796 cites the text four different times and with great emphasis,[52] a fact kindly brought to my attention by Celia Chazelle. Surely the iconography of this ivory, with its Isaiah prophecy and concentration upon Christ's miracles, has contemporary political resonance.

❖

Another ivory carving, this one made for Charles the Bald, raises the issue of the political relevance of Carolingian works of art in a rather different and—most today would say—more direct way, since the previous examples bear primarily upon what now would be called ecclesiastical matters with only secondary political overtones and connections. The ivory carving at the center of the jeweled back cover of Charles's Psalter, now in Paris, B.N. cod. lat. 1152, shows a dramatic episode in the life of David (fig. 11),[53] the well-known episode of his sinful affair with Bathsheba, which caused him to fall from favor with the Lord. The story is told in 2 Samuel 11–12. From his roof David saw the beautiful Bathsheba in her bath, was overcome by lust for her, lay with her and conceived a child, and, abusing his royal powers, deliberately and maliciously gave orders that led to the death of her husband, Uriah. The prophet Nathan comes to David in his royal palace and speaks at first indirectly of the actions of an unnamed rich man who, wishing to have a sheep with which to make an offering, took one not from his own large flocks but instead seized the single lamb belonging to a poor man. David angrily denounces the pitiless rich man, at which point Nathan tells him that he has condemned himself ("Thou art the man"), and as punishment explains that David's own sons will rise against him and that Bathsheba's child will die. This rebuke is the occasion for David's great Psalm of Repentance, Psalm 50(51), in which he begs for cleansing mercy while saying, "I acknowledge my transgressions; and my sin is ever before me."

The ivory illustrates this story from Samuel and also the *titulus* to Psalm 50,[54] depicting the parable of the rich man and the poor man in the lower register. In the larger upper scene, Nathan bursts in from one side and

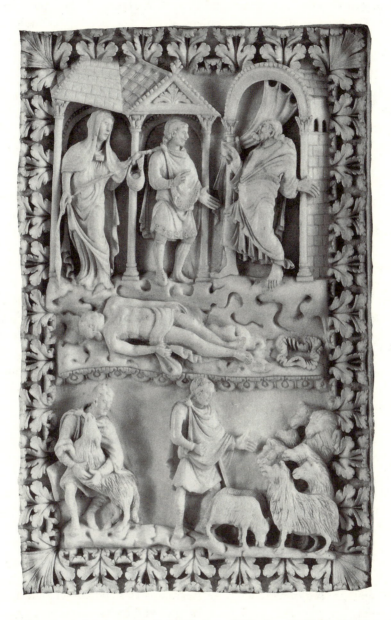

FIGURE 11. Ivory cover of the Psalter of Charles the Bald: David and Bathsheba before Nathan. Paris, Bibliothèque Nationale, MS lat. 1152. Reproduced by permission of the Bibliothèque Nationale.

points to the corpse of Uriah, and Bathsheba apparently seeks to retain David entwined in her snare, perhaps literally her weaving, as the two stand before what must be taken to represent the royal palace. David himself is caught at a moment of decision: should he deny his crime and punish Nathan, or admit his fault and beg forgiveness?

It is precisely because he chooses the latter course of humility and penitence that David is a proper model for a Carolingian ruler, guided by the man of God, aware of his own sin. Sedulius Scottus uses the episode in his treatise *De rectoribus christianis (On Christian Rulers)*, written between 855 and 859 for either Charles the Bald himself or for his nephew King Lothair II, in which David is both contrasted with the "impious King Saul of Israel [who] was deprived of his kingdom and his life because he did not stand before the Lord as a faithful minister," and praised for his submission to Nathan, when he "bewailed himself with bitter penance."[55] Archbishop Hincmar of Reims cites the Nathan passage to Lothair II in his treatise against Lothair's divorce, cites it again to Charles the Bald in his important and pervasively Augustinian comprehensive work of 873 on the royal office and duties, and indeed cites the passage yet once more in a letter to Pope Hadrian II, along with ecclesiastical canons and decretals and Augustinian injunctions concerning the proper duty of ecclesiastics to bring accusation against the sins and errors of their rulers.[56]

The image on the ivory cover of Charles the Bald's Psalter was commissioned by or presented to the king at an undetermined moment before 869, and presents an example of a royal sin that must be avoided, not royal glory to be imitated. Its selection can be explained in many ways. Least satisfactory is the notion that since Psalm 50 begins the second of three parts into which early medieval Psalter manuscripts were often divided, its selection reflects the particular importance of illustrations of that psalm in the pictorial tradition. If this as it were unthinkingly "automatic" explanation of the choice of Psalm 50 had any validity, one should expect to see Psalm 1 or Psalm 100 decorating the other ivory cover on the front of the book, not Psalm 56, as is in fact the case.[57] That other carving illustrates not the *titulus* but the psalm text itself (verses 5 and 7, respectively), specifically showing the Psalmist "delivered from the midst of the young lions . . . and the sons of men, whose teeth are weapons and arrows, and their tongue a sharp sword," while at the bottom of the panel the enemies who have dug a pit as a snare fall into it themselves. Clearly the two covers make a program, arguing that if the ruler acts justly—specifically, does not confiscate the property of the powerless (or the church!)—he will be given victory over his enemies.

Certainly the image of Nathan's rebuke of David is by no means rare and may be found in a substantial percentage of the preserved early medieval Psalters in both Latin and Greek worlds, as in the well-known miniature of the tenth-century Byzantine Paris Psalter.[58] Yet in that manuscript the episode is but one in a substantial series of scenes from David's life, and neither there nor in any other work is the sin and penitence of David given such prominence as in Charles the Bald's Psalter, where it is one of only two psalms illustrated. In this instance we can even say with some confidence that the choice of this scene cannot have been due to the chance availability of a model for that scene and no other, since, as was already noted by Goldschmidt,[59] the ivory cover of Charles the Bald's Psalter appears to have had its direct source in the profusely illustrated Utrecht Psalter,[60] which could have provided the artist and program designer with a model for any of the 150 psalms, not for Psalm 50 only. Clearly Psalm 50 was deliberately chosen by the artist or designer of the program of the Psalter of Charles the Bald; moreover, in taking the composition of the Utrecht Psalter for Psalm 50 as its essential inspiration, the artist of the ivory has altered the composition so as to place the dead body of Uriah in a very prominent position at the center of the ivory panel. Surely, especially in the case of a work of such superlative quality of expression and composition, such concentration upon the effect of David's sin cannot be dismissed as accidental.

The special bearing of Psalm 50 and the penitence of King David upon contemporary political thinking has recently been indicated by Christoph Eggenberger in his study of the late ninth-century Carolingian Golden Psalter of Saint Gall, a very richly illustrated book, yet one in which the Bathsheba episode is absent altogether. Eggenberger dismisses, rightly in my opinion, the possibility that the psalm is not illustrated in that magnificent book because no model was available to the artists, who demonstrably drew upon a wide variety of sources. Eggenberger suggests that the image of the sin and penitence of David was deliberately excluded from that illustrative cycle because the humility theme was not considered desirable for a book designed to be used by various important visitors to the monastery, that it was perhaps too provocative.[61] As Eggenberger shows, drawing upon liturgical and exegetical sources, this psalm had a particularly important monitory function as one of the penitential psalms.

Although images sometimes could and did de-emphasize David's sin—as in the later Byzantine example already mentioned and in the earlier Carolingian Corbie and Zurich Psalters—by depicting his praiseworthy humble penitence without showing Bathsheba or the dead body of Uriah,

which were the causes of that penitence, the cover of the Psalter of Charles
the Bald gives Uriah and especially Bathsheba great prominence. It must
also be remembered that the designer of the program for the ivory cover
deliberately chose this psalm with its penitential theme, where he could
have followed earlier Carolingian royal tradition by placing David as author and musician on the cover, as on the Dagulf Psalter.[62] Surely also the
theme of the penitence of David was chosen, and the sin which preceded
the penitence emphasized, on the cover of Charles the Bald's Psalter because the conception of royal humility was so important to the ideal of
rulership preached in the ninth-century *Fürstenspiegel*,[63] based ultimately
upon Augustine's picture of the humility of Theodosius in his *City of God*,
book 5, chapter 26.[64] Indeed, immediately after citing to Lothair II the
proper penitence and humility of David after being rebuked for his sin
with Bathsheba, Sedulius Scottus cites at great length the episode of "the
wonderful humility and penance of the glorious prince Theodosius,"
which Augustine had so prominently featured.[65]

Sedulius Scottus' close linkage of David and Theodosius as royal
models supports the view that the program of images developed for
Charles the Bald's Psalter extends to the miniatures inside the volume.
There Charles appears in an enthroned portrait image, wearing a crown
and holding a scepter and an orb, while the hand of God reaches down
toward him. The inscription above the king says that he is like Josiah and
Theodosius.[66] Why are these two figures cited, rather than Moses, David,
or, conceivably, Constantine?

Josiah was the king of Judah who, during the time of the prophet Isaiah, came to the throne as a boy of eight after his wicked father, Amon,
had been slain by his own household. Josiah subsequently rebuilt the dam-
aged temple in Jerusalem and found there the books of Moses (2 Kings
21–23), the "books of the Law," which he read to the people,[67] whom he
attempted to lead in a religious revival by destroying all the altars and idols
that had been established by his predecessors since the time of David. Indeed, Josiah is said to have "walked in the ways of his father David" (2
Kings 22:2). Josiah in this sense forms a natural model for emulation by a
Frankish king concerned, as Charles the Bald and others had been, with
legislation seeking to reform the Christian church and the moral life of the
people in their care. Josiah had been cited earlier as such a model, along
with Moses, David, and Samuel, by Theodulf of Orléans in his poem *Contra iudices*, addressed to Charlemagne.[68] On the other hand, Josiah's story
also carries a subversive subtext, for his virtues did not prevent the Lord's

continuing anger with the people of Judah from allowing him to be killed in battle against the Egyptians and, in the time of his sons, allowing Jerusalem to be taken by Nebuchadnezzar, the Temple destroyed, and the people taken into captivity in Babylon. Josiah was good, but not triumphant, a model especially appropriate for a king besieged by powerful enemies and not always victorious.

Why is Josiah linked with Theodosius as a model for Charles the Bald? Theodosius is a different but no less difficult figure. First is a problem of simple identification. It is not altogether clear whether Theodosius I or Theodosius II is meant by the inscription, and either is a possibility; indeed it may well be that the two were either confused or erroneously merged in the ninth century.

Theodosius II is often considered to be the emperor represented in this miniature, for his name is attached to the greatest codification of Roman law before Justinian. Theodosius II is specified in an early ninth-century North Italian manuscript, with an inscription reading *Theodosius iunior imperator* in the portrait showing him enthroned and accompanied by the teeming bishops attending the Council of Ephesus.[69] Theodosius II had also undoubtedly been represented in an early Carolingian miniature contained in a law book, without any inscription specifying which Theodosius is shown but presumably identifiable on the basis of the legal text with which he is linked and because of the lawyers who surround him.[70]

However, Theodosius I "the Great" was also a well-known figure in the Carolingian period, paired with Constantine as a predecessor of the Carolingian kings in a description of wall paintings in the royal hall at Ingelheim written in the late 820s by Ermoldus Nigellus, in which Theodosius' great deeds *(actis praeclaris)* are mentioned.[71] When Lupus of Ferrières wrote to Charles the Bald in 844, he refers to a "very brief summary of the deeds of the emperors [that he had] presented to Your Majesty," in which he especially commends Trajan and Theodosius "because you can most profitably find many things among their deeds to imitate."[72] Theodosius is here unnumbered, but the elder emperor is presumably intended, because the reference is to his great deeds, as in the Ingelheim poem of Ermoldus.

One could argue that the common denominator between Josiah and Theodosius, and between each and Charles the Bald, is the idea of law. Josiah discovered and promulgated the "books of the Law"; Theodosius II was a law codifier; and Charles was actively interested in the law. Were the miniatures the frontispiece to a law book—as they could well have been,

since we know of some luxuriously decorated legal codices from the time
and the circle of Charles the Bald[73]—this would be the more likely interpretation. However, the manuscript is a Psalter, indeed a private Psalter of
the sort that could be and presumably was intended to be used for private
devotions by the king.

The image of David and Bathsheba is certainly an appropriately devo-
tional image, a call to humility and penance, Psalm 50 being one of the
seven penitential Psalms. Hence, it seems more than likely that the invoca-
tion of Theodosius in connection with Charles the Bald's portrait should
share the same theme and reflect the identification of Theodosius I as not
only the doer of great deeds but also the shining example of a ruler's humility and penance, as cited by Augustine in the *City of God* and reiterated
by such contemporary authors as Sedulius Scottus, as already mentioned.

Augustine praises both the great deeds and the humility of Theodosius
in the same chapter, and that chapter deserves further scrutiny for four additional themes that connect it to the artistic decoration of Charles the
Bald's Psalter. First, Augustine also praises Theodosius for having consulted the prophetic hermit John for advice before proceeding against the
tyrannical Maxentius, a theme analogous to that on the ivory cover of
David hearing the prophet Nathan, and one of obvious attractiveness for a
clerical program designer. Second, Augustine praises Theodosius for casting down the statues of Jupiter that had been set up in the Alps by his
enemies, recalling Josiah's actions in casting down the idols from the high
places, as described in the Old Testament. Third, Augustine praises Theodosius for not having confiscated the property of his defeated enemies'
heirs, a theme recalling the sin of David and Nathan's parable and gently
evoking Carolingian churchmen's claims for the inviolability of church
property against the actions of some rulers' attempts to reclaim land.
Finally, the overarching theme of Augustine's discussion, in which Theodosius serves as an exemplum, is the idea of personal salvation far out-
weighing any earthly good:

> These and other similar good works, which it would be long to tell,
> he carried with him from the world of time, where the greatest hu-
> man nobility and loftiness are but vapour. Of these works the re-
> ward is eternal happiness, of which God is the giver, though only
> to those who are sincerely pious. But all other blessings and privi-
> leges of this life, as the world itself, light, air, earth, water, fruits,
> and the soul of man himself, his body, sense, mind, life, He lavishes
> on good and bad alike. And among these blessings is also to be

reckoned the possession of an empire, whose extent He regulates according to the requirements of His providential government at various times.[74]

How appropriate a thought to be evoked by the reference to Theodosius in the portrait miniature in a royal Psalter! Surely this section of Augustine's *City of God*, which has been termed by a recent scholar *"the* Christian Fürstenspiegel par excellence,"[75] would have been known to Charles the Bald himself, as well as to the as-yet-unidentified designer of the program of images for his Psalter.[76] The Augustinian passage articulated a fundamental conception underlying the intended significance of the portrait of Charles as "like Josiah and Theodosius."

In what context would such a program of images, such a concatenation of themes and allusions, have been particularly appropriate? The themes include the death of a favored son, to be supplanted by another borne by a new wife; rejection of idolatry; protection, rather than confiscation, of the property of the "poor and defenseless," however those might be construed; and the defeat of the righteous king because of God's anger at his ancestors and people. Many of those themes must have had contemporary resonance. The king's duty to protect rather than confiscate ecclesiastical property is a major theme of ninth-century writers; indeed that duty was sometimes linked with the often reiterated call to defend the rights of widows and orphans.[77]

Such frequent reiteration suggests abuse, and Charles the Bald followed a long family tradition in assigning ecclesiastical estates to lay followers. Lupus of Ferrières' many letters over a period of eight years begging for restitution of the cell of Saint Josse are only one of the best known examples of this phenomenon.[78] The possibility that the Lord's anointed king might be defeated in battle by infidels, as happened to Josiah, cannot have been a point of merely antiquarian interest in Charles the Bald's kingdom. The Viking raids and indeed invasions had already begun in earnest in the early days of Charles's rule, in the 840s, and grew in intensity thereafter, with the great invasions of 856–62 providing a high or low point, depending upon the point of view.[79]

The prophecy of Nathan concerning the sons of David must also have been a reference with special resonance for one of the sons of Louis the Pious, as was Charles the Bald. A dominant factor in Carolingian history during the second quarter of the ninth century was the revolt of Louis's sons, who had indeed, like David's son Absalom, repeatedly rebelled against paternal authority, causing their father to be deposed, imprisoned, and humiliated—a revolt, also in an analogous manner, prompted in very large part by the father's new marriage to a beautiful woman, in this case Charles's own mother, Judith. Although the first child of David and Bathsheba died as a result of God's anger at David's sin, it is also true that the second son of that union was Solomon, the great future king destined to succeed to the throne of all Israel and to build the Temple.

In terms of the narrative situation, Judith's son Charles the Bald thus stands as a parallel to Bathsheba's son Solomon. Are we really to imagine that no such connection ever occurred to the man who designed the program of this cover, or to Charles the Bald, for whom it was intended? To take such a view seems to me to require that we imagine a particularly dense stupidity on the part of the Carolingian king and court, and in my view the surviving evidence suggests nothing of the kind. Indeed, it has been observed by Joachim Gaehde and others that the frontispiece miniature for the Book of Kings in the great Bible given by Charles the Bald to the pope in 875, on the occasion of his imperial coronation in Rome (now preserved in the monastery of San Paolo fuori le mura in that city), shows Solomon seated upon his throne (fig. 12) looking very much indeed like portraits of Charles the Bald in such works as the Codex Aureus of St. Emmeran, produced likewise in the early 870s.[80]

I must admit that I have used such usefully vague terms as "resonance" to gloss the issue of direct topical political reference in the imagery of the Psalter of Charles the Bald's ivory cover and portrait miniature.[81] I have not been able to uncover any specific evidence that would allow the program to be linked exclusively with a particular event or moment. I could easily imagine it being commissioned in the dark days of 858, when Charles's kingdom was invaded by both the Vikings and his own brother Louis the German; I could also imagine it being commissioned in celebration of Charles's survival of the latter threat, with the help of Hincmar of Reims and other churchmen who refused to abandon their king. The problem is that the imagery is not strictly allegorical, but rather more loosely allusive—as it were, metaphorical. The program is also unusual and difficult to interpret, thereby nicely reflecting the fact that it must have been unusual and difficult to interpret in the ninth century. The combination of Psalms 50 and 56, each reflecting a quite different evocation of the king's relationship to God, his people, and the church, with the citation of Josiah and (unspecified) Theodosius cannot have been thought to be straightforward by the program's designer. Evidently the program was meant to provoke extended thought, or perhaps one should say reflection, on the part of its prime audience, the king himself. In fact, the audience for

FIGURE 12. Illustration from the Bible of Charles the Bald at San Paolo fuori le mura, Rome: Solomon seated upon the throne. Rome, San Paolo fuori le mura, fol. 188v. Photo: I.C.C.D. Roma, neg. E47522.

such a work was most severely restricted, numbering no more than the king and intimate members of his family and court, who would have been in the fortunate position, which we do not share, of knowing the date and context of the commission and therefore being able to interpret the manuscript's imagery in that specific context.

We are in a double bind in trying to determine the context (that is, on the simplest level, the date) and the interpretation at once, when the two are interdependent. Only a terminus ante quem seems to be securely fixed, as the manuscript was given by Charles the Bald to the cathedral of Metz (together with the so-called Vivian Bible) in 869. The Vivian Bible was at that time nearly twenty years old, so there is no reason to think a date near 869 either likely or unlikely for the Psalter. The circumstances of the gift do, however, suggest that the Psalter was thought of by the king in a political context. It is probably not an accident that the donation to Metz followed upon Charles's coronation there, by Bishop Arnulf of Toul and by Archbishop Hincmar of Reims, as king of Lothair II's realm.[82] The triumphant outcome of Charles's ancient desire to possess his nephew's kingdom no doubt encouraged him to believe, incorrectly as later events proved, that he was one of the lucky few chosen rulers who would be successful in his earthly career and also merit heavenly salvation thereafter. The monitory content of the imagery of the Psalter that he offered as a gift on the occasion suggests that he humbly recognized his shortcomings and had been exalted in part for that reason, as David and Theodosius before him.

�֍

The monitory content of the cover of Charles the Bald's Psalter is not an isolated example of an image embodying a monitory or implicitly critical address to a Carolingian monarch that may perhaps be closely related to a specific historical situation. One of the most famous and most beautiful artworks of the Carolingian period is the magnificent rock crystal of King Lothair II (fig. 13), decorated with a series of narrative scenes from the Old Testament story of Susanna, beginning with the two evil Elders peering over the garden wall at the young woman preparing to take her bath.[83] At the center of the crystal in a medallion appears the enthroned judge, usually interpreted as Daniel, vindicating the innocent young woman against her perjured accusers. This scene is clearly unusual, not being called for by the biblical text and given special prominence by its central location and framing. Since the inscription *Lotharius Rex Francorum* . . . *[me] [f]ieri iussit* (Lothair King of the Franks ordered me to be made) ap

FIGURE 13. Lothair crystal: Scenes from the life of Susanna. London, British Museum. Reproduced by permission of the British Museum.

pears immediately above this scene, it seems more than likely that some parallelism between Lothair and the just judge of the Old Testament is intended, the royal connection of the image being further underscored by the compositional similarity of the canopy-like coffered vault on four columns above the scene to a similar feature in the portrait of Charles the Bald from the Codex Aureus of St. Emmeran.[84]

Since the early years of this century it has become traditional for scholars to see a link between the production of this quite extraordinary work of art and the attempt by Lothair II—younger son of Emperor Lothair, ruler from 855 to 869 of the central Carolingian territories (stretching along the western bank of the Rhine from the Low Countries to Switzerland), and Charles the Bald's nephew—to win a divorce from his barren wife Teutberga.[85] This notorious cause célèbre of the period involved the accusation that, prior to her marriage to Lothair, Teutberga was guilty of committing incest with her brother and inducing an abortion, and although once vindicated by ordeal, the queen was ultimately pressured into confessing to her crimes before an ecclesiastical council and was sent to a nunnery. The actions in this matter of Lothair and of the Council of Aachen of 860 were condemned most outspokenly by Hincmar of Reims in a treatise already mentioned, *De divortio Lotharii regis et Tetbergae reginae*,[86] and by Pope Nicholas I, and Lothair was compelled by the church—very much against his will—to take back Teutberga and to repudiate his much-loved mistress.[87] Obviously, the cases of Teutberga and Susanna, two women unjustly accused of sexual transgressions by "seniors" of considerable stature but ultimately vindicated, are at least in broad terms similar.

Although Genevra Kornbluth has rightly pointed out a number of differences between the Old Testament and contemporary legal cases, has justly criticized the superficiality of the analysis devoted to the connection between the Susanna crystal and this contemporary political situation in previous scholarly literature, which treats it as virtually self-evident, and has indicated the extreme implausibility of the view that the crystal was made at the order of Lothair as a kind of public apology to his aggrieved queen, it nonetheless seems to me that the crystal need not then be simply interpreted as a rather abstract exemplum of royal justice. It may well be that, through the crystal's iconographic program, Lothair is urged to be like Daniel in justice, as Kornbluth argues, but clearly the program at the same time warns him to be unlike the Elders and provides the linked positive and negative models for the Carolingian ruler propounded in such texts as Hincmar's *De cavendis vitiis et virtutibus exercendis* (On vices to be avoided and virtues to be practiced), which was dedicated to Charles the Bald.[88] Given the contemporary political situation, this allusion cannot have failed to be a pointed, albeit (thinly) disguised, reference to Lothair's personal difficulties, even though it is equally true that the relationships are not to be seen as fully developed allegories to be read as if the judge represents Lothair, Susanna represents Teutberga, and the two Elders represent the archbishops of Trier and Cologne, the key figures in condemning Teutberga.

The proper and, I think, intended reading of the work by contemporaries would have been more indirect and ironic, as is also indicated by formal qualities of the crystal. It is noteworthy that the compositional arrangement undercuts the closeness of the parallel between the just judge of the crystal and the Carolingian king, since despite the formal analogy to near-contemporary Carolingian ruler portraiture already adduced, it can hardly be merely coincidental that the judge of the crystal does not occupy the central space, here given over to Susanna, and is presented in profile. Carolingian ruler portraits, including not only those already mentioned but many others as well, habitually portray the king frontally in some variation of the "majesty" formula, and disguised portrayals of Carolingian rulers through Old Testament prototypes use the same formula. Thus when, in the Bible of San Paolo fuori le mura, the frontispiece miniature for the book of Proverbs shows Solomon enthroned beneath just such a canopy-vault as is the judge on the Susanna crystal, Solomon, who is providing wise and just judgment for the two women quarreling over a child depicted below him, is portrayed frontally at the center of the image (see fig. 12). Evidently, had the Carolingian artist wished to make a similarly direct association between contemporary ruler and Old Testament prototype he could have done so, and we are entitled to suspect that when he used a different manner of presentation he wished to make a rather different point.

The Susanna crystal is clearly not an insult to Lothair II nor an apology by him but remains, in my view, a pointed warning to him of the danger of failing to execute properly his royal responsibilities. Surely, if simple flattery and praise were intended by the designer of the Susanna crystal, they were managed very awkwardly indeed, and Lothair II of all men is unlikely to have been unreservedly delighted with a gift telling him of his duty to vindicate women against unjust accusations of sexual misconduct!

❖

Scholars today, including art historians, are well aware of the difficulties in establishing the original intention of the artists and patrons of any historical moment, including the present one, to say nothing of the Carolingian past. I am sufficiently old-fashioned to think that, impossible as it may be fully to recapture creative intention, it is possible to deduce at least some portion of avowed conscious intention, and very likely something of unconscious significance as well. In any event, the search seems to me well worth the effort, and I am not apologetic for sharing with you some examples of what appear to me the intent of Carolingian artists and patrons to reflect and convey specific and occasionally complex and subtle political messages through works of art. At the same time, we cannot confuse intent of the artist with reception by contemporary audiences. We must not too simply and schematically reduce the diversity and complexity of the Carolingian audience, or indeed audiences, for works of art, which were presumably and, in my view, demonstrably as variable as those today. Complex meanings and programs may well have been incomprehensible to contemporaries, even to the relatively learned, to say nothing of later observers. Perhaps an example will clarify my point.

The majority of the profile portrait coins of Charlemagne with which I began my remarks bear on the reverse an image of a Roman temple (fig. 14), derived demonstrably from late antique Roman series, such as the example of a coin of Maxentius of about 308. Here, clearly, we have a reference to Rome, but with a cross replacing the cult image of the ancient coins, another cross surmounting the temple facade, and the legend *Cristiana Religio*, all testifying to the importance of regarding Charlemagne's assumption of the imperial title and style as a Christian conversion of the originally pagan Roman tradition.[89] This idea of Hugh Fallon, who showed the origin of the *Cristiana Religio* term and theme in the *Libri Carolini* text, is to me not only a just assessment but an important one. These coins bear a coherent political program uniting obverse and reverse in a meaningful way, and I think they were intended to do so, having been elaborated in some official setting, presumably at the court, for manufacture at the important mint at Frankfurt, where all were produced. Yet already in Charlemagne's reign, other mints copied the obverse portrait but replaced the meaningful reverse image and legend with a local emblem, such as the ship of the port at Quentovic and the city gate of the old Ro-

FIGURE 14. Carolingian coin (reverse of fig. 3): image of a Roman temple. Staatliche Museen zu Berlin. Reproduced by permission of the Staatliche Museen Preussischer Kulturbesitz.

man city of Trier, destroying the meaning of the program.[90] Evidently even highly placed contemporaries either failed to receive or deliberately rejected the political program or message intended by the original issue of the series, or the figures at the court who designed the original program were resigned to its significance being opaque in the provinces in any event, so that alteration of the reverse image would not actually be a loss.

The original intent was not lost altogether, however, and could be recovered and restated by later issues, as on the temple coins with profile portraits issued by Charlemagne's son Louis the Pious. Even here, however, the reproduction of the same image and legend types was very likely intended to carry a rather different meaning. Fallon suggested, I think persuasively, that the Charlemagne temple coins carried a sharply anti-Byzantine message still in the tradition of the diatribes of the *Libri Carolini*, but it would be difficult to see such a meaning being intended by Louis the Pious roughly two decades later, if I rightly understand important recent work by Thomas Noble on Louis's relations with Byzantium.[91] The interpretive and historical ground here provides very tricky footing, in other words, and we should tread upon it with great circumspection.

❈

If Aristotle is right in defining man as "by nature a political animal,"[92] then even Carolingian art must be in some sense political too; the difficulty is apparently in defining politics and manner. Recently Janet Nelson has argued that Carolingian politics was more than a matter of parties and campaigns, but "an affair of the guts and of the soul." Specifically addressing Carolingian royal ritual, which seems far less varied and changing than Carolingian art, she held that it was indeed political.[93] Perhaps, as well as reflecting the hoary historiographical tradition of holding the "dark ages" in low regard, the denial of the political relevance of Carolingian art bespeaks a narrower definition of politics than she would allow. Documentation of artistic works as immediate responses to particular political events is very difficult in this period, but probably not only because of the quantity of our evidence. Works of art are abundant, as are written sources, bearing upon such issues as the imperial coronation of Charlemagne, the revolts of Louis the Pious's sons, or the attempted divorce of Lothair II, but the two can seldom be brought together in a relationship so exclusive as to rule out alternative explanations. Carolingian thinking is not, I would argue, vague and unfocused, but it is elastic and often multivalent, repeatedly employing familiar concepts and stories drawn from Scripture and the Fathers but deploying them in new contexts to carry new mes-

sages. Carolingians might in this sense be regarded as postmodernists before their time, as rejecting the modernist univocal hermeneutic attitude.
It was therefore not troubling to Carolingian authors, and presumably artistic patrons, that, for example, the David and Bathsheba story might be
authoritatively interpreted both as royal sin and abuse of power and as the
marriage of the Savior with Ecclesia.[94]

Notes

This essay has been extensively revised since it was given as a lecture at The Ohio
State University in 1989, but I have tried to maintain the essential structure and
something of the tone of the original lecture. A few important publications that
appeared in and after 1992 have been noted here, but the text has not been
revised again to respond to their contributions. I am grateful to members of the
original audience at Columbus for their helpful comments, as well as to an
anonymous reviewer of the early written version. Biblical quotations are from the
Douay Rheims Version.

1. See *Karl der Grosse: Werk und Wirkung*, nos. 12–25, and the illustration on
   the cover of the catalogue.
2. For a brief discussion of the Renaissance question, see Lawrence Nees, *A
   Tainted Mantle: Hercules and the Classical Tradition at the Carolingian Court*,
   pp. 3–17, with further literature.
3. Philip Grierson, "Money and Coinage under Charlemagne," esp. pp. 518–
   20.
4. It should be noted, however, that although the coin portrait seems to
   presuppose the imperial coronation, it does not directly follow that event
   and may have other, more immediate causes; for a finely balanced discussion
   of this work and of the entire class of royal images, see Donald A. Bullough,
   "'Imagines Regum' and Their Significance in the Early Medieval West," esp.
   pp. 247–48.
5. The interesting study of Stanley Morison, *Politics and Script: Aspects of
   Authority and Freedom in the Development of Graeco-Latin Script from the Sixth
   Century B.C. to the Twentieth Century A.D.*, makes useful comments about
   the Carolingian reform of script but makes this a parallel to a very general
   political development rather than a response to specific individuals and
   events.
6. No studies are wholly devoted to the question of the imperial coronation's
   impact upon art, although the issue was addressed by John Beckwith,
   "Byzantine Influence on Carolingian Art," and there are important cau-
   tionary remarks in Bullough, "'Imagines Regum,'" pp. 244–49. One
   interesting example of the problem is presented by the Gatehouse or
   Torhalle of Lorsch. Richard Krautheimer made this an important point in
   his justly famous article seeking to connect various aspects of early Carolingian architecture with the imitation of Rome, dating it close to 800
   because it was so Roman; see "The Carolingian Revival of Early Christian

Architecture." More recently, Werner Jacobsen has persuasively proposed a much later date and different interpretation; see his "Die Lorscher Torhalle: Zum Problem ihrer Datierung and Deutung."

7. Rosamond McKitterick, *The Carolingians and the Written Word*, p. 30. The miniature is Utrecht, Bibliotheek der Rijksuniversiteit, cod. 32 (*olim* cod. Script. eccles. 484), fol. 90v, for which see Koert van der Horst and Jacobus H. A. Engelbregt, eds., *Utrecht-Psalter: Vollständige Faksimile Ausgabe in Originalformat der Handschrift 32 aus dem Besitz der Bibliotheek der Rijksuniversiteit te Utrecht.* A more convenient reproduction may be found in Jean Hubert, Jean Porcher, and Wolfgang Fritz Volbach, *The Carolingian Renaissance*, trans. James Emmons, Stuart Gilbert, and Robert Allen, fig. 88, along with an interpretation that the artist "selected, assembled [from earlier Mediterranean models], and dashed down his vivid figurations, in which nothing was really new but the zest giving them such vibrant life" (p. 105). It is interesting to note that since these remarks were written, this same miniature has been the subject of an important study by Celia Chazelle, presented as a lecture at the 26th International Congress of Medieval Studies at Kalamazoo in 1991 and to be published in the near future. Chazelle offers a strong argument that the miniature contains specific details of costume and setting that connect it with Carolingian ecclesiastical ceremonies and political contexts.

8. Herbert Kessler, "On the State of Medieval Art History," esp. p. 182.

9. Ibid., p. 178. It should be noted that in a series of important recent works Kessler has in fact vigorously propounded the importance of the cultural and political content of several Carolingian images. See his "An Apostle in Armor and the Mission of Carolingian Art"; "A Lay Abbot as Patron: Count Vivian and the First Bible of Charles the Bald"; and "'Facies bibliotheca revelata': Carolingian Art as Spiritual Seeing."

10. Georg Wilhelm Friedrich Hegel, *The Philosophy of History*, trans. J. Sibree, pp. 341–42.

11. A recent study of Carolingian arms and armor argues, against the earlier prevailing view, that Carolingian imagery usually depicts contemporary weaponry with considerable accuracy, and does not simply follow earlier iconographic models; see Simon Coupland, "Carolingian Arms and Armor in the Ninth Century," esp. p. 50: "Carolingian ivories and manuscript illumination are a more reliable guide to contemporary armament than has hitherto been believed . . . even though certain features may have been influenced by late Roman or Byzantine pictorial traditions, ninth-century Frankish illustrations depicted current forms of helmets, shields, swords, sword-mounts and spears." I have, in another recent study, attempted to address the issue of "invented" images; see Nees, "The Originality of Early Medieval Artists."

12. Two recent studies that deserve mention are Joan S. Cwi, "A Study in Carolingian Political Theology: The David Cycle at St. John, Müstair"; and the important article by Kessler, "An Apostle in Armor," p. 35.

13. See Bullough, "'Imagines Regum,'" p. 243 and n. 88; and Bullough, "Alcuin and the Kingdom of Heaven: Liturgy, Theology, and the

Carolingian Age," esp. pp. 13–15. For the Vienna manuscript, see Kurt Holter, ed., *Der goldene Psalter "Dagulf-Psalter": Vollständige Faksimile-Ausgabe im Originalformat von Codex 1861 der Österreichischen National-bibliothek.* For the dates of the manuscript and more on its credal collection, see my review of Holter's *Der goldene Psalter* in *Art Bulletin* 67 (1985): 681–90. On the date of the *Libri Carolini* and related questions, see Ann Freeman, "Carolingian Orthodoxy and the Fate of the *Libri Carolini.*"

14. For more on this theme, see chap. 7 in this volume, by Thomas F. X. Noble.

15. See Adolph Goldschmidt, *Die Elfenbeinskulpturen aus der Zeit der karolingischen und sächsischen Kaiser*, vol. 1, nos. 3–4; and Holter, ed., *Goldene Psalter*, 2:58–65. For a recent discussion of such David iconography, see Christoph Eggenberger, *Psalterium Aureum Sancti Galli: Mittelalterliche Psalterillustration im Kloster St. Gallen*, pp. 39–54.

16. For a thorough discussion of the ivories' sources, see Thomas P. F. Hoving, "The Sources of the Ivories of the Ada School," pp. 71–78. Although he notes that the Dagulf images in fact diverge from those few earlier works that treat the same subject, and that some of its features are "purely Carolingian," Hoving assumes that the ivories must follow a lost model. Since he thinks the style of the ivories indicates a model of the Theodosian period, Hoving suggests that the Carolingian work closely copies a lost original of that period.

17. In general on the political context of the image and Adoptionist controversies, see McKitterick, *The Frankish Kingdoms under the Carolingians, 751–987*, p. 59; and Bullough, "Alcuin and the Kingdom of Heaven," pp. 31–40. See also Freeman, "Carolingian Orthodoxy," pp. 90–91, on *Libri Carolini*, bk. 1, chap. 6, which gives an unprecedented statement of papal authority and in fact illustrates this theme with Jerome's appeal to the pope even on a grammatical point.

18. Nees, *The Gundohinus Gospels*, esp. pp. 132–44.

19. Hubert, Porcher, and Volbach, *The Carolingian Renaissance*, pp. 71–74.

20. See Wolfgang Braunfels, "Karolingischer Klassizismus als politisches Programm und karolingischer Humanismus als Lebenshaltung."

21. See Wilhelm Koehler, *Die karolingischen Miniaturen*, vol. 2: *Die Hofschule Karls des Grossen*, pp. 88–100 and pls. 99–116. For a complete facsimile publication, see Braunfels, *Das Lorscher Evangeliar*.

22. For the former, see Nees, *Gundohinus Gospels*, pl. 35, and for the latter, see Hubert, Porcher, and Volbach, *The Carolingian Renaissance*, fig. 78.

23. Nees, *Gundohinus Gospels*, pp. 83–129. In general for this iconography, see Albert Boeckler, "Die Evangelistenbilder der Ada-Gruppe"; and Elizabeth Rosenbaum, "The Evangelist Portraits of the Ada School and Their Models."

24. For the Calendar of 354, see Henri Stern, *Le Calendrier de 354: Etude sur son texte et ses illustrations*, including a discussion of the Carolingian copies of this lost manuscript.

25. Florentine Mütherich and Joachim E. Gaehde, *Carolingian Painting*, p. 9.

26. On the absence of flanking angels: Nees, *Gundohinus Gospels*, fig. 70; and

Braunfels, *Lorscher Evangeliar*, p. 36. On imperial iconography: for example, on the famous silver plate of Emperor Theodosius I from the late fourth century, see Volbach, *Early Christian Art*, pl. 53; and Kurt Weitzmann, ed., *Age of Spirituality: Late Antique and Early Christian Art, Third to Seventh Century*, no. 64. On angels substituting for soldiers: see in general André Grabar, *L'Empereur dans l'art byzantin*, esp. pp. 196–205; and Grabar, *Christian Iconography: A Study of Its Origins*, pp. 42–44.

27. The miniature is reproduced in Peter Bloch, "Das Apsismosaik von Germigny-des-Prés: Karl der Grosse und der Alte Bund," fig. 5. For the manuscript's presence at Tours, see Grabar, "Fresques romanes copiés sur les miniatures du Pentateuque de Tours," showing the presence of the manuscript at Tours by the eleventh century; and Bezalel Narkiss, "Towards a Further Study of the Ashburnam Pentateuch (Pentateuque de Tours)," esp. p. 58, for the suggestion that the erasure of the heterodox "second Creator" by ninth-century monks in the Tours scriptorium may have been a response to the Adoptionist controversy. For a more recent study of the manuscript, see Franz Rickert, *Studien zum Ashburnham Pentateuch (Paris, Bibl. Nat. NAL. 2334)*.

28. Ann Freeman, "Theodulf of Orléans and the *Libri Carolini*," esp. pp. 699–701.

29. *Libri Carolini*, bk. 1, chaps. 15 and 20, and bk. 2, chap. 26, which specifically reject the equation of making images with making the images of the cherubim for the Ark; see *Libri Carolini sive Caroli Magni Capitulare de Imaginibus*, ed. Hubert Bastgen, MGH, Concilia 2, Supplementum (Hannover, 1924), pp. 34–37, 45–48, and 85–86, respectively. For a discussion of the *Libri Carolini*'s view of those things that can properly be described as holy, see Chazelle, "Matter, Spirit, and Image in the *Libri Carolini*," esp. pp. 165–70. For a convenient illustration and a brief discussion of the Germigny mosaic, see Hubert, Porcher, and Volbach, *Carolingian Renaissance*, pp. 11–14 and figs. 10–11. The Germigny mosaic itself probably carried a more pointedly political message than is generally recognized. Bloch, "Apsismosaik," pp. 258–59, touches upon this in linking it to a broader tendency to appeal to and evoke the Old Testament in Charlemagne's circle, especially linking Charlemagne to David and Solomon and, in a broader sense, the Franks to the Israelites as God's chosen people. It is important that, in praising the special character and power of the ark and not of images, Theodulf in *Libri Carolini*, ed. Bastgen, bk. 2, chap. 26, pp. 85–86, speaks of the ark's ability to defeat God's enemies, and mentions that the king and prophet [David, at 2 Sam. 6:14–23] was not ashamed to dance before the ark. Not previously noted is the passage in Isaiah 37:16–38 in which King Hezekiah prays to the "Lord of hosts, God of Israel, who sittest upon the cherubims," for help against the Assyrians, singling out as the Assyrians' crime their worship of gods that "were not gods, but the works of men's hands, of wood and stone." The ark is the visible sign of God's military support for his chosen people; on the early Frankish emphasis on prayers for military victory, see Michael McCormick, *Eternal Victory: Triumphal Rulership in Late Antiquity, Byzantium, and the Early*

Medieval West, pp. 344–58, arguing that Theodulf himself on several occasions referred to and promoted this linkage, which became a regular practice in the 790s.

30. For this text, see Paul Meyvaert, "Excerpts from an Unknown Treatise of Jerome to Gaudentius of Brescia," attributing the work to Jerome; and Yves-Marie Duval, "Le 'Liber Hieronymi ad Gaudentium': Rufin d'Aquilée, Gaudence de Brescia et Eusèbe de Crémone," arguing rather for an attribution to Rufinus. Meyvaert has informed me that he accepts the correction.

31. Nees, "Image and Text: Excerpts from Jerome's 'De trinitate' and the *Maiestas Domini* Miniature of the Gundohinus Gospels"; treated more briefly in Nees, *Gundohinus Gospels*, pp. 178–88.

32. Goldschmidt, *Elfenbeinskulpturen*, no. 5; *Karl der Grosse: Werk und Wirkung*, no. 519; and Volbach, *Elfenbeinarbeiten der Spätantike und des frühen Mittelalters*, no. 221.

33. Goldschmidt, *Elfenbeinskulpturen*, no. 1; and Volbach, *Elfenbeinarbeiten*, no. 217. For recent literature and an interesting and plausible suggestion that the ivory might have been executed in the southeastern part of the Carolingian territories, see Carol Neuman de Vegvar, "The Origin of the Genoels-Elderen Ivories."

34. Goldschmidt, *Elfenbeinskulpturen*, no. 13; *Karl der Grosse: Werk und Wirkung*, no. 521; and Volbach, *Elfenbeinarbeiten*, no. 223.

35. For these ivories, see Volbach, *Elfenbeinarbeiten*, nos. 112 and 113. The relationship was noted by Goldschmidt, *Elfenbeinskulpturen*, p. 10 and fig. 6.

36. Hoving, "Sources," p. 31, notes the six pots and states that this is the "common number from the sixth century." Thereby Hoving implies that although we in fact have the Carolingian artist's direct model before us, with four jugs, he carved six, not because he corrected his model by reference to the text, but because for this specific feature he followed a different model.

37. Ibid., p. 32, noting the displacement.

38. Ibid., p. 34.

39. Weitzmann, *Late Antique and Early Christian Book Illustration*, pl. 29, the figure at the lower right being Isaiah. For a facsimile of the manuscript, see Guglielmo Cavallo, Jean Gribomont, and William C. Loerke, *Codex purpureus Rossanensis: Museo dell'Arcivescovado, Rossano Calabro* (Rome and Graz, 1987), esp. p. 122 for discussion.

40. Mütherich and Gaehde, *Carolingian Painting*, pl. 3.

41. Weitzmann, "A Tabula Odysseaca" (repr. in his *Studies in Classical and Byzantine Manuscript Illumination*, esp. p. 18).

42. I am forced to imagine the basis for separating the book from its cover; in *Karl der Grosse: Werk und Wirkung*, no. 519, it is simply asserted that "die Handscrift ursprünglich wohl nicht zugehörig."

43. Goldschmidt, *Elfenbeinskulpturen*, no. 5, p. 10.

44. *Karl der Grosse: Werk und Wirkung*, no. 519, with literature.

45. For the standard Latin edition of Alcuin's letters to Gisla, see *Alcuini sive Albini Epistolae*, nos. 15, 84, 154, 195, 196, 213, 214, 216, and 228, ed. Ernst Dümmler, MGH, Epp. 4 (Berlin, 1895), pp. 40–42, 127, 249, 322–23, 354–57, 359–60, and 371–72. A translation of some of the letters into

English is in Stephen Allott, *Alcuin of York, His Life and Letters* (York, 1974), nos. 87–91, 93–94.

46. See Alcuin, *Commentarium in Joannem*, in PL 100:665–1008. On the commentary, see Bullough, "Alcuin and Kingdom of Heaven," pp. 59–62.

47. Bernhard Bischoff, "Die Kölner Nonnenhandscriften und das Skriptorium von Chelles."

48. Winfried Böhne, "Beobachtungen zur Perikopenreihe des Godescalc-Evangeliars."

49. See Böhne, "Beobachtungen," pp. 149, 160–61.

50. Bullough, "Alcuin and the Kingdom of Heaven," p. 56.

51. Hoving, "Sources," p. 33.

52. Paulinus of Aquileia, *Contra Felicem*, PL 99:343–468; citations at cols. 371b–72a, 393c–94a, 394d, and 447c.

53. Goldschmidt, *Elfenbeinskulpturen*, no. 40; Danielle Gaborit-Chopin, *Elfenbeinkunst im Mittelalter*, no. 54.

54. That miniatures should be based upon the *tituli* of the Psalms rather than upon the Psalm text itself is neither unprecedented nor uncommon; for a discussion of the issue in the context of the later Carolingian Psalter, Saint Gall cod. 22, whose miniatures consistently illustrate the *tituli*, see Eggenberger, *Psalterium aureum*, esp. pp. 9–11.

55. S. Hellmann, ed., *Sedulius Scottus* (Munich, 1906), chap. 3, p. 29; and *Sedulius Scottus: On Christian Rulers and the Poems*, trans. Edward Gerard Doyle, Medieval and Renaissance Texts and Studies 17 (Binghampton, N.Y., 1983), p. 56. For the controversial question of the ruler for whom the work was written, see most recently Dean Simpson's introduction to *Sedulii Scotti collectaneum miscellaneum*, ed. Simpson, CC cont. med. 67 (Turnhout, 1988), p. xxiv. I am grateful to David Ganz for having kindly brought Simpson's edition to my attention.

56. On Lothair's divorce: Hincmar of Reims, *De divortio Lotharii regis et Tetbergae reginae*, PL 125:760. On royal office and duties: Hincmar, *De regis persona et regio ministerio*, chap. 30, PL 125:854. Unfortunately there is no modern edition of this text. For a discussion of the work and this passage, see Karl F. Morrison, *The Two Kingdoms: Ecclesiology in Carolingian Political Thought*, pp. 123–24, and 10–11, n. 14. On the letter to Pope Hadrian: Hincmar, *Epistolae*, in PL 126:178.

57. See Goldschmidt, *Elfenbeinskulpturen*, no. 40; and Gaborit-Chopin, *Elfenbeinkunst*, p. 62.

58. The standard publication remains Hugo Buchthal, *The Miniatures of the Paris Psalter: A Study in Middle Byzantine Painting*. For a useful tabulation of the subjects in early medieval Psalter illustrations, see Suzy Dufrenne, *Tableaux synoptiques des 15 psautiers médiévaux à illustrations intégrales issues du texte*.

59. Goldschmidt, *Elfenbeinskulpturen*, p. 24 and fig. 11.

60. See van der Hoerst and Engelbregt, eds., *Utrecht-Psalter*.

61. Eggenberger, *Psalterium aureum*, pp. 162–65.

62. Goldschmidt, *Elfenbeinskulpturen*, nos. 3 and 4; for discussion, see also Holter, ed., *Goldene Psalter*.

63. On this important genre of texts in the Carolingian period, see Hans

Hubert Anton, *Fürstenspiegel und Herrscherethos in der Karolingerzeit*. For the image of the Carolingian ruler's humility in art, see the fundamental article by Robert Deschman, "The Exalted Servant: The Ruler Theology of the Prayerbook of Charles the Bald."

64. *Sancti Aurelii Augustini De civitate Dei*, bk. 5, chap. 26, ed. Bernard Dombart and Alphonse Kalb, CCSL 47, pt. 14, 1 (Turnhout, 1955), p. 162; and Saint Augustine, *City of God*, trans. Marcus Dods (New York, 1950), p. 180.

65. See n. 55, above, for reference.

66. *Cum sedeat Karolus magno coronatus honore / Est Iosiae similes parque Theodosio.* On the miniature, see also William Diebold, "Verbal, Visual, and Cultural Literacy in Medieval Art: Word and Image in the Psalter of Charles the Bald."

67. On Josiah's career and involvement with the text of the Bible, see Richard Elliott Friedman, *Who Wrote the Bible?* pp. 96–116.

68. For the text of this poem, see *Contra iudices*, ed. Ernst Dümmler, MGH, Poetae 1 (Berlin, 1881), pp. 493–517; and Nicolai Alexandrenko, "The Poetry of Theodulf of Orleans: A Translation and Critical Study," p. 161. I discuss this poem in *A Tainted Mantle*, pt. 2. For other examples of the citation of Josiah in connection with Carolingian kings, see Anton, *Fürstenspiegel*.

69. Vercelli, Biblioteca Capitolare, MS CLXV; see Hubert, Porcher, and Volbach, *Europe of the Invasions*, fig. 158.

70. Paris, B.N., cod. lat. 4404, fols. 1v–2; for a color plate, see Porcher, "La Peinture provinciale," p. 63 (a rather bizarre diatribe against the perceived poor quality of the painting style) and pl. 27.

71. I discuss this text at length in *A Tainted Mantle*, pp. 270–77. The text is published in *Ermold le Noir: Poème sur Louis le Pieux et Epîtres au roi Pépin*, ed. Edmond Faral, Les classiques de l'histoire de France au moyen âge 14 (Paris, 1964), pp. 164–65. For this section only of the text and an English translation and commentary, see Peter Godman, *Poetry of the Carolingian Renaissance*, pp. 254–55.

72. See *The Letters of Lupus of Ferrières*, no. 37, trans. Graydon W. Regenos (The Hague, 1966), pp. 53–55; for the Latin text, see *Servati Lupi Epistulae*, no. 93, ed. Peter K. Marshall, Bibliotheca Scriptorum Graecorum et Romanorum Teubneriana (Leipzig, 1984), pp. 90–91. After this chapter had been written, Janet Nelson kindly sent me a copy of her article "Translating Images of Authority: The Christian Roman Emperors in the Carolingian World," which admirably discusses the confusion of the two emperors and the emulation of both, especially Theodosius I, in the laws of Charles the Bald.

73. See Nees, "Unknown Carolingian Drawings of Hercules from the Scriptorium of Reims, and the *Cathedra Petri* Ivories," esp. pp. 48–50, and figs. 3, 4, and 15.

74. *De civitate Dei*, bk. 5, chap. 26, ed. Dombart and Kalb, pp. 162–63 (pp. 180–81 in the English trans.).

75. Anton, *Fürstenspiegel*, p. 99, speaking of the influence of the immediately

preceding chapter of the same book upon Alcuin's *Vita Willibrordi* terms the
section "*dem* christlichen Fürstenspiegel par excellence.*"

76. See Nees, *A Tainted Mantle*, pp. 83–84 and 238, on the knowledge of Au-
    gustine's *City of God* in the Carolingian period. In the present context it is
    especially noteworthy that Hincmar of Reims in his treatise of 879 addressed
    to Charles the Bald, *De regis persona et regio ministerio*, PL 125:833–56, esp.
    cols. 839–40, transcribes most of Augustine's bk. 5, chap. 24, on the happi-
    ness of the Christian ruler.

77. Discussed by Nelson, "Kingship and Empire," p. 220. Here also (pp. 217–
    19) for a discussion of the *Prospice* prayer used in royal consecrations and
    other contexts, which emphasized the royal duty to comfort churches and
    monasteries. Unfortunately I received too late for consideration in this study
    the important new book by Nelson, *Charles the Bald* (London and New
    York, 1992).

78. For a brief discussion and sources, in the context of the broader problem of
    the royal need to secure military and political support through the bestowal
    of benefices upon which the king could lay his hands, see McKitterick,
    Frankish Kingdoms, pp. 181–82. See also Nelson, "Charles the Bald and the
    Church in Town and Countryside" (repr. in Nelson, *Politics and Ritual in
    Early Medieval Europe*, esp. pp. 77–82).

79. For a summary of events and literature, see McKitterick, *Frankish Kingdoms*,
    pp. 231–36.

80. See Joachim Gaehde, "The Bible of San Paolo fuori le mura in Rome:
    Its Date and Its Relation to Charles the Bald"; and Gaehde, "The Picto-
    rial Sources of the Illustrations of the Books of Kings, Proverbs, Judith
    and Maccabees in the Carolingian Bible of San Paolo Fuori Le Mura
    in Rome," esp. pp. 373–78, and fig. 92. See also William Diebold, "The
    Ruler Portrait of Charles the Bald in the S. Paolo Bible," especially p. 12
    and fig. 4.

81. I have not attempted to address the issues raised by the other two miniatures
    in the book. The portrait of David shows him not enthroned as a king and
    prophet, perhaps in part because the portrait of Charles occupies that icono-
    graphic niche, but dancing with his musicians; for a convenient reproduc-
    tion, see Hubert, Porcher, and Volbach, *The Carolingian Renaissance*, fig.
    134. This image is complex but evidently shows David, surrounded by four
    musicians, dancing and playing his psaltery. One famous biblical text evoked
    by the image is of David "leaping and dancing before the Lord" when the
    Ark of the Covenant was brought to Jerusalem, and his rejection of his wife
    Michal, who castigated him for appearing so undignified and unkingly.
    David responded (2 Sam. 6:20–21), "Before the Lord, who chose me . . . I
    will both play and make myself meaner than I have done; and I will be little
    in my own eyes." For discussion of the related iconography in the Saint Gall
    Psalter, see Eggenberger, *Psalterium aureum*, pp. 39–53. The image of St.
    Jerome on the facing page poses even more difficult interpretive problems,
    which will not be addressed here; the Saint Gall Psalter also has a Jerome
    image (Hubert, Porcher, and Volbach, *The Carolingian Renaissance*, fig. 136)
    and is discussed by Eggenberger, *Psalterium aureum*, pp. 54–60, with

literature, and most recently by Diebold, "Verbal, Visual, and Cultural Literacy."

82. See Nelson, "The Lord's Anointed and the People's Choice: Carolingian Royal Ritual," pp. 137–80, esp. pp. 163–64, with sources.

83. For this work, see the illustrations and earlier literature in Percy Ernst Schramm and Florentine Mütherich, *Denkmale der deutschen Könige und Kaiser*, no. 31, pp. 125–26; and the study by Hans Wentzel, "Der Bergkristall mit der Geschichte der Susanna." The Carolingian engraved rock crystals were studied as a group by Genevra A. Kornbluth, "Carolingian Treasure: Engraved Gems of the Ninth and Tenth Centuries," no. 1 and pp. 278–306. I am grateful to the author for having provided me with a copy of her dissertation, and I have learned even more from the preliminary draft of her article recently published as "The Susanna Crystal of Lothar II: Chastity, the Church, and Royal Justice."

84. Hubert, Porcher, and Volbach, *The Carolingian Renaissance*, fig. 137; Schramm and Mütherich, *Denkmale*, no. 92; and more recently Horst Fuhrmann and Mütherich, *Das Evangeliar Heinrich des Löwen und das mittelalterliche Herrscherbild*, pl. 3. For royal portraits in Carolingian books, see most recently John Lowden, "The Royal/Imperial Book and the Image or Self-Image of the Medieval Ruler."

85. P. Lauer, "Le Joyau carolingien de Waulsort-sur-Meuse."

86. Hincmar, *De divortio*, PL 125:619–772.

87. For a discussion of this complicated affair, see Peter R. McKeon, *Hincmar of Laon and Carolingian Politics*, pp. 39–58.

88. Hincmar, *De cavendis*, PL 125:857–930.

89. For this coin type, see esp. Hugh C. Fallon, "Imperial Symbolism on Two Carolingian Coins." For this and related coins, along with some related seals and other material, see Schramm, *Die deutschen Kaiser und Könige in Bildern ihrer Zeit, 751–1190*, esp. pp. 148–50, with earlier literature.

90. For a discussion of the various types and an assessment of the chronology and issues of this series, see Grierson, "Money and Coinage under Charlemagne," esp. pp. 518–27.

91. Thomas F. X. Noble, "Louis the Pious, the Papacy and the Byzantines in the Second Iconoclastic Controversy," presented as a lecture at a meeting of the Delaware Valley Medieval Association held at the University of Pennsylvania in 1986.

92. Aristotle, *Politics* 1.2 (quoted from the trans. by Benjamin Jowett, in *The Basic Works of Aristotle*, ed. Richard McKeon [New York, 1941], p. 1129).

93. Nelson, "The Lord's Anointed," p. 175.

94. For this interpretation, see *S. Gregorii Magni Moralia in Job*, bk. 3, chap. 28, para. 55, ed. Marc Adriaen, CCSL 143 (Turnhout, 1979), pp. 148–50. The passage was discussed by Morrison, *The Mimetic Tradition of Reform in the West*, p. 102.

7

Tradition and Learning in Search of Ideology:
The Libri Carolini

THOMAS F. X. NOBLE

The text called by modern scholars the *Libri Carolini*, the Caroline books, that is to say, Charlemagne's books, is puzzling in many ways.[1] It is not clear, for example, in what sense this treatise can be ascribed to Charlemagne. It is hard to say exactly what kind of treatise the *Libri Carolini* really is. Sometimes the work is called the *Capitulare de imaginibus*, but it is not a capitulary.[2] François Louis Ganshof refused to accept the *Libri Carolini* as a capitulary in his authoritative treatment of those quasi-legislative texts.[3] It was published by the Monumenta Germaniae Historica in the Concilia series as a supplement, not in the Capitularia series, but this is not helpful either because the treatise was not the product of conciliar deliberations. Is the work actually about images? Is one of its customary titles at least half right? This deceptively simple question requires investigation too, but it can be said right away that much of what is most important in the *Libri Carolini* has nothing to do with images. The oldest surviving manuscript of the *Libri Carolini* lacks all titular and prefatory material, but a slightly later and complete text calls the work, if I may be permitted some nondistorting abridgement, *Opus Caroli contra synodum*.[4] Here is Charles again, but now he has issued neither *libri* nor *capitularia*, but rather an *opus*. And this time it is *contra synodum* not *de imaginibus*. The synod referred to is the Second Council of Nicaea, held in 787, and it is perfectly clear, on the plain and copious testimony of the text, that that synod figured largely in the discussions that produced the

Libri Carolini. But, once again, there is much in the *Libri Carolini* that is only loosely connected with Second Nicaea. Confusing titles by both original authors and modern editors have sent readers scurrying down several divergent paths in their attempts to understand the *Libri Carolini*.

The *Libri Carolini* is a big book by any measure that might be applied to it: 228 quarto pages in the standard printed edition. It has, I think, been more often characterized than read, more often interpreted than studied. There have been battles over who wrote it, although it appears that the guns have been stilled on at least this field of contention as a result of Ann Freeman's compelling demonstration that Theodulf, the later bishop of Orléans, was the author.[5] It has been suggested that the Carolingians completely misunderstood the subtleties of the theological positions embraced at Nicaea and that they responded with a misguided and intemperate diatribe that was largely irrelevant to the issues at hand. Some have tried to exculpate Charlemagne and his associates by saying that they worked from such a bad translation of the conciliar *acta* that they could not possibly have come to grips with the issues that had been raised in 787. There are those who think that the *Libri Carolini* was mainly a proud assertion by Charlemagne of his regal and sacerdotal position, while others counter by saying that Charlemagne did not wish to embarrass Pope Hadrian I and that he laid his great book aside without publishing it.[6]

It would be easy, and perhaps instructive, to go on and on pointing out puzzles, but it is more important to try to solve at least a few of them. In the process of offering solutions, some bold claims will be advanced on behalf of the *Libri Carolini*. In defense of such claims, I can say only this: I am going to try to tackle the *Libri Carolini* as a whole and in its historical context. I take my lead from a remark by Walter Goffart in his brilliant study of early medieval historical writing. He says that "like us, Jordanes, Gregory and the others meant to write what they did and were well aware of what they said and why."[7] Although poststructuralist critics have warned us that texts can be polysemic and that authorial intent may be an illusion, I proceed on the assumption that Theodulf had both the means and the will to articulate his own views and those of his contemporaries and associates. The central purpose of this study, therefore, is to work out what Theodulf said and why he said it. I am confident that this investigation will demonstrate that the *Libri Carolini* is a work of great power and sophistication that must be understood as a whole and on its own terms, and that it is a book that reveals a great deal about the cultural life of the Carolingian world in the last decades of the eighth century.

My discussion of the *Libri Carolini* will proceed along three paths. First,

I shall say a little about how the book came to be written and how the circumstances surrounding its composition provide some clues as to its meaning. Second, I shall give my reading of the text itself, laying particular stress on the organization of the work and on the several major lines of argument that it develops. In the course of this discussion, I shall attempt to assess the kinds of learning on which the *Libri Carolini* depended. Third and finally, I shall offer a series of interpretations of the *Libri Carolini* based on its preparation, historical setting, and intellectual foundations.

⁂

Ostensibly the *Libri Carolini* represents a response of some kind to the issues involved in the Second Council of Nicaea of 787. Let us, as a beginning, make a brief investigation of how that synod came to be called, what its central concerns were, and how the synod and its concerns came to the attention of the Franks.

Byzantine Iconoclasm, inaugurated in the 720s by Emperor Leo III, proceeded through two distinct phases in the eighth century. First, during Leo's reign and the early years of that of his son and successor, Constantine V, icons were destroyed on imperial orders. The principal objection to icons in this early period of Iconoclasm was that they were idolatrous. Orthodox theologians, chiefly John of Damascus, were able to show that idols and icons were fundamentally different, and also to assert that there were profound theological grounds, to be found in the realms of soteriology and Christology, for defending the use of icons in the church. At this juncture, a major council was held at Hiereia in 754, and icons were now condemned on ecclesiastical and theological authority with, of course, complete imperial approval. The charge of idolatry was not abandoned, but it was now supplemented by arguments whose bases were Christological, and which sought to respond to the defense of images advanced by John of Damascus. In 775 the arch-Iconoclast Constantine V died, and five years later he was followed to the grave by his son and successor, Leo IV. Leo left behind a minor son, Constantine VI, and a remarkable and resourceful widow, Irene.[8]

Almost immediately upon assuming her regency, Irene embarked upon a series of diplomatic initiatives. Her efforts toward the East are of no direct concern to us here, but highly significant was her opening to the West, which took the form of a proposed marriage alliance between her son Constantine and Charlemagne's daughter Rotrud. Irene and the old patriarch Paul IV had already been making some subtle moves against Iconoclasm, and without these the empress could have had no hope of reconciliation, let alone of alliance, with the pope and the Franks. For two generations the popes and their protectors and allies, the Carolingians, had steadfastly opposed Byzantine Iconoclasm. That opposition had played a role in the papal alienation from Byzantium, the Franko-papal alliance, and the reconfiguration of the political map of Italy. Apparently, then, Irene was signaling her willingness to recognize the permanent loss to the Byzantine Empire of all of northern and central Italy, while also hoping to make Charlemagne guarantor of the continued imperial possession of the duchy of Naples and of Sicily. Where the pope was concerned, Irene primarily wished to tell him that as soon as possible there would be an end to Iconoclasm. Essentially, Irene was leading the Byzantine state out of the diplomatic and ecclesiastical isolation in which it had found itself for a half century.[9]

It is frustrating that, because of lack of sources, we cannot know more precisely the momentum and motivations of change in Constantinople. The approach to Charlemagne and the first one to Rome came in 781. By 784 Irene had decided to call an ecumenical council to condemn Iconoclasm, and in 785 she duly notified Pope Hadrian of her intentions and invited him to attend or to send representatives to the council.[10] Hadrian responded in October of 785 with a long letter in which he expressed his pleasure at the forthcoming condemnation of heretical Iconoclasm, raised a number of ecclesiastical concerns, and agreed to send legates to a council.[11] Hadrian also received, perhaps along with Irene's letter, a synodical letter and profession of faith from the newly elected (25 December 784), and firmly iconodule, patriarch Tarasius.[12] Irene convened her council in Constantinople in 786, but it was almost immediately disbanded by troops loyal to Iconoclasm.[13] About a year later, and well outside the capital, at Nicaea, the council assembled again and this time completed its work in six full sessions, with a brief final session in the Magnaura Palace in Constantinople.[14] Leaving aside rituals and protocols, the work of the council consisted of two major accomplishments. The first was a review of the place of images in Christian history, with a view to showing that ancient and authentic traditions approved their use. The second was a detailed and systematic refutation of the *horos*, the definition, and of the biblical and patristic proof-texts advanced at Hiereia in 754. The council did not offer anything new. Its intention from the outset was to restore the status quo *ante* Iconoclasm.

Hadrian's representatives brought the conciliar *acta* back to Rome, probably very late in 787. According to the *Liber Pontificalis*, a Latin translation of the Greek *acta* was prepared and placed in the Lateran archives.[15]

Two things only are known with certainty about that translation: it was poorly done and it somehow found its way into Charlemagne's hands. There is not a scrap of surviving evidence to the effect that Hadrian sent the *acta* to the king, and there are hints that Charlemagne thought he had gotten his text directly from Constantinople.[16] While I am not optimistic that we shall ever know exactly how Charlemagne got his copy of the Nicene *acta*, I am quite convinced that it cannot have been later than 788 when the king first heard of the proceedings of Nicaea and Constantinople. Let us note that from 781 to 789 Charles's daughter was affianced to Irene's son. In addition, the Franks and the Greeks were involved in a complicated set of political and diplomatic intrigues in southern Italy. Finally, the papal and Frankish courts were in almost constant contact throughout the period that concerns us. In 789 the Franko-Byzantine marriage alliance was broken off, probably as a result of the decisions taken, or thought by the Franks to have been taken, at Nicaea. Much was going on in these years that has left no trace in the scanty records.

By 790 or 791 Theodulf had begun work on a text that would come to be known as the *Libri Carolini*.[17] In 792 a decision was made at the Frankish court to send the recently condemned Adoptionist heretic, Felix of Urgel, to Rome in the custody of Angilbert of Saint-Riquier. Apparently it was also decided, rather hastily, to inform Hadrian about the deliberations at the Frankish court concerning Second Nicaea. A very brief version, perhaps involving no more than chapter titles, of the *Libri Carolini* as a work-in-progress accompanied Angilbert to Rome. This document is usually called the *Capitulare adversus synodum*.[18] In, probably, 793 a massive response from Hadrian arrived at the Frankish court.[19] In angry and exasperated terms Hadrian rejected point after point the Frankish condemnation of Second Nicaea. This response appears to have been wholly unexpected, and its immediate result was to put an end to the discussions at court surrounding the *Libri Carolini*.

The *Libri Carolini* is, therefore, a book prepared at the court of Charlemagne between about 790 and 793. A happy accident has preserved the actual, working copy of the *Libri Carolini*: MS Vaticanus Latinus 7207. Close studies of that original manuscript, plus some scattered bits of ninth-century evidence, make it possible to form a reasonably good impression of how the book came to be composed.

It is to Ann Freeman, and to a lesser degree to Walter Schmandt, that we are indebted for our understanding, not only of the composition of the *Libri Carolini*, but also for precious insights into the way in which Charlemagne's court theologians attacked the problems posed by the council of

Nicaea.[20] Theodulf of Orléans was assigned the task of preparing a first draft of the Frankish response to the Byzantines. That draft was pretty well advanced when the *Capitulare adversus synodum* was dispatched to Rome. Meanwhile, serious work continued, apparently in two stages. Theodulf's draft, now the Vatican manuscript, a text that lacks the preface and the beginning of book 1 as well as the whole of book 4, was subjected to intense scrutiny at court. This truncated manuscript contains no fewer than 3,400 corrections.[21] The heavily corrected sections stop at book 2, chapter 29, and after book 3, chapter 13 there is a marked decline in the quality of the parchment and script.[22] These changes almost certainly betoken the arrival of Hadrian's disheartening response. At some point in the proceedings, actual argumentation was carried out in Charlemagne's presence,[23] and his reactions were recorded in marginal notations that were subsequently erased and replaced with Tironian notes.[24] Thus, in sum, there was a three-step process: composition by Theodulf, review by other theologians, and approval by Charlemagne. The work can, therefore, be said to be official in the sense that it had the king's explicit endorsement, but it must be remembered that it was the intellectual product of a series of spirited and sophisticated exchanges.

Manuscript Vat. Lat. 7207 arrived in Rome in 1784 and was already mutilated.[25] In its tattered and corrected state, it had been put in the palace archives, where Hincmar saw it in the 820s[26] and where it might have been consulted in connection with the renewed image controversy that culminated in the Council of Paris in 825.[27] Around the middle of the century Hincmar had a copy made for himself, and this manuscript, containing the complete text of the *Libri Carolini*, survives as Paris Arsenal 663.[28] Angelo Mercati was able to trace the presence in the papal library of a copy of the *Libri Carolini* in the fifteenth and sixteenth centuries, but it is not known what happened to this manuscript.[29] A few years ago, Bernhard Bischoff discovered on the flyleaf of a Paris manuscript a single folio from another copy of the *Libri Carolini* that was made at Corbie in the middle of the ninth century.[30] All in all, then, only four copies of the book can be shown to have been in existence. This represents an extremely limited dissemination indeed for a book of such evident importance and powerful associations. It has been published a number of times since the middle of the sixteenth century but never satisfactorily. A new and truly critical edition by Ann Freeman is presently in press at the Monumenta Germaniae Historica.

It will be clear now why I spoke at the outset of puzzles. A full consideration of the *Libri Carolini* would require a careful assessment of all the evidentiary problems that I have only alluded to here. Obviously this is not the place for that assessment. But there is one puzzle that cannot be passed over in silence. It is this: why was so much effort and such great learning lavished upon a work that seems never to have been published and never to have been disseminated? And why was this work so apparently uninfluential until, ironically, it was embraced by Protestants in the sixteenth century and placed on the Index of Forbidden Books until 1900? Most of the rest of this paper will constitute an attempt to answer those questions.

Schmandt has quite correctly called the *Libri Carolini* a *Staatsschrift* (political tract),[31] but the implications of his observations have often been missed. An old tradition holds that the *Libri Carolini* and the Synod of Frankfurt in 794 represented the high point of Carolingian Caesaropapism and a deep humiliation for the pope.[32] Another tradition holds that the *Libri Carolini* was, in fact, shelved—this accounting for its weak dissemination—either because the Franks did not wish to embarrass the pope or because Hadrian commanded the Franks to give up their opposition to his official position.[33]

Each of these views is anachronistic. Charlemagne never treated the popes in the haughty way that Roman or Byzantine emperors did, and the plain testimony of the *Libri Carolini* speaks respectfully of the papacy.[34] Moreover, no early medieval pope possessed or claimed the kind of jurisdictional primacy in matters of dogma that high medieval popes routinely asserted. It was only with the professionalization of theological learning and the hardening of jurisdictional lines by the canonists and decretalists that there emerged a sharply Rome-centered source of dogmatic definition.[35] In the very period that concerns us, the Franks and the popes agreed to disagree on a doctrinal matter of some significance: the procession of the Holy Spirit, or the *filioque* controversy.[36] Charlemagne and Hadrian had some rather sharp differences of opinion about the nature and dimensions of the territorial settlements in Italy that resulted from the demise of the Lombard kingdom, but here also they managed to work together amicably to achieve a just and lasting solution.[37]

Amicable cooperation is indeed the spirit that I detect in the whole period when the *Libri Carolini* was being prepared. Let us consider some of the relevant actions of both the king and the pope. The preface to the *Libri Carolini*, a section written in 790 and never revised,[38] says that when the Franks learned of the synod of the Greeks and its horrible decisions, they immediately set to work in defense of the faith and the church.[39] It is interesting to note that the procedure followed was exactly the same as that used in the Adoptionist and *filioque* controversies. That is, when a problem was brought to Charlemagne's attention, he, as a loyal son of the church, gathered his clergy so that they, with his blessing and under his authority, might assemble the necessary scriptural and patristic texts to settle the matter.[40] As in the cases of Adoptionist and Trinitarian strife, so too in the matter of images; the results of Frankish deliberations were sent to Rome. Nowhere in any of the pertinent sources is there a remark to the effect that the Franks were, in any of these instances, attempting to dictate to the pope. Nor is there anywhere a hint that the Franks felt in some sense legally obligated to lay their work before the pope. They had acted in defense of the church and the faith, and their recourse to Rome was a mark of profound respect.

After Hadrian's response to the *Capitulare adversus synodum* arrived at court, plans were continued for the great synod and public assembly of Frankfurt that was held in 794. Papal legates did attend Frankfurt. The *acta* say that the council was held "with apostolic authority," and that the council's second canon pronounced a condemnation of sorts upon Second Nicaea. Thus, it might seem that the Franks imposed their views upon Rome. Closer inspection shows that such was not the case, however. In the first place, Frankfurt was one of the most significant councils held in the whole of Charlemagne's reign and it dealt with a huge agenda of business.[41] Nicaea was certainly not the first item on that agenda. Indeed, the initial topic was Adoptionism, and Nicaea came second.[42]

That is significant by itself, but two further aspects of Frankfurt's treatment of Nicaea are even more revealing. The first of these concerns the language of the canons themselves. Canon one, dealing with Adoptionism, says "sanctissimi patres . . . contradixerunt atque . . . statuerunt" (the most holy fathers . . . contradict and . . . declare), and canon two, dealing with Nicaea, says "sanctissimi patres nostri . . . contempserunt atque . . . condempnaverunt" (our most holy fathers . . . despise and . . . condemn). Canon three handled the affairs of the rebellious Duke Tassilo of Bavaria. Its dispositive language says that Tassilo was "made to stand up in the midst of the most holy council" and that after all the charges were read "dominus noster" (our lord), that is, Charlemagne himself, pronounced his punishments: "indulsit" (he indulged), "concessit" (he conceded), "precepit" (he instructed), and "iussit" (he ordered).

The dispositive language in subsequent canons is more like that of canon three than of canons one and two. For example, canon four reads "Statuit piissimus domnus noster rex" (Our most pious lord king declared), and canon six says "Statutum est a domno rege et sancta synodo" (It was decreed by the lord king and by the holy synod).[43] It appears that a clear distinction was being drawn between the first two canons and all the others. As Hans Barion argued long ago, "dogmatic issues were being independently decided legally by the bishops."[44] In the very canons where papal authority is emphasized, episcopal authority is much to the fore. Another structural aspect of these canons is striking. Canon one says that Adoptionism "exortum est" (arose), while canon two says that the image question "Allata est in medio" (was brought forward), and, finally, canon three says of Tassilo that "definitum est capitulum" (a decision was spelled out). Each of these cases was complex, and so the language dealing with them does not reflect the clear, crisp, business-like dispositions of the rest of the canons. Here it is as if crucial issues were decided openly and only after due deliberation.[45]

The second issue that requires careful analysis touches the actual words used at Frankfurt concerning Nicaea. In a slightly tortured bit of Latin, the council fathers accused their Nicaean counterparts of anathematizing anyone who would not pay to images of the saints exactly the same honor that was to be accorded to the Trinity.[46] At Nicaea, Bishop Constantine of Cyprus had explicitly condemned a statement that the same honor should be paid to images as to the Trinity, but his words had been garbled in the translation sent to the Franks. At Frankfurt, only Constantine's words were condemned, and it cannot have been too difficult for the pope's legates to agree to this condemnation. The Latin translation of the text had been prepared in Rome, after all, and it may have been that all parties thought that Constantine of Cyprus had indeed said something reprehensible in the midst of a council that otherwise met with papal, but not Frankish, approval. Thus, at Frankfurt, one remarkably minute issue was fixed upon for condemnation.[47] The pope, through his legates, was not asked to condemn all that was done at Nicaea, and the Franks got at least a measure of papal approval for their dissatisfaction with Nicaea.

The papal legates went home laden with gifts,[48] and the Franks do seem to have taken at least some of Hadrian's objections to heart in carrying out their revisions of the *Libri Carolini*.[49] Here again one detects a spirit of cooperation and compromise. This same spirit is evident in Hadrian's massive letter to the Franks. It contains no less than two diplomatic safety valves for the Franks. In one, Hadrian promised Charlemagne that he might yet declare the Greeks heretics if they did not restore to the church provinces and revenues that had been seized many years before by Leo III.[50] Hadrian did not promise to repudiate Nicaea, but the Franks got some hope of a condemnation of the Greeks. In the other, Hadrian attempted to dissociate Charlemagne from the totality of the *Libri Carolini* and to associate him personally with only a very limited reading of the famous letter of Gregory I to Serenus of Marseilles concerning images. Hadrian was saying, in effect, that Charlemagne was surely correct in all his thinking, but his bishops had gotten a bit carried away in the heat of the argument.[51]

The pope gave Charlemagne, in other words, a diplomatic opportunity to distance himself from the very documents he had dispatched to Rome in the first place, while telling the king that his understanding of the papal view of images was impeccable. Finally, it has been suggested recently that Hadrian may have taken Frankish views on sacred art into consideration in Rome in the years after about 790. When, before Hadrian's pontificate, the *Liber Pontificalis* makes one of its numerous mentions of images, it does so with no reference to aesthetic considerations. The spiritual, or theological, significance of images was stressed. In Hadrian's time, however, modifying adjectives denoting size, color, or beauty begin to appear to signify aesthetic or even decorative, but not spiritual, value attached to images. This was the argument of the *Libri Carolini*.[52]

Einhard says that Charlemagne wept when he heard of Hadrian's death in 795.[53] Well might he have done so. He and the old pope had been friends and allies for more than two decades. They sometimes disagreed with one another but they never had a major break in relations. The whole affair surrounding the *Libri Carolini* did not provoke a rift in Franko-papal relations because it was not meant to do so and because the pope and the Frankish king knew very well how to compromise and cooperate.

The *Libri Carolini* was a *Staatsschrift* in the sense that it represented a core of ideological values and ideas that were prominent at the Carolingian court in the 780s and 790s. But it was more like a treatise, like a *liber*, than like a capitulary or other public act of the will of the king. It received no wider dissemination than other treatises written in the Carolingian period, for example, the books on kingship written by Jonas of Orléans, Smaragdus of Saint-Mihiel, Hincmar of Reims, and Sedulius Scottus, or the volumes of ethical advice prepared by Paulinus of Aquileia, Alcuin, Hrabanus Maurus, and Hincmar. But the *Libri Carolini* was official because it reflected the views of Charlemagne and his most influential associates at a key moment in the reign.

❧

Let us turn now to what the *Libri Carolini* actually says or, more precisely, to the major themes it develops. There are four of these, and each is tied closely to a particular type of tradition. For purposes of discussion I shall call these themes biblical, ecclesiastical, papal, and Christian-imperial. Although these labels are notionally accurate, none actually appears in just this way in the *Libri Carolini*. The four traditions are woven so tightly into the text that it is not easy to disentangle them without rending the fabric. With due care, then, we shall attempt in what follows to trace four particular threads.

The *Libri Carolini* was composed in four books, the original intention having been to produce books of thirty chapters, each book preceded by a preface. The surviving version departs slightly from this scheme, but the discrepancies are not such as to require comment.[54] Book 1 begins with an attack on the eastern emperors and goes on to say that the Greeks misunderstand images in a fundamental way. The flaws in their reasoning are particularly attributable to a deficient understanding of the Old Testament. Patriarch Tarasius is also severely criticized, and then more scorn is heaped on Byzantine misunderstandings of the Old Testament. Book 2 begins by carrying on the attack against Byzantine mishandling of the Bible and then turns to a series of searing indictments of the mistakes of a number of Greek Fathers and of the misuse of those Fathers at Nicaea. Book 3 begins with a Frankish *confessio fidei* and then goes on to another condemnation of Tarasius, which blames him for misleading his church. Next there are several rejections of Byzantine theological errors, followed by sharp criticisms of the theological positions of a group of eastern theologians. After this we find a neat bit of ecclesiological criticism of Second Nicaea, a pointed attack on Irene, and then a remarkable set of observations on what images are, what they are not, and what place they hold in the church. The fourth and last book continues the theological reasoning begun in book 3 but is, in a sense, more systematic and less historical, exegetical, and ecclesiological—at least until the very end. Here we read that the Byzantines do not understand what an image truly is or what images are for and do not know how to establish or to verify evidence concerning images. The work ends with a ringing denunciation of the failure of the Byzantines to adhere to the universal traditions of the Church.

Again and again the *Libri Carolini* refers to Second Nicaea, and the problem of images appears in some fashion on almost every page. But I believe that Nicaea provided an opportunity, and images provided an issue, that enabled the Carolingians to crystallize their thinking on a host of concerns that reached far beyond the immediate historical circumstances that had set Theodulf and his colleagues to working in the first place. An investigation based upon the four traditions enumerated above will enable us to test the validity of that belief.

First, then, let us look at the biblical tradition. The first two books especially of the *Libri Carolini* contain a series of specific and programmatic
condemnations of Byzantine readings of the Old Testament. In specific
terms, they reject a long set of passages that were adduced at Nicaea in
defense of images. For example, they say that Abraham did not adore the
sons of Heth, Moses did not adore Jethro, and Jacob did not adore pha-
raoh.[55] Likewise, Jacob did not erect his pillow stone as an image, nor did
he treat Joseph's cloak in this way. Jacob's staff was not an image, and neither was the Ark of the Covenant. Bezeleel did not build images, and the
story of Moses and the hyacinths has no more to do with images than does
the tale of Moses' bronze staff. The account of Joshua and the twelve
stones does not authorize images.[56] Extensive attention is paid to the alleged misuse of the psalms by the Byzantines. In particular, Eastern interpretations of eleven psalms (4, 9, 11, 25, 29, 47, 73, 74, 84, 98, and 124)
are explicitly criticized.[57] The minute attention devoted to the psalms in
this section of *Libri Carolini* is probably attributable to the prominent
place occupied by these biblical prayer-poems in the public worship of the
Western church.

The more programmatic comments are of two kinds. In one, the Byzantines are hectored for failing to understand the vocabulary and grammar of
the Old Testament.[58] The second kind is more serious and sustained.
Again and again the Franks condemn the Byzantines for reading passages
in the Old Testament literally and for quoting those passages in connection
with images when, in reality, all such passages are to be understood typo-
logically as referring to Christ or to the church.[59]

The Byzantines certainly did not need a lesson in typological exegesis,
and at least some of the Carolingians' criticisms of the Greeks were occasioned by misunderstandings of their own prompted by the poor translation of Nicaea's *acta* from which they were working. To some extent the
controversy was created by the fact that the Byzantines generally hewed
close to the more literalist Antiochene school of exegesis while the West
had a preference for the allegorical school of Alexandria. But it takes very
little imagination to see that Theodulf and his associates were really giving
voice to a central set of preoccupations in the Carolingian court. It is to
those concerns that one must turn in order to understand the context and
meaning of the exegetical and interpretive arguments that fill most of the
first two books of the *Libri Carolini*.

At just the time when the *Libri Carolini* was being prepared, Charlemagne's massive program of educational reform and spiritual revival was
coming into full swing. It would be no exaggeration to say that that pro-

gram was focused directly on the Bible.[60] The whole idea of the reform was to communicate biblical truths to the people so that all might be led to salvation. In order for the clergy to preach the Bible, and for the people to understand what was being preached to them, books had to be obtained and copied, teachers had to be trained, schools had to be formed, and pupils had to be recruited.[61] In many respects, the whole program demanded that the right things had to be taught and understood. Where the Old Testament was concerned, this meant that it had to be seen as having foreshadowed the New Testament and also, as we shall see below, the Frankish people and their kings.

It cannot be mere coincidence that just in the years when the *Libri Carolini* was being prepared, there arose among Charlemagne's key advisers a potent association between the great Frank and the kings of the Old Testament. In the preface to the *Admonitio generalis* of 789, Charlemagne is compared to Josiah because, like him, he sought "by visitation, correction and admonition to recall the kingdom which God had given him to the worship of the true God" (cf. 2 Kings:22–23).[62] As early as 775 Charlemagne had been addressed as both Solomon and David by Cathwulf,[63] and Charlemagne's throne at Aachen, in the chapel on which construction had begun in about 788, was consciously modeled on that of Solomon.[64] To Alcuin, Charlemagne was like Solomon both because of his wisdom and because he erected a complex of buildings like the Temple once built in Jerusalem.[65] Paul the Deacon called Charlemagne David in about 787, as had Cathwulf earlier, albeit in a numerical riddle.[66] By about 794, however, it had become common to refer to Charlemagne as David.[67] These sources, whether poetic or epistolary, sought to draw a parallel between Charlemagne's and David's prophetic wisdom and strength in defense of Israel and the faith.[68] The precise significance of these references to Old Testament kings can be grasped from the very first chapter of the *Libri Carolini*, where the emperors of Byzantium are accused of failing to rule as David and Solomon had done.[69] It may well have been known at Charlemagne's court that in the East the emperor was called *allos Dabid* (the second David).

The point of the careful Old Testament exegesis in the *Libri Carolini*, coupled with the designation of Charlemagne as David, was precisely to make the Frankish ruler, and him alone, the authentic representative of and heir to the Davidic kingship of Israel.[70] Pope Paul I had called the Franks a "new Israel"[71] and at about the same time, in the second prologue to the Salic Law, the Franks had referred to themselves in the same terms.[72] In the *Libri Carolini* the Franks say, "we are not the carnal but the spiritual Israel."[73] Beginning in the late 780s, the Franks are called, in sources of all kinds, the *populus Christianus*.[74] The newly defined "Christian people" was none other than the new Frankish Israel led by the new Carolingian David.

A correct understanding of the Old Testament, therefore, pointed in a palpably historical way to the Franks. At the same time, a proper typological exegesis of the Old Testament pointed to the age of Christ, the apostles, and the church. For purposes of discussion, I label these, taken together, the ecclesiastical tradition to which the *Libri Carolini* draws attention.

The *Libri Carolini* developed its arguments on ecclesiastical traditions in ways that were based on doctrine, practice, and institutions, although it is not always easy to make sharp distinctions between these categories. Where doctrine is concerned, the biblical foundation was crucial. Theodulf says indeed that one must follow the teachings of the prophets, the Lord, and the apostles.[75] The end of book 2 presents an interesting set of arguments to the effect that everything that is needed for every possible kind of knowledge is available in Scripture.[76] Always, priority was given to the word of God.[77] But over a long period of time, God's word had been interpreted, made accessible, and kept inviolate by a series of authoritative teachers. In fact, the Scriptures could only be understood in the light of the "writings of the holy fathers."[78] Thus book 3 contains a long series of attacks on various Greek theologians, or the way in which those theologians were understood—or even misunderstood—at Nicaea.[79] But the argument is not carried purely by negation. Jerome, Ambrose, Augustine, and Gregory are repeatedly cited as having held to the correct line in matters of faith, and there is a remarkable statement in book 2 that "after the writings of the prophets, evangelists and apostles we are very content with the teachings of the illustrious Latin doctors whose life and teaching are known to us, as well as with those Greeks who were Catholic and who have been translated by Catholics into our language."[80] It is perfectly true that the Carolingians sometimes were muddled about what had been said at Nicaea.[81] And on a few occasions they admitted to being unfamiliar with texts and authors cited there.[82] But this is beside the point. What is clear is that Theodulf and those who worked with him saw a straight line of teaching running from the time of Jesus to that of Charlemagne, and as they looked back along that line they could see that the Byzantines had at some point departed from it, that "they had severed the bond of ecclesiastical unity."[83]

This is also the argument advanced in the matter of practices or customs. To take first a fairly obvious example, images, the *Libri Carolini* takes a rather simple line. Tradition has always permitted the possession of images for purposes of ornamentation or commemoration, but nothing more.

> We do not reject images put up to remind us of great deeds or to beautify churches since we know they were put up thus by Solomon and Moses, although only as type figures, but we object to their adoration which is contrary to custom and indeed more than superstitious; and we cannot find this worship ever to have been instituted by patriarchs or prophets or apostolic men.[84]

The Byzantines cannot seem to get this straight. They think the Old Testament talks about images when it does no such thing.

Byzantine failures in this regard are twofold. First, they do not study the Old Testament correctly. If they did so, they would know that every passage has three levels of meaning: historical, spiritual, and allegorical (or mystical).[85] Thus they are led to suppose that when the psalmist spoke (Ps. 4:7) of the "countenance" *(vultus)* of the Lord, he meant an image, when he simply cannot have been referring to a manufactured thing.[86] Or when the psalmist said, "Lord I have loved the beauty of your house" (Ps. 25:8), he supposed an image to have been implied, whereas "the house of the Lord is to be understood according to allegory as the church, or according to anagogy as the celestial homeland, or according to tropology as the soul of man."[87] Their second failure is to reject the universal tradition of the church, which refuses to worship God in images.[88] The Greeks also misread the Fathers, who never command or even permit the worship of images.[89] Theodulf and his associates could even be a bit devious in separating the Byzantines from patristic tradition. For example, Theodulf gives an extensive citation from one of the famous letters of Gregory I to Serenus of Marseilles on images but only to argue that Gregory forbade the adoration and destruction of images. All the rest of Gregory's highly nuanced argument for the didactic values of images is silently omitted.[90] And of course Byzantium spent a half century destroying images only to turn around and command worship of them.

Other religious practices are brought up as well. The Franks understand the customary place of relics and why they are holy. They are the actual, physical remains of the saints, or else objects closely associated with them during their lives.[91] The Greeks think images are holy when they are merely senseless objects made by men.[92] It has never been the universal practice of the church to worship God through mere objects, and only

God is to be worshiped in the first place.[93] The Franks, apparently alone, understand that certain objects are actually in some sense holy: relics, the cross, and the sacred vessels, for example.[94] These objects are holy because they are consecrated by prayers, used in the worship of God, and approved by tradition. But they are never worshiped for themselves, as the Greeks insist that images can, indeed must, be.[95]

The Carolingian position was that, ever since apostolic times, there had been certain universal traditions with respect to customary Christian practices, and that time and time again the Byzantines had departed from those traditions and then, having departed, had had the temerity to insist that others join them on their wayward path. The Carolingian view was somewhat less than fair to the Greeks and somewhat less than accurate in its reading of Christian history but, once again, that is beside the point if our goal is to understand the argument of the *Libri Carolini*.[96]

Insofar as ecclesiastical tradition refers to institutions, similar points were made, although in this realm some very new, and heretofore poorly understood, arguments were advanced. Actually, it seems to me that a minor and a major argument are made on the institutional front. The minor one turns on the position of Tarasius. On two separate occasions, the *Libri Carolini* addresses the election of the patriarch of Constantinople. In book 1 Tarasius is criticized because he "was promoted extraordinarily from the lay state to the sacerdotal dignity, from the military habit to the religious, from the circus to the altar, from the forum to the pulpit, from the clash of arms to the performance of sacred mysteries." Not surprisingly, therefore, Tarasius was unprepared for his office and thus led his people "from spiritual to carnal, from invisible things to visible ones, from the truth to images, from a body to a shadow, from the living spirit to a dead letter."[97] Later Tarasius is accused of fabricating the whole image controversy to cover up his irregular election.[98] At this point, Theodulf is less concerned with images per se than with drawing a comparison between Tarasius and a proper bishop. Book 3, after telling of Tarasius's theological misadventures, quotes St. Paul and then Gregory I on how a bishop ought to be chosen and on what sort of person a bishop ought to be.[99] A comparison of Tarasius and a hypothetically correct bishop was inevitably a comparison between the Greeks and the Franks.

Ever since the commencement of the Bonifatian reforms, the Carolingians had been working hard and successfully to erect a proper ecclesiastical hierarchy. The major Frankish ecclesiastical legislation, from the 740s to the great capitularies of Charlemagne in 789 and 794, called for bishops who were learned, wise, and humble; bishops who would be both leaders and models for those entrusted to their care. In other words, only the bishops of Charlemagne's realm represented the ideal bishop of both St. Paul and Pope Gregory I. The irregular situation of Tarasius, as the Franks wished to view it, indicated yet again a Byzantine departure from the traditions of the church and marked the precise Frankish adherence to those traditions.

The major and much more historically significant institutional issue turned around a central ecclesiological problem, namely, the nature of synods and the relationship of synods to the *catholica fides*. A generation or two ago it was customary to argue that the Franks were offended because the Byzantines called Nicaea universal and they had not been invited.[100] Then, in a more refined view, it was maintained that what the Franks objected to in Nicaea was its departure from what they believed the Catholic faith to be and to demand of its adherents. In other words, Nicaea falsely called itself universal, not because the Franks were absent, but because it was untrue to the universal faith.[101] In reality, the *Libri Carolini* sketches out a fascinating and new conciliar theory that constitutes nothing less than a recasting of a whole series of traditional positions.

It is true that some of what the *Libri Carolini* says is quite conventional. A couple of points, however, at first reading suggest something a little odd. We are told that Nicaea was held "carelessly" and "indiscreetly," and that a synod should only be held to deal with "serious" problems and should confine itself to taking only those actions that are strictly necessary.[102] What can this mean? Was not the removal of the Iconoclastic heresy serious and necessary? Yes and no. Constantine VI and Irene, as Wilhelm de Vries has astutely pointed out, were in a precarious position. They wished to restore images, but the Iconoclasts were still numerous and powerful. Moreover, the official Byzantine church was completely isolated from all the other churches of the East and West. Nothing less than a properly ecumenical council would solve their theological and political problems. But for the Franks, and, perhaps initially at least, for Hadrian as well, Iconoclasm was merely a local heresy. No official council, Hiereia having been roundly condemned, had proclaimed it, and so no ecumenical council was needed to renounce it. The Byzantine church needed only to put its own house in order.[103] This alone might well explain why the Franks considered the Greeks arrogant for calling Nicaea ecumenical, but there is even more to it than this.

Theodulf and his colleagues took the opportunity to engage in a bit of reflection on ecumenicity and universality. The ancient church had built up a conciliar theory that had both "vertical" and "horizontal" dimensions. The vertical ones involved authoritative, accepted teaching reaching back through the Fathers to the Bible. The horizontal ones meant representation and acceptance by the "pentarchy" of ancient patriarchates (Jerusalem, Antioch, Alexandria, Constantinople, and Rome) and the churches they represented. The Franks accepted the vertical argument but added a new twist. They raised an argument based on the twin principles of *scrutinium* and *ratio*.[104] As we have seen, they sharply rejected the Byzantine reading of Scripture and patristic teaching. In other words, they said it is not enough merely to cite precedents or to claim adherence to tradition. No, every text adduced must be examined closely to see what it means and if it is truly relevant.[105] This will explain why the Franks submitted text after text to their own powerfully reasoned scrutiny.

The vertical conciliar theory was not a static measure but a constantly evolving and rationally founded standard. As to the horizontal theory, the Franks found its received version inadequate. They complained that the issues raised at Nicaea, if they had to be discussed at all, ought to have been submitted to "each and every part of the church."[106] The Franks were adjusting conciliar theory to historical reality. The old pentarchy had arisen before the Franks had come on the scene. They did not feel that their "monarch," the pope, adequately represented them. They deserved representation of their own. They were not offended materially at having gotten no invitation to Nicaea, but formally at the idea that the pope alone could represent the whole Western church. In the end there are two issues here: the very different views the Franks and the Byzantines had of what a synod was and of how the church was organized in the world.

So the Old Testament had pointed to the New, and the New had pointed to the church. Only the Franks had so far been faithful in all respects to these two links in an unbroken chain of tradition. The Byzantines had fallen away in both instances. Christ himself, in his words to Peter (Mt. 16:16–18), had instituted a guarantor of his traditions. We turn now to a third tradition, the papal, to which, according to the *Libri Carolini*, the Franks had been faithful and the Byzantines, faithless.

Very early the *Libri Carolini* sets about emphasizing the importance of communion with Rome. At the end of the fifth chapter of book 1 we read that "among all other churches, the Holy Roman Church is held in special veneration concerning matters of the faith."[107] The following chapter is the most rigorously papal of the whole treatise. It makes three very simple, direct arguments: the Roman church has from the beginning been set before all other churches; only books used in Rome and teachings that hold authority there are to be admitted; and although many people have at some time broken from Rome's communion, the Franks never have. Indeed, they struggle mightily to bring new peoples, such as the Saxons, into the Roman fold.[108] Elsewhere in the text, on one occasion the teaching authority of Pope Sylvester is affirmed,[109] while on another occasion some debating points are scored against the Byzantines by pointing out that even so great a scholar as St. Jerome did not hesitate to turn for instruction to Pope Damasus.[110] Pope Gregory I was cited as an authority on images and the ordination of bishops.[111] The citation at Nicaea of the alleged correspondence between Jesus and Abgar of Edessa was rejected on the authority of Pope Gelasius.[112] Theodulf also mentions St. Peter's leadership of the apostolic church.[113] The position of the papacy as the culmination and guarantee of ecclesiastical traditions can be set off neatly against the irregular and schismatic situation of Tarasius.

The broad context within which Theodulf was writing serves to shed even more light on the relationship between the Franks and the Roman church. In book 1, Theodulf said that the Franks had turned to Rome for instruction in liturgical chant "so that there would be no difference in singing between those who were alike in believing."[114] What Theodulf is referring to, of course, is the extraordinarily lively liturgical exchange between Rome and the Frankish court that began under Pepin III in the 760s and carried on well into the ninth century.[115] In 774, or shortly after, Charlemagne got from Rome a copy of the *Dionysio-Hadriana*, which was then regarded by the Franks as the definitive collection of canon law.[116] In around 787, Charlemagne turned to Rome for an authentic copy of the Rule of St. Benedict in order to promote monastic reform in his realm.[117] In about 791, while Theodulf was drafting the *Libri Carolini*, Charlemagne ordered a collection to be made of his and his predecessors' correspondence with Rome. The result was the book known as the *Codex Carolinus*.[118] In 794 Charlemagne requested from Rome a copy of the letters of Pope Gregory I, another sure sign of the Frankish adherence to Roman and papal traditions.[119] A few years earlier, Charlemagne showed his attachment to Roman and Petrine traditions by commissioning Paul the Deacon to write a history of the bishops of Metz.[120] Paul stressed, as no one before him had done, the connection between the Carolingians and the see of Metz and the connection between Metz and St. Peter, the see allegedly having been founded by a disciple.[121] This passion for doing things *more Romano* (in the Roman fashion) was not confined to liturgy and law, in other words to books. It has long been recognized that Carolingian architecture, whether the rebuilding of Saint-Denis with occidentation and an annular crypt, or the modeling of parts of the Aachen complex on the Lateran baptistery, owed a great deal to genuine or putative Roman exemplars.[122]

The remarks in the *Libri Carolini* about the papacy are in perfect agreement with what was going on at the Carolingian court. Donald Bullough has sagely observed that the massive Carolingian educational reform sought authentic books and that, to those associated with Charlemagne and his court, authentic meant "Roman" and Roman meant "papal."[123] Josef Flechenstein has also shown that the Carolingian emphasis on authentic books and proper traditions, as well as correct (or corrected) books and teachers, had its source in papal Rome. Zachary had written to urge Pepin to adhere to the "norma rectitudinis," a phrase that surely needs no translation and very little explanation.[124] The synod of Verneuil in 755 referred to a need to get back to "rectissima norma."[125] In promoting his religious reforms, Chrodegang of Metz often used such phrases as "norma rectitudinis" and "linea rectitudinis."[126] The *Admonitio generalis* of 789, the circular letter *De litteris colendis* (which must date from around 789), the correspondence of Alcuin, and the *Libri Carolini* are replete with the word *recte* (rightly) in all its various forms. And doing it right, whatsoever "it" happened to be, meant doing it *more Romano*, the way the pope did. In all their words and deeds, the Franks clung steadfastly to the traditions of papal Rome, while the perfidious Byzantines attacked the popes, ignored their teachings, and challenged their authority. Those who have argued that Charlemagne somehow set out to humiliate Hadrian or to subordinate him to the Frankish royal power have simply ignored the radically papalist current in Carolingian thought and action in the 780s and 790s.[127] It is ironic but nevertheless true that the Carolingians, much more than the popes themselves, placed the pope at the center of the church, enhanced papal powers, and evoked papal pretensions.

One final line of historical development is worked out in the *Libri Carolini*. It might be called Christian-imperial. The *Libri Carolini* talks fairly often about rulership, and virtually everything it says involves implicit or explicit comparisons of good and bad rulership. The Byzantine rulers, often derisively titled "kings," are called arrogant and uncharitable.[128] The point of these criticisms is to drive home the distinction between the Byzantines and the Franks, whose royal theory demanded that rulers be humble, loving servants of God and his people.[129] At one point, Theodulf remarks that David was a humble minister of God, and even of Christ, whose type he bore.[130] The Old Testament kings, as we have seen, were in many respects appropriated as models by Theodulf and the Carolingians.

The reason why the Byzantines got their image of rulership out of focus was that they drew their inspiration from the world of pagan Rome. This led them to call themselves *divos* and their official acts *divalia*. They had the hauteur to compare their own images to those of Christ, and to call themselves the "equal of the apostles" *(isapostolos)*.[131] These were traditional epithets and protocols at Byzantium, inheritances from antiquity.[132] Theodulf and his associates fixed upon them with a vengeance, however, because they provided a pretext for elaborating a new view of history. By viewing the Bible as the record of salvation history, the Franks could insist that the old sequence of kingdoms running from Babylon to Rome had been broken. Theodulf explicitly stated that Rome, by which he meant Byzantium, was the heir of Babylon.[133] Byzantium was, in other words, the heir to the order that had been overthrown. Charlemagne was the true heir of the salvation history first revealed in the Bible.[134]

Rome's pagan inheritance from Babylon was not, however, the only potential Frankish legacy from Rome. There was also the Rome of Constantine. It was Constantine's Rome, not that of the Caesars, that Charlemagne sought to evoke. This was a Rome whose first emperor turned for instruction to Pope Sylvester[135] and whose most recent ruler, Pope Hadrian, had addressed Charlemagne himself as a "new Constantine."[136] Charlemagne's chapel at Aachen, which is almost exactly contemporary with the *Libri Carolini*, expressed well the program of that treatise and its contrasting of Byzantium and the Franks. It can be compared with the imperial *Chrysotryklinos*, a room almost certainly known to at least some at the Carolingian court through diplomatic exchanges. In Constantinople, the emperor's throne was placed in the east, behind the altar and before a *maiestas* image. At Aachen, the altar was in the east, but the throne—modeled, as we saw earlier, on that of Solomon—was in the west. A mosaic of Christ in Majesty (or possibly an image of the Lamb of God) was placed in the cupola, regnant over the whole scene.[137] These comparisons served to demonstrate, first, that only Christ truly ruled; earthly potentates acted in his name and on his behalf but never reigned.[138] Second, Constantine was a complex and ambiguous symbol for the Carolingians. It may be true, as Richard Krautheimer said, that "it seems as though Antiquity were epitomized in the Christian Rome of Constantine and Sylvester."[139] But Constantine was an Arian heretic and a Roman. It was not until the ninth century, a generation after Charlemagne, that the Carolingians became comfortable with the ideal of the first Christian emperor.[140] What was not ambiguous at all was that, according to the *Libri Carolini* and the ideas prevailing at the Carolingian court, only the Franks had been true to the correct ideal of Christian rulership.

❊

It is time to conclude. The *Libri Carolini* represents one masterfully de-signed strategy in the Carolingian fight for history. It was only natural that the Carolingians felt compelled to wage that fight. Ever since the fourth century, Christians had been obliged to locate themselves in history.[141] The very fact of conversion meant the discovery of a new history, which began with Adam and Eve and continued down to current events.[142] For a long time, Christian and Roman universalism converged. Then the west-ern provinces of the old Roman Empire were divided among *gentes* who had had no previous place in biblical or classical schemes of temporal reck-oning. As these peoples were converted to Christianity, they learned to think in universal terms while separating those terms from the referents of the vanished Roman order.[143] The Byzantine view of history was paradox-ical, implying at once a dramatic change, represented by the adoption of Christianity, and a total absence of change, implicit in Roman continu-ity.[144] So it was that the *Libri Carolini* "proclaimed, on biblical-typological grounds, a Christian universalism which directly opposed the constitu-tionally fixed Byzantine claims upon world rulership."[145] For the Car-olingians to take their place as Christians in the roll of nations, they had to battle the Byzantines. To do this, they contested them on every field that really mattered; the biblical, the apostolic, the ecclesiastical, and the institutional.

A few widely chosen examples may help to show that the historical con-cerns evidenced by the *Libri Carolini* were by no means unique to that book. We have already mentioned the parallels drawn between the kings of the Old and New Israels. Notice was taken, too, of Paul the Deacon's his-tory of the see of Metz. The Sacramentary of Gellone, written in the last decade of the eighth century, contains a litany for the dead that begins with Noah and goes down to Peter and Paul. The point of these prayers was to create a sense of community "not only among the attendants at the death, but between them and those who had preceded them in sacred his-tory."[146] Carolingian collections of canon law tended to be "historical" rather than "systematic." That is, they organized their material chronologi-cally according to the councils from which the canons were taken instead of topically according to the subject matter treated.[147] An episcopal statute from the early ninth century mentions four great epochs of law giving: natural law before the fall; the Mosaic law of the Old Testament; Christ's law and the New Testament; and the legislation of the Frankish Church.[148] Even Carolingian library collections were organized historically.[149] There is need for a big study of the Carolingian idea of history, and the intense historical-mindedness of Charlemagne and his key advisers will doubtless play a key role in that inquiry.

The *Libri Carolini* constitutes an elegant metahistory that can in every way bear favorable comparison with the more famous works of Eusebius and Orosius and even, in a way, with that of Augustine. It is a metahistory that seeks to locate the Franks in their own time but also in all time. This is why I insist that Nicaea and the issue of images merely provided an opportunity for deeper reflections on larger themes. Can anyone be surprised that a few years after the *Libri Carolini* was written Charlemagne was crowned emperor? This magnificent book had already prepared for that event by demonstrating that God's covenant with Abraham had been communicated to the church, preserved by the popes, and transferred to the Franks. The Byzantines, who alone in the late eighth century could have competed with the Franks on grounds of spiritual and historical universalism, had to be written out of history, as it were. This was done in two ways. First, they were made objects of almost unspeakable scorn. They and their teachings were called arrogant, contemptible, damnable, laughable, stupid, foolish, silly, inadequate, inappropriate, incautious, superficial—I could go on and on. At Byzantium, a physical mutilation rendered a person ineligible for high office. The Franks rendered the Byzantines ineligible for historical participation by verbal mutilation. Second, and more significantly, the *Libri Carolini* neatly sets aside all possibility that the Byzantines could be regarded as the heirs of Israel, the Old Testament, apostolic traditions, the ancient councils, the Roman papacy, and the Christian Roman Empire. When Theodulf laid down his quill, all of history had been made to point to the very court in which he had been working.

What is the argument of the *Libri Carolini*? It is a simple one that goes like this: Abraham was a Frank, and David was a Carolingian. God in heaven rules the world and his agent on earth is Charlemagne. This book was not put on the shelf for fear that it would humiliate Hadrian, because there was little in its central thesis, quite apart from its details, that would have offended the pope. And it was in a sense published and disseminated because its basic arguments were preached from the pulpits of the cathedral and monastic and parish churches that played in all ways so decisive a role in spreading the Carolingian reform. If the events of Christmas Day, 800, have any meaning at all, then certainly the ideas contained in the *Libri Carolini* were official. The book has been called a *Staatsschrift* and a

Streitschrift (polemic).[150] Both characterizations are accurate but incomplete, for the *Libri Carolini* went beyond politics and polemics to become an exceptionally learned work of history that contained nothing less than the fullest single expression of the ideological program of the court of Charlemagne during the most creative years of his long reign.

Notes

1. *Libri Carolini sive Caroli Magni capitulare de imaginibus,* ed. Hubert Bastgen, MGH, Concilia, pt. 2, Supplementum (Hannover, 1924), hereafter *LC.* A new edition is being prepared for the MGH by Ann Freeman.
2. This is the title given to the work by Bastgen (cited n. 1) and often adopted by modern scholars.
3. François Louis Ganshof, *Recherches sur les capitulaires.*
4. Paris, Bibliothèque de l'Arsenal, MS 663, fol. 1. For a reproduction of this manuscript's title page, see *Karl der Grosse: Werk und Wirkung,* pl. 33 and p. 193.
5. See Ann Freeman, "Theodulf of Orléans and the *Libri Carolini*"; "Further Studies in the *Libri Carolini* I–II"; "Further Studies in the *Libri Carolini* III: The Marginal Notes in *Vaticanus Latinus 7207*"; and "Theodulf of Orléans and the Psalm Citations of the 'Libri Carolini.'" Freeman's great opponent was Luitpold Wallach, whose studies are conveniently assembled in his *Diplomatic Studies in Latin and Greek Documents from the Carolingian Age.* Wallach maintained, at different times, that Alcuin was either the author or the editor of the *Libri Carolini.* For an assessment of the authorship problem, see Paul J. Meyvaert, "The Authorship of the 'Libri Carolini': Observations Prompted by a Recent Book." Donald Bullough has taken a slightly different line, arguing that Alcuin played a role in the revision of the text at the court. His evidence consists primarily of a demonstration that texts prepared by Alcuin in his campaign against the Adoptionists found their way into, at the least, book 4 of the *LC*; see his "Alcuin and the Kingdom of Heaven: Liturgy, Theology, and the Carolingian Age," esp. pp. 34–38 (repr. in Bullough, *Carolingian Renewal: Sources and Heritage,* esp. pp. 180–87). Freeman, "Additions and Corrections to the *Libri Carolini*: Links with Alcuin and the Adoptionist Controversy," says that Bullough's approach "commands respect." There is another intriguing problem discussed by John Marenbon, *From the Circle of Alcuin to the School of Auxerre: Logic, Theology, and Philosophy in the Early Middle Ages,* pp. 35ff. The problem is that the so-called *dicta Albini,* some philosophical fragments of Alcuin, turn up in the *Libri Carolini,* where they are, in one instance, attributed to Augustine. The questions are: Where did Theodulf get this material? Did he know it was by his contemporary and fellow courtier? Did it enter the *LC* during revision? Answers to these questions will have to await further research.
6. The most valuable studies of the *LC* are Wolfram von den Steinen,

"Entstehungsgeschichte der Libri Carolini"; von den Steinen, "Karl der Grosse und die Libri Carolini: Die tironischen Noten zum Codex"; Walter Schmandt, *Studien zu den Libri Carolini* (I am grateful to Paul Meyvaert for providing me a copy of this study); and Freeman, "Carolingian Orthodoxy and the Fate of the *Libri Carolini*." Several very widely held views can be traced back to three sources: Karl Hampe, "Hadrians I Vertheidigung der zweiten nicaeanischen Synode gegen die Angriffe Karls des Grossen"; Albert Hauck, *Kirchengeschichte Deutschlands*, 2:327–43; and Georg Ostrogorsky, "Rom und Byzanz im Kampf um die Bilderverehrung." Among many other works that might be cited, these seem pertinent: Edward James Martin, *A History of the Iconoclastic Controversy*, pp. 222–57; Gert Haendler, *Epochen karolingischer Theologie: Eine Untersuchung über die karolingischen Gutachten zum byzantinischen Bilderstreit*, pp. 27–43, 67–101; Stephen Gero, "The Libri Carolini and the Image Controversy"; and Girolamo Arnaldi, "La questione dei Libri Carolini."

7. Walter Goffart, *The Narrators of Barbarian History: Jordanes, Gregory of Tours, Bede, and Paul the Deacon*, p. ix.

8. This is hardly the place for a full bibliographical assessment of the first period of Byzantine Iconoclasm. The interpretation offered here is based on my study, "John Damascene and the History of the Iconoclastic Controversy," which cites much older literature. Not mentioned in my earlier work but very valuable are Hans-Georg Beck, *Von der Fragwürdigkeit der Ikone*; Paul Speck, "Ikonoklasmus und die Anfänge der makedonischen Renaissance"; Speck, "Weitere Überlegungen und Untersuchungen über die Ursprünge der byzantinischen Renaissance"; Antonio Carile, "L'iconoclasmo fra bisanzio e l'Italia"; and Peter Schreiner, "Der byzantinische Bilderstreit: Kritische Analyse der zeitgenössischen Meinungen und das Urteil der Nachwelt bis heute."

9. The critical decade of the 780s in Byzantium has recently been the subject of several important studies: Speck, *Kaiser Konstantin VI*; Judith Herrin, *The Formation of Christendom*, pp. 408–66; and Warren Treadgold, *The Byzantine Revival, 780–842*, pp. 60–126. An interesting assessment of Empress Irene is Steven Runciman, "The Empress Irene the Athenian."

10. Mansi, *Concilia*, 12:984–86.

11. Mansi, *Concilia*, 12:1056–72; and Philippus Jaffé, *Regesta Pontificum Romanorum*, no. 2448 (hereafter Jaffé, *RP*).

12. Venance Grumel, *Les Regestes des actes du patriarchat de Constantinople*, no. 351; Mansi, *Concilia*, 12:1077–84; and Jaffé, *RP*, no. 2449.

13. Treadgold, *Byzantine Revival*, pp. 49–81, with full references at p. 400, n. 9; and Treadgold, "The Empress Irene's Preparation for the Seventh Ecumenical Council."

14. The *acta* of Second Nicaea are published in Mansi, *Concilia*, 12:991–1154, 13:1–418. Extended discussions of the council may be found in Charles Joseph Hefele and Henri Leclercq, *Histoire des conciles*, pp. 601–804; Gervais Dumeige, *Nicée II*; F. Boespflug and N. Lossky, eds., *Nicée II, 787–1987: Douze siècles d'images religieuses*; Josef Wohlmuth, ed., *Streit um das Bild: Das zweite Konzil von Nicäa (787) in ökumenischer Perspektive*; Wilhelm

de Vries, "Die Struktur der Kirche gemäss dem II Konzil von Nicäa (787)"; and Vittorio Fazzo, "Il II Concilio di Nicea nella storia cristiana ed i rapporti fra Roma e Bisanzio." There is a valuable English translation of, and commentary upon, the sixth session (which gave the *horos* of 754, its refutation, and the *horos* of 787) in Daniel J. Sahas, *Icon and Logos: Sources in Eighth-Century Iconoclasm.*

15. *Le Liber Pontificalis*, ed. Louis Duchesne, vol. 1, 2nd ed. (Paris, 1955): "Quam synodum iamdicti missi in greco sermone secum deferentes una cum imperialibus sacris manibus propriis subscriptis, praedictus egregius antistes in latino eam translatari iussit, et in sacra bibliotheca pariter recondi, dignam sibi orthodoxe fidei memoriam aeternam faciens" (p. 512).

16. Gero, "Libri Carolini," has emphasized (and perhaps exaggerated) the importance of the poor translation. He also believes that the Franks may have had no more than extracts of the *acta* of the council. In the ninth century, Hincmar of Reims said that Charlemagne had gotten his copy of the *acta* from the pope; see *Opuscula et epistolae quae spectant ad causam Hincmari Laudunensis*, PL 126:360a–b. Freeman, "Carolingian Orthodoxy," p. 68, thinks that Hincmar based his account of events on the entry in the *Annales regni Francorum* pertaining to the Synod of Frankfurt in 794 (ed. Friedrich Kurze, MGH, SS rer. Germ. [Hannover, 1895], p. 94). I suspect that she is right in general, but the *Annales* say nothing about the *acta*. Hincmar was either guessing or else he had another source of information of which we are ignorant. (Pseudo-)Simeon of Durham, *anno* 792, ed. R. Pauli, MGH, SS 13 (Hannover, 1881), says "Karolus rex Francorum misit sinodalem librum ad Britanniam sibi a Constantinopoli directum" (p. 155). Scholars have concluded that the York annals as quoted above are substantially reliable (for a full discussion, see Freeman, "Carolingian Orthodoxy," pp. 77–78, with nn. 42–48), but Constantinople cannot have been the direct source for Charlemagne. The *LC*, a letter of Hadrian to Charlemagne (discussed below), and documents from the renewed discussion of images undertaken at Paris in 825 all cite the Latin translation, itself no longer extant, to which the *Liber Pontificalis* refers. The preface to the *LC* merely refers to "textus . . . ad nos usque pervenit" without elaboration (p. 5).

17. *LC, Praef.*: "Gesta praeterea est ferme ante triennium et altera synodum" (p. 3). As Freeman, "Carolingian Orthodoxy," p. 71, carefully reasons, this statement dates only the preface. Because the word "ferme" is imprecise, it is possible to think of Theodulf as having begun work in about 790 or 791, though Freeman would prefer 790.

18. This is Freeman's reconstruction of the chronology of events; see her "Carolingian Orthodoxy," pp. 71–75. She points out, and I agree, that the most difficult of all problems concerns precisely why the Franks went to work at all on the *LC* if they had known Hadrian had embraced the decisions of Second Nicaea. Given that Theodulf did labor so assiduously on the text, it would seem that the Franks either did not get their copy of the *acta* directly from the pope, or else they did not think the copy that had

been sent to them bore the official stamp of papal approval. For an ingenious but unpersuasive reconstruction of the chronology of these years, consisting essentially of an attempt to move the *LC* to around 794, see Arnaldi, "La questione dei Libri Carolini."

19. *Epistolae Hadriani I. papae*, no. 2, ed. Ernst Dümmler, MGH, Epp. 5 (Berlin, 1899), pp. 5–57.
20. See the studies cited above, nn. 5 and 6, esp. those by Freeman.
21. Schmandt, *Studien*, p. 6.
22. Freeman, "Carolingian Orthodoxy," p. 86.
23. Such was the belief of the bishops who gathered in Paris in 825 for a new discussion of images; *Concilia aevi karolini*, no. 44, ed. Albert Werminghoff, MGH, Concilia, pt. 2 (Hannover, 1908): "Eandem porro synodum cum sanctae memoriae genitor vester [this was addressed to Louis the Pious] coram se suisque perlegi fecisset et multis in locis, ut dignum erat, reprehendisset" (p. 481).
24. See esp. Freeman, "Further Studies III," pp. 597–612.
25. Freeman, "Carolingian Orthodoxy," p. 96 and n. 125.
26. Hincmar's testimony is cited by Freeman, "Carolingian Orthodoxy" (from Paris, B.N., lat. 2865): "Non modicum volumen, quod in palatio adolescentulus legi" (p. 96, n. 121).
27. Freeman, "Carolingian Orthodoxy," pp. 100–105, points out that nowhere in the rich testimony from 825 is there a single reference to *LC*.
28. Ibid., pp. 96–99.
29. Angelo Mercati, "Per la storia del codice Vaticano dei Libri Carolini," pp. 112–19. Freeman argues, plausibly, that this manuscript was destroyed in the riot after the death of Paul IV in 1559, when a mob sacked the Holy Office and burned all the books they could find; see "Carolingian Orthodoxy," p. 97, n. 127.
30. Paris, B.N., lat. 12125, fol. 157. See Freeman, "Further Studies I–II," pp. 218–19; and Freeman, "Carolingian Orthodoxy," p. 66.
31. Schmandt, *Studien*, p. 1.
32. Hampe and Hauck, as in n. 6, above; and Johannes Haller, *Das Papsttum: Idee und Wirklichkeit*, 2:15. Haller's highly influential work is still in print, recently in paperback.
33. See the works of von den Steinen, Freeman, and Arnaldi (cited n. 6, above).
34. Charlemagne and Hadrian were allies and cooperated in many ventures. On this alliance, see my *The Republic of St. Peter: The Birth of the Papal State, 680–825*, pp. 256–76. A quick consultation of Jaffé, *RP*, no. 2467ff, will suffice to show that Charlemagne and Hadrian carried on all sorts of routine business during the whole period when the *LC* was in preparation. For some representative statements from the *LC* on the papacy, see, *LC* 1.5–6, pp. 19, 20–22.
35. See, e.g., R. I. Moore, *The Formation of a Persecuting Society*, pp. 69, 134.
36. For a summary of the *filioque* struggle in the age of Charlemagne, see Richard Haugh, *Photius and the Carolingians: The Trinitarian Controversy*, pp. 41–81. And *LC* 3.3, pp. 110–13, mentions the *filioque* issue.

37. Noble, *Republic of St. Peter*, pp. 138–83.
38. Freeman, "Carolingian Orthodoxy," pp. 72–73, n. 31; see also Meyvaert, "Authorship," pp. 40–42.
39. *LC, Praef.*, esp. pp. 2–3.
40. *LC, Praef.*: "cum conhibentia sacerdotum in regno a Deo nobis concesso catholicis gregibus praelatorum" (p. 5). For the Adoptionist issue, see *Concilia aevi karolini*, no. 19, ed. Werminghoff, MGH, Concilia, pt. 1 (Hannover and Leipzig, 1906), pp. 110–64; for *filioque*, ibid., no. 33, pp. 235–44.
41. Ganshof, "Observations sur le synode de Francfort de 794."
42. *Concilia aevi karolini*, no. 19, ed. Werminghoff, MGH, Concilia, pt. 1, p. 165.
43. Ibid., pp. 165–66.
44. Hans Barion, *Das fränkisch-deutsche Synodalrecht des Frühmittelalters*, pp. 252–53, 265–66.
45. Freeman, "Carolingian Orthodoxy," offers the interesting speculation that "there is reason to think that when the Council assembled the image question was not on the agenda" (p. 92). It is certainly true that it was not emphasized.
46. *Concilia aevi karolini*, no. 19, ed. Werminghoff, MGH, Concilia, pt. 1: "Allata est in medio de nova Grecorum synodo, quam de adorandis imaginibus Constantinopolim fecerunt; in qua scriptum habebatur, ut qui imagines sanctorum ita ut deificam trinitatem servitio aut adorationem non inpenderent, anathema iudicaverunt" (p. 165).
47. Freeman, "Carolingian Orthodoxy," pp. 92–95, gives a very careful reading of these events.
48. *Annales regni Francorum*, anno 793, ed. Kurze, p. 94.
49. Freeman, "Carolingian Orthodoxy," pp. 87–92.
50. *Ep. Hadriani I*, no. 2, ed. Dümmler, p. 57.
51. Ibid., pp. 55–56.
52. Maria Andoloro, "Il Liber Pontificalis et le questione delle immagini da Sergio I a Adriano I." Her views will have to await confirmation, but if there is anything to them, they would point to an extremely politic gesture on Hadrian's part, particularly because, as Florentine Mütherich and Henry Mayr-Hartung have argued, it is very difficult to show that the *LC* had any clear impact on Frankish art; see, respectively, "I Libri Carolini e la miniatura carolingia"; and "Charlemagne as a Patron of Art."
53. *Eginhard, Vie de Charlemagne*, chap. 19, ed. and trans. Louis Halphen, 4th ed. (Paris, 1967), p. 60.
54. The work has a general preface, and then books 2 through 4 have briefer individual prefaces. The books contain the following number of chapters: bk. 1 = 30; bk. 2 = 31; bk. 3 = 31; bk. 4 = 28.
55. *LC* 1.9, pp. 26–28.
56. *LC* 1.10, 1.12, 1.13, 1.15, 1.16, 1.17, 1.18, 1.21, pp. 28–29, 31–32, 32–33, 34–37, 37–39, 39–42, 42–44, 48–49.
57. *LC* 1.22, 1.23, 1.25, 1.26, 1.29, 1.30, 2.1–2, 2.3, 2.4, 2.5, 2.7–8, pp. 50–52, 53–54, 54–55, 56–57, 57–59, 60, 63–64, 64–65, 65–66, 66–68,

69. For a discussion of the extensive corrections in this section of the *LC*, see Freeman, "Further Studies I–II," pp. 214–15.

58. For some examples: *LC* 1.9, 1.29, 2.1, pp. 26–28, 57–59, 63.

59. *LC* 1.5, 1.15, 1.17, 1.18, 1.19, 1.20, pp. 18–19, 34–37, 39–42, 42–44, 44–45, 48. Most of the passages cited in n. 57 are relevant here as well. In fact, virtually every chapter in books 1 and 2 concerns exegetical matters.

60. John J. Contreni, "Carolingian Biblical Studies," esp. pp. 71–77; Robert E. McNally, *The Bible in the Early Middle Ages*, pp. 20ff., esp.: "The Carolingian renaissance can be characterized as a rebirth of the Christian aspiration for biblical spirituality and biblical studies" (p. 20).

61. The three sources that spell out most clearly the contours of Charlemagne's program are: the preface to the *Admonitio generalis* (MGH, Capit., no. 22, ed. Alfred Boretius, vol. 1 [Hannover, 1883], pp. 53–54); the *Epistola de litteris colendis* (ibid., no. 29, p. 79); and the cyclical letter sent out with Paul the Deacon's revision of the lectionary (ibid., no. 30, pp. 80–81). For the wider context of Charlemagne's educational program, see Contreni's chapter in this volume, chap. 3, and the literature cited by him.

62. *Admonitio generalis*, MGH, Capit., no. 22, ed. Boretius, 1:53–54. The preface to the *Admonitio* is almost certainly the work of Alcuin; see Friedrich-Carl Scheibe, "Alcuin und die Admonitio Generalis." Bullough accepts Scheibe's arguments; see his "Alcuin and the Kingdom of Heaven," p. 24; and "*Aula Renovata:* The Carolingian Court before the Aachen Palace," p. 294 (repr. in Bullough, *Carolingian Renewal*, p. 142). I do not share the reservations of Rosamond McKitterick, *The Frankish Church and the Carolingian Reforms, 789–895*, p. 1. I wish to thank Katy Cubitt and Patrick Wormald for interesting and helpful discussions of this matter.

63. *Epistolae variorum Carolo Magno regnante scriptae*, no. 7, ed. Dümmler, MGH, Epp. 4 (Berlin, 1895), p. 503.

64. Heinrich Fichtenau, "Byzanz und die Pfalz zu Aachen," pp. 25–26; Horst Appuhn, "Zum Thron Karls des Grossen," pp. 127–29; and Roderich Schmidt, "Zur Geschichte des fränkischen Königsthrons."

65. *Alcvini Epistolae*, no. 145, ed. Dümmler, MGH, Epp. 4:235.

66. *Pauli et Petri Diaconorum Carmina*, no. 14, ed. Ernst Dümmler, MGH, Poetae 1 (Berlin, 1881), p. 52. See Fichtenau, "Pfalz," p. 29 and n. 144.

67. Most famously in the dedicatory verses to the Dagulf Psalter: MGH, Poetae 1:90–91; and in the poem by Angilbert with the frequent refrain "David amat vates," ibid., pp. 360–63. There is a Latin text and English translation of this poem in Peter Godman, *Poetry of the Carolingian Renaissance*, pp. 112–19. For the date of the Dagulf Psalter, see Lawrence Nees's review of Kurt Holter, ed., *Der goldene Psalter "Dagulf Psalter,"* in *Art Bulletin* 67 (1985): 681–90. Another David appellation from the same period may be found in *Alcvini Epistolae*, no. 41, ed. Dümmler, MGH, Epp. 4:84.

68. Peter Godman, *Poets and Emperors: Frankish Politics and Carolingian Poetry*, pp. 65–66.

69. *LC* 1.1, p. 9.

70. Fichtenau, "Pfalz," pp. 30, 32–34.

71. *Codex Carolinus*, no. 39, ed. Wilhelm Gundlach, MGH, Epp. 3 (Berlin, 1892), p. 552.
72. *Lex Salica*, ed. Karl Augustus Eckhardt, MGH, Legum Sectio I, Legum Nationum Germanicarum, vol. 4, pt. 2 (Hannover, 1969), pp. 1–9.
73. *LC* 1.19, p. 44. On the Franks as a New Israel, see Eugen Ewig, "Zum christlichen Königsgedanken im Frühmittelalter," pp. 39–45; and Robert Folz, *The Coronation of Charlemagne 25 December 800*, pp. 97–100.
74. For some examples: *Admonitio generalis*, MGH, Capit., no. 22, chap. 62, ed. Boretius, 1:58; *Annales regni Francorum, anno* 791, ed. Kurze, p. 88; Paulinus of Aquileia, *Libellus adversus Elipandum,* ed. Werminghoff, MGH, Concilia, pt. 1, p. 142; *Alcvini Epistolae,* no. 41, ed. Dümmler, MGH, Epp. 4:84. Claudio Leonardi has developed a fascinating argument for the centrality of Alcuin to the universalizing and historicizing efforts at the court; see his "Alcuino e la scuola palatina: Le ambizioni di una cultura unitaria," 1:459–96. Surely Alcuin had little to teach Theodulf along these lines.
75. *LC* 2.25, pp. 84–85.
76. *LC* 2.30–31, pp. 92–102, esp. 95–96. The ultimate source for this point of view is the work of Augustine, esp. *De doctrina christiana.*
77. So McKitterick, "Text and Image in the Carolingian World."
78. *LC* 1.5, p. 19.
79. *LC* 3.4, 3.6, 3.7, 3.10, 3.17, 3.18, 3.19, 3.20, 3.26, pp. 113–15, 116–19, 119–20, 122–23, 138–40, 140–42, 143–45, 158–61.
80. *LC* 2.17, p. 77.
81. For example, in *LC* 2.27, p. 87, Theodulf criticizes the Greeks for claiming that the body and blood of Christ were images. In fact, at Second Nicaea the Council of Hiereia was condemned for this teaching. Another example concerns the refutation in 787 of the 754 teachings by the deacon Epiphanios, who was taken by the Carolingians to have advanced the very argument he was refuting; see *LC* 4.15, pp. 201–2.
82. *LC* 2.17, p. 76, contains an admission that the Franks know neither Gregory of Nyssa nor his works, while 2.20, p. 79, admits unfamiliarity with a book of Cyril of Alexandria.
83. *LC, Praef.*, p. 3.
84. *LC* 2.9, p. 70. This is the basic argument of *LC*; cf. *Praef.*, p. 3; 2.13, 3.16, pp. 73, 138.
85. *LC* 1.17, p. 41.
86. *LC* 1.23, p. 51.
87. *LC* 1.29, p. 57.
88. *LC* 4.2, p. 175.
89. *LC, Praef.*, p. 4.
90. *LC* 2.23, pp. 81–82. On the actual meaning of Gregory's letter, see Celia M. Chazelle, "Pictures, Books and the Illiterate: Pope Gregory I's Letters to Serenus of Marseilles." For a brilliant discussion of a thousand years of interpretation of Gregory's letters, see Lawrence G. Duggan, "Was Art Really the 'Book of the Illiterate'?"
91. *LC* 1.18, 2.21, 3.16, pp. 40–42, 80, 136–38. For an illuminating

discussion of this subject, see David Appleby, "Holy Relic and Holy Image: Saints' Relics in the Western Controversy over Images in the Eighth and Ninth Centuries."

92. *LC*, bk. 4, *praef.*, p. 169.

93. *LC* 4.2, p. 175.

94. *LC* 3.16, 3.24, 4.3, 4.16, pp. 136, 153–55, 177, 203.

95. *LC* 4.16, p. 203, is a clear presentation of this argument, but it comes up again and again. For an interpretation of the place of these holy objects in the *LC*, see Chazelle, "Matter, Spirit and Image in the *Libri Carolini*," esp. pp. 165–70.

96. Bullough, *The Age of Charlemagne*, p. 111, stresses that the Carolingians could, and here probably did, engage in willful misunderstanding.

97. *LC* 1.20, p. 45–46.

98. *LC* 3.2, pp. 108–9.

99. *LC* 3.2, pp. 109–10.

100. Bastgen, "Das Kapitulare Karls des Grossen über die Bilder oder dis sogennanten Libri Carolini," pp. 664–66; Hans von Schubert, *Geschichte der christlichen Kirche im Frühmittelalter*, p. 384; and Hauck, *Kirchengeschichte Deutschlands*, 2:343. From these basic sources the idea lived on for a generation or more in many general works.

101. Barion, "Der kirchenrechtliche Charakter des Konzils von Frankfurt 794," esp. pp. 148–51; and Werner Ohnsorge, "Orthodoxus Imperator: Vom religiösen Motiven für das Kaisertum Karls des Grossen." This is perhaps the reigning view today. Often it is coupled with the observation that no Frank had been present at the earlier ecumenical councils and yet the decisions of those councils were fully accepted by the Franks.

102. *LC*, *Praef.*, 3.11, 3.12, 3.14, 4.13, 4.28, pp. 3, 123–27, 130–33, 193–99, 227–29.

103. de Vries, "Die Struktur der Kirche."

104. Hermann Josef Sieben, *Die Konzilsidee der alten Kirche*, pp. 307–43. Bullough, "Alcuin and the Kingdom of Heaven," pp. 36–38, accepts Sieben's arguments. On the pentarchy the key study is Vittorio Peri, "La pentarchià: Istituzione ecclesiale (IV–VII sec.) e teoria canonico-teologia," 1:209–311. See also Klaus Schatz, "Oecuménicité du concile et structure de l'église à Nicée II et dans les *Livres carolins*." For another view of the complex problems involved in interpreting the scriptural and patristic *paradosis*, see Walter Brandmüller, "*Traditio Scripturae Interpres*: The Teaching of the Councils on the Right Interpretation of Scripture up to the Council of Trent."

There is an interesting puzzle here. The Synod of Frankfurt seems not to have embraced the synodal theory of the *LC*; see Wilfried Hartmann, *Die Synoden der Karolingerzeit im Frankenreich und in Italien*, pp. 105–10. Certainly not all Frankish bishops would have accepted such a novel view, and the *LC* was directed more against the Greeks than against a traditional Western reading of the Christian past. It may be that the views expressed in the *LC* were Theodulf's own and very much rooted in Spanish traditions; see Elisabeth Dahlhaus-Berg, *Nova Antiquitas et Antiqua Novitas: Typologische*

Exegese und isidorianisches Geschichtsbild bei Theodulf von Orléans, pp. 199–200; and Consuelo Maria Aherne, "Late Visigothic Bishops, Their Schools and the Transmission of Culture." Be that as it may, the argument that was developed in the *LC* is still plainly to be seen and, although the last chapter of the work adopted a slightly more traditional line on conciliar history (4.28), the earlier and more radical chapters were neither altered nor expunged; they must have won some adherents.

105. *LC* 4.8, 11, 12, pp. 187–88, 190–92, 192–93. These are good, representative examples of "scrutiny." *Ratio* (see bk. 4, *praef.*, p. 169) is what drives the whole scrutiny. It is the "reason" for it, the "reason" that guides it, and the goal or objective toward which it tends.

106. *LC* 3.11, p. 123: "Uniuscuiusque partis ecclesiae."

107. *LC* 1.5, p. 19.

108. *LC* 1.6, pp. 20–22.

109. *LC* 2.13, p. 73. It is significant that the story being told is first of all challenged as potentially inauthentic and then held up as an example of an emperor properly deferring to the teaching office of the pope.

110. *LC* 1.6, p. 21.

111. *LC* 2.23, 3.2, pp. 81–82, 109. Invidious comparisons with Tarasius could not have been missed.

112. *LC* 4.10, p. 189. Of course, the "Gelasius" in question was the pseudo-Gelasian decree *De libris recipiendis et non recipiendis,* but the Franks, like everyone else, regarded this text as both authentic and authoritative. See McKitterick, *The Carolingians and the Written Word*, pp. 202–4.

113. *LC* 1.6, pp. 20, 22.

114. *LC* 1.6, p. 21.

115. For general discussion of these liturgical exchanges, see Cyrille Vogel, "Les Echanges liturgiques entre Rome et les pays francs jusqu'à l'époque de Charlemagne"; and Vogel, "Les Motifs de la romanisation du culte sous Pépin le Bref (751–768) et Charlemagne (774–814)." The greatest product of these interactions was the so-called Gregorian Sacramentary sent to Charlemagne by Hadrian in 786/7. The text has been edited with copious commentary by Jean Deshusses, *Le Sacramentaire grégorien: Les Principales Formes d'après les plus anciennes manuscrits* (2nd ed., vol. 1, 1979). Against the traditional date of 784/5, see Bullough, "Ethnic History and the Carolingians: An Alternative Reading of Paul the Deacon's *Historia Langobardorum*," p. 102, n. 6 (repr. in his *Carolingian Renewal*, pp. 99 and 116, n. 6). The redating itself depends on the redating of *Codex Carolinus,* no. 89, ed. Gundlach, MGH, Epp. 3:626. In light of all else, it is surely not without significance that the Carolingians requested not only a Roman but indeed a Gregorian sacramentary.

116. Hubert Mordek, "Kirchenrechtliche Autoritäten im Frühmittelalter." Substantial extracts from the collection were promulgated in 789 as part of the *Admonitio generalis*; MGH, Capit., no. 22, ed. Boretius, 1:52–57.

117. *Epistula ad regem Karolum de monasterio sancti Benedicti directa et a Paolo dictata*, ed. Kassius Hallinger, Corpus Consuetudinum Monasticarum, vol. 1 (Siegburg, 1963), pp. 157–75.

118. *Codex Carolinus, Praef.*, ed. Gundlach, MGH, Epp. 3:476. The text says it was also intended to collect the letters "de imperio," but none of these survive in the two extant manuscripts of the *Codex Carolinus.* It seems safe to suggest that the plan was to contrast good and bad rulers in their faithfulness and faithlessness to Rome. Dahlhaus-Berg, *Nova Antiquitas,* pp. 187–88, has drawn an explicit connection between the *LC* and the *Codex Carolinus.* So too Walter Mohr, *Die karolingische Reichsidee*, p. 47.

119. See Thomas F. X. Noble, "Literacy and the Papal Government in Late Antiquity and the Early Middle Ages," pp. 90–91 and n. 38.

120. *Pauli Warnefridi Liber de episcopis Mettensibus,* ed. George Henry Pertz, MGH, SS 2 (Hannover, 1829), pp. 260–70.

121. Otto Gerhard Oexle, "Die Karolinger und die Stadt des heiligen Arnulf," pp. 299–301.

122. I owe most to Richard Krautheimer, "The Carolingian Revival of Early Christian Architecture." See also Carol Heitz, "More Romano: Problèmes d'architecture et liturgie carolingiennes." Artistic and architectural connections between Aachen and Rome are given their fullest, though by no means definitive, treatment by Mario D'Onofrio, *Roma e Aquisgrana.* Issues pertaining to Aachen have not been comprehensively revisited since Ludwig Falkenstein, "Zwischenbilanz zur aachener Pfalzenforschung." For general details, see Kenneth John Conant, *Carolingian and Romanesque Architecture, 800 to 1200*, pp. 43–55.

123. Bullough, "Roman Books and Carolingian *Renovatio.*"

124. Josef Fleckenstein, *Die Bildungsreform Karls des Grossen als Verwicklichung der norma rectitudinis.*

125. MGH, Capit., no. 14, ed. Boretius, 1:33.

126. Chrodegang, *Regula Canonicorum,* prologue, chap. 20, PL 89:1057c.

127. Against the still widely influential Haller (and all his predecessors), *Das Papsttum,* 2:15, I prefer: Etienne Delaruelle, "Charlemagne et l'église," esp. pp. 187–89; Folz, *Coronation of Charlemagne*, p. 94; and Marcel Pacaut, *La Papauté, des origines au concile de Trente*, pp. 76–77.

128. *LC* 1.1, 2, 3, pp. 8–16; 2.31, pp. 130–32; 4.5, p. 180.

129. Ewig, "Zum christlichen Königsgedanken," esp. pp. 59–61; Janet L. Nelson, "The Lord's Anointed and the People's Choice: Carolingian Royal Ritual," with abundant references to the older literature.

130. *LC* 1.22, p. 50.

131. *LC* 1.3, 4.20, pp. 14–16, 212–13.

132. Otto Hiltbrunner, "Die Heiligkeit des Kaisers." The full and brilliant study of these issues is Otto Treitinger, *Die oströmische Kaiser- und Reichsidee nach ihrer Gestaltung im höfischen Zeremoniell.* Stimulating is Nelson, "Symbols in Context: Rulers' Inauguration Rituals in Byzantium and the West in the Early Middle Ages."

133. *LC* 3.15, p. 135.

134. Dahlhaus-Berg, *Nova Antiquitas,* pp. 196–97.

135. *LC* 2.13, p. 73.

136. *Codex Carolinus*, no. 60, ed. Gundlach, MGH, Epp. 3:587.

137. Fichtenau, "Byzanz und die Pfalz," pp. 7–16. The existence in

Charlemagne's time of a *maiestas* in the Aachen cupola was challenged by Hermann Schnitzler, "Das Kuppelmosaik der aachener Pfalzkapelle." Schnitzler's arguments were refuted by H. Schrade, "Zum Kuppelmosaik der aachener Pfalzkapelle." The existence of the *maiestas* is accepted by J. M. Wallace-Hadrill, *Early Germanic Kingship in England and on the Continent*, pp. 194–95; and by Bullough, "'Imagines Regum' and Their Significance in the Early Medieval West," pp. 241–42 (repr. in his *Carolingian Renewal*, p. 57).

138. Franz Kampers, "Rex et Sacerdos"; Fichtenau, "Karl der Grosse und das Kaisertum," pp. 279–80; Ewig, "Zum christlichen Königsgedanken," pp. 57ff.; Karl F. Morrison, *The Two Kingdoms: Ecclesiology in Carolingian Political Thought*, pp. 26–36; Dahlhaus-Berg, *Nova Antiquitas*, p. 196; and Nelson, "The Lord's Anointed," pp. 154–57.

139. Krautheimer, "Carolingian Revival," p. 236.

140. The key study remains Ewig, "Das Bild Constantins des Grossen in den ersten Jahrhunderten des abendländischen Mittelalters."

141. Robert Markus, *Saeculum: History and Society in the Theology of St. Augustine*, pp. 3–4.

142. Arnaldo Momigliano, "Pagan and Christian Historiography in the Fourth Century A.D.," p. 110.

143. Karl Hauck, "Von einer spätantiken Randkultur zum karolingischen Europa"; and Wolfgang Fritze, "Universalis gentium confessio: Formeln, Träger und Wege universalmissionarischen Denkens im 7. Jahrhundert."

144. A. J. Gurevich, *Categories of Medieval Culture*, p. 140.

145. Dahlhaus-Berg, *Nova Antiquitas*, p. 201.

146. Frederick S. Paxton, *Christianizing Death: The Creation of a Ritual Process in Early Medieval Europe*, pp. 118–19.

147. Mordek, "Kirchenrechtlichen Authoritäten," pp. 249–50.

148. McKitterick, *Frankish Church*, p. 66.

149. McKitterick, *Carolingians and the Written Word*, pp. 165–210, esp. 196–98.

150. The former by Schmandt, *Studien*, p. 1, and the latter by Gero, "Libri Carolini," p. 9.

8

Conclusion:
Visions of Carolingian Education, Past, Present, and Future

DAVID GANZ

I n his remarkable life of St. Helena, the mother of the emperor Constantine, the Carolingian abbot of Hautvillers offered a challenging view of the goals of educational inquiry. In his account of Helena's search for the true cross, Abbot Altmann, a pupil of John Scottus Eriugena, explained how Christian education could achieve what the pagans had failed to accomplish. He describes how, while a pagan, Helena strove to explore the cults of all races, observing their diversity of customs and rites. She wished to understand the word of God, the creation of the world, the origin and immortality of the soul, and the coming judgment and resurrection of the body. To find answers she first consulted Jews and then Christians, and, after her son's conversion, she was guided to the relics of the true cross.[1]

Helena's quest is not unlike the shared search that brought some two hundred scholars to The Ohio State University in Columbus in February 1989 to hear and discuss the important series of papers on Carolingian education and learning that inspired this volume. Their questions were about the context, schools, patristic tradition, art, music, and search for ideology in the Carolingian world.

Too many accounts of Carolingian education and learning have ignored the tensions between spiritual fulfillment and resistance to ecclesiastical authority, or between the values of monks and the aristocratic world they often left. Richard E. Sullivan, who has established Carolingian studies in

North America on a secure footing among colleagues as closely linked by loyalty and friendship as were Alcuin's pupils, has not shied away from such questions. Defining the intellectual program of the monastery of Hautvillers, where relics of Helena were preserved, Altmann praised the program's height of speculation, broad charity, and profundity of wisdom, both divine and human, all of which raised the monastery above Athens as a center of learning. Similar aims have shaped this volume. It is important to recognize the change in ideological approach that those aims imply, the new directions for research that have emerged from the explorations of Carolingian cultural activity in the past, and the ultimate significance of the studies included in this volume.

※

The Carolingian cultural achievement is presently evaluated through the use of a tacit ideology, long in the making and sustained by the selective quotation of those Carolingian sources that tend to develop and establish the myths this ideology entails. Textbooks neither explain nor justify the term "Carolingian renaissance," a phrase that has had an unusually long life as a code signifying that something significant happened in the cultural realm during the reign of the Carolingian dynasty. Those primers simply cite royal pronouncements commanding that a *renovatio* should be under-taken and, as proof that it was, offer comments to the effect that Einhard imitated Suetonius or that Charlemagne's favorite book was Augustine's *City of God*. Students of art history are shown some dozen images of Ca-rolingian works of art ostensibly linking Carolingian artists with ancient models, examples that have barely changed since the appearance of Franz von Reber's *History of Medieval Art*, translated into English in 1887.[2]

Because the historiography of Carolingian education and learning has more frequently relied on views that have been inherited than it has con-cerned itself with tracing or challenging those views, scholars have often ignored those who have chosen to doubt the myth of Charlemagne the lover of wisdom and the fiction of careers open to talent derived from a ideologically inspired reading of Notker's description of the clientele at-tending the palace school.[3] Too often those investigators have failed to see that what they have inherited has stemmed from evaluations of the Caro-lingian accomplishment cast in terms of the needs and ideologies of those who produced these interpretations. One result is that the Carolingian achievement is now the subject of reification: concepts such as literacy, dramatic narrative, or "the social function of *grammatica*" are applied to the sources in an effort to discover original insights. In delight at such originality, factual errors and distortions pass unchallenged, cocooned in the language of indefinitude.[4]

As Chris Wickham has recently reminded us, "As society and politics changed, the social memory of Charlemagne changed to fit."[5] By surveying the changes in social memory that Charlemagne's educational legacy underwent, it is possible to see what different epochs have found useful in that legacy. The medieval legend of Charlemagne, nurtured by bellettrists, polemicists, and visual artists, had little to say about education and learning until that legend became the property of historians, but one of the liturgical lections used at St. Emmeran in Regensberg from the fifteenth century praised Charles's love of letters and his attempts to learn to write;[6] and Alexander von Roes, in his *Memoriale de prerogativa imperii Romani*, started the myth that Charlemagne had founded the University of Paris.[7]

The finest tribute to Charlemagne's educational achievement may be Montaigne's sentence: "In this way Cyrus can be honoured by his farming and Charlemagne for his eloquence and knowledge of good letters."[8] A brief survey of the historiography of Charles the patron of learning reveals the biases and hopes of his admirers.[9] The most constant feature is the use of Notker Balbulus's stories of the Irishmen who arrived on Charlemagne's shores selling wisdom and of Charlemagne the inspector of schools.[10] Albertus Krantz was the first to praise Charlemagne as the man who brought the liberal arts to the Saxons.[11] The first extended account of Charlemagne's educational policies was written by Jean Launoy in 1672; it ended the myth of the Carolingian University of Paris, but suggested that Charlemagne was responsible for many cathedral schools.[12] Jacques Bénigne Bossuet's *Discours sur l'histoire universelle*, published in 1681, not only validated this view but also made it widely accessible. In 1750 Frobenius Forster, who had been professor of philosophy at Salzburg, was appointed librarian of St. Emmeran and strove to produce an edition of the works of Alcuin as a part of the work of the Societas Literaria Benedictina. In 1777 his edition appeared, and subsequent work has confirmed the quality of his texts. Frobenius's introduction praises Charlemagne's attack on entrenched barbarism and ignorance and explains Alcuin's share in this program.[13]

Frobenius's concern for texts was rare in the eighteenth century. Rather than labor with the sources, historians were inclined to dismiss the distant Carolingian past in terms of the cultural values of the Enlightenment. In a general history, William Robertson's *History of the Reign of Charles V*, published in 1769, the outline in the opening chapter of the progress of society in Europe gives Charlemagne a single sentence. Like Alfred he "gave his subjects a short glimpse of light and knowledge. But the ignorance of the age was too powerful for their efforts and institutions."[14] Voltaire had already belittled the emperor in his *Essai sur les moeurs* (1769), but despite stressing Charlemagne's illiterate cruelty, Voltaire conceded that "he conceived by the force of his genius how much literature was necessary."[15] In chapter 49 of his *History of the Decline and Fall of the Roman Empire*, Gibbon, relying on Gabriel Gaillard's four-volume *Histoire de Charlemagne* (Paris, 1782), noted that "the literary merits of Charlemagne are attested by the foundation of schools. . . . The grammar and logic, the music and astronomy, of the times were only cultivated as the handmaids of superstition; but the curiosity of the human mind must ultimately tend to its improvement, and the encouragement of learning reflects the purest and most pleasing lustre on the character of Charlemagne."[16] In 1818 Henry Hallam affirmed that "a strong sympathy for intellectual excellence was the leading characteristic of Charlemagne."[17] Leaders of the Enlightenment saw Charlemagne as a precursor of their heavenly city, but they acknowledged, indeed celebrated, the deep gulf between his cultural ideals and their own.

Hegel in his *Vorlesungen über die Philosophie der Geschichte* (lectures given from 1822 to 1831, published posthumously in 1837) devoted a chapter to Charlemagne's empire. He described how the emperor sought to restore learning, which was almost completely decayed, by requiring the establishment of schools in towns and villages.[18] But Hegel explains that Charlemagne could not create a state; this would have required reactions, by nations and individuals, to the continual lies that ruled the Middle Ages and a repudiation of the division of reality that governed the medieval worldview.[19]

Charlemagne had been compared to Peter the Great and Napoleon,[20] but his importance as a political figure increased as a result of the case advanced by François Guizot and Jules Michelet. In his lectures of 1828–30 on European civilization, Guizot's bourgeois-oriented history saw Charlemagne as the leader of "the battle against the barbaric state" and the embodiment of "the spirit of civilization."[21] In 1833 Michelet, inspired by Vico's historical categories, published his own Collège de France lectures as the start of his *Histoire de France*. Michelet's account of Charlemagne in book 2 has left unacknowledged traces on much subsequent historiography, but its evaluation was more critical than many suspect: "No less pedantic and barren was the attempt at literary reform directed by Alcuin." Michelet retells Notker's story of the Irishmen who sold wisdom, but after many extracts from Notker his verdict remains: "While Char-

lemagne discoursed on theology, dreamed of the Roman Empire and studied grammar, the domination of the Franks collapsed little by little." In the
reign of Charles the Bald "feudalism was founded; scholastic philosophy
was at least being prepared for," as evidenced by Paschasius Radbertus,
Gottschalk, and John Scottus, who was "the renewal of the free Celtic
spirit."[22]

Michelet inspired J.-J. Ampère's literary history of France, and in volume 3 Ampère treated Charlemagne's renaissance, which he saw as the result of the influence of one man.[23] The *De litteris colendis* was "the charter
of modern thought." Charlemagne aimed at universal instruction, and unlike Napoleon his achievement was a lasting one. "Charlemagne latinized
the West."[24]

In A. F. Ozanam's *La Civilisation chrétienne chez les Francs*, Charlemagne
is clearly a model fulfilling a mission relevant for Catholics opposed to
the revolutionary ideology of Michelet.[25] Avoiding the dangers of lay
power and armed with the heroism of the Christian monarch, he converts
pagans and seeks the peaceful glories of letters; he is the instrument of
providence and humanity. Ozanam repeats Ampère's translation of the *De
litteris colendis* and concludes that "the destiny of the human spirit was assured."[26] In his *Charlemagne et sa cour*, B. Hauréau, following Ampère,
sees Charlemagne as the restorer of arts and letters and devotes a chapter
to his palace school.[27]

Arno Borst has traced the development of Leopold von Ranke's view of
Charlemagne as reflected in his lectures delivered from 1826 to 1865. In
1825 Ranke regarded Charles's greatest achievement as the conquest of
Saxony. After reading Michelet, he defended Charlemagne's greatness
against French attacks, and he valued the court as a cultural center and
Charlemagne's more systematic revival of culture.[28] In a less nationalistic
vein, Jacob Burckhardt in 1851 placed Charlemagne in his typology of renaissances, and in lectures on Charlemagne he regarded Carolingian education as "the soul of Karl's system." While the value of Charlemagne's
culture might be challenged, it was certain that between 732 and 830 culture was again possible.[29]

The first treatment in English of Charlemagne's achievement in education was the prize essay by J. Bass Mullinger, *The Schools of Charles the
Great and the Restoration of Education in the Ninth Century* (London,
1877). The subject was chosen for the Kaye Prize at Cambridge as a question "relating to ancient Ecclesiastical History." Mullinger claimed that he
was treating of "the true boundary line between ancient and modern
history." Separate chapters discuss Alcuin, Hrabanus, Lupus, and John

Scottus. "The younger members of the Palace School seem to have required to be at once instructed and amused, much after the way that would now seem well adapted to a night-school of Somersetshire rustics."[30] He relied chiefly on Ampère, Francis Monnier's study entitled *Alcuin et Charlemagne* (2nd ed., Paris, 1863), and Léon Maître's *Les Ecoles épiscopales et monastiques de l'occident depuis Charlemagne jusqu'à Philippe-Auguste (768–1180)* (Paris, 1866).[31]

The names Georg Wilhelm Pertz and Ranke evoke a shift in the approach toward the history of Carolingian education. A part of their legacy included the editions of Carolingian capitularies, charters, letters, poems, and annals that are one of the glories of the Monumenta Germaniae Historica.[32] Those editions were the fruit of a critical approach that focused on reconstructing authentic versions of historical sources through a rigorous methodology applied to manuscript remains. The sharpened focus of scholarly attention on the sources and their decipherment gave new impetus to reconstructing the past based on an objective gleaning of the "facts" from the sources and the arrangement of those facts into a narrative that would reveal the past "as it actually happened."

The fruits of the change heralded by Pertz and Ranke were reflected in the work of scholars who were among the editors of Carolingian texts. Ernst Dümmler, for instance, published a general history of the East Frankish kingdom that reflected an effort to embrace all the data contained in the sources into a narrative account that would embrace the totality of Carolingian civilization.[33] Along another line, Ludwig Traube trained students to explore the manuscript evidence and reconstruct the transmission of classical texts. The study of Carolingian education was transformed by new evidence of how texts were read and which texts were read. Traube was a close friend of E. von Steinmeyer, whose systematic edition of Old High German glosses revealed what evidence survived of the activities of the schoolroom, and an admirer of Johann K. Zeuss and Heinrich Zimmer's collection of Irish glosses, some of which were written in Carolingian Europe.[34] The study of vernacular glosses, as Traube recognized, was crucial to understanding the language of Carolingian education.

The first chapters entitled "The Carolingian Renaissance" are found in works by Gabriel Monod (1898) and Karl Lamprecht (1891). While Monod is concerned with Charlemagne's role in promoting and leading the revival of learning, Lamprecht offers an important and original analysis of Carolingian culture, including a long section on Carolingian art and especially its choice of ornament. Lamprecht was concerned with the problems of expressing ideas in Latin rather than the vernacular, and with the veneration of the formal content of education in which phrases were more important than meanings. "The mental sphere of the Germans of this time was still completely intuition, the coexistence of all things, but not understanding, not the superimposition of one thing over another." He noted that Old High German borrowed from Latin only for its religious vocabulary, and he contrasted the culture of the eastern and western parts of the empire.[35]

The impact of the Nazi triumph in 1933 left traces in the writings of Hermann Aubin, Albert Brackmann, Johannes Haller, Feodor Schneider, and Gerd Tellenbach, who all saw Charlemagne as the embodiment of "a chiefly Germanic world" ("ein vornehmlich germanische Welt").[36] Hitler noted that "the German people did not emerge solely as a product of the classical idea and Christianity, but as a product of force, the classical idea, and Christianity." For Charlemagne, "Cultural activity was collective activity" ("Kulturarbeit sei Zusammenarbeit").[37] In 1935 Karl Hampe could affirm that "he [Charlemagne] was far too much an original Germanic layman to be absorbed totally in this ecclesiastical-classical educational ideal," a view Carl Erdmann had the courage to oppose.[38]

In the face of such orthodoxy, the courage and capacity for change of Hermann Heimpel were neither common nor influential.[39] Those concerned with the history of Carolingian education also must pay tribute to scholars who were victims of the darker side of this orthodoxy: to the work of Traube, long denied tenure because of his Jewish origins, and to that of Wilhelm Levison, excluded from German universities after 1935.[40] Charlemagne's 1200th birthday was celebrated on 2 April 1942, after historians had explained how his empire and his eastern campaigns were models.[41] After the Second World War, Charlemagne became the model of all those who sought a united Europe; the effort to evaluate his work from this perspective culminated in the Aachen exhibition of 1965 and the "Karl der Grosse Festschrift."[42] Since 1950 the city of Aachen has awarded a Charlemagne prize for services to Europe, whose recipients for the most part have been conservative politicians.[43]

It appears, then, beyond question that to write about Charlemagne entails an ideological stance. It might be argued that happy are those who are unconscious of how they attained such a position. But this quick review of the various ideological perspectives that have been brought to bear on Carolingian educational and cultural history in the past suggests that consciousness on the part of any scholar of his or her ideological bent and its

potential impact on the reconstruction of that history might expose some
of the myths that still cause distortion in our understanding of the Carolingian educational and cultural achievement.

⚜

Despite being pulled one way or another by ideological concerns, the
long-standing effort to assess the nature and import of Carolingian educational and cultural activity has left many matters still open for investigation; some of them seem likely to occupy the major attention of
Carolingian scholars in the foreseeable future.

The effort to see the Carolingian educational and cultural scene in holistic terms has challenged a succession of scholars to try their hand at syntheses. In 1924 Erna Patzelt, a student of Alfons Dopsch, published the
only book devoted to the Carolingian renaissance, making a case for continuity instead of innovation.[44] M. L. W. Laistner did much the same in his
survey of thought and letters in Western Europe from 500 to 900, first
published in 1931; his effort was prompted by the lack of any work in
English that did justice to "the immense debt we owe to the Carolingian
Age for the preservation of classical and post-classical Latin literature, that
era and the centuries that preceded it were a formative period without
which it is impossible either to understand or to explain the full achievement of medieval culture at its zenith."[45] Walter Ullmann, in his Birkbeck
lectures of 1968–69, emphasized that the Carolingian renaissance cannot
be seen in isolation from Charlemagne's policies for the reform of society.[46] Another important recent synthesis is that of Pierre Riché, who set
the Carolingian renaissance in a continuous line of development that highlighted evolutionary developments within the Carolingian era.[47]

Akin to these general syntheses have been recent efforts, often collaborative, to reconstruct a picture of Carolingian cultural life at particular
moments during the eighth and ninth centuries.[48] Historians continue
their efforts to fix Carolingian cultural activity more firmly in the larger
context of Carolingian history and to assess the impact of the Carolingian
renaissance on society as a whole.[49] Beyond doubt, the effort to see the
Carolingian cultural achievement whole and in context will continue to
challenge scholars.

Access to good editions of Carolingian sources remains an important
item on the agenda of Carolingianists to which contemporary scholars
continue to respond. Postwar editors have made new texts available, especially the writings of Gottschalk and Paschasius Radbertus and the Latin
glosses to Bede's computistical writings.[50] Editors are increasingly taking

advantage of computer technology to expedite analyses of the sources.[51] The number of translations of Carolingian sources into modern languages appears to be increasing, perhaps a reflection not only of a decline in competence in Latin but also an expanding interest in Carolingian civilization. What the impact of reading Carolingian sources in a modern language might be on the interpretation of Carolingian cultural history provides ground for interesting speculation.[52] Perhaps the greatest challenge facing scholars interested in Carolingian cultural life is to increase the availability of quality reproductions of Carolingian visual and aural sources and to expand the competence of Carolingian scholars in general in utilizing such materials.[53]

The most fruitful developments in the study of Carolingian education have been the attempts to reconstruct the libraries and intellectual life of major cultural centers at Tours, St. Gall, Freising, Tegernsee, Regensburg and Salzburg, Würzburg, Lorsch, Laon, Corbie, Auxerre, and Fleury.[54] This work has been shaped by the profound knowledge of the paleography and contents of Carolingian manuscripts which Bernhard Bischoff accumulated over sixty years; when his catalogue of Carolingian manuscripts is published, systematic comparative studies of Carolingian library growth will become possible.[55] We need to explore how easy or difficult it was for libraries to obtain specific texts and the extent to which there were standard texts for the study of grammar, poetry, and theology.[56]

The history of how particular texts were read and annotated has provided details about the study of grammar, computus, and the classics, and this approach is now being extended to the study of patristic writers. No one has yet compared Carolingian glosses on Martianus Capella or Boethius to those on Virgil in order to explore how far Carolingian readers were still in touch with the late antique legacy of Servius or Donatus, but John J. Contreni has shown that at least one of them put notes on Virgil and Sedulius into the same manuscript.[57] And sometimes glosses on classical authors refer to contemporary events or to the teachings of a Carolingian master.[58] The spread of sets of glosses throughout the Carolingian realms may reveal how few people were involved in close study of texts, but it may also suggest that some texts were widely considered as the best authorities.[59]

But the question of how to identify a "schoolbook" is still unresolved: The presence of glosses need not always entail teaching.[60] And even if we think we have a schoolbook, it does not always lead us into a classroom: we cannot be sure whether Lupus of Ferrières taught anyone other than Heiric of Auxerre.[61] In part the problem results from the nature of our evidence; manuscripts preserve the notes and text of one or more scribes, but references to teaching come chiefly from biographies and letters. The pedagogical handbooks of the Carolingians were concerned with content, not educational practice. The classification of manuscripts, texts, and glosses can reveal how ideas circulated and hint at the contacts between friends and pupils that gave Carolingian education the charm that shared learning retains. Manuscripts of Horace or Juvenal, Priscian or Martianus Capella or Boethius can preserve references to the teachings of named masters. But no one has yet attempted to assemble this evidence.

Recent work has shown that the Carolingian world was fringed with contacts to other traditions. Knowledge of Greek and Hebrew and interest in Slavic and runic writings was never extensive, but often important.[62] While earlier scholars evaluated medieval schools for their preservation and transformation of Latin culture, we are now more ready to set that culture beside its rivals and explore the syncreticisms of Carolingian thinkers. When Rudolf of Fulda used Tacitus to describe the beliefs of his pagan ancestors, he was giving them a legitimacy that an oral culture could not provide.[63] In the same way, when the poets of German biblical epics used the vernacular, they explained, in Latin prefaces, why this was a legitimate activity.[64] The close comparison of their works with the Latin epic and exegetical sources can reveal the clash of two sets of values and the tensions of transferring Christian vocabulary into a language still in the throes of conversion. Carolingianists are often immune to comparative history, but they can learn much from work on education in other worlds.

As the different complexions of schools become clearer, it seems probable that not only the personalities of teachers but the pressures on their teaching affected those complexions. Carolingian education was conceived to meet specific needs, and to study it in terms of an evolutionary paradigm of growing enlightenment is to distort it.

We still need studies of the nature of Carolingian classicism, the reasons for the study and correction of works of Cicero, but also of authors like Valerius Maximus and Aulus Gellius, and the nature of imitation of classical models by Carolingian authors.[65] In the same way, fuller studies of borrowings from particular authors must distinguish between respect for authority and the process of selecting what seemed especially appropriate among a range of possible sources. Only when we can see Carolingian scholars choosing their authorities will we understand their thought. We are far from certain how far we can speak of a canon of authors studied throughout the empire.[66] Too little work has been done on the study of mathematics and natural science, though treatises on computus were some of the most popular school texts.[67] Mathematics was linked to music theory, but musicologists seldom attempt to integrate their discoveries so as to clarify educational procedures.[68]

All too little work on the teaching of medieval medicine has been assimilated by students of Carolingian education. But much of the compiling of medical texts was done in monasteries. Recent work on the Lorscher Arzneibuch has suggested that it was compiled by Richbod, the abbot of Lorsch from 784 to 791. The work contains a history of medicine and its divisions, a list of the *dies aegyptiaci*, tables of medical weights, a list of Greek medicines, and over 560 recipes, including dietary rules, a treatise on the origins of spices, and a work on the preparation of remedies.[69] More than 200 recipes have been lost. Scholars distinguish between the longer and shorter types of recipe and suggest that the latter may have been designed for oral transmission. A selection of the short recipes is found in a Saint Gall manuscript folded in a way that suggests that it was carried by a doctor.[70] It uses a question and answer formula for its first page, so it may also have been used for teaching. The clearest evidence for medical instruction is found in Agnellus's commentary on Galen, which survives in Carolingian manuscripts in Munich and Karlsruhe.[71] This work is clearly designed to treat medicine as one of the liberal arts.

If we contrast Carolingian education with the picture of the twelfth century presented by Peter Classen and his pupils, it becomes possible to specify what the Carolingians failed to achieve.[72] We assume that Carolingian students were less mobile and that their curiosity was more restricted. Nor did they have the same chances to profit from their learning at royal, papal, or episcopal courts. The most crucial distinction is that Carolingian scholars seldom thought of themselves as a group with common interests; instead they were monks, clerics, or bishops. And monastic schools were designed to provide readings for meditation and prayer.

But Carolingian schools, supported by royal and imperial legislation and free from the dramatic expansion and diversity of twelfth-century religious foundations, should have flourished. We have very inadequate information about the people involved in teaching, even in major abbeys.[73] The commentary on the Rule of St. Benedict by Hildemar, a monk of Corbie who taught in northern Italy, gives important information on how oblates were trained and quotes a decree of Pope Eugenius II on the need to learn the liberal arts.[74] But though he describes how bright pupils are to converse with guests about chant, computus, grammar, or some art, the training envisaged is spiritual and not intellectual. The vision of a meritocracy described by Notker was an ideal and not a reality.[75]

✤

Obviously, this brief assessment of current scholarly concerns with respect to the broad area of Carolingian cultural life makes it clear that there is much yet to be done. Not unlike the inhabitants of a crowded Carolingian *villa*, contemporary scholars looking outward from the clearing fashioned by their scholarly predecessors behold a formidable and mysterious forest whose clearance promises its own rewards in terms of understanding better a distant age. It needs hardly be said that now, as has been the case for a long time, Carolingianists are extending their vision and spending their energy moving beyond the settled lands into the unknown. Perhaps we can conclude by asking to what extent and in what ways the chapters in this volume are attuned to received wisdom about Carolingian education and learning and in what ways they reflect a productive foray into the forest to clear new and fertile land.

The studies assembled here are an eloquent testimony to the tensions between the ideal and the real in Carolingian cultural life. Those tensions emerge most vividly when cultural "events" are put in their context. Sullivan has reminded us in general terms that Carolingian learning cannot be seen merely in the idealizing perspective imposed by a search for precedent; it has context. Each of the other studies reinforces this vital point with respect to a specific situation, be it what gave shape to the curriculum of schools, the performance of music, the perception of a revered Biblical scholar, the selection of a program for an art work, or coping with heterodox ideas. To read these chapters in this light will give pause to those who are tempted by the siren call of poststructuralist critical theory to dismiss as irrelevant to the understanding of cultural artifacts the context in which "texts" are set.

These chapters make a strong case that the cultural history of the Carolingian age will be understood more clearly only to the extent that those studying it immerse themselves more fully in an exploration of its context; and conversely, Carolingian civilization in general will be better comprehended only when cultural factors are given a central place in assessing its nature. In making that point, these studies mute some of the intellectual trends that in recent times have spread chaos in the arena of cultural history and point the way toward giving that field new vitality by reassessing the nexus between society and culture.

In adding to his previous helpful accounts of Carolingian teachers and pupils a treatment of the goals of Carolingian education, which includes a discussion of how women were educated, John J. Contreni alerts us to a dimension of Carolingian cultural history that will surely warrant attention in the future.[76] In drawing attention to the place of women in the educational system he invites us to ask whether the circle of people affected in some way by the Carolingian cultural revival was more extensive than heretofore allowed. Once that thought enters our mind, we find ourselves wondering whether the intellectual and artistic creations treated in the other papers were aimed at audiences with whom Carolingianists have heretofore been little concerned. Once the potential audience for cultural creations is expanded, another question arises quite logically: are there substantive aspects of Carolingian cultural life that have heretofore escaped the attention of historians because it never occurred to them that there might be an audience that would be affected in some way by such matters? Again these chapters leave little doubt that there is new ground to be discovered in the record that has survived to mark the Carolingian cultural effort. As is the case with contemporary historical inquiry in general, Carolingian cultural history will continue to be enriched by the identification of new participants and by a new array of activities that can properly be annexed to the realm of cultural history.

The chapters of Bernice M. Kaczynski and Richard L. Crocker remind us of two matters that will undoubtedly play a role in future studies of Carolingian cultural life. They show us the ways in which received tradition—be it in music, scriptural exegesis, or doctrinal discourse—was transformed into new forms of cultural expression that in the long run made a significant impact on the cultural history of western Europe. And they remind us of an array of cultural figures—such as anonymous cantors (whose potential creative role was stunningly illustrated by Crocker's virtuoso performance of Carolingian chant), choir singers, preachers, translators, scribes, and manuscript illuminators—who had a role in shaping the cultural environment for which they have been given little attention. In a sense these dimensions of Carolingian intellectual and artistic life present a version of Carolingian culture "from the bottom up." A firmer grasp on Carolingian cultural history depends on the willingness of future scholars to pursue this line of inquiry on as broad a range as possible.

Thomas F. X. Noble's account of the *Libri Carolini* focuses our attention on the innovative aspects of the cultural program of Charlemagne's court; his interpretation of that text must now be set beside Ann Freeman's account of how far the *Libri Carolini* was a failure.[77] His reading of the *Libri Carolini* only serves to highlight what is implicit in all the other essays: there were dimensions of Carolingian cultural activity that broke new intellectual and aesthetic ground. Such creative efforts were responses made by individuals who saw thought and expression as means of resolving real problems facing real people. Future cultural historians must continue the effort to identify the innovative aspects of the Carolingian cultural revival and put it into its appropriate place in the total stream of cultural history.

Lawrence Nees provides sure guidance to the considerable array of Carolingianists who suffer to a greater or lesser degree from visual illiteracy. His skilled reading of visual artifacts in search of the message their creators sought to convey about the real world in which they lived provides a highly instructive guide to how to decode visual images and a powerful reminder of what visual sources have to say about what people thought and felt.[78] Hardly less impressive on this same score is Crocker's exploitation of musical documents as sources of information for the cultural historian. These studies leave no doubt that in the future effective historians of Carolingian culture must develop skills in reading visual and aural as well as literary texts.

It need hardly be said that these chapters collectively highlight the ongoing importance of source criticism that is at once disciplined and imaginative, traditional and innovative. Without asserting undue claims to the possession of critical infallibility by virtue of adherence to one or another contemporary school of criticism, each author has subjected a "text" or a group of "texts" to the kind of scrutiny that at once honors the long tradition of treating sources as vessels containing a message about something that really happened while at the same time it takes into account contemporary critical insights relating to the nature of language, the processes governing human discourse, how texts are created, how their structure determines their message, and how their reception shapes their meaning. The authors' efforts in this realm highlight the importance of critical awareness to the advance of knowledge about Carolingian cultural life. It might be argued that a more overt and conscious collective cultivation of textual criticism among Carolingianists would be a fruitful enterprise.

Each of these studies confirms Sullivan's reminder that we must acknowledge the importance of the particularities of the Carolingian intellectual and artistic enterprise. That situation is obvious whatever aspect of cultural life one deals with: schoolbooks, curricula, teaching methods, the practices of different scriptoria, the performance of antiphons, the reception of classical and patristic authors, the interpretation of the past. Scholars need to continue their efforts to discern and describe these particularities. And they must remain patient in formulating generalizations about Carolingian cultural life until they have mastered all its particularistic aspects.

But we must also recognize the truth of Sullivan's remark in chapter 2 that "at stake [in Carolingian society] was control of the traditions that defined by whom, through what means, in what ways, and to what ends Christian society should be directed." An investigation of that control, its costs in financial but also in social terms, its flaws, and its consequences is implied in all of these chapters. To escape the triumphalism of previous treatments of Carolingian cultural life it is worth trying to focus on what Carolingians were quarreling about. Lupus of Ferrières was more concerned with the cell of St. Josse than with the text of Cicero. That he regarded both tasks as compatible is the measure of what Carolingian tradition could encompass. Altmann explains how the Christian Helena is superior to Helen of Troy and reminded his readers that Christ's apostles were not orators skilled in the splendors of eloquence or laden with worldly riches, for they were judged by the state of their souls, not the fluency of their words.[79] The standard Christian formula for excusing faults of style is also a reminder of the Christian transformation of educational values. That transformation of power, embodied in the powers of the relics of Helena, is one symbol of how Carolingian education in particular and cultural life in general controlled the institutions and values of the Frankish empire. The essays collected here treat aspects of that control, and it is in searching for the visions of power they explore that we come closest to how to read them.

Notes

I am very grateful to Richard E. Sullivan for inviting me to write this piece, and for his meticulous and patient assistance in making it more lucid.

1. *Acta Sanctorum*, Aug. 3 (Paris, 1737), cols. 580–99. On Altmann, see André Wilmart, "La Lettre philosophique d'Altmann et son contexte littéraire." Relics of Helena were venerated at Hautvillers.

2. I owe my knowledge of von Reber and of the survival of his canon in such standard texts as H. W. Janson's *History of Art*, 4th ed., rev. and exp. (New York, 1991), or Helen Gardner's *Art through the Ages*, 9th ed. (San Diego, 1991), to a paper presented by William Dieboldt at the International Congress on Medieval Studies held at Kalamazoo, Michigan, in 1992.

3. For that account, see *Notkeri Balbvli Gesta Karoli Magni Imperatoris*, bk. 1, chap. 3, ed. Hans F. Haefele, MGH, SS rer. Germ., new ser., 12 (Berlin, 1959; repr. Munich, 1980), pp. 4–5; English translation in *Einhard and*

Notker the Stammerer: Two Lives of Charlemagne, trans. Lewis Thorpe, pp. 95–96.

4. Such efforts are not always lacking in merit; see, e.g., Joaquin Martinez Pizarro, *A Rhetoric of the Scene: Dramatic Narrative in the Early Middle Ages*, pp. 129–50, which is stimulating on the historical writings of Paul the Deacon, Agnellus, and Notker.

5. James Fentress and Chris Wickham, *Social Memory*, p. 161. The Charlemagne whose twelve peers were recalled by the Contestado of Brazil in 1914 (ibid., p. 107) cannot be linked with education, yet the values he shared with his younger knights would have been recognized as a proper part of a *schola* by Bede and Hildemar.

6. Robert Folz, *Etudes sur le culte liturgique de Charlemagne dans les églises de l'empire*, p. 102.

7. Alexander von Roes, *Memoriale de prerogativa imperii Romani*, chap. 25, in *Die Schriften des Alexander von Roes*, ed. Herbert Grundmann and Hermann Heimpel, Deutsches Mittelalter, Kritische Studientexte der Monumenta Germaniae Historica 4 (Weimar, 1949), p. 48 (cf. Folz, *Le Souvenir et la légende de Charlemagne dans l'Empire germanique médiéval*, pp. 389–90), with a later development by a fifteenth-century schoolmaster, J. Birl, noted in Folz, *Le Souvenir*, p. 483. The fullest account of Charlemagne's "foundation" of the University of Paris is in C. du Boulay, *Historia Universitatis Parisiensis . . .* , vol. 1 (Paris, 1665; repr. Frankfurt, 1966), pp. 91–130.

8. Montaigne, *Essais*, bk. 1, chap. 40, ed. Pierre Villey (Paris, 1965): "De cette façon faict honneur à Cyrus l'agriculture et à Charlemagne l'eloquence et connoissance de bonnes lettres" (p. 250).

9. This account draws on Arno Borst, "Das Karlsbild in der Geschichtswissenschaft vom Humanismus bis heute"; and Siegfried Epperlein, "Karl der Grosse in der deutschen bürgerlichen Geschichtsschreibung."

10. For a background of Notker's vision of Charlemagne, see Theodor Siegrist, *Herrscherbild und Weltsicht bei Notker Balbulus: Untersuchungen zu den Gesta Karoli*; and my own "Humour as History in Notker's *Gesta Karoli Magni.*"

11. Albertus Krantzius, *Saxonia*, pp. 29–43. The work was composed in 1502.

12. Jean Launoy, *De scholis celebrioribus seu a Carolo Magno et seu post eundum Carolum in occidentem instauratis Liber.* Launoy made extensive use of the *De litteris colendis* and surveyed the history of monastic schools until the death of Charles the Bald.

13. PL 100:42–55. For Frobenius's career, see Bernhard Bischoff, *Salzburger Formelbücher und Briefe aus tassilonischer und karolingischer Zeit*, pp. 3–7.

14. William Robertson, *The Progress of Society in Europe: A Historical Outline from the Subversion of the Roman Empire to the Beginning of the Sixteenth Century*, p. 21.

15. "Il conçut par la force de son génie combien les belles lettres étaient nécessaires." Voltaire, *Essai sur les moeurs et l'esprit des nations*, 12:277. See also his *Annales de l'empire depuis Charlemagne*, 13:233–34.

16. Edward Gibbon, *The History of the Decline and Fall of the Roman Empire*, 5:286.

17. Henry Hallam, *View of the State of Europe during the Middle Ages*, 1:13.
18. G. W. F. Hegel, *Vorlesung über die Philosophie der Geschichte*, p. 438 (pp. 363–64 in the English trans.).
19. Ibid, pp. 440–67 (pp. 366–89 in the English trans.).
20. I know the works of Count Wackerbarth (comparing Charlemagne and Peter the Great) and of Barbet du Pertaud (comparing Charlemagne and Napoleon) only from library catalogues, but see C. H. Castille, *Parallèle entre César, Charlemagne et Napoléon: L'Empire et la démocratie, philosophie de la légende impériale*.
21. "La luttre contre l'état barbare" and "l'esprit de civilisation." François Guizot, *Histoire de la civilisation en Europe*, p. 109. See also Pierre Rosanvallon, *Le Moment Guizot*.
22. Quotations from Jules Michelet, *Oeuvres complètes*, vol. 4: *Histoire de France*: "Non moins pédantesque et inféconde fut la tentative de réforme littéraire dirigée par Alcuin" (pp. 285–86). "Pendant que Charlemagne disserte sur la théologie, rêve d'Empire romain et étudie la grammaire, la domination des Francs croule tout doucement" (p. 291). "La féodalité se fonda; la philosophie scholastique fut au moins preparée" (p. 309). And "la rénovation du libre génie celtique" (p. 311). For a contemporary German treatment of Charlemagne's educational policy, see J. C. Pfister, *Geschichte der Teutschen*, using Notker: "So wurden die Klosterschulen zu St. Gallen und Fulda die ersten lichten Puncte in den teutschen Waldern" [So the monastic schools at St. Gall and Fulda were the first points of light in the Germanic forests] (1:455–57).
23. J.-J. Ampère, *Histoire littéraire de la France avant le douzième siècle*: "Par là, je suis amené à considerer le régne de Charlemagne sous son véritable point de vue, c'est à-dire comme une renaissance. . . . La première renaissance est la mère des deux autres" [In that way, I am led to consider the reign of Charlemagne from its true point of view, that is to say, as a renaissance. . . . The first renaissance is the mother of the other two] (3:32). As Lucien Febvre has shown, the word "renaissance" was first used by Michelet; see his *Michelet et la Renaissance* (Paris, 1992), pp. 155–96.
24. Ampère, *Histoire littéraire*, 3:25, 27. "Charlemagne a latinisé l'Occident" (3:35).
25. A. F. Ozanam, *La Civilisation chrétienne chez les Francs: Recherches sur l'histoire ecclésiastique, politique et littéraire des temps mérovingiens, et sur le règne de Charlemagne*, pp. 245 and 251, for a discussion of Charlemagne's mission, and pp. 315 and 337, where there is a treatment of the "grand dessein." He devotes a chapter to schools from Donatus to the Carolingians (pp. 406–582). Cf. L. Baunard, *Ozanam d'après sa correspondance*.
26. "Les destinées de l'esprit humain sont assurées." Ozanam, *La Civilisation chrétienne*, pp. 560–63.
27. B. Hauréau, *Charlemagne et sa cour*, pp. 21–45; quotation from Ampère is at p. 32. The chapter on the palace school is at pp. 198–228. Hauréau attributes to Charlemagne the desire to create a new Athens; see p. 203. (This work went through four editions from 1854 to 1888 in the Bibliothèque des chemins de fer).

28. Borst, "Ranke und Karl der Grosse."

29. I rely on a transcript of unpublished lectures on Charlemagne by Burckhardt, which survives in Basel. The text will be edited in the forthcoming Gesamtausgabe of Burckhardt's writings.

30. J. Bass Mullinger, *The Schools of Charles the Great and the Restoration of Education in the Ninth Century*, p. 83.

31. Monnier, who was trained at the Ecole des Chartres, describes the renaissance of Gaul under Charlemagne, listing schools in each diocese and reprinting library catalogues. I have been unable to examine Maître's work.

32. In addition to the MGH editions, Philippus Jaffé's editions of texts related to Charlemagne and of the letters and other works of Alcuin, in his *Bibliotheca Rerum Germanicarum*, 6 vols. (Berlin, 1864–73), vols. 4 (texts related to Charlemagne) and 6 (Alcuin's works) deserve particular mention, as do the reasons for his suicide. On Jaffé, see Gabriel Silagi, "Jaffé, Philipp," in *Neue Deutsche Biographie* (Berlin, 1974), 10:292–93.

33. Ernst Dümmler, *Geschichte des ostfränkischen Reiches*.

34. Ludwig Traube, *Einleitung in die lateinische Philologie des Mittelalters*, 2:57. Traube discusses Carolingian latinity on pp. 51–52 and 132–34.

35. "Das geistige Feld der Germanen dieser Zeit war noch durchaus die Anschauung, das Nebeneinander, nicht aber das Verständnis, das Übereinander." Karl Lamprecht, *Deutsche Geschichte*, 2:46–83. It is instructive to compare Lamprecht's picture with that of the novelist and cultural historian Gustav Freytag, who, after citing the same quotations from Notker, Angilbert, and Alcuin, affirmed that "the king had an unbounded reverence in the presence of all higher learning and understood exactly and quickly" ("Der Konig hatte eine unbegrenzte Ehrfurcht vor allem edelen Wissen und fasste sharf und schnell"); see *Bilder aus der deutschen Vergangenheit*, vol. 1, chap. 6, pp. 314–48, at p. 337. Freytag described Charlemagne using the present tense! There is a chapter entitled "La Renaissance carolingienne" in Gabriel Monod, *Etudes critiques sur les sources de l'histoire carolingienne*, pp. 37–67, emphasizing Charlemagne's contribution and suggesting decline had set in by the reign of Charles the Bald.

36. K. Schreiner, "Führertum, Rasse, Reich: Wissenschaft von der Geschichte nach der nationalsozialistischen Machterergreifung," pp. 163–252. At p. 189 the author notes as typical of these historians the idea that "without Charlemagne today there would be no German people and no German history" ("Ohne Karl den Grossen gabe es heute kein deutsches Volk und keine deutsche Geschichte").

37. "Das deutsche Volk sei auch nicht lediglich als ein Produkt von antiker Idee und Christentum, sondern als ein Produkt von Gewalt, antiker Idee und Christentum enstanden. . . . Kulturarbeit sei Zusammenarbeit." Henry Picker, ed., *Hitlers Tischgespräche im Führerhauptquartier* (Stuttgart, 1976), pp. 166–67. Charlemagne has no place in *Mein Kampf*, but Hitler regarded him as a great German emperor. While Hitler seems to have read little more than his school textbooks, his ignorance made his stance all too clear, and others followed his lead.

38. "Er [Charlemagne] selbst aber war viel zu sehr urwüchsig-germanischer Laie, um in diesem kirchlich-klassischen Bildungsideal aufzugehen." Karl Ferdinand Werner, *Das NS-Geschichtsbild und die deutsche Geschichtswissenschaft*, pp. 74–78, discussing *Karl der Grosse oder Charlemagne? Acht Antworten deutscher Geschichtsforscher*. Most recently, see Karen Schönwalder, *Historiker und Politiker: Geschichtswissenschaft im Nationalsozialismus*, pp. 75–76.

39. "In Memoriam Hermann Heimpel," *Göttinger Universitätsreden* 83 (1989), esp. pp. 34–42, with an account of Heimpel at the 1937 Historikertag. Heimpel was a student of S. Hellmann, the author of classic studies of Einhard and Sedulius Scottus, who was killed in a concentration camp.

40. Levison's seminal work was *England and the Continent in the Eighth Century*, esp. the lecture entitled "Learning and Scholarship," pp. 132–73. On Levison, see Theodor Schieffer in *Rheinische Vierteljahresblätter* 40 (1976): 225–42.

41. Extracts from the speeches of Paul Sethe and Kurt Reich on this occasion are printed by Friedrich Schneider, *Die neueren Anschauungen der deutschen Historiker über die deutsche Kaiserpolitik des Mittelalters and die mit ihr verbundene Ostpolitik*, pp. 39–40. The Franks did not think like the Carolingians (p. 37).

42. On the Aachen exhibition: *Karl der Grosse: Werk und Wirkung*. On the "Festschrift": Wolfgang Braunfels, et al., eds., *Karl der Grosse: Lebenswerk und Nachleben*. Most helpful on Carolingian education and cultural life is vol. 2, *Das geistige Leben*, ed. Bischoff.

43. Winston Churchill, Konrad Adenauer, Jean Monnet, Helmut Kohl, and François Mitterand, among others. It is relevant that the prize was not awarded to Willy Brandt.

44. Erna Patzelt, *Die karolingische Renaissance*.

45. M. L. W. Laistner, *Thought and Letters in Western Europe, A.D. 500 to 900*; the quotation is from the preface of the first edition as reprinted in the revised edition, p. 5.

46. Walter Ullmann, *The Carolingian Renaissance and the Idea of Kingship: The Birkbeck Lectures, 1968–1969*.

47. Pierre Riché, *Ecoles et enseignement dans le haut moyen âge: Fin du Ve siècle–milieu du XIe siècle*. Riché's earlier monograph, entitled *Education et culture dans l'Occident barbare, 6e–8e siècles*, is an indispensable collection of material for those who wish to evaluate whether there was a Carolingian renaissance of learning. Other recent surveys are Anita Guerreau-Jalabert, "La 'Renaissance carolingienne': Modèles culturels, usages linguistiques et structures sociales"; and Johannes Fried, *Der Weg in die Geschichte: Die Ursprünge Deutschlands bis 1024*, pp. 263–96. The treatment of Carolingian cultural life in the forthcoming vol. 2 of *The New Cambridge Medieval History* should be a valuable addition to these efforts to provide an overview of the Carolingian cultural achievement.

48. The best example is the five-volume work entitled *Karl der Grosse: Lebenswerk und Nachleben*, cited in n. 42, above. Others include Peter Godman and Roger Collins, eds., *Charlemagne's Heir: New Perspectives on the Reign of Louis*

the Pious (814–840), esp. pp. 487–687; Margaret T. Gibson and Janet L. Nelson, eds., *Charles the Bald: Court and Kingdom*; and Rosamond McKitterick, ed., *Carolingian Culture: Emulation and Innovation*.

49. Illustrative are Donald A. Bullough, *The Age of Charlemagne*; Friedrich Heer, *Charlemagne and His World*; Riché, *Les Carolingiens: Une famile qui fit l'Europe*; and Arnold Angenendt, *Das Frühmittelalter: Die abendländische Christenheit von 400 bis 900*.

50. For Gottschalk, whose grammatical writings await an adequate study, see his *Oeuvres théologiques et grammaticales de Godescalc d'Orbais*, ed. Cyrille Lambot. For Paschasius, see the editions of his works by Bede Paulus, E. Ann Matter, and Albert Ripberger, CC cont. med. 16, 56, 56A–C, 85, 94, 97 (Turnhout, 1969, 1984, 1985, 1988, 1990, 1991); and the important review by A. Hardelin in *Kyrkohistorisk Arsskrift* 87 (1987): 23–36. For Carolingian glosses to Bede, see *Bedae Venerabilis Opera*, pt. 6, *Opera didascalica*, ed. Charles W. Jones, 3 vols., CCSL, 123A–C (Turnhout, 1975–80), which incorporates editions of the glosses; and Steven B. Killion, "Bede's Irish Legacy: Knowledge and Use of Bede's Works in Ireland from the Eighth through the Sixteenth Century," which treats the Old Irish glosses that circulated in the Carolingian world. On the matter of publication of improved editions of Carolingian sources, the products of the Corpus Christianorum series and of the MGH are of crucial importance to Carolingianists.

51. On this matter, see the remarks of Sullivan above, chap. 1.

52. What is noteworthy about recent translations is the growing availability of materials that once might have been thought esoteric in the main stream of Carolingian studies, chiefly because these works dealt primarily with cultural pursuits. As examples of such works translated into English, one thinks of Wilbur Samuel Howell, ed., *The Rhetoric of Alcuin and Charlemagne: A Translation with an Introduction, the Latin Text, and Notes,* Princeton Studies in English 23 (Princeton, N.J., 1941); *The Letters of Lupus of Ferrières*, trans. Graydon W. Regenos; *Walafrid Strabo, Hortulus*, trans. Raef Payne, Hunt Facsimile Series 2 (Pittsburgh, Pa., 1966); the writings of Sedulius Scottus in *Sedulius Scottus: On Christian Rulers and the Poems*, trans. Edward Gerard Doyle (Binghampton, N.Y., 1983); the anthology of Carolingian poetry available in Peter Godman, *Poetry of the Carolingian Renaissance*; and Dhuoda, *Handbook for William: A Carolingian Woman's Counsel for Her Son*, trans. Carol Neel (Lincoln, Nebr., and London, 1991). An anthology illustrating the point is Paul Edward Dutton, ed., *Carolingian Civilization: A Reader*. A useful tool for beginners in Carolingian studies would be a compilation of all Carolingian texts available in translation in all modern languages.

53. The importance of such "editing" for understanding the Carolingian renaissance will become obvious to anyone who spends a few moments surveying Jean Hubert, Jean Porcher, and Wolfgang Fritz Volbach, *L'Empire carolingien*; or Marcel Durliat, *Des barbares à l'an mil*.

54. Tours: E. K. Rand, *A Survey of the Manuscripts of Tours*. Saint Gall: A. Bruckner, *Scriptoria Helvetica Medii Aevi*. Freising, Tegernsee, Regensburg, and Salzburg: Bischoff, *Die südostdeutschen Schreibschulen und Bibliotheken*.

Würzburg: Bischoff and Josef Hoffmann, *Libri sancti Kyliani: Die Würzburger Schreibschule and die Dombibliothek im VIII. und IX. Jahrhundert.* Lorsch: Bischoff, *Die Abtei Lorsch im Spiegel ihrer Handschriften.* Laon: John J. Contreni, *The Cathedral School of Laon from 850 to 930: Its Manuscripts and Masters.* Corbie: David Ganz, *Corbie in the Carolingian Renaissance.* Fleury: Marco Mostert, *The Library of Fleury: A Provisional List of Manuscripts.* Mostert is engaged in a full study of Fleury.

55. For an account of Bischoff's life and work and a full bibliography, see *Bernhard Bischoff, 1907–1991*, privately published by the MGH in 1992. For suggestions about the systematic study of libraries, see McKitterick, *The Carolingians and the Written Word*, pp. 165–210; and my chapter, "Book Production," to appear in the forthcoming *New Cambridge Medieval History*, vol. 2.

56. Louis Holtz, *Donat et la tradition de l'enseignement grammatical: Etude sur l'"Ars Donati" et sa diffusion (IVe–IXe siècle) et édition critique*, is the model. Günter Glauche, *Schullektüre im Mittelalter: Entstehung und Wandlungen des Lektürekanons bis 1200 nach den Quellen dargestellt*, shows how a canon of authors developed. But his evidence of lists must be supplemented by a study of the manuscripts of the authors listed.

57. Contreni, ed., *Codex Laudunensis 468: A Ninth-Century Guide to Virgil, Sedulius, and the Liberal Arts.*

58. The Virgil glosses in MS Bern 165 identify the Daci with the Northmen and refer to the teachings of Master Berno.

59. While vernacular glosses have been expertly studied, Latin glosses still need editors. For an insight into the problems, see W. M. Lindsay, *The Corpus, Epinal, Erfurt, and Leiden Glossaries*; and for the complexity of one tradition, see Charles E. Murgia, *Prolegomena to Servius*, vol. 5: *The Manuscripts*. For Boethius, see Gibson, "Boethius in the Carolingian Age"; for Priscian, see Gibson, "Milestones in the Study of Priscian, circa 800–circa 1200."

60. For two views of how to identify a "schoolbook," see Michael Lapidge, "The Study of Latin Texts in Late Anglo-Saxon England, 1: The Evidence of Latin Glosses"; and Gernot Wieland, "The Glossed Manuscript: Classbook or Library Book?"

61. On Lupus and Heiric, see the contributions to Dominique Iogna-Prat, Colette Jeudy, and Guy Lobrichon, eds., *L'Ecole carolingienne d'Auxerre de Murethach à Rémi, 830–908.*

62. For Greek, see Walter Berschin, *Greek Letters and the Latin Middle Ages: From Jerome to Nicholas of Cusa*; and the important papers in Michael W. Herren, ed., *The Sacred Nectar of the Greeks: The Study of Greek in the West in the Early Middle Ages.*

63. Rudolf of Fulda, *Translatio S. Alexandri*, ed. Bruno Krusch, *Die Übertragung des Heiligen Alexander von Rom nach Wildeshausen durch den Enkel Widukinds 851: Die älteste niedersächsische Geschichtsdenkmal*, Nachrichten von der Gesellschaft der Wissenschaften zu Göttingen, phil.-hist. Klasse 2, 13 (Berlin, 1933), pp. 405–36. The Hannover MS I 186 was reproduced in facsimile with an introduction by H. Hartel in 1979.

64. Jürgen Eichhoff and Irmengard Rauh, eds., *Der Heiland*; and Gisela Vollmann-Profe, *Kommentar zu Otfrids Evangelienbuch*, pt. 1, pp. 1–148.

65. Louis Holtz, "La Redécouverte de Virgile aux VIIIe et IXe siècles d'après les manuscrits conservés"; and Robert A. Kaster, *The Tradition of the Text of the "Aeneid" in the Ninth Century.*

66. On the circulation of the works of Augustine, see Alain J. Stoclet, "Le *De civitate dei* de St. Augustin"; and the studies by M. Gorman summarized in his "The Manuscript Tradition of St. Augustine's Major Works." For Jerome, see Bernard Lambert, *Bibliotheca Hieronymiana Manuscripta: La Tradition manuscrite des oeuvres de saint Jérôme,* which provides a full list of all extant manuscripts including the *spuria.*

67. The proceedings of the 1991 Aachen colloquium, Paul Leo Butzer and Dietrich Lohrmann, eds., *Science in Western and Eastern Civilization in Carolingian Times,* make an important contribution in filling this gap. See also Wesley M. Stevens, *Bede's Scientific Achievement: The Jarrow Lecture, 1985,* with a list of all extant manuscripts of Bede's *De temporum ratione*; and Bruce S. Eastwood, "Plinian Astronomical Diagrams in the Early Middle Ages." H. le Bourdelles, "De Astronomia more Christiano," edits a Carolingian treatise on the zodiac, though the author's claim to have established that it was composed by Paschasius Radbertus is neither convincing nor probable.

68. Peter Jeffery, "The Oldest Sources of the Gradual: A Preliminary Checklist of Manuscripts Copied before about 900 A.D."; Kenneth Levy, "On the Origin of the Neumes"; and J. Hourlier and Michel Huglo, "Notation paléofranque."

69. Gundolf Keil and Paul Schnitzler, eds., *Das Lorscher Arzneibuch und die frühmittelalterliche Medizin.* There is a helpful introduction in M. L. Cameron, "The Sources of Medical Knowledge in Anglo-Saxon England."

70. P. Köpp, ed., *Vademecum eines frühmittelalterlichen Arztes.*

71. Agnellus of Ravenna, *Lectures on Galen's De Sectis: Latin Text and Translation by Seminar Classics 609, State University of New York at Buffalo,* Arethusa Monographs 8 (Buffalo, N.Y., 1981). I have not seen Walter Wiedemann, *Untersuchungen zu dem frühmittelalterlichen medizinischen Briefbuch des Codex Bruxelliensis 3701–3715.*

72. Peter Classen, "Die hohen Schulen und die Gesellschaft im 12. Jahr-hundert"; and Fried, ed., *Schulen und Studium im soziale Wandel des hohen und späten Mittelalters,* esp. the paper by Peter Johanek entitled "Klosterstudien im 12. Jahrhundert," pp. 35–68.

73. For Tours, see E. Mabille, "Les Invasions normandes dans la Loire et les pérégrinations du corps de St. Martin"; a charter of 894, printed on p. 434, gives a history of the *scola Sancti Martini* from the reign of Charlemagne. For Fulda, see Mechthild Sandmann, "Wirkungsbereich fuldische Mönche," pp. 760–63, where there is a discussion of the *magistri.*

74. Mayke de Jong, "Growing up in a Carolingian Monastery: Magister Hildemar and His Oblates."

75. For an acute characterization of early medieval education, see Detlef Illmer, "Totum namque in sola experientia usque consistit: Eine Studie zur monas-tischen Erziehung und Sprache"; and Illmer, *Formen der Erziehung und und Wissensvermittlung im frühen Mittelalter: Quellenstudien zur Frage der*

Kontinuität des abendländischen Erziehungswesens. The challenge Illmer presents to Riché's account of early medieval education has remained unanswered.

76. Seventeen of his articles are collected in Contreni, *Carolingian Learning, Masters, and Manuscripts.* In addition he is the author of a chapter entitled "The Carolingian Renaissance, Education, and Literary Culture" to appear in the forthcoming *New Cambridge Medieval History*, vol. 2.

77. Ann Freeman, "Carolingian Orthodoxy and the Fate of the *Libri Carolini*"; and Celia M. Chazelle, "Images, Scripture, the Church, and the Libri Carolini."

78. Lawrence Nees is also a contributor to the forthcoming *New Cambridge Medieval History*, vol. 2. I have offered a sketch of an alternative approach to Carolingian art in "'Pando quod ignoro': In Search of Carolingian Artistic Experience."

79. *Acta Sanctorum*, Aug. 3, col. 580.

Selected Bibliography

Primary Sources

Recent editions of the writings of the major Carolingian authors, important musical texts, and photographic reproductions of basic art works are provided in the notes appended to each of the essays in this collection. The fundamental guide to Carolingian written sources is Wilhelm Wattenbach, Wilhelm Levison, and Heinz Löwe, *Deutschlands Geschichtsquellen im Mittelalter: Vorzeit und Karolinger*. A convenient brief listing can be found in Arnold Angenendt, *Das Frühmittelalter: Die abendländischen Christenheit von 400 bis 900*, pp. 462–65. Helpful information about Carolingian primary sources can be found in the articles related to Carolingian cultural figures and to Carolingian cultural activities published in two recent historical encyclopedias: *Lexikon des Mittelalters*, vols. 1– (Munich and Zurich, 1900–), and *Dictionary of the Middle Ages*, 13 vols. (New York, 1982–89). Invaluable guidance in utilizing the basic sources is provided by the many volumes published in the series entitled *Typologie des sources du moyen âge*, ed. Léopold Genicot (Turnhout, 1972–). Each volume in this series (more than sixty have now been published) deals with a separate genre of source materials, seeking to identify its unique features, describe the kind of information that can be gleaned from it, and highlight the methodological problems inherent in utilizing the genre. The surest way to keep abreast of new publications of basic Carolingian source materials is to review the annual bibliographies published in *Revue d'histoire ecclésiatique* or in *Medioevo latino: Bulletino, bibliografico della cultura europae del secolo VI al XIII*, ed. Claudio Leonardi, et al., vols. 1– (Spoleto, 1980–).

Secondary Sources

ABEL, Sigurd, and Bernhard Simson. *Jahrbücher des fränkischen Reiches unter Karl dem Grossen*. 2 vols. Leipzig, 1883–88.

AFFELDT, Werner. "Untersuchungen zur Königserhebung Pippins: Das

Papsttum und die Begründung des karolingischen Königtum im Jahre 751." *Frühmittelalterliche Studien* 14 (1980): 95–187.

AHERNE, Consuelo Maria. "Late Visigothic Bishops, Their Schools and the Transmission of Culture." *Traditio* 22 (1966): 435–44.

"*AHR Forum*: The Old History and the New." *American Historical Review* 94 (1989): 654–98.

AIGRAIN, René. *L'Hagiographie: Ses sources, ses méthodes, son histoire*. Paris, 1953.

ALEXANDRENKO, Nicolai. "The Poetry of Theodulf of Orleans: A Translation and Critical Study." Ph.D. diss., Tulane University, 1971.

ALLARD, Guy-H., ed. *Jean Scot écrivain*. Montreal, 1986.

ALLGEIER, Arthur. "Das Psalmenbuch des Konstanzer Bischofs Salomon III. in Bamberg: Eine Untersuchung zur Frage der mehrspaltigen Psalterien." In *Jahresbericht der Görresgesellschaft 1938* (Cologne, 1939): 104–5.

ALLOTT, Stephen. *Alcuin of York, His Life and Letters*. York, 1974.

ALTANER, Berthold, and Alfred Stuiber. *Patrologie: Leben, Schriften und Lehre der Kirchenväter*. 8th ed. Freiburg, 1978.

AMANN, Emile. *L'Epoque carolingienne*. Histoire de l'Eglise 6. Edited by Augustin Fliche and Victor Martin. Paris, 1947.

AMPÈRE, J.-J. *Histoire littéraire de la France avant le douzième siècle*. 3 vols. Paris, 1839–40.

ANDERSON, Perry. *Passages from Antiquity to Feudalism*. London, 1974.

ANDOLORO, Maria. "Il Liber Pontificalis et la questione delle immagini da Sergio I a Adriano I." In *Roma e l'età carolingi*, pp. 69–77.

ANGENENDT, Arnold. *Das Frühmittelalter: Die abendländische Christenheit von 400 bis 900*. Stuttgart, Berlin, and Cologne, 1990.

———. *Monachi Peregrini: Studien zu Pirmin und den monastischen Vorstellungen der frühen Mittelalters*. Münstersche Mittelalter-Schriften 6. Munich, 1972.

ANTON, Hans Hubert. *Fürstenspiegel and Herrscherethos in der Karolingerzeit*. Bonner historische Forschungen 32. Bonn, 1968.

———. "Zum politischen Konzept karolingischer Synoden und zur karolingischen Brüdergemeinschaft." *Historisches Jahrbuch* 99 (1979): 55–132.

APEL, Willi. *Gregorian Chant*. Bloomington, Ind., 1958.

APPLEBY, David. "Holy Relic and Holy Image: Saints' Relics in the Western Controversy over Images in the Eighth and Ninth Centuries." *Word and Image* 8 (1992): 333–43.

APPUHN, Horst. "Zum Thron Karls des Grossen." *Aachener Kunstblätter* 24/25 (1962/63): 127–36.

ARCARI, Paola Maria. *Idee e sentimenti politici dell'alto medioevo*. Università di Cagliari, Publicazioni della Facoltà di Giurisprudenza, serie 2, Scienze politiche 1. Milan, 1968.

ARIÈS, Philippe. "L'Histoire des mentalités." In *La Nouvelle Histoire*, edited by Jacques Le Goff, et al., pp. 402–23.

ARLT, W., et al., eds. *Gattungen der Musik in Einzeldarstellungen*. Bern, 1973.

ARNALDI, Girolamo. "La questione dei Libri Carolini." In *Culto cristiano,* pp. 61–86.

ARQUILLIÈRE, H.-X. *L'Augustinisme politique: Essai sur la formation des théories politiques du moyen âge.* L'Eglise et l'état au moyen-âge 2. 2nd ed. Paris, 1955.

"L'Art et la société à l'époque carolingienne: Actes des XXIIIe Journées romanes de Cuxa." *Les Cahiers de Saint-Michel de Cuxa* 23 (1992): 3–131.

ATKINSON, Charles. "The *Parapteres: Nothi* or Not?" *Musical Quarterly* 68 (1982): 32–59.

ATTRIDGE, Derek, Geoff Bennington, and Robert Young, eds. *Post-structuralism and the Question of History.* Cambridge and New York, 1987.

AUDA, Antoine. *L'Ecole musicale liègeoise au Xe siècle: Etienne de Liège.* Académie royale de Belgique, Classe des beaux arts, Mémoires 2/1. Brussels, 1923.

AUERBACH, Erich. *Literary Language and Its Public in Late Antiquity and the Early Middle Ages.* Translated by Ralph Mannheim. Bollingen Series 74. New York, 1965.

Aus der Welt des Buches: Festgabe zum 70. Geburtstag von Georg Leyh. Leipzig, 1950.

BAILEY, Terence. "Accented and Cursive Cadences in Gregorian Psalmody." *Journal of the American Musicological Society* 29 (1976): 463–71.

BAKER, Derek, ed. *The Church in Town and Countryside.* Studies in Church History 16. Oxford, 1979.

———, ed. *Medieval Women.* Studies in Church History, Subsidia 1. Oxford, 1978.

———, ed. *The Orthodox Churches and the West.* Studies in Church History 13. Oxford, 1976.

———, ed. *Renaissance and Renewal in Christian History.* Studies in Church History 14. Oxford, 1977.

BALDOVIN, John. *The Urban Character of Christian Worship: The Origins, Development, and Meaning of Stational Liturgy.* Orientalia Christiana Analecta 228. Rome, 1987.

BANNIARD, Michel. *Viva Voce: Communication écrite et communication orale du IVe au IXe siècle en occident latin.* Collection des études augustiniennes, série moyen-âge et temps modernes 25. Paris, 1992.

BARBERA, A., ed. *Music Theory and Its Sources: Antiquity and the Middle Ages.* Notre Dame, Ind., 1990.

BARION, Hans. *Das fränkisch-deutsche Synodalrecht des Frühmittelalters.* Kano-nistische Studien und Texte 5–6. Bonn, 1931.

———. "Der kirchenrechtliche Charakter des Konzils von Frankfurt 794." *Zeitschrift der Savigny-Stiftung für Rechtsgeschichte, kanonistische Abteilung* 19 (1930): 139–70.

BARK, William Carroll. *Origins of the Medieval World.* Stanford Studies in History, Economics, and Political Science 14. Stanford, Calif., 1958.

BARZUN, Jacques. *Clio and the Doctors: Psycho-History, Quanto-History, and History*. Chicago, 1974.

BASTGEN, Hubert. "Das Kapitulare Karls des Grossen über die Bilder oder die sogennanten Libri Carolini." *Neues Archiv* 36 (1911): 629–66.

BATTISTI, Carlo. "Latini e germani nella Gallia del nord nei secoli VII e VIII." In *Caratteri del secolo VII in Occidente*, 2:445–83, 509–18.

BAUNARD, L. *Oznam d'après sa correspondance*. Paris, 1912. Published in English as *Ozanam in His Correspondence*. Dublin, 1925.

BECHER, Matthias. "Drogo und die Königserhebung Pippins." *Frühmittelalterliche Studien* 23 (1989): 131–53.

BECK, Hans-Georg. *Von der Fragwürdigkeit der Ikone*. Bayerische Akademie der Wissenschaften, phil.-hist. Klasse, Sitzungberichte, Jahrgang 1975, Heft 7. Munich, 1975.

BECKER, H., and R. Kaczynski, eds. *Liturgie und Dichtung: Ein interdisziplinäres Kompendium*. 2 vols. Pietas liturgica 2. S. Ottilien, 1983.

BECKWITH, John. "Byzantine Influences on Carolingian Art." In *Karl der Grosse: Lebenswerk und Nachleben*, edited by Wolfgang Braunfels, et al., 3:288–300.

BEIERWALTES, Werner, ed. *Eriugena: Studien zur seinen Quellen, Vorträge des III. Internationalen Eriugena-Colloquiums, Freiburg im Breisgau, 27.–30. August 1979*. Heidelberger Akademie der Wissenschaften, Abhandlungen, phil.-hist. Klasse, Jahrgang 1980, Heft 3. Heidelberg, 1980.

BELTING, Hans. *The End of the History of Art?* Translated by Christopher S. Wood. Chicago, 1987.

BERGMANN, Werner. "Dicuils *De mensura orbis terrae*." In *Science in Western and Eastern Civilization in Carolingian Times*, edited by Paul Leo Butzer and Dietrich Lohrmann, pp. 525–37.

BERNHEIM, Ernst. *Lehrbuch der historischen Methode*. Leipzig, 1889.

BERNT, Günter, Fidel Rädel, and Gabriel Silagi, eds. *Tradition und Wertung: Festschrift für Franz Brunhölzl zum 65. Geburtstag*. Sigmaringen, 1988.

BERSCHIN, Walter. *Biographie und Epochenstil im lateinischen Mittelalter*. 3 vols. Stuttgart, 1986–91.

———. *Greek Letters and the Latin Middle Ages: From Jerome to Nicholas of Cusa*. Translated by Jerold C. Frakes. Rev. and exp. ed. Washington, D.C., 1988.

———. "Salomons III. Psalterium quadrupartitum in Köln und Heidelberg." In *Kaiserin Theophanu*, edited by Anton von Euw and Peter Schreiner, 1:327–34.

BETZ, Werner. "Karl der Grosse und die Lingua Theodisca." In *Karl der Grosse: Lebenswerk und Nachleben*, edited by Wolfgang Braunfels, et al., 2:300–306.

BEUMANN, Helmut. *Ideengeschichtliche Studien zu Einhard und anderen Geschichtsschreibern des früheren Mittelalters*. Darmstadt, 1962.

BEZZOLA, Reto R. *Les Origines et la formation de la littérature courtoise en occident (500–1200)*. 3 vols. Bibliothèque de l'Ecole des Hautes Etudes, IVe section, Sciences historiques et philologiques 286, 313, 319–20. Paris, 1944–63.

BILLANOVICH, Giuseppe. "Dall'antica Ravenna alle biblioteche umanistiche." *Università cattolica del Sacro Cuore, Annuario* (1955–56): 73–107.

Bisanzio, Roma e l'Italia nell'alto medioevo. 2 vols. Settimane 34. Spoleto, 1988.

BISCHOFF, Bernhard. *Die Abtei Lorsch im Spiegel ihrer Handschriften.* 2nd enl. ed. Geschichtsblätter Kreis Bergstrasse, Sonderband 10. Lorsch, 1989.

———. "Elementarunterricht und Probationes Pennae in der ersten Hälfte des Mittelalters." In Bischoff, *Mittelalterliche Studien*, 1:74–87.

———. "Die Hofbibliothek unter Ludwig dem Frommen." In Bischoff, *Mittelalterliche Studien*, 3:170–86.

———. "Die Kölner Nonnenhandschriften und das Skriptorium von Chelles." In *Karolingische und ottonische Kunst: Werden, Wesen, Wirkung*, pp. 395–411. Repr. in Bischoff, *Mittelalterliche Studien*, 1:16–34.

———. *Mittelalterliche Studien: Ausgewählte Aufsätze zur Schriftkunde und Literaturgeschichte.* 3 vols. Stuttgart, 1966–81.

———. "Paläographische Fragen deutschen Denkmäler der Karolingerzeit." *Frühmittelalterliche Studien* 5 (1971): 101–34.

———. "Panorama der Handschriftenüberlieferung aus der Zeit Karls des Grossen." In *Karl der Grosse: Lebenswerk und Nachleben*, edited by Wolfgang Braunfels, et al., 2:233–54.

———. *Salzburger Formelbücher und Briefe aus tassilonischer und karolingischer Zeit.* Bayerische Akademie der Wissenschaften, Sitzungberichte, 1973, Heft 4. Munich, 1973.

———. "Eine Sammelhandschrift Walahfrid Strabos (Cod. Sangall. 878)." In Bischoff, *Mittelalterliche Studien*, 2:34–51.

———. "The Study of Foreign Languages in the Middle Ages." In Bischoff, *Mittelalterliche Studien*, 2:227–45.

———. *Die südostdeutschen Schreibschulen und Bibliotheken.* Vol. 1: *Die bayerischen Diözesen.* Vol. 2: *Die vorwiegend österreichischen Diözesen.* Stuttgart, 1974, 1980.

———. "Theodulf und der Ire Cadac-Andreas." In Bischoff, *Mittelalterliche Studien*, 2:19–25.

BISCHOFF, Bernhard, and Josef Hoffmann. *Libri sancti Kyliani: Die Würzburger Schreibschule und die Dombibliothek im VIII. und IX. Jahrhundert.* Quellen und Forschungen zur Geschichte des Bistums und Hochstifts Würzburg 6. Würzburg, 1952.

BISHOP, T. A. M. "The Scribes of the Corbie a–b." In *Charlemagne's Heir*, edited by Peter Godman and Roger Collins, pp. 521–36.

BJORK, David. "The Kyrie Repertory in Aquitanian Manuscripts of the Tenth and Eleventh Centuries." 2 vols. Ph.D. diss., University of California at Berkeley, 1976.

BLOCH, Peter. "Das Apsismosaik von Germigny-des-Prés: Karl der Grosse and der Alte Bund." In *Karl der Grosse: Lebenswerk und Nachleben*, edited by Wolfgang Braunfels, et al., 3:234–61, and fig. 5.

BLOCH, Peter, and Hermann Schnitzler. *Die ottonische Kölner Malerschule*. 2 vols. Düsseldorf, 1967–70.

BLUMENTHAL, Uta-Renate, ed. *Carolingian Essays: Andrew W. Mellon Lectures in Early Christian Studies*. Washington, D.C., 1983.

BOECKLER, Albert. "Die Evangelistenbilder der Ada-Gruppe." *Münchener Jahrbuch der bildenden Kunst*, 3rd ser., 3–4 (1952–53): 121–44.

BOESPFLUG, F., and N. Lossky, eds. *Nicée II, 787–1987: Douze siècles d'images religieuses*. Paris, 1987.

BÖHNE, Winfried. "Beobachtungen zur Perikopenreihe des Godescalc-Evangeliars." *Würzburger Diözesansblätter* 37/38 (1975): 149–67.

BOLGAR, R. R. *The Classical Heritage and Its Beneficiaries from the Carolingian Age to the End of the Renaissance*. London and New York, 1954; repr., New York, 1964.

BORST, Arno. "Alkuin und die Enzyklopädie von 809." In *Science in Western and Eastern Civilization in Carolingian Times*, edited by Paul Leo Butzer and Dietrich Lohrmann, pp. 53–78.

———. "Das Karlsbild in der Geschichtswissenschaft vom Humanismus bis heute." In *Karl der Grosse: Lebenswerk und Nachleben*, edited by Wolfgang Braunfels, et al., 4:364–402.

———. *Lebensform im Mittelalter*. Frankfurt, 1973.

———. "Ranke und Karl der Grosse." In *Dauer und Wandel der Geschichte*, edited by Rudolf Vierhaus and Manfred Botzenhart, pp. 448–82.

———, ed. *Mönchtum, Episkopat und Adel zur Gründungzeit des Klosters Reichenau*. Vorträge und Forschungen 20. Sigmaringen, 1974.

BOSHOF, Egon. *Erzbischof Agobard von Lyon: Leben und Werk*. Kölner historische Abhandlungen 17. Cologne, 1969.

BOSSE, Detlov. *Untersuchungen einstimmiger mittelalterlicher Melodien zum Gloria in excelsis*. Erlangen, 1954.

BOUCHARD, Constance B. "The Origins of the French Nobility: A Reassessment." *American Historical Review* 86 (1981): 501–32.

BOUHOT, Jean-Paul. *Ratram de Corbie: Histoire littéraire et controverses doctrinales*. Paris, 1976.

BOUMAN, C. A. *Sacring and Crowning: The Development of the Latin Ritual for the Anointing of Kings and the Coronation of an Emperor before the Eleventh Century*. Bijdragen van het Instituut voor Middeleeuwse Geschiednis der Rijks-Universiteit te Utrecht 30. Groningen, 1957.

BRANDMÜLLER, Walter. "*Traditio Scripturae Interpres*: The Teaching of the Councils on the Right Interpretation of Scripture up to the Council of Trent." *Catholic Historical Review* 73 (1987): 523–40.

BRAUNFELS, Wolfgang. "Karolingischer Klassizismus als politisches Programm und karolingischer Humanismus als Lebenshaltung." In *Nascita dell'Europa ed Europa carolingia*, 2:821–49.

————. *Das Lorscher Evangeliar*. Munich, 1967.

BRAUNFELS, Wolfgang, et al., eds. *Karl der Grosse: Lebenswerk und Nachleben.* 5 vols. Vol. 1: *Persönlichkeit und Geschichte,* edited by Helmut Beumann. 2nd ed. Vol. 2: *Das geistige Leben,* edited by Bernhard Bischoff. 2nd ed. Vol. 3: *Karolingische Kunst,* edited by Braunfels and Hermann Schnitzler. 3rd ed. Vol. 4: *Das Nachleben,* edited by Braunfels and Percy Ernst Schramm. Vol. 5: *Registerband,* edited by Braunfels. Düsseldorf, 1966–68.

BREISACH, Ernst. *Historiography: Ancient, Medieval, and Modern.* Chicago and London, 1983.

BROOK, Thomas. *The New Historicism and Other Old-Fashioned Topics.* Princeton, N.J., 1991.

BROOKS, Nicholas, ed. *Latin and the Vernacular Languages in Early Medieval Britain.* Studies in the Early History of Britain. Leicester, 1982.

BROWN, Giles. "Introduction: The Carolingian Renaissance." In *Carolingian Culture,* edited by Rosamond McKitterick, pp. 1–51.

BRUCKNER, A. *Scriptoria Helvetica Medii Aevi.* Vols. 2–3. Geneva, 1936–38.

BRUNHÖLZL, Franz. "Der Bildungsauftrag der Hofschule." In *Karl der Grosse: Lebenswerk und Nachleben,* edited by Wolfgang Braunfels, et al., 2:28–41.

————. *Geschichte der lateinischen Literatur des Mittelalters.* Vol. 1: *Von Cassiodor bis zum Ausklang der karolingischen Erneuerung.* Munich, 1975.

BUCHTHAL, Hugo. *The Miniatures of the Paris Psalter: A Study in Middle Byzantine Painting.* Studies of the Warburg Institute 2. London, 1938.

BÜHLER, Arnold. "Capitularia Relecta: Studien zur Entstehung und Überlieferung der Kapitularien Karls des Grossen und Ludwig des Frommen." *Archiv für Diplomatik, Schriftgeschichte, Siegel- und Wappenkunde* 32 (1986): 305–501.

BÜLL, F. "Die Klöster Franken bis zum IX. Jahrhundert." *Studien und Mitteilungen zur Geschichte des Benediktiner-Ordens und seiner Zweige* 104 (1993): 9–40.

BULLOUGH, Donald A. *The Age of Charlemagne.* 2nd ed. London, 1973.

————. "Alcuin and the Kingdom of Heaven: Liturgy, Theology, and the Carolingian Age." In *Carolingian Essays,* edited by Uta-Renate Blumenthal, pp. 1–69. Repr. with revisions in Bullough, *Carolingian Renewal,* pp. 161–240.

————. "*Aula Renovata*: The Carolingian Court before the Aachen Palace (Raleigh Lecture on History, 1985)." *Proceedings of the British Academy* 71 (1985): 267–301. Repr. with revisions in Bullough, *Carolingian Renewal,* pp. 123–60.

————. *Carolingian Renewal: Sources and Heritage.* Manchester and New York, 1991.

————. "Ethnic History and the Carolingians: An Alternative Reading of Paul the Deacon's *Historia Langobardorum.*" In *The Inheritance of Historiography, 350–900,* edited by Christopher Holdsworth and T. P. Wiseman, pp. 85–105. Repr. in Bullough, *Carolingian Renewal,* pp. 97–122.

————. *"Europae Pater*: Charlemagne and His Achievements in the Light of Recent Scholarship." *English Historical Review* 85 (1970): 59–105.

————. "'Imagines Regum' and Their Significance in the Early Medieval West." In *Studies in Memory of David Talbot Rice*, edited by Giles Robertson and George Henderson, pp. 223–76. Repr. in Bullough, *Carolingian Renewal*, pp. 39–96.

————. "Roman Books and Carolingian *Renovatio*." In *Renaissance and Renewal in Christian History*, edited by Derek Baker, pp. 23–50. Repr. in Bullough, *Carolingian Renewal*, pp. 1–33.

BULLOUGH, Donald A., and Alice L. H. Corrêa. "Texts, Chant, and the Chapel of Louis the Pious." In *Charlemagne's Heir*, edited by Peter Godman and Roger Collins, pp. 489–508. Repr. with revisions in Bullough, *Carolingian Renewal*, pp. 241–71.

BURKE, Peter, ed. *New Perspectives on Historical Writing*. Cambridge, 1991.

BURNS, C. Delisle. *The First Europe: A Study of the Establishment of Medieval Christendom, A.D. 400–800*. London, 1947.

BUTZER, Paul Leo, and Dietrich Lohrmann, eds. *Science in Western and Eastern Civilization in Carolingian Times*. Basel, 1993.

CABANISS, Allen. *Agobard of Lyons: Churchman and Critic*. Syracuse, N.Y., 1953.

The Cambridge History of Later Greek and Early Medieval Philosophy. Edited by A. H. Armstrong. Cambridge, 1970.

The Cambridge History of Medieval Political Thought, c. 350–c. 1450. Edited by J. H. Burns. Cambridge and New York, 1988.

The Cambridge History of the Bible. Edited by G. W. H. Lampe. 3 vols. Cambridge, 1963–69.

The Cambridge Illustrated History of the Middles Ages. Vol. 1: *350–950*. Edited by Robert Fossier. Translated by Janet Sondheimer. Cambridge and New York, 1989. Originally published as Robert Fossier, et al., *La Moyen âge*, vol. 1: *Les Mondes nouveaux* (Paris, 1982).

CAMERON, M. L. "The Sources of Medical Knowledge in Anglo-Saxon England." *Anglo-Saxon England* 11 (1983): 133–55.

CANNADINE, David, and Simon Price, eds. *Rituals of Royalty: Power and Ceremonial in Traditional Societies*. Cambridge, 1987.

CANTELLI, Silvia. *Angelomo e la scuola esegetica di Luxeuil*. 2 vols. Biblioteca di "Medioevo Latino." Collana della "Società internazionale per lo studio del medioevo latino" 1. Spoleto, 1990.

————. "L'Esegesi al tempo di Ludovico il Pio e Carlo il Calvo." In *Giovanni Scoto nel suo tempo: L'organizzazione del sapere in età carolingi*, edited by Claudio Leonardi and Enrico Menestò, pp. 261–336.

CANTOR, Norman F. *Inventing the Middle Ages*. New York, 1991.

CAPPUYNS, Maïeul. *Jean Scot Erigène: Sa vie, son oeuvre, sa pensée*. Louvain, 1933.

Caratteri del secolo VII in Occidente. 2 vols. Settimane 5. Spoleto, 1958.

CARDINE, Eugene. *Gregorian Semiology.* Translated by R. Fowels. Solesmes, 1982.

CARILE, Antonio. "L'iconoclasmo fra bisanzio e l'Italia." In *Culto delle immagini e crisi iconoclasta,* pp. 13–54.

CAROZZI, Claude. Introduction to *Adalbéron de Laon: Poème au roi Robert,* edited by Carozzi, pp. ix–cxl. Les classiques de l'histoire de France au Moyen Age 32. Paris, 1979.

CARRARD, Philippe. *Poetics of the New History: French Historical Discourse from Braudel to Chartier.* Parallax: Re-visions of Culture and Society. Baltimore, Md., 1992.

CASTILLE, C. H. *Parallèle entre César, Charlemagne et Napoléon: L'Empire et la démocratie, philosophie de la légende impériale.* Paris, 1858.

CAVALLO, Guglielmo, Jean Gribomont, and William C. Loerke. *Codex purpureus Rossanensis: Museo dell'Arcivescovado, Rossano Calabro.* Rome and Graz, 1987.

CHADWICK, Henry. *Boethius: The Consolations of Music, Logic, Theology, and Philosophy.* Oxford and New York, 1981.

CHAZELLE, Celia M. "Images, Scripture, the Church, and the *Libri Carolini.*" *Proceedings of the PMR Conference* 16/17 (1992–93): 53–76.

———. "Matter, Spirit, and Image in the *Libri Carolini.*" *Recherches augustiniennes* 21 (1986): 163–84.

———. "Pictures, Books and the Illiterate: Pope Gregory I's Letters to Serenus of Marseilles." *Word and Image* 6 (1990): 138–53.

———, ed. *Literacy, Politics, and Artistic Innovation in the Early Medieval West: Papers Delivered at a Symposium on Early Medieval Culture, Bryn Mawr College.* Lanham, Md., and London, 1992.

CHÉLINI, Jean. *L'Aube du moyen âge: Naissance de la chrétienté occidentale: La Vie religieuse des laïcs dans l'Europe carolingienne (750–900).* Paris, 1991.

La chiesa nei regni dall'Europa occidentale e i loro rapporti con Roma sino all'800. 2 vols. Settimane 7. Spoleto, 1960.

CHIOVARO, F., et al., eds. *Histoire des saints et de la sainteté chrétienne.* Vol. 4: *Les Voies nouvelles de la sainteté, 605–814,* edited by Pierre Riché. Vol. 5: *Les Saintetés dans les empires rivaux, 815–1053,* edited by Pierre Riché. Paris, 1986.

CLASSEN, Peter. "Die hohen Schulen und die Gesellschaft im 12. Jahrhundert." *Archiv für Kulturgeschichte* 48 (1966): 155–80. Repr. in Classen, *Studium und Gesellschaft im Mittelalter,* pp. 1–26.

———. *Studium und Gesellschaft im Mittelalter.* Edited by Johannes Fried. MGH, Schriften 29. Stuttgart, 1983.

———, ed. *Recht und Schrift im Mittelalter.* Vorträge und Forschungen 23. Sigmaringen, 1977.

CLIVIO, Gianrenzo P., and Riccardo Massano, eds. *Civiltà del Piemonte: Studi in onore di Renzo Gandolfo nel suo settantacinquesimo compleanno.* Turin, 1975.

CLOVER, F. M., and R. S. Humphreys, eds. *Tradition and Innovation in Late Antiquity*. Wisconsin Studies in Classics. Madison, Wis., 1989.

COCKS, Geoffrey, and Travis L. Crosby, eds. *Psycho/History: Readings in the Method of Psychology, Psychoanalysis, and History*. New Haven, Conn., and London, 1987.

COHEN, G. A. *Karl Marx's Theory of History: A Defence*. Oxford, 1978.

COLISH, Marcia L. "Carolingian Debates over *Nihil* and *Tenebrae*: A Study in Theological Method." *Speculum* 59 (1984): 757–95.

COLLINS, Roger. *Early Medieval Europe, 300–1000*. New York, 1991.

Committenti e produzione artistico-letteraria nell'alto medioevo occidentale. 2 vols. Settimane 39. Spoleto, 1992.

CONANT, Kenneth John. *Carolingian and Romanesque Architecture, 800 to 1200*. The Pelican History of Art. 2nd integrated ed., rev. Harmondsworth, 1978; repr., 1990.

CONGAR, Yves M.-J. *L'Ecclésiologie du haut moyen âge de saint Grégoire le Grand à le désunion entre Byzance et Rome*. Paris, 1968.

———. *Tradition and Traditions: An Historical and a Theological Essay*. Translated by Michael Naseby and Thomas Rainborough. New York, 1967.

CONSTABLE, Giles. *Medieval Monasticism: A Select Bibliography*. Toronto Medieval Bibliographies 6. Toronto, 1976.

CONTAMINE, Geneviève, ed. *Traduction et traducteurs au moyen âge*. Actes du colloque international du Centre national de la recherche scientifique organisé à Paris, les 26–28 mai 1986. Institut de recherche et d'histoire des textes. Paris, 1989.

CONTRENI, John J. "Carolingian Biblical Studies." In *Carolingian Essays*, edited by Uta-Renate Blumenthal, pp. 71–98. Repr. in Contreni, *Carolingian Learning, Masters, and Manuscripts*, chap. 5.

———. *Carolingian Learning, Masters, and Manuscripts*. Variorum Collected Studies Series, CS363. Aldershot, England, 1992.

———. "The Carolingian Renaissance." In *Renaissances before the Renaissance*, edited by Warren Treadgold, pp. 59–74. Repr. in Contreni, *Carolingian Learning, Masters, and Manuscripts*, chap. 3.

———. "The Carolingian School: Letters from the Classroom." In *Giovanni Scoto nel suo tempo: L'organizzazione del sapere in età carolingia*, edited by Claudio Leonardi and Enrico Menestò, pp. 81–111. Repr. in Contreni, *Carolingian Learning, Masters, and Manuscripts*, chap. 11.

———. *The Cathedral School of Laon from 850 to 930: Its Manuscripts and Masters*. Münchener Beiträge zur Mediävistik und Renaissance-Forschung 29. Munich, 1978.

———. "Inharmonius Harmony: Education in the Carolingian World." *Annals of Scholarship: Metastudies of the Humanities and Social Sciences* 1 (1980): 81–96. Repr. in Contreni, *Carolingian Learning, Masters, and Manuscripts*, chap. 4.

———. "John Scottus, Martin Hiberniensis, the Liberal Arts, and Teaching." In

Insular Latin Studies, edited by Michael W. Herren, pp. 23–44. Repr. in Contreni, *Carolingian Learning, Masters, and Manuscripts*, chap. 6.

———"Learning in the Early Middle Ages." In Contreni, *Carolingian Learning, Masters, and Manuscripts*, chap. 1.

———. "The Tenth Century: The Perspective from the Schools." In *Haut moyen âge: Culture, éducation, et société: Etudes offertes à Pierre Riché*, edited by Michel Sot, pp. 379–97. Repr. in Contreni, *Carolingian Learning, Masters, and Manuscripts*, chap. 12.

———, ed. *Codex Laudunensis 468: A Ninth-Century Guide to Virgil, Sedulius, and the Liberal Arts*. Armarium Codicum Insignium 3. Turnhout, 1984.

La conversione al cristianesimo nell'Europa dell'alto medioevo. Settimane 14. Spoleto, 1967.

COPELAND, Rita. *Rhetoric, Hermeneutics, and Translation in the Middle Ages: Academic Traditions and Vernacular Texts*. Cambridge, 1991.

CORBIN, Solange. *Die Neumen*. Palaeographie der Musik 1/3. Cologne, 1977.

COUPLAND, Simon. "Carolingian Arms and Armor in the Ninth Century." *Viator* 21 (1990): 29–50.

CRISTIANI, Marta. *Dall'unanimitas all'universitas da Alcuino a Giovanni Eriugena: Lineamenti ideologici e terminologia politica della cultura del secolo IX*. Istituto storico per il medio evo, Studi storici, fasc. 100–102. Rome, 1978.

Cristianizzazione ed organizzazione ecclesiatica delle campagne nell'alto medioevo: Espanzione e resistenze. 2 vols. Settimane 28. Spoleto, 1982.

CROCKER, Richard L. "Chants of the Roman Mass." In *The Early Middle Ages to 1300*, edited by Crocker and David Hiley, pp. 196–214.

———. "Chants of the Roman Office." In *The Early Middle Ages to 1300*, edited by Crocker and David Hiley, pp. 146–73.

———. *The Early Medieval Sequence*. Berkeley, 1977.

———. "Gloria in excelsis." In *The New Grove Dictionary of Music and Musicians*, 7:450–52.

———. "Hucbald." In *The New Grove Dictionary of Music and Musicians*, 8:758–59.

———. "Kyrie eleison." In *The New Grove Dictionary of Music and Musicians*, 10:331–33.

———. "Liturgical Materials of Roman Chant." In *The Early Middle Ages to 1300*, edited by Crocker and David Hiley, pp. 115–45.

———. "Matins Antiphons at St. Denis." *Journal of the American Musicological Society* 39 (1986): 441–90.

———. "Medieval Chant." In *The Early Middle Ages to 1300*, edited by Crocker and David Hiley, pp. 225–309.

———. "The Sequence." In *Gattungen der Musik in Einzeldarstellungen*, edited by W. Arlt, et al., pp. 269–322.

CROCKER, Richard L., and David Hiley, eds. *The Early Middle Ages to 1300*. 2nd ed. New Oxford History of Music 2. Oxford and New York, 1990.

CRUZIUS, Irene, ed. *Beiträge zu Geschichte und Struktur der mittelalterlichen*

Germania Sacra. Veröffentlichungen des Max-Planck-Instituts für Geschichte 93; Studien zu Germania Sacra 17. Göttingen, 1989.

CULLER, Jonathan. *On Deconstruction: Theory and Criticism after Structuralism.* Ithaca, N.Y., 1982.

Culto cristiano: Politica imperiale carolingia. Convegni del Centro di Studi sulla spiritualità medievale, Università degli Studi di Perugia 18. Todi, 1979.

Culto delle immagini e crisi iconoclasta. Atti del convegno di studi Catania, 16–17 maggio 1984. Palermo, 1986.

La cultura antica nell'occidente latino dal VII all'XI secolo. 2 vols. Settimane 22. Spoleto, 1975.

Cultura e società nell'Italia medievale: Studi per Paolo Brezzi. 2 vols. Studi storici, fasc. 184–92. Rome, 1988.

CWI, Joan S. "A Study in Carolingian Political Theology: The David Cycle at St. John, Müstair." In *Riforma religiosa e arti nell'epoca Carolingia*, edited by Alfred A. Schmid, pp. 117–27.

DAHLHAUS-BERG, Elisabeth. *Nova Antiquitas et Antiqua Novitas: Typologische Exegese und isidorianisches Geschichtsbild bei Theodulf von Orléans.* Kölner historische Abhandlungen 23. Cologne, 1975.

DAWSON, Christopher. *The Making of Europe: An Introduction to the History of European Unity.* New York, 1945.

DÉCARREAUX, Jean. *Moines et monastères à l'époque de Charlemagne.* Paris, 1980.

DE CLERCQ, Carlo. *La Législation religieuse franque: Etude sur les actes de conciles et les capitulaires, les statuts diocésains et les règles monastiques.* Vol. 1: *De Clovis à Charlemagne (507–814).* Vol. 2: *De Louis le Pieux à la fin du IXe siècle (814–900).* Louvain and Antwerp, 1936 and 1958.

DE JONG, Mayke. "Growing up in a Carolingian Monastery: Magister Hildemar and His Oblates." *Journal of Medieval History* 9 (1983): 99–128.

DEKKERS, E., ed. *Clavis Patrum Latinorum.* 2nd ed. Steenbrugge, 1961.

DELARUELLE, Etienne. "Charlemagne et l'église." *Revue d'histoire de l'église de France* 39 (1953): 165–99.

DERRIDA, Jacques. *Of Grammatology.* Translated by Gayatri Chakravorty Spivak. Baltimore, Md., 1976.

DESCHMAN, Robert. "The Exalted Servant: The Ruler Theology of the Prayerbook of Charles the Bald." *Viator* 11 (1980): 385–417, and figs. 1–22.

DESHUSSES, Jean. *Le Sacramentaire grégorien: Les Principales Formes d'après les plus anciennes manuscrits.* 3 vols. Spicilegium Friburgensis 16, 24, 28. Freiburg, 1971–82; 2nd ed., vol. 1, 1979.

DEVISSE, Jean. *Hincmar, Archevêque de Reims, 845–882.* 3 vols. Travaux d'histoire ethico-politique 29. Geneva, 1975–76.

DE VOGÜÉ, Adalbert. *Le Règle de saint Benoît.* Vol. 7: *Commentaire doctrinal et spirituel.* Paris, 1977. Published in English as *The Rule of St. Benedict: A Doctrinal and Spiritual Commentary*, translated by John B. Hasbrouck, Cistercian Studies 54 (Kalamazoo, Mich., 1983).

DE VRIES, Wilhelm. "Die Struktur der Kirche gemäss dem II Nicäa (787)." *Orientalia Christiana Periodica* 33 (1967): 47–71.

DEVROEY, Jean-Pierre. "'Ad utilitatem monasterii': Mobiles et préoccupations de gestion dans l'économie monastique du monde franc." *Revue bénédictine* 103 (1993): 224–40.

Dictionary of the Middle Ages. 13 vols. New York, 1982–89.

DIEBOLD, William. "The Ruler Portrait of Charles the Bald in the S. Paolo Bible." *Art Bulletin* 76 (1994): 6–18.

———. "Verbal, Visual, and Cultural Literacy in Medieval Art: Word and Image in the Psalter of Charles the Bald." *Word and Image* 8 (1992): 89–99.

DIERKENS, Alain. "Pour une typologie des missions carolingiennes." In *Propagande et contrapropagande religieuses*, edited by J. Marx, pp. 77–93.

DINZELBACHER, Peter. "Die Bedeutung des Buches in der Karolingerzeit." *Archiv für Geschichte des Buchwesens* 24 (1983): 257–88.

DIONISOTTI, A. C. "Greek Grammars and Dictionaries in Carolingian Europe." In *The Sacred Nectar of the Greeks*, edited by Michael W. Herren, pp. 1–56.

DODWELL, C. R. *The Pictorial Arts of the West, 800–1200.* Pelican History of Art. New Haven, Conn., and London, 1993.

D'ONOFRIO, Mario. *Roma e Aquisgrana.* Collana di studi di storia dell'arte 4. Rome, 1983.

DOPSCH, Heinz, and Roswitha Ruffinger, eds. *Virgil von Salzburg, Missionär und Gelehrter: Beiträge des internationalen Symposiums von 21.–24. September 1984 in der Salzburger Residenz.* Salzburg, 1985.

DOSSE, François. *L'histoire en miettes: Des "Annales" à la "nouvelle histoire."* Armillaire. Paris, 1987.

DOYLE, Edward Gerard. Introduction to *Sedulius Scottus: On Christian Rulers and the Poems*, translated by Doyle, pp. 9–48. Medieval and Renaissance Texts and Studies 17. Binghamton, N.Y., 1983.

DRAAK, Maartje. "Construe Marks in Hiberno-Latin Manuscipts." *Mededelingen der koninklijke nederlandse Akademie van Wetenschappen, afd. Letterkunde*, new ser., 20, no. 10 (1957): 216–82.

———. "The Higher Teaching of Latin Grammar in Ireland during the Ninth Century." *Mededelingen der koninklijke nederlandse Akademie van Wetenschappen, afd. Letterkunde*, new ser., 30, no. 4 (1967): 100–144.

DREVES, Guido Maria. *Lateinische Hymnendichter des Mittelalters.* Analecta hymnica medii aevi 50. Leipzig, 1907; repr., New York and London, 1961.

DUCHEZ, Marie-Elisabeth. "Jean Scot Erigène, premier lecteur du De institutione musica de Boèce?" In *Eriugena: Studien zu seinem Quellen*, edited by Werner Beierwaltes, pp. 165–87.

DUCKETT, Eleanor Shipley. *Carolingian Portraits: A Study in the Ninth Century.* Ann Arbor, Mich., 1962.

DUFRENNE, Suzy. *Tableaux synoptiques des 15 psautiers médiévaux à illustrations intégrales issues du texte.* Paris, 1978.

DUGGAN, Anne J., ed. *Kings and Kingship in Medieval Europe*. London, 1993.

DUGGAN, Lawrence G. "Was Art Really the 'Book of the Illiterate'?" *Word and Image* 5 (1989): 227–51.

DUMEIGE, Gervais. *Nicée II*. Histoire des conciles ecuméniques 4. Paris, 1978.

DÜMMLER, Ernst. *Geschichte des ostfränkischen Reiches*. 3 vols. 2nd ed. Leipzig, 1887–88; repr., Hildesheim, 1960.

DUPREE, A. Hunter. "The Significance of the Plan of St. Gall to the History of Measurement: A Link between Roman, and English and American Systems of Measurement." In Walter Horn and Ernest Born, *The Plan of St. Gall*, 3:131–40.

DURLIAT, Marcel. *Des barbares à l'an mil*. Paris, 1985.

DUTTÓN, Paul Edward, ed. *Carolingian Civilization: A Reader*. Peterborough, Ontario, 1993.

DUVAL, Yves-Marie. "Le 'Liber Hieronymi ad Gaudentium': Rufin d'Aquilée, Gaudence de Brescia et Eusèbe de Crémone." *Revue bénédictine* 97 (1987): 163–86.

DUVAL, Yvette. *Auprès des saints corps et âme: L'Inhumation "ad sanctos" dans le chrétienté d'orient et d'occident du IIIe au VIIe siècle*. Paris, 1988.

EAGLETON, Terry. *Literary Theory: An Introduction*. Minneapolis, 1983.

EASTWOOD, Bruce S. "The Astronomy of Macrobius in Carolingian Europe: Dungal's Letter of 811 to Charles the Great." *Early Medieval Europe* 3 (1994): 117–34.

———. "Medieval Science Illustrated." *History of Science* 24 (1986): 183–209.

———. "Plinian Astronomical Diagrams in the Early Middle Ages." In *Mathematics and Its Applications to Science and Natural Philosophy in the Middle Ages*, edited by Edward Grant and John P. Murdoch, pp. 141–72.

EBENBAUER, Alfred. *Carmen Historicum: Untersuchungen zur historischer Dichtung im karolingischen Europa*. Vol. 1. Philologica Germanica 4. Vienna, 1978.

EBERHARDT, Otto. *Via Regia: Der Fürstenspiegel Smaragds von St.-Mihiel und seine literarische Gattung*. Münstersche Mittelalter-Schriften 28. Munich, 1977.

EDELSTEIN, Wolfgang. *Eruditio und Sapientia: Weltbild und Erziehung in der Karolingerzeit: Untersuchungen zu Alcuins Briefen*. Freiburg im Breisgau, 1965.

EDWARDS, Cyril. "German Vernacular Literature: A Survey." In *Carolingian Culture*, edited by Rosamond McKitterick, pp. 141–70.

EGGENBERGER, Christoph. *Psalterium Aureum Sancti Galli: Mittelalterliche Psalterillustration im Kloster St. Gallen*. Sigmaringen, 1987.

EICHHOFF, Jürgen, and Irmengard Rauh, eds. *Der Heiland*. Wege der Forschung 321. Darmstadt, 1973.

ENRIGHT, Michael J. *Iona, Tara and Soissons: The Origin of the Royal Anointing Ritual*. Arbeiten zur Frühmittelalterforschung, Schriftenreihe des Instituts für Frühmittelalterforschungen der Universität Münster 17. Berlin and New York, 1985.

E P P E R L E I N, Siegfried. "Karl der Grosse in der deutschen bürgerlichen Geschichtsschreibung." *Zeitschrift für Geschichtswissenschaft* 13 (1965): 235–61.

E R D M A N N, Carl. *Die Entstehung des Kreuzzugsgedankens.* Stuttgart, 1965. Published in English as *The Origin of the Idea of Crusade,* translated by Marshall W. Baldwin and Walter Goffart (Princeton, N.J., 1977).

E S P O S I T O, Mario. "An Unpublished Astronomical Treatise by the Irish Monk Dicuil." *Proceedings of the Royal Irish Academy* 26C (1907): 378–446.

E S T I N, Colette. "Les Traductions du Psautier." In *Le Monde latin antique et la Bible,* edited by Jacques Fontaine and Charles Pietri, pp. 77–88.

E V A N S, Michael. "The Geometry of the Mind." *Architectural Association Quarterly* 12, no. 4 (1980): 32–55.

E V A N S, Paul. *The Early Trope Repertory of Saint Martial de Limoges.* Princeton, N.J., 1970.

E W I G, Eugen. "Beobachtungen zur Entwicklung der fränkischen Reichskirche unter Chrodegang von Metz." *Frühmittelalterliche Studien* 2 (1968): 67–77. Repr. in Ewig, *Spätantikes und fränkisches Gallien,* 2:220–31.

———. "Das Bild Constantins des Grossen in den ersten Jahrhunderten des abendländischen Mittelalters." *Historisches Jahrbuch* 75 (1956): 1–46. Repr. in Ewig, *Spätantikes und fränkisches Gallien,* 1:72–113.

———. *Spätantikes und fränkisches Gallien: Gesammelte Schriften (1952–1973).* Edited by Hartmut Atsma. 2 vols. Beihefte der Francia 3, 1–2. Munich, 1976, 1979.

———. "Zum christlichen Königsgedanken im Frühmittelalter." In *Das Königtum: Seine geistigen und rechtlichen Grundlagen,* edited by Theodor Mayer, pp. 7–73. Repr. in Ewig, *Spätantikes und fränkisches Gallien,* 1:3–71.

F A L K E N S T E I N, Ludwig. "Zwischenbilanz zur aachener Pfalzenforschung." *Zeitschrift der aachener Geschichtsverein* 80 (1970): 7–71.

F A L L O N, Hugh C. "Imperial Symbolism on Two Carolingian Coins." *American Numismatic Society, Museum Notes* 8 (1958): 119–31.

F A S S L E R, Margot E. "The Office of Cantor in Early Western Monastic Rules and Customaries: A Preliminary Investigation." *Early Music History* 5 (1985): 29–52.

F A Z Z O, Vittorio. "Il II Concilio di Nicea nella storia cristiana ed i rapporti fra Roma e Bisanzio." In *Cultura e società nell'Italia medievale,* 1:345–60.

F E L T E N, Franz J. *Äbte und Laienäbte im Frankenreich: Studie zum Verhältnis von Staat und Kirche im früheren Mittelalter.* Monographien zur Geschichte des Mittelalters 20. Stuttgart, 1980.

———. "Herrschaft des Abtes." In *Herrschaft und Kirche,* edited by Friedrich Prinz, pp. 147–296.

F E N T R E S S, James, and Chris Wickham. *Social Memory.* New Perspectives on the Past. Oxford, 1992.

F E R G U S O N, Wallace K. *The Renaissance in Historical Thought: Five Centuries of Interpretation.* Boston, 1948.

FICHTENAU, Heinrich. "Byzanz und die Pfalz zu Aachen." *Mitteilungen des Instituts für österreichische Geschichtsforschung* 59 (1951): 1–54.

———. "Karl der Grosse und das Kaistertum." *Mitteilungen des Instituts für österreichische Geschichtsforschung* 61 (1953): 257–334.

———. *Lebensordnungen des 10. Jahrhunderts: Studien über Denkart und Existenz im einstigen Karolingerreich.* 2 vols. Stuttgart, 1984. Published in English as *Living in the Tenth Century: Mentalities and Social Orders*, translated by Patrick J. Geary (Chicago and New York, 1991).

FISCHER, Bonifatius. *Die Alkuin-Bibel.* Aus der Geschichte der lateinischen Bibel 1. Freiburg, 1957.

———. "Bibeltext und Bibelreform unter Karl dem Grossen." In *Karl der Grosse: Lebenswerk und Nachleben*, edited by Wolfgang Braunfels, et al., 2:156–216. Repr. in Fischer, *Lateinische Bibelhandschriften im frühen Mittelalter*, pp. 101–202.

———. *Lateinische Bibelhandschriften im frühen Mittelalter.* Aus der Geschichte der lateinischen Bibel 11. Freiburg, 1985.

FLECKENSTEIN, Josef. *Die Bildungsreform Karls des Grossen als Verwicklichung der norma rectitudinis.* Bigge-Ruhr, 1953.

FLINT, Valerie I. J. *The Rise of Magic in Early Medieval Europe.* Princeton, N.J., 1991.

FOKKEMA, D. W., and Elrud Kunne-Ibsch. *Theories of Literature in the Twentieth Century: Structuralism, Marxism, Aesthetics of Reception, Semiotics.* New York, 1977.

FOLZ, Robert. *Le Couronnement impérial de Charlemagne, 25 décembre 800.* Trente journées qui ont fait la France 3. Paris, 1964. Published in English as *The Coronation of Charlemagne 25 December 800*, translated by J. E. Anderson (London, 1974).

———. *Etudes sur le culte liturgique de Charlemagne dans les églises de l'empire.* Publications de la Faculté des lettres de l'Université de Strasbourg 115. Paris, 1951.

———. *L'Idée d'empire en occident du Ve au XIVe siècle.* Collection historique. Paris, 1953. Published in English as *The Concept of Empire in Western Europe from the Fifth to the Fourteenth Century*, translated by Sheila Ann Ogilvie (London, 1969).

———. *Le Souvenir et la légende de Charlemagne dans l'empire germanique médiéval.* Paris, 1950.

Les fonctions des saints dans le monde occidental (IIIe–XIIIe siècle): Actes du colloque organisé par l'Ecole française de Rome avec le concours de l'Université de Rome 'La Sapienza,' Rome, 27–29 octobre 1988. Collection de L'Ecole française de Rome 149. Rome, 1991.

FONTAINE, Jacques. "De la pluralité à l'unité dans le 'latin carolingien'?" In *Nascita dell'Europa ed Europa carolingia*, 2:765–818.

———. *Isidore de Séville et la culture classique dans l'Espagne wisigothique.* 3 vols. Paris, 1959–83.

————. "La Naissance difficile d'une latinité médiévale (500–744): Mutations, étapes et pistes." *Bulletin de l'Association Guillaume Budé*, 1981, pp. 360–68.

FONTAINE, Jacques, and J. N. Hillgarth, eds. *Le Septième Siècle: Changements et continuités: Actes du colloque bilatéral franco-brittanique tenu au Warburg Institute les 8–9 juillet 1988/The Seventh Century: Change and Continuity: Proceedings of Joint French and British Colloquium held at the Warburg Institute 8–9 July 1988.* Studies of the Warburg Institute 42. London, 1992.

FONTAINE, Jacques, and Charles Pietri, eds. *Le Monde latin antique et la Bible.* Bible de Tous les Temps 2. Paris, 1985.

La Fortune historiographique des thèses d'Henri Pirenne. Actes du colloque organisé à l'occasion du cinquantenaire de la mort de l'historien belge, à l'initiative de G. Despy et A. Verhulst, 10–11 mai 1985. Brussels, 1986.

FOSSIER, Robert, et al. *Le Moyen Age*, 3 vols. Paris, 1982–83. Vol. 1, *Les Mondes nouveaux*, translated as *The Cambridge Illustrated History of the Middle Ages*, vol. 1: *350–950.* Edited by Robert Fossier. Translated by Janet Sondheimer.

FOUCAULT, Michel. *The Archaeology of Knowledge.* Translated by A. M. Sheridan Smith. New York, 1972.

FOURNIER, Paul, and Gabriel Le Bras. *Histoire des collections canoniques en occident depuis les Fausses Décrétales jusqu'au Décret de Gratian.* 2 vols. Bibliothèque d'histoire des droit 4–5. Paris, 1931–32.

FRAKES, Jerold C. *The Fate of Fortune in the Early Middle Ages: The Boethian Tradition.* Studien und Texte zur Geistesgeschichte des Mittelalters 23. Leiden, New York, and Copenhagen, 1988.

FRANK, Karl Suso. "Vom Kloster als schola dominici servitii zum Kloster als servitium imperii." *Studien und Mitteilungen zur Geschichte des Benediktiner-Ordens und seiner Zweige* 91 (1980): 80–97.

FREEDBERG, David. *The Power of Images: Studies in the History and Theory of Response.* Chicago, 1989.

FREEMAN, Ann. "Additions and Corrections to the *Libri Carolini*: Links with Alcuin and the Adoptionist Controversy." In *Scire Litteras*, edited by Sigrid Krämer and Michael Bernhard, pp. 159–69.

————. "Carolingian Orthodoxy and the Fate of the *Libri Carolini*." *Viator* 16 (1985): 65–108.

————. "Further Studies in the *Libri Carolini* I–II." *Speculum* 40 (1965): 203–89.

————. Further Studies in the *Libri Carolini* III: The Marginal Notes in *Vaticanus Latinus 7207*." *Speculum* 46 (1971): 597–612.

————. "Theodulf of Orléans and the *Libri Carolini*." *Speculum* 32 (1957): 663–705.

————. "Theodulf of Orléans and the Psalm Citations of the 'Libri Carolini.'" *Revue bénédictine* 97 (1987): 195–224.

FREISE, Eckhard. "Kalendarische und annalistische Grundformen der

Memoria." In *Memoria*, edited by Karl Schmid and Joachim Wollasch, pp. 527–34.

FREYTAG, Gustav. *Bilder aus der deutschen Vergangenheit*. Vol. 1: *Aus dem Mittelalter*. In Freytag, *Gesammelte Werke*, vol. 17. 2nd ed. Leipzig, 1897.

FRIED, Johannes. *Der Weg in die Geschichte: Die Ursprünge Deutschlands bis 1024*. Berlin, 1994.

————, ed. *Schulen und Studium im soziale Wandel des hohen und späten Mittelalters*. Vorträge und Forschungen 30. Sigmaringen, 1986.

FRIEDMAN, Richard Elliott. *Who Wrote the Bible?* New York, 1987.

FRITZE, Wolfgang. "Universalis gentium confessio: Formeln, Träger und Wege universalmissionarischen Denkens im 7. Jahrhundert." *Frühmittelalterliche Studien* 3 (1969): 78–130.

FUHRMANN, Horst. *Einfluss und Verbreitung der pseudoisidorischen Fälschungen: Von ihrem Auftauchen bis in die neuere Zeit*. 3 vols. Schriften der MGH 24, 1–3. Stuttgart, 1972–74.

FUHRMANN, Horst, and Florentine Mütherich. *Das Evangeliar Heinrich des Löwen und das mittelalterliche Herrscherbild*. Munich, 1986.

GABORIT-CHOPIN, Danielle. *Elfenbeinkunst im Mittelalter*. Translated from the French by Gisela Bloch and Roswitha Beyer. Berlin, 1978.

GAEHDE, Joachim E. "The Bible of San Paolo fuori le mura in Rome: Its Date and Its Relation to Charles the Bald." *Gesta* 5 (1966): 9–21.

————. "The Pictorial Sources of the Illustrations of the Books of Kings, Proverbs, Judith and Maccabees in the Carolingian Bible of San Paolo Fuori Le Mura in Rome." *Frühmittelalterliche Studien* 9 (1975): 359–89.

————. "The Turonian Sources of the Bible of San Paolo Fuori Le Mura in Rome." *Frühmittelalterliche Studien* 5 (1971): 359–400.

GAMBER, Klaus. "Die Textgestalt des Gloria in excelsis." In *Liturgie und Dichtung*, edited by H. Becker and R. Kaczynski, 1:227–56.

GANSHOF, François L. *The Carolingians and the Frankish Monarchy: Studies in Carolingian History*. Translated by Janet Sondheimer. Ithaca, N.Y., 1971.

————. "L'Historiographie dans le monarchie franque sous les mérovingiens et les carolingiens: Monarchie franque unitaire et Francie Occidentale." In *La storiografia altomedievale*, 2:631–85, 743–50.

————. "Louis the Pious Reconsidered." *History* 42 (1957): 171–80. Repr. in Ganshof, *The Carolingians and the Frankish Monarchy*, pp. 261–72.

————. "Observations sur le synode de Francfort de 794." In *Miscellanea Historica in honorem Alberti de Meyer*, 1:306–18.

————. *Recherches sur les capitulaires*. Paris, 1958.

GANZ, David. *Corbie in the Carolingian Renaissance*. Beihefte der Francia 20. Sigmaringen, 1990.

————. "Heiric d'Auxerre: Glossateur du *Liber glossarum*." In *L'Ecole carolingienne d'Auxerre de Murethach à Rémi, 830–908*, edited by Dominique Iogna-Prat, Colette Jeudy, and Guy Lobrichon, pp. 297–312.

———. "Humour as History in Notker's *Gesta Karoli Magni.*" In *Monks, Nuns, and Friars in Mediaeval Society*, edited by Edward B. King, Jacqueline T. Schaefer, and William B. Wadley, pp. 171–83.

———. "The 'Liber Glossarum': A Carolingian Encyclopedia." In *Science in Western and Eastern Civilization in Carolingian Times*, edited by Paul Leo Butzer and Dietrich Lohrmann, pp. 127–35.

———. "'Pando quod ignoro': In Search of Carolingian Artistic Experience." In *Intellectual Life in the Middle Ages*, edited by Lesley Smith and Benedicta Ward, pp. 25–32.

———. "The Preconditions for Caroline Minuscule." *Viator* 18 (1987): 23–44.

———. "A Tenth-Century Drawing of Philosophy Visiting Boethius." In *Boethius, His Life, Thought, and Influence*, edited by Margaret Gibson, pp. 275–77.

GAY, Peter. *Freud for Historians*. New York, 1985.

GEERTZ, Clifford. *The Interpretation of Culture: Selected Essays*. New York, 1973.

GENICOT, Léopold, "'Mahomet et Charlemagne' après 50 ans." *Revue d'histoire ecclésiastique* 82 (1987): 277–81.

———. "La Noblesse dans la société médiévale: A propos des dernières études aux terres d'empire." *Le Moyen Age* 71 (1965): 539–60.

———. "La Noblesse médiévale: encore!" *Revue d'histoire ecclésiastique* 88 (1993): 173–201.

———. "La Noblesse médiévale: Pans de lumière et zones obscures." *Tijdschrift voor Geschiedenis* 93 (1988): 341–56.

GERBERDING, Richard A. *The Rise of the Carolingians and the "Liber Historiae Francorum."* Oxford Historical Monographs. New York, 1987.

GERO, Stephen. "The Libri Carolini and the Image Controversy." *Greek Orthodox Theological Review* 18 (1973): 7–34.

GEUENICH, Dieter. "Die volkssprachige Überlieferung des Karolingerzeit aus der Sicht des Historikers." *Deutsches Archiv für Erforschung des Mittelalters* 39 (1983): 104–30.

GIACONE, Roberto. "Giustificazione degli 'Studia liberalia' dalla sacralizzazione alcuiniana all'immanentismo di Giovanni Scoto Eriugena." In *Civiltà del Piemonte*, edited by Gianrenzo P. Clivio and Riccardo Massano, pp. 823–32.

GIBBON, Edward. *The History of the Decline and Fall of the Roman Empire*. Edited by J. B. Bury. 7 vols. London, 1897–1900.

GIBSON, Margaret T. "Boethius in the Carolingian Age." *Transactions of the Royal Historical Society*, 5th ser., 32 (1982): 43–56.

———. "Milestones in the Study of Priscian, circa 800–circa 1200." *Viator* 23 (1992): 17–33.

———. "RAG Reads Priscian." In *Charles the Bald*, edited by Margaret T. Gibson and Janet L. Nelson, pp. 261–66 (1990 ed.).

———, ed. *Boethius, His Life, Thought and Influence*. Oxford, 1981.

GIBSON, Margaret T., and Janet L. Nelson, eds., *Charles the Bald: Court and Kingdom*. British Archaeological Reports 101. London, 1981; 2nd rev. ed., Aldershot, England, 1990.

GLAUCHE, Günter. *Schullektüre im Mittelalter: Entstehung und Wandlungen des Lektürekanons bis 1200 nach den Quellen dargestellt*. Münchner Beiträge zur Mediävistik und Renaissance-Forschung 5. Munich, 1970.

GNEUSS, H. *Hymnar und Hymnen im englischen Mittelalter*. Tübingen, 1968.

GODMAN, Peter. "Louis 'the Pious' and His Poets." *Frühmittelalterliche Studien* 19 (1985): 239–89.

———. *Poetry of the Carolingian Renaissance*. London, 1985.

———. *Poets and Emperors: Frankish Politics and Carolingian Poetry*. Oxford, 1987.

GODMAN, Peter, and Roger Collins, eds. *Charlemagne's Heir: New Perspectives on the Reign of Louis the Pious (814–840)*. Oxford, 1990.

GOETZ, Hans-Werner. "'Nobilis': Der Adel im Selbstverständnis der Karolingerzeit." *Vierteljahrschrift für Sozial- und Wirtschaftsgeschichte* 70 (1983): 153–91.

———. "Regnum: Zum politischen Denken der Karolingerzeit." *Zeitschrift der Savigny-Stiftung für Rechtsgeschichte, germanistische Abteilung* 104 (1987): 110–89.

———, ed. *Weibliche Lebensgestaltung im frühen Mittelalter*. Cologne, 1991.

GOEZ, Werner. *Translatio Imperii: Ein Beitrag zur Geschichte des Geschichtsdenkens und der politischen Theorien des Mittelalter und der frühen Neuzeit*. Tübingen, 1958.

GOFFART, Walter. *The Narrators of Barbarian History: Jordanes, Gregory of Tours, Bede, and Paul the Deacon*. Princeton, N.J., 1988.

GOLDSCHMIDT, Adolph. *Die Elfenbeinskulpturen aus der Zeit der karolingischen und sächsischen Kaiser*. 4 vols. Berlin, 1914–26.

GOMBRICH, E. H. *Ideals and Idols: Essays on Values in History and in Art*. 5th ed. London, 1977.

GOODY, Jack. *The Interface between the Written and the Oral*. Studies in Literacy, Family, Culture, and the State. Cambridge and New York, 1987.

———, ed. *Literacy in Traditional Societies*. Cambridge, 1968.

GORMAN, M. "The Manuscript Tradition of St. Augustine's Major Works." In *Congresso internazionale su S. Agostino nel XVI centenario della conversione, Roma, 15–20 settembre 1986, Atti*. Vol. 1: *Cronaca del congresso, sezioni generali, sezione di studio*, pp. 381–412. Studia Ephemeridis "Augustinianum" 24. Rome, 1987.

GÖSCHL, Johann B. "Der gegenwärtige Stand der semiologischen Forschung." *Beiträge zur Gregorianik* 1 (1985): 43–103.

GOTTSCHALK. *Oeuvres théologiques et grammaticales de Godescalc d'Orbais*. Edited by Cyrille Lambot. Spicilegium Sacrum Lovaniense, Etudes et documents 20. Louvain, 1945.

GOUILLARD, Jean. "Aux origines de l'iconoclasme: La Témoignage de

Grégoire II?" In *Travaux et Mémoires*, pp. 276–97. Centre de recherche d'histoire et civilisations byzantines 3. Paris, 1968.

GRABAR, André. *L'Art de la fin de l'antiquité et du moyen âge.* 3 vols. Paris, 1968.

———. *Christian Iconography: A Study of Its Origins.* Princeton, N.J., 1968.

———. *L'Empereur dans l'art byzantin.* Paris, 1936.

———. "Fresques romanes copiés sur les miniatures du Pentateuque de Tours." *Cahiers archéoloqigues* 9 (1957): 329–41. Repr. in Grabar, *L'Art de la fin de l'antiquité*, 2:1037–43.

GRAFF, Harvey J. *The Legacies of Literacy: Continuities and Contradictions in Western Culture and Society.* Bloomington and Indianapolis, Ind., 1987.

GRANT, Edward, and John E. Murdoch, eds. *Mathematics and Its Applications to Science and Natural Philosophy in the Middle Ages: Essays in Honor of Marshall Claggett.* Cambridge, 1987.

GREEN, D. H. "Orality and Reading: The State of Research in Medieval Studies." *Speculum* 65 (1990): 267–80.

GRIBOMONT, Jean. "The Translations: Jerome and Rufinus." In *Patrology*, edited by Johannes Quasten and Angelo DiBerardino, 4:212–46.

GRIERSON, Philip. *Dark Age Numismatics: Selected Studies.* London, 1979.

———. "Money and Coinage under Charlemagne." In *Karl der Grosse: Lebenswerk und Nachleben*, edited by Wolfgang Braunfels, et al., 1:501–36. Repr. in Grierson, *Dark Age Numismatics: Selected Studies*, no. 18.

GROTZ, Hans. "Beobachtungen zu den zwei Briefen Papst Gregors II. an Leo III." *Archivum Historiae Pontificae* 18 (1980): 9–40.

———. "Weitere Beobachtungen zu den zwei Briefen Papst Gregors II. an Kaiser Leo III." *Archivum Historiae Pontificae* 24 (1986): 365–75.

GRUMEL, Venance. *Les Regestes des actes du patriarchat de Constantinople.* Vol. 1: *Les Actes des patriarches.* Fasc. 2: *Les Registres de 715 à 1043.* Paris, 1936.

GRUNDMANN, Herbert. "*Literatus—illiteratus*: Der Wandlung einer Bildungsnorm von Altertum zum Mittelalter." *Archiv für Kulturgeschichte* 40 (1958): 1–65.

GUERREAU-JALABERT, Anita. "La 'Renaissance carolingienne': Modèles culturels, usages linguistiques et structures sociales." *Bibliothèque de L'Ecole des chartes* 139 (1981): 5–35.

GUIZOT, François. *Histoire de la civilisation en Europe.* Paris, 1985.

GUREVICH, A. J. *Categories of Medieval Culture.* Translated by George Campbell. London and Boston, 1985.

GUSHEE, Lawrence A. "Questions of Genre in Medieval Treatises on Music." In *Gattung der Musik in Einzeldarstellungen*, edited by W. Arlt, et al., pp. 365–433.

HAENDLER, Gert. *Epochen karolingischer Theologie: Eine Untersuchung über die karolingischen Gutachten zum byzantinischen Bilderstreit.* Theologische Arbeiten 10. Berlin, 1958.

HÄGERMANN, Dieter. "Die Abt als Grundherr: Kloster und Wirtschaft im frühen Mittelalter." In *Herrschaft und Kirche*, edited by Friedrich Prinz, pp. 345–85.

HAHN, Heinrich. *Jahrbücher des fränkischen Reiches, 741–752.* Berlin, 1863.

HALLAM, Henry. *View of the State of Europe during the Middle Ages.* 3 vols. London, 1872.

HALLER, Johannes. *Das Papsttum: Idee und Wirklichkeit.* 5 vols. 2nd ed. Stuttgart, 1950–53.

HALPHEN, Louis. *Etudes critiques sur l'histoire de Charlemagne.* Paris, 1921.

HAMMER, Carl I., Jr. "Country Churches, Clerical Inventories and the Carolingian Renaissance in Bavaria." *Church History* 49 (1980): 5–17.

HAMPE, Karl. "Hadrians I Vertheidigung der zweiten nicaeanischen Synode gegen die Angriffe Karls des Grossen." *Neues Archiv* 21 (1895): 83–113.

HANSSENS, John Michael. Introduction to *Amalarii episcopi Opera liturgica omnia*, edited by Hanssens, 1:39–224. Studi e Testi 138. Vatican City, 1948.

HARLAN, David. "Intellectual History and the Return of Literature." *American Historical Review* 94 (1989): 581–609.

HARTMANN, Wilfried. *Die Synoden der Karolingerzeit im Frankenreich und in Italien.* Konziliengeschichte, edited by Walter Brandmüller. Reihe A, Darstellungen. Paderborn, Munich, Vienna, and Zurich, 1989.

———. "Vetera et nova: Altes und neues Kirchenrecht in den Beschlüssen karolingischer Konzilien." *Annuarium Historiae Conciliorum* 15 (1983): 79–95.

HASELBACH, Irene. *Aufstieg und Herrschaft der Karlinger in der Darstellung der sogenannten Annales Mettensis priores: Ein Beitrag zur Geschichte der politischen Ideen im Reich Karls des Grossen.* Historische Studien 412. Lübeck and Hamburg, 1970.

HASKELL, Francis. *History and Its Images: Art and the Interpretation of the Past.* New Haven, Conn., 1993.

HAUCK, Albert. *Kirchengeschichte Deutschlands.* 5 vols. 8th ed. Berlin and Leipzig, 1954.

HAUCK, Karl. *Karolingische Taufpfalzen im Spiegel hofnaher Dichtung: Überlegungen zur Ausmalung von Pfalzkirchen, Pfalzen und Reichsklöstern.* Akademie der Wissenschaften in Göttingen, Nachrichten, phil.-hist. Klasse, 1985, Heft 1. Göttingen, 1985.

———. "Von einer spätantiken Randkultur zum karolingischen Europa." *Frühmittelalterliche Studien* 1 (1967): 3–93.

HAUG, Walter, and Benedikt Konrad Vollmann, eds. *Frühe deutsche Literatur und lateinische Literatur in Deutschlands, 800–1150.* Bibliothek des Mittelalters 1. Frankfurt, 1991.

HAUGH, Richard. *Photius and the Carolingians: The Trinitarian Controversy.* Belmont, Mass., 1975.

HAURÉAU, B. *Charlemagne et sa cour.* Paris, 1854.

HAVELOCK, Eric A. *The Muse Learns to Write: Reflections on Orality and Literacy from Antiquity to the Present.* New Haven, Conn., 1986.

————. *Origins of Western Literacy*. Toronto, 1976.

HEARD, Edmund Brooks. "Alia Musica: A Chapter in the History of Medieval Music Theory." Ph.D. diss., University of Wisconsin, 1966.

HEER, Friedrich, *Charlemagne and His World*. New York, 1975.

HEFELE, Charles Joseph, and Henri Leclercq. *Histoire des Conciles*. Vol. 3, pt. 2. Paris, 1910.

HEGEL, Georg Wilhelm Friedrich. *Vorlesung über die Philosophie der Geschichte*. Theorie Ausgabe 12. Frankfurt, 1970. Published in English as *The Philosophy of History*, translated by J. Sibree (1899; repr., New York, 1956).

HEINZELMANN, Martin. "Bischof und Herrschaft vom spätantiken Gallien bis zu den karolingischen Hausmeieren: Die institutionallen Grundlagen." In *Herrschaft und Kirche*, edited by Friedrich Prinz, pp. 23–82.

————. *Bischofsherrschaft in Gallien: Zur Kontinuität römischer Führungsschicten vom 4. bis zum 7. Jahrhundert: Sociale, prosopographische und bildungs-geschichtliche Aspekte*. Beihefte der Francia 5. Zurich and Munich, 1976.

————. "La Noblesse du haut moyen âge (VIIIe–XIe siècles): Quelques problèmes à propos d'ouvrages récents." *Le Moyen Age* 83 (1977): 131–44.

HEINZLE, Joachim, ed. *Geschichte der deutschen Literatur von den Anfängen bis zum Beginn der Neuzeit*. Vol. 1: *Von den Anfängen zum hohen Mittelalter*, pt. 1, *Die Anfängen: Versuche volkspachiger Schriftlichkeit im frühen Mittelalter (ca. 700–1050/60)*, by Wolfgang Haubrichs. Frankfurt am Main, 1988.

HEITZ, Carol. *L'Architecture religieuse carolingienne: Les Formes et leurs functions*. Paris, 1980.

————. *La France pré-romane: Archéologie et architecture religieuse du haut moyen âge du IVe siècle à l'an mil*. Paris, 1987.

————. "More Romano: Problèmes d'architecture et liturgie carolingiennes." In *Roma e l'età carolingia*, pp. 27–37.

————. "Renaissances éphémères du haut moyen âge (VIIe–XIe siècles)." In *De Tertullien aux Mozarabes*, edited by Louis Holtz, Jean-Claude Fredouille, and Marie Hélène Jullien, 2:129–40.

HEITZ, Carol, and Jean Roubier. *Gallia Praeromanica: Die Kunst der merowingischen, karolingischen und frühromanischen Epoche in Frankreich*. Vienna, 1982.

HENNING, E. M. "Archaeology, Deconstruction, and Intellectual History." In *Modern European Intellectual History*, edited by Dominick LaCapra and Steven L. Kaplan, pp. 153–96.

HERREN, Michael W., ed. *Insular Latin Studies: Papers on Latin Texts and Manuscripts of the British Isles, 500–1066*. Papers in Mediaeval Studies 1. Toronto, 1981.

————, ed. *The Sacred Nectar of the Greeks: The Study of Greek in the West in the Early Middle Ages*. King's College London Medieval Studies 2. London, 1988.

HERRIN, Judith. *The Formation of Christendom*. Princeton, N.J., 1987.

HESBERT, René Jean. *Antiphonale missarum sextuplex*. Brussels, 1935.

————. *Corpus antiphonalium officii.* Rerum ecclesiasticarum documenta, Series maior, Fontes VII–IX. Vols. 1–6. Rome, 1963–79.

HEYSE, Elisabeth. *Hrabanus Maurus' Enzyklopädia "De Rerum Naturis": Untersuchungen zu den Quellen und zur Methode der Kompilation.* Münchener Beiträge zur Mediävistik und Renaissance-Forschung 4. Munich, 1969.

HILDEBRANDT, M. M. *The External School in Carolingian Society.* Education and Society in the Middle Ages and Renaissance 1. Leiden and New York, 1992.

HILEY, David. "Recent Research on the Origins of Western Chant." *Early Music* 16 (1988): 203–13.

————. *Western Plainchant: A Handbook.* Oxford, 1993.

HILTBRUNNER, Otto. "Die Heiligkeit des Kaisers." *Frühmittelalterliche Studien* 2 (1968): 1–30.

HIMMELFARB, Gertrude. *The New History and the Old.* Cambridge, Mass., and London, 1987.

HIRST, Paul Q. *Marxism and the Writing of History.* London, 1985.

HODGES, Richard, and David Whitehouse. *Mohammed, Charlemagne, and the Origins of Europe: Archaeology and the Pirenne Thesis.* London, 1983.

HOFFMANN, Hartmut. *Untersuchungen zur karolingischen Annalistik.* Bonner historische Forschungen 10. Bonn, 1958.

HOLDSWORTH, Christopher, and T. P. Wiseman, eds. *The Inheritance of Historiography, 350–900.* Exeter Studies in History 12. Exeter, 1986.

HOLLINGER, David A. "The Return of the Prodigal: The Persistence of Historical Knowing." *American Historical Review* 94 (1989): 610–21.

HOLTER, Kurt, ed. *Der Goldene Psalter "Dagulf-Psalter": Vollständige Faksimile-Ausgabe im Originalformat von Codex 1861 der Österreichischen National-bibliothek.* 2 vols. Codices Selecti Phototypice Impressi, Fascimile vol. 69, Commentarium vol. 69*. Graz, 1980.

HOLTZ, Louis. *Donat et la tradition de l'enseignement grammatical: Etude sur l'"Ars Donati" et sa diffusion (IVe–IXe siècle) et édition critique.* Documents, études et répertoires publiés par l'Institut de recherche et d'histoire des textes. Paris, 1981.

————. "La Redécouverte de Virgile aux VIIIe et IXe siècles d'après les manu-scrits conservés." In *Lectures médiévales de Virgile,* pp. 9–30.

————. "Le Retour aux sources de la latinité du milieu du VIIIe s. à l'an mil," *Bulletin de l'Association Guillaume Budé,* 1981, pp. 369–88.

HOLTZ, Louis, Jean-Claude Fredouille, and Marie Hélène Jullien, eds. *De Tertullien aux Mozarabes: Mélanges offerts à Jacques Fontaine à l'occasion de son 70e anniversaire, par ses élèves, amis et collègues.* 2 vols. Collection des études augustiniennes, série moyen-âge et temps modernes 26. Paris, 1992.

HORN, Walter, and Ernest Born. *The Plan of St. Gall: A Study of the Architecture and Economy of, and Life in a Paradigmatic Carolingian Monastery.* 3 vols. University of California Studies in the History of Art 19. Berkeley, 1979.

Hourlier, J., and Michel Huglo. "Notation paléofranque." *Etudes grégoriennes* 2 (1957): 212–19.

Hoving, Thomas P. F. "The Sources of the Ivories of the Ada School." Ph.D. diss., Princeton University, 1959.

Hoyt, Robert Stuart, ed. *Life and Thought in the Early Middle Ages*. Minneapolis, Minn., 1967.

Hubert, Jean. "Les Prémisses de la renaissance carolingienne au temps du Pépin III." *Francia* 2 (1974): 49–58.

Hubert, Jean, Jean Porcher, and Wolfgang Fritz Volbach. *L'Empire carolingien*. Paris, 1968. Published in English as *The Carolingian Renaissance*, translated by James Emmons, Stuart Gilbert, and Robert Allen, The Arts of Mankind (New York, 1970). Also published as *Carolingian Art* (London, 1970).

———. *L'Europe des invasions*. Paris, 1967. Published in English as *Europe of the Invasions*, translated by Stuart Gilbert and James Emmons, The Arts of Mankind (New York, 1969). Also published as *Europe in the Dark Ages* (London, 1969).

Hucke, Helmut. "Gregorianische Fragen." *Die Musikforschung* 41 (1988): 304–30.

———. "Karolingische Renaissance und gregorianische Gesang." *Die Musikforschung* 28 (1975): 4–18.

———. "Musikalische Formen der Officiumsantiphonen." *Kirchenmusikalisches Jahrbuch* 37 (1953): 7–33.

Hughes, David. "Evidence for the Traditional View of the Transmission of Gregorian Chant." *Journal of the American Musicological Society* 40 (1987): 377–404.

Huglo, Michel. "Antiphon." In *The New Grove Dictionary of Music and Musicians*, 1:471–81.

———. "Les Remaniements de l'Antiphonaire grégorien au IXe siècle: Hélisachar, Agobard, Amalaire." In *Culto cristiano*, pp. 87–120.

———. *Les Tonaires: Inventaire, analyse, comparaison*. Paris, 1971.

Hunt, Lynn. "French History in the Last Twenty Years: The Rise and Fall of the *Annales* Paradigm." *Journal of Contemporary History* 21 (1986): 209–24.

———, ed. *The New Cultural History*. Studies on the History of Society and Culture. Berkeley, Los Angeles, and London, 1989.

Huygens, R. B. C. *Accessus ad auctores*. Collection Latomus 15. Berchem-Brussels, 1954.

I, Deng-Su. *L'opera agiografica di Alcuino*. Spoleto, 1983.

Iggers, Georg G. *New Directions in European Historiography*. 2nd ed. Middletown, Conn., 1984.

Iggers, Georg G., and Harold T. Parker, eds. *International Handbook of Historical Studies: Contemporary Research and Theory*. Westport, Conn., 1979.

Illmer, Detlef. *Formen der Erziehung und Wissensvermittlung im frühen Mittelalter: Quellenstudien zur Frage der Kontinuität des abendländischen*

Erziehungswesens. Münchener Beiträge zur Mediävistik und Renaissance-Forschung 7. Munich, 1971.

———. "Totum namque in sola experientia usque consistit: Eine Studie zur monastischen Erziehung und Sprache." In *Mönchtum und Gesellschaft im Frühmittelalter*, edited by Friedrich Prinz, pp. 430–55.

IOGNA-PRAT, Dominique, Colette Jeudy, and Guy Lobrichon, eds. *L'Ecole carolingienne d'Auxerre de Murethach à Rémi, 830–908*. Paris, 1991.

ITALIANI, Giuliana. *La tradizione esegetica nel Commento ai Re di Claudio di Torino*. Quaderni dell'Istituto di filologia classica "Giorgio Pasquali" dell'Università degli studi di Firenze 3. Florence, 1979.

JACOBSEN, Werner. "Die Lorscher Torhalle: Zum Problem ihrer Datierung und Deutung." *Jahrbuch des Zentralinstituts für Kunstgeschichte* 1 (1985): 9–75.

JACOBY, Russell. "A New Intellectual History?" *American Historical Review* 97 (1992): 405–24.

JAFFÉ, Philippus. *Regesta Pontificum Romanorum*. Vol. 1. 2nd ed. Leipzig, 1885.

JANKUHN, Herbert. *Einführung in die Siedlungsarchäologie*. Berlin and New York, 1977.

JANKUHN, Herbert, and Reinhard Wenskus, eds. *Geschichtswissenschaft und Archäologie: Untersuchungen zur Siedlungs-, Wirtschafts-, und Kirchengeschichte*. Vorträge und Forschungen 22. Sigmaringen, 1979.

JARNUT, Jörg. "Bonifatius und die fränkischen Reformkonzilien (743–748)." *Zeitschrift der Savigny-Stiftung für Rechtsgeschichte, kanonistische Abteilung* 65 (1979): 1–26.

———. "Chlodwig und Chlothar: Anmerkungen zu den Namen zweier Söhne Karls des Grossen." *Francia* 12 (1984): 645–51.

JEAUNEAU, Edouard. "Jean Scot Erigène et le grec." *Archivum Latinitatis Medii Aevi (Bulletin du Cange)* 41 (1979): 5–50.

———. "Jean Scot Erigène: Grandeur et misère du métier de traducteur." In *Traduction et traducteurs au moyen âge*, edited by Geneviève Contamine, pp. 99–108.

———. *Quatre thèmes érigéniens*. Conférence Albert-le-Grand, 1974. Paris, 1978.

JEDIN, Hubert, ed. *Handbuch der Kirchengeschichte*. Vol. 3: *Die mittelalterliche Kirche*, pt. 1, *Vom kirchlichen Frühmittelalter zur gregorianischen Reform*, by Friedrich Kempf, et al. Freiburg, Basel, and Vienna, 1966. Published in English as *Handbook of Church History*. Edited by Jedin and Joseph Dolan. Vol. 3: *The Church in the Age of Feudalism*, by Kempf, et al. Translated by Anselm Biggs. London and New York, 1969.

JEFFERY, Peter. "The Oldest Sources of the Gradual: A Preliminary Checklist of Manuscripts Copied before about 900 A.D." *Journal of Musicology* 2 (1983): 316–21.

———. *Re-Envisioning Past Musical Cultures: Ethnomusicology in the Study of Gregorian Chant*. Chicago, 1992.

JEUDY, Colette. "Le Florilège grammatical inédit du manuscrit 8° 8 de la bibliothèque d'Erfurt." *Archivum Latinitatis Medii Aevi (Bulletin du Cange)* 44–45 (1985): 91–128.

———. "Le *Scalprum Prisciani* et sa tradition manuscrite." *Revue d'histoire des textes* 12–13 (1982–83): 181–93.

JOLIVET, Jean. *Godescalc d'Orbais et la Trinité: La Méthode de la théologie à l'époque carolingienne.* Etudes de la philosophie médiévale 47. Paris, 1958.

JONES, Charles W. Introduction to *Bedae Opera de temporibus*, edited by Jones, pp. 3–172. Mediaeval Academy of America Publications 41. Cambridge, Mass., 1943.

———. Introduction to *De temporum ratione Liber*, edited by Jones. In *Bedae Venerabilis opera*, pt. 6, *Opera didascalica*, 2:241–61. CCSL 123B. Turnhout, 1977.

JUNGBLUT, Renate. *Hieronymus: Darstellung und Verehrung eines Kirchenvaters.* Tübingen, 1967.

KACZYNSKI, Bernice M. "Greek Glosses on Jerome's *Ep. CVI, Ad Sunniam et Fretelam*, in Ms. Berlin (East), Deutsche Staatsbibliothek, Phillipps 1674." In *The Sacred Nectar of the Greeks*, edited by Michael W. Herren, pp. 215–27.

———. *Greek in the Carolingian Age: The St. Gall Manuscripts.* Speculum Anniversary Monographs 13. Cambridge, Mass., 1988.

———. "Medieval Translations: Latin and Greek." In *Medieval Latin Studies*, edited by F. A. C. Mantello and A. G. Rigg, forthcoming.

KAISER, Reinhold. "Königtum und Bischofsherrschaft im frühmittelalterlichen Neustrien." In *Herrschaft und Kirche*, edited by Friedrich Prinz, pp. 83–108.

KAMESAR, Adam. *Jerome, Greek Scholarship, and the Hebrew Bible: A Study of the "Quaestiones Hebraicae in Genesim."* Oxford, 1993.

KAMMEN, Michael, ed. *The Past Before Us: Contemporary Historical Writing in the United States.* Ithaca, N.Y., 1980.

KAMP, Norbert, and Joachim Wollasch, eds. *Tradition als historische Kraft: Interdisziplinäre Forschungen zur Geschichte des früheren Mittelalters.* Berlin and New York, 1982.

KAMPERS, Franz. "Rex et Sacerdos." *Historisches Jahrbuch* 45 (1925): 495–515.

KANTOROWICZ, Ernst H. *Laudes Regiae: A Study in Liturgical Acclamations and Mediaeval Ruler Worship.* University of California Publications in History 33. Berkeley and Los Angeles, 1946.

Karl der Grosse oder Charlemagne? Acht Antworten deutscher Geschichtsforscher. Probleme der Gegenwart. Berlin, 1935.

Karl der Grosse: Werk und Wirkung. Exhibition catalogue. Aachen, 1965.

Karolingische und ottonische Kunst: Werden, Wesen, Wirkung: VI. internationaler Kongress für Frühmittelalterforschung. Forschungen zur Kunstgeschichte und christliche Archäologie 3. Wiesbaden, 1957.

KASTEN, Brigitte. *Adalhard von Corbie: Die Biographie eines karolingischen Politikers und Klostervorstehers.* Studia humaniora 3. Düsseldorf, 1985.

KASTER, Robert A. *The Tradition of the Text of the "Aeneid" in the Ninth Century.* New York and London, 1990.

KEIL, Gundolf, and Paul Schnitzler, eds. *Das Lorscher Arzneibuch und die frühmittelalterliche Medizin*. Verhandlungen des medizinhistorischen Symposiums im September 1989 in Lorsch. Geschichtsblätter Kreis Bergstrasse, Sonderband 12. Lorsch, 1991.

KELLEY, Donald R. "Horizons of Intellectual History: Retrospect, Circumspect, Prospect." *Journal of the History of Ideas* 48 (1987): 143–69.

KELLY, J. N. D. *Jerome: His Life, Writings, and Controversies*. London, 1975.

KENNEY, James F. *The Sources for the Early History of Ireland, Ecclesiastical: An Introduction and Guide*. New York, 1929; repr., New York, 1966.

KESSLER, Herbert L. "An Apostle in Armor and the Mission of Carolingian Art." *Arte medievale*, 2nd ser., 4 (1990): 17–39.

———. "'Facies bibliotheca revelata': Carolingian Art as Spiritual Seeing." In *Testo e immagine nell'alto medioevo*, 2:533–94.

———. *The Illustrated Bibles from Tours*. Studies in Manuscript Illumination 7. Princeton, N.J., 1977.

———. "A Lay Abbot as Patron: Count Vivian and the First Bible of Charles the Bald." In *Committenti e produzione artistico-letteraria nell'alto medioevo occidentale*, 2:647–79.

———. "On the State of Medieval Art History." *Art Bulletin* 70 (1988): 166–87.

KIESEL, Georges, and Jean Schroeder, eds. *Willibrord, Apostel der Niederlande, Gründer der Abtei Echternach: Gedenkgaben zum 1250. Todestag des angelsächsischen Missionars*. Luxemburg, 1987.

KILLION, Steven B. "Bede's Irish Legacy: Knowledge and Use of Bede's Works in Ireland from the Eighth through the Sixteenth Century." Ph.D. diss., University of North Carolina at Chapel Hill, 1992.

KING, Edward B., Jacqueline T. Schaefer, and William B. Wadley, eds. *Monks, Nuns, and Friars in Mediaeval Society*. Sewanee Mediaeval Studies 4. Sewanee, Tenn., 1989.

KING, Margot H., and Wesley M. Stevens, eds. *Saints, Scholars, and Heroes: Studies in Medieval Culture in Honour of Charles W. Jones*. 2 vols. Collegeville, Minn., 1979.

KING, P. D., trans. *Charlemagne: Translated Sources*. Kendal, 1987.

KOCH, Josef. *Artes Liberales von der antiken Bildung zur Wissenschaft des Mittelalters*. Studien und Texte zur Geistesgeschichte des Mittelalters 5. Leiden, 1959.

KOEHLER, Wilhelm. *Die karolingischen Miniaturen*. Vol. 1: *Die Schule von Tours*. Berlin, 1933; repr., Berlin, 1963. Vol. 2: *Die Hofschule Karls des Grossen*. Berlin, 1958. Vol. 5 (with Florentine Mütherich): *Die Hofschule Karls des Kahlen*. Berlin, 1982.

KÖPP, P., ed. *Vademecum eines frühmittelalterlichen Arztes: Die gefaltete lateinische Handschrift medizinischen Inhalts im Codex 217 und der Fragmentensammlung 1396 der Stiftsbibliothek in St. Gallen*. Veröffentlichungen der

Schweizerischen Gesellschaft für Geschichte der Medizin und der Natur-
wissenschaften 34. Aurau, 1980.

KORNBLUTH, Genevra A. "Carolingian Treasure: Engraved Gems of the
Ninth and Tenth Centuries." Ph.D. diss., University of North Carolina,
1986.

———. "The Susanna Crystal of Lothar II: Chastity, the Church, and Royal
Justice." *Gesta* 31 (1992): 25–39.

KOTTJE, Raymund. *Die Bussbücher Halitgars von Cambrai und des Hrabanus
Maurus: Ihre Überlieferung und ihre Quellen.* Beiträge zur Geschichte und
Quellenkunde des Mittelalters 8. Berlin and New York, 1980.

KOTTJE, Raymund, and Helmut Maurer, eds. *Monastische Reform im 9. und 10.
Jahrhundert.* Vorträge und Forschungen 38. Sigmaringen, 1989.

KOTTJE, Raymund, and Harald Zimmermann, eds. *Hrabanus Maurus: Lehrer,
Abt und Bischof.* Akademie der Wissenschaft und der Literatur, Mainz;
Abhandlungen der geistes- und sozialwissenschaftlichen Klasse,
Einzelveröffentlichung 4. Wiesbaden, 1982.

KOZICKI, Henry, ed. *Developments in Modern Historiography.* New York,
1993.

KRÄMER, Sigrid, and Michael Bernhard, eds. *Scire Litteras: Forschungen zum
mittelalterlichen Geistesleben.* Munich, 1988.

KRANTZIUS, Albertus. *Saxonia.* Frankfurt, 1575.

KRAUTHEIMER, Richard. "The Carolingian Revival of Early Christian
Architecture." *Art Bulletin* 24 (1942): 1–38. Repr. with appendix in
Krautheimer, *Studies in Early Christian, Medieval, and Renaissance Architecture,*
pp. 203–56.

———. *Studies in Early Christian, Medieval, and Renaissance Architecture.* New
York, 1969.

KRIEGER, Leonard. *Time's Reason: Philosophies of History Old and New.*
Chicago, 1989.

KUCHENBUCH, Ludolf. *Bäuerliche Gesellschaft und Klosterherrschaft im 9.
Jahrhundert: Studien zur Sozialstruktur der Familie der Abtei Prüm.* Vierteljahrschrift für Sozial- und Wirtschaftsgeschichte, Beihefte 66. Wiesbaden,
1978.

———. "Die Klostergrundherrschaft im Frühmittelalter: Eine Zwischenbilanz."
In *Herrschaft und Kirche,* edited by Friedrich Prinz, pp. 297–343.

KÜNZEL, Rudi. "Paganisme, syncrétisme et culture religieuse populaire au haut
moyen âge: Réflexions de méthode." *Annales: Economies, sociétés, civilisations* 47
(1992): 1055–69.

LaCAPRA, Dominick. *History and Criticism.* Ithaca, N.Y., 1985.

LaCAPRA, Dominick, and Steven L. Kaplan, eds. *Modern European Intellectual
History: Reappraisals and New Perspectives.* Ithaca, N.Y., and London, 1982.

LAISTNER, M. L. W. "The Study of St. Jerome in the Early Middle Ages." In
A Monument to Saint Jerome, edited by Francis X. Murphy, pp. 233–56.

————. *Thought and Letters in Western Europe*, A.D. *500 to 900*. Rev. ed. Ithaca, N.Y., 1957.

LAMBERT, Bernard. *Bibliotheca Hieronymiana Manuscripta: La Tradition manuscrite des oeuvres de saint Jérôme*. 4 vols. in 6. Instrumenta Patristica 4. Steenbrugge, 1969–72.

LAMPRECHT, Karl. *Deutsche Geschichte*. Vol. 2. Freiburg, 1904.

LANDWEHR-MELNICKI, Margareta. *Das einstimmige Kyrie des lateinischen Mittelalters*. Forschungsbeiträge zur Musikwissenschaft 1. Regensburg, 1968.

LANGLOIS, Charles-Victor, and Charles Seignobos. *Introduction aux études historiques*. Paris, 1898. Published in English as *Introduction to the Study of History*, translated by G. G. Berry (New York, 1898).

LAPIDGE, Michael. "The Study of Latin Texts in Late Anglo-Saxon England, 1: The Evidence of Latin Glosses." In *Latin and the Vernacular Languages in Early Medieval Britain*, edited by Nicholas Brooks, pp. 99–140.

LAPIDGE, Michael, and Richard Sharpe. *A Bibliography of Celtic-Latin Literature, 400–1200*. Dublin, 1985.

Latin vulgaire—latin tardif: Actes du Ier Colloque international sur le latin vulgaire et tardif (Pécs, 2–5 septembre 1985). Edited by Jósef Herman. Tübingen, 1987.

Latin vulgaire—latin tardif: Actes du IIe Colloque international sur le latin vulgaire et tardif (Bologna, 29 août–2 septembre 1988). Edited by G. Calboli. Tübingen, 1990.

Latin vulgaire—latin tardif: Actes du IIIe Colloque international sur le latin vulgaire et tardif (Innsbruck, 2–5 septembre 1991). Edited by M. Iliescu and W. Marxgut. Tübingen, 1992.

LAUER, P. "Le Joyau carolingien de Waulsort-sur-Meuse." *Bulletin de la Société nationale des antiquaires de France* (1908): 102–7.

LAUNOY, Jean. *De scholis celebrioribus seu a Carolo Magno et seu post eundum Carolum in occidentem instauratis Liber*. Paris, 1672.

LAW, Vivien. *The Insular Latin Grammarians*. Woodbridge, 1982.

————. "The Study of Grammar." In *Carolingian Culture*, edited by Rosamond McKitterick, pp. 88–110.

LE BOURDELLES, H. "De Astronomia more Christiano." *Studi Medievali*, 3rd ser., 32 (1991): 385–444.

LECLERCQ, Jean. *The Love of Learning and the Desire for God: A Study of Monastic Culture*. Translated by Catharine Misrahi. 3rd ed. New York, 1982; repr., 1988.

LECLERCQ, Jean, François Vandenbroucke, and Louis Bouyer. *La Spiritualité du moyen âge*. Histoire de la spiritualité chrétienne 2. Paris, 1961. Published in English as *The Spirituality of the Middle Ages*, A History of Spirituality 2 (New York, 1982).

Lectures médiévales de Virgile: Actes du colloque organisé par L'Ecole française de Rome (Rome, 25–28 octobre 1982). Collection de L'Ecole française de Rome 80. Rome, 1985.

LE GOFF, Jacques. "Les Mentalités: Une Histoire ambiguë." In *Faire de l'histoire*, edited by Le Goff and Pierre Nora, 3:79–94. Published in English as "Mentalities: A History of Ambiguities," translated by David Denby, in *Constructing the Past*, edited by Le Goff and Nora, pp. 166–80.

LE GOFF, Jacques, and Pierre Nora, eds. *Faire de l'histoire*. 3 vols. Paris, 1974; 2nd ed., 1986. A selection of these essays was published in English as *Constructing the Past: Essays in Historical Methodology*, edited by Le Goff and Nora (Cambridge and New York, 1985).

LE GOFF, Jacques, et al., eds. *La nouvelle histoire*. Les encyclopédies de savoir moderne. Paris, 1978; new ed., Brussels, 1988.

LEHMANN, Paul. *Mittelalterliche Bibliothekskataloge Deutschlands und der Schweiz*. 2 vols. Munich, 1918–28.

LENTRICCHIA, Frank. *After the New Criticism*. Chicago, 1980.

LEONARDI, Claudio. "Alcuino e la scuola palatina: Le ambizioni di una cultura unitaria." In *Nascita dell'Europa ed Europa carolingia*, 1:459–506.

———. "I codici de Marziono Capella." *Aevum* 33 (1959): 443–89; 34 (1960): 1–99, 411–524.

———. "Martianus Capella et Jean Scot: Nouvelle présentation d'un vieux problème." In *Jean Scot écrivain*, edited by Guy-H. Allard, pp. 187–207.

LEONARDI, Claudio, and Enrico Menestò, eds. *Giovanni Scoto nel suo tempo: L'organizzazione del sapere in età carolingia*. Atti dei convegni dell'Accademia Tudertina e del Centro di studi sulla spiritualità medievale, new ser., 1. Spoleto, 1989.

LEONARDI, Claudio, et al., eds. *Medioevo latino: Bulletino bibliografico della cultura europea del secolo VI al XIII*. Vols 1–. Spoleto, 1980–.

LESNE, Emile. *Histoire de la propriété ecclésiastique en France*. Vol. 4: *Les Livres, "scriptoria" et bibliothèques du commencement du VIIIe à la fin du XIe siècle*. Vol. 5: *Les Ecoles de la fin du VIIIe siècle à la fin du XIIe siècle*. Mémoires et travaux publiés par des professeurs des facultés catholiques de Lille 46, 50. Lille, 1938, 1940.

LEVISON, Wilhelm. *England and the Continent in the Eighth Century (The Ford Lectures)*. Oxford, 1946.

LEVY, Kenneth. "Charlemagne's Archetype of Gregorian Chant." *Journal of the American Musicological Society* 40 (1987): 1–30.

———. "On Gregorian Orality." *Journal of the American Musicological Society* 43 (1990): 185–227.

———. "On the Origin of the Neumes." *Early Music History* 7 (1987): 59–90.

LEWIS, Archibald R. *Emerging Medieval Europe, A.D. 400–1000*. New York, 1967.

La Lexicographie du latin médiévale et ses rapports avec les recherches actuelles sur la civilisation du moyen âge. Colloques internationaux du Centre national de la recherche scientifique 589. Paris, 1981.

Lexikon des Mittelalters. Vols. 1. Munich and Zurich, 1980–.

LEYSER, K. "The German Aristocracy from the Ninth to the Early Twelfth Century: A Historical and Cultural Sketch." *Past and Present* 41 (1968): 25–53.

LIGHT, Laura. "Versions et révisions du texte biblique." In *Le Moyen Age et la Bible*, edited by Pierre Riché and Guy Lobrichon, pp. 55–93.

LINDSAY, W. M. *The Corpus, Epinal, Erfurt, and Leiden Glossaries*. Publications of the Philological Society 8. London and New York, 1921.

LOEWE, Raphael. "The Medieval History of the Latin Vulgate." In *The Cambridge History of the Bible*, edited by G. W. H. Lampe, 2:102–54.

LOEWENBERG, Peter. *Decoding the Past: The Psychohistorical Approach*. New York, 1983.

LOHRMANN, Dietrich. "Alcuins Korrespondenz mit Karl dem Grossen über Kalender und Astronomie." In *Science in Western and Eastern Civilization in Carolingian Times*, edited by Paul Leo Butzer and Lohrmann, pp. 79–114.

LOT, Ferdinand. "A quelle époque a-t-on cessé de parler latin?" *Archivum Latinitatis Medii Aevi (Bulletin du Cange)* 6 (1931): 97–159.

———. "Quels sont les dialectes romans que pouvaient connaître les Carolingiens?" *Romania* 64 (1938): 433–53.

LOT, Ferdinand, and Robert Fawtier, eds. *Histoire des institutions françaises au moyen âge*. Vol. 3: *Institutions ecclésiastiques*, by Jean-François Lemarignier, Jean Gaudemet, and Guillaume Mollat. Paris, 1962.

LOURDAUX, W., and D. Verhelst, eds. *Benedictine Culture, 750–1050*. Medievalia Lovaniensia, ser. 1, Studia 11. Leuven, 1983.

LOWDEN, John. "The Royal/Imperial Book and the Image or Self-Image of the Medieval Ruler." In *Kings and Kingship in Medieval Europe*, edited by Anne J. Duggan, pp. 213–40.

LÖWE, E. A. *Codices Latini Antiquiores: A Palaeographical Guide to Latin Manuscripts Prior to the Ninth Century*. 11 vols. and Suppl. Oxford, 1934–71.

LÖWE, Heinz, ed. *Die Iren und Europe im früheren Mittelalter*. 2 vols. Veröffentlichungen des Europa-Zentrums Tübingen, Kulturwissenschaftliche Reihe. Stuttgart, 1982.

LOYN, H. R., and John Percival, trans. *The Reign of Charlemagne: Documents on Carolingian Government and Administration*. Documents of Medieval History 2. London, 1975.

LUNDGREEN, Peter, ed. *Wissenschaft im dritten Reich*. Frankfurt, 1984.

MABILLE, E. "Les Invasions normandes dans la Loire et les pérégrinations du corps de St. Martin." *Bibliothèque de L'Ecole des chartes* 30 (1870): 149–94, 425–69.

MCCORMICK, Michael. *Eternal Victory: Triumphal Rulership in Late Antiquity, Byzantium, and the Early Medieval West*. Past and Present Publications. Cambridge and Paris, 1986.

MCCULLOH, John M. Introduction to *Rabani Mauri Martyrologium*, edited by McCulloh, pp. xi–xxiv. CC cont. med. 44. Turnhout, 1979.

McGurk, Patrick. "Carolingian Astrological Manuscripts." In *Charles the Bald*, edited by Margaret T. Gibson and Janet L. Nelson, pp. 317–32 (1981 ed.).

MacKenzie, Mary Margaret, and Charlotte Roueché, eds. *Images of Authority: Papers Presented to Joyce Reynolds on the Occasion of Her 70th Birthday.* Cambridge, 1989.

McKeon, Peter R. *Hincmar of Laon and Carolingian Politics.* Urbana, Ill., 1978.

McKinnon, James. "Christian Antiquity." In *Antiquity and the Middle Ages*, edited by McKinnon, pp. 68–87.

———. "Emergence of Gregorian Chant in the Carolingian Era." In *Antiquity and the Middle Ages*, edited by McKinnon, pp. 88–119.

———, ed. *Antiquity and the Middle Ages.* Englewood Cliffs, N.J., 1990.

McKitterick, Rosamond. *The Carolingians and the Written Word.* Cambridge and New York, 1989.

———. *The Frankish Church and the Carolingian Reforms, 789–895.* Royal Historical Society Studies in History. London, 1977.

———. *The Frankish Kingdoms under the Carolingians, 751–987.* London and New York, 1983.

———. "Frauen und Schriftlichkeit im Frühmittelalter." In *Weibliche Lebensgestaltung im frühen Mittelalter*, edited by Hans-Werner Goetz, pp. 65–118.

———. "The Palace School of Charles the Bald." In *Charles the Bald*, edited by Margaret T. Gibson and Janet L. Nelson, pp. 326–39 (1990 ed.).

———. "Le Rôle culturel des monastères dans les royaumes carolingiens du VIIIe au Xe siècle." *Revue bénédictine* 103 (1993): 117–30.

———. "Royal Patronage of Culture in the Frankish Kingdoms under the Carolingians: Motives and Consequences." In *Committenti e produzione artistico-letteraria nell'alto medioevo occidentale*, 1:93–129.

———. "The Study of Frankish History in France and Germany in the Sixteenth and Seventeenth Centuries." *Francia* 8 (1980): 556–72.

———. "Text and Image in the Carolingian World." In *The Uses of Literacy in Early Mediaeval Europe*, edited by Rosamond McKitterick, pp. 319–33.

———, ed. *Carolingian Culture: Emulation and Innovation.* Cambridge, 1994.

———, ed. *The Uses of Literacy in Early Mediaeval Europe.* Cambridge, 1990.

McNally, Robert E. *The Bible in the Early Middle Ages.* Westminster, Md., 1959; repr., Atlanta, 1986.

Madec, Goulven. *Jean Scot et ses auteurs: Annotations érigéniennes.* Paris, 1988.

Magoun, Francis P., Jr. "Otfrid's *ad Liutbertum*." *PMLA* 58 (1943): 869–90.

Mähl, Sibylle. *Quadriga Virtutum: Die Kardinaltugenden in der Geistesgeschichte der Karolingerzeit.* Archiv für Kulturgeschichte, Beihefte 9. Cologne and Vienna, 1969.

Maître, Léon. *Les Ecoles épiscopales et monastiques de l'occident depuis Charlemagne jusqu'à Philippe-Auguste (768–1180).* Paris, 1866.

MANITIUS, MAX. *Geschichte der lateinischen Literatur des Mittelalters.* Vol. 1: *Von Justinian bis zur Mitte des zehnten Jahrhunderts.* Munich, 1911; repr., 1959.

MANN, Michael. *The Sources of Social Power.* Vol. 1: *A History of Power from the Beginning to A.D. 1760.* Cambridge and New York, 1986.

MANTELLO, F. A. C., and A. G. Rigg, eds. *Medieval Latin Studies: An Introduction and Bibliographical Guide.* Washington, D.C., forthcoming.

MARENBON, John. *Early Medieval Philosophy (480–1150): An Introduction.* Rev. ed. London and New York, 1988.

——. *From the Circle of Alcuin to the School of Auxerre: Logic, Theology, and Philosophy in the Early Middle Ages.* Cambridge Studies in Medieval Life and Thought, 3rd ser., 15. Cambridge and New York, 1981.

MARILIER, J., and J. Roumailhac. "Mille ans d'épigraphie dans les cryptes de Saint-Germain d'Auxerre (857–1857)." *Bulletin de la Société de fouilles archéologiques et des monuments historiques de l'Yonne* 5 (1989): 1–30.

MARKUS, Robert. *Saeculum: History and Society in the Theology of St. Augustine.* Rev. ed. Cambridge, 1988.

MARTIN, Edward James. *A History of the Iconoclastic Controversy.* London, 1930.

MARTINDALE, Jane. "The French Aristocracy in the Early Middle Ages: A Reappraisal." *Past and Present* 75 (1977): 5–45.

MARX, J., ed. *Propagande et contrapropagande religieuses.* Problèmes d'histoire du Christianisme, fasc. 17. Brussels, 1987.

MASTRELLI, Carlo Alberto. "Vicenda linguistiche del secolo VIII." In *I problemi dell'occidente nel secolo VIII*, 2:803–31, 861–68.

MAYER, Theodor, ed. *Das Königtum: Seine geistigen und rechtlichen Grundlagen.* Vorträge und Forschungen 3. Lindau and Constance, 1956.

MAYR-HARTUNG, Henry. "Charlemagne as a Patron of Art." In *The Church and the Arts*, edited by Diana Wood, pp. 43–77.

MAZLISH, Bruce. *The Leader, the Led, and the Psyche: Essays in Psychohistory.* Hanover, N.H., 1990.

——, ed. *Psychoanalysis and History.* Rev. ed. New York, 1971.

MEGILL, Allan. *Prophets of Extremity: Nietzsche, Heidegger, Foucault, Derrida.* Berkeley, 1985.

——. "The Reception of Foucault by Historians." *Journal of the History of Ideas* 48 (1987): 117–41.

MELVILLE, Gert, ed. *Institutionen und Geschichte: Theoretische Aspekte und mittelalterliche Befunde.* Norm und Struktur 1. Cologne, 1992.

MERCATI, Angelo. "Per la storia del codice Vaticano dei Libri Carolini." *Bessarione* 37 (1921): 112–19.

MEYERS, Jean. "Le Latin carolingien: Mort ou renaissance d'une langue?" *Le Moyen Age* 96 (1990): 385–410.

MEYVAERT, Paul J. "The Authorship of the 'Libri Carolini': Observations Prompted by a Recent Book." *Revue bénédictine* 89 (1979): 29–57.

————. "Excerpts from an Unknown Treatise of Jerome to Gaudentius of Brescia." *Revue bénédictine* 96 (1986): 203–18.

MICHELET, Jules. *Oeuvres complètes*. Vol. 4: *Histoire de France*. Edited by P. Viallaneix. Paris, 1974.

MICHELS, Helmut. "Zur Echtheit der Briefe Papst Gregors II. an Kaiser Leon III." *Zeitschrift für Kirchengeschichte* 99 (1988): 376–91.

MILLER, David Harry. "Sacral Kingship, Biblical Kingship, and the Elevation of Pepin the Short." In *Religion, Culture, and Society in the Early Middle Ages*, edited by Thomas F. X. Noble and John J. Contreni, pp. 131–54.

Miscellanea historica in honorem Alberti de Meyer. 2 vols. Université de Louvain, Recueil de travaux d'histoire et de philologie, 3rd ser., fasc. 22–23. Louvain, 1946.

MITCHELL, John. "Literacy Displayed: The Use of Inscriptions at the Monastery of San Vincenzo al Volturno in the Early Ninth Century." In *The Uses of Literacy in Early Mediaeval Europe*, edited by Rosamond McKitterick, pp. 186–225.

MOHR, Walter. *Die karolingische Reichsidee*. Aevum Christianum 5. Münster, 1962.

MOHRMANN, Christine. *Etudes sur le latin des chrétiens*. 4 vols. Rome, 1958–77.

————. "Die Kontinuität des Lateins vom 6. bis zum 13. Jahrhundert." *Wiener Studien* 89, new ser., 10 (1976): 239–55.

MÖLLER, Helmut, and Rudolf Stephan, eds. *Die Musik des Mittelalters*. Neues Handbuch der Musikwissenschaft 2. Laaber, 1991.

MOMIGLIANO, Arnaldo. "Pagan and Christian Historiography in the Fourth Century A.D." In Momigliano, *Essays in Ancient and Modern Historiography*, pp. 107–26. Middletown, Conn., 1982.

Il monachesimo nell'alto medioevo e la formazione della civiltà occidentale. Settimane 4. Spoleto, 1957.

MONNIER, Francis. *Alcuin et Charlemagne*. 2nd ed. Paris, 1863.

MONOD, Gabriel. *Etudes critiques sur les sources de l'histoire carolingienne*. Bibliothèque de L'Ecole des hautes études, IVe section, Sciences historiques et philologiques 119. Paris, 1898.

MOORE, Michael Edward. "A Sacred Kingdom: Royal and Episcopal Power in the Frankish Realms (490–846)." Ph.D. diss., University of Michigan, 1993.

MOORE, R. I. *The Formation of a Persecuting Society*. Oxford, 1987.

MORAN, Dermot. *The Philosophy of John Scottus Eriugena: A Study of Idealism in the Middle Ages*. Cambridge, New York, and New Rochelle, 1989.

MORDEK, Hubert. "Kanonistische Aktivität in Gallien in der ersten Hälfte des 8. Jahrhunderts: Eine Skizze." *Francia* 2 (1974): 19–25.

————. "Karolingische Kapitularien." In *Überlieferung und Geltung normativer Texte des frühen und hohen Mittelalters*, edited by Mordek, pp. 25–50.

————. *Kirchenrecht und Reform im Frankenreich: Die Collectio Vetus Gallica, die älteste systematische Kanonenssammlung des fränkischen Gallien, Studien und Edition*. Beiträge zur Geschichte und Quellenkunde des Mittelalters 1. Berlin and New York, 1975.

―――. "Kirchenrechtliche Autoritäten im Frühmittelalter." In *Recht und Schrift im Mittelalter*, edited by Peter Classen, pp. 237–55.

―――, ed. *Überlieferung und Geltung normativer Texte des frühen und hohen Mittelalters: Vier Vorträge, gehalten auf dem 35. Deutschen Historikertag 1984 in Berlin*. Quellen und Forschungen zum Recht im Mittelalter. Sigmaringen, 1986.

MORISON, Stanley. *Politics and Script: Aspects of Authority and Freedom in the Development of Graeco-Latin Script from the Sixth Century B.C. to the Twentieth Century A.D. The Lyell Lectures, 1957*. Oxford, 1972.

MORRISON, Karl F. "The Church, Reform and Renaissance in the Early Middle Ages." In *Life and Thought in the Early Middle Ages*, edited by Robert Stuart Hoyt, pp. 143–59. Repr. in Morrison, *Holiness and Politics in Early Medieval Thought*, chap. 3.

―――. *Holiness and Politics in Early Medieval Thought*. London, 1985.

―――. "Incentives for Studying the Liberal Arts." In *The Seven Liberal Arts in the Middle Ages*, edited by David L. Wagner, pp. 32–57.

―――. "'Know Thyself': Music in the Carolingian Renaissance." In *Committenti e produzione artistico-letteraria nell'alto medioevo occidentale*, 1:369–483.

―――. *The Mimetic Tradition of Reform in the West*. Princeton, N.J., 1982.

―――. *Tradition and Authority in the Western Church, 300–1140*. Princeton, N.J., 1969.

―――. *The Two Kingdoms: Ecclesiology in Carolingian Political Thought*. Princeton, N.J., 1964.

―――. "Unum ex multis: Hincmar of Rheims' Medical and Aesthetic Rationales for Unification." In *Nascita dell'Europa ed Europa carolingia*, 2:583–718.

MOSS, H. St. L. B. *The Birth of the Middle Ages, 395–814*. London, 1935.

MOSTERT, Marco. *The Library of Fleury: A Provisional List of Manuscripts*. Middeleeuwse Studies en bronnen 3. Hilversum, The Netherlands, 1989.

MULLINGER, J. Bass. *The Schools of Charles the Great and the Restoration of Education in the Ninth Century*. London, 1877.

MURGIA, Charles E. *Prolegomena to Servius, 5: The Manuscripts*. University of California Publications in Classical Studies. Berkeley, 1975.

MURPHY, Francis X., ed. *A Monument to Saint Jerome: Essays on Some Aspects of His Life, Works, and Influence*. New York, 1952.

MURPHY, James J. *Rhetoric in the Middle Ages: A History of Rhetorical Theory from Saint Augustine to the Renaissance*. Berkeley, 1974.

Die Musik in Geschichte und Gegenwart: Allgemeine Enzyklopädie der Musik. 17 vols. Kassel, 1949–86.

MÜTHERICH, Florentine. "I Libri Carolini et la miniatura carolingia." In *Culto cristiano*, pp. 281–301.

Mütherich, Florentine, and Joachim E. Gaehde. *Carolingian Painting.* New York, 1976.

Nahmer, Dieter von der. "*Dominici scola seruitii*: Über Schultermini in Klosterregeln." *Regula Benedicti Studia: Annuarium Internationale* 12 (1983–85): 143–85.

Narkiss, Bezalel. "Towards a Further Study of the Ashburnam Pentateuch (Pentateuque de Tours)." *Cahiers archéologiques* 19 (1969): 45–60.

Nascita dell'Europa ed Europa carolingia: Un'equazione da verificare. 2 vols. Settimane 27. Spoleto, 1981.

Nees, Lawrence. *The Gundohinus Gospels.* Medieval Academy of America Books 95. Cambridge, Mass., 1987.

———. "Image and Text: Excerpts from Jerome's 'De Trinitate' and the *Maiestas Domini* Miniature of the Gundohinus Gospels." *Viator* 18 (1987): 1–21.

———. "The Originality of Early Medieval Artists." In *Literacy, Politics, and Artistic Innovation in the Early Medieval West*, edited by Celia M. Chazelle, pp. 77–109.

———. *A Tainted Mantle: Hercules and the Classical Tradition at the Carolingian Court.* Philadelphia, 1991.

———. "Unknown Carolingian Drawings of Hercules from the Scriptorium of Reims, and the *Cathedra Petri* Ivories." *Journal of the Walters Art Gallery* 46 (1988): 37–54.

———. Review of Kurt Holter, ed., *Der goldene Psalter "Dagulf Psalter." Art Bulletin* 67 (1985): 681–90.

Neff, Karl, ed. *Die Gedichte des Paulinus Diaconus.* Quellen und Untersuchungen zur lateinischen Philologie des Mittelalters 3, pt. 4. Munich, 1908.

Nelson, Janet L. *Charles the Bald.* London and New York, 1992.

———. "Charles the Bald and the Church in Town and Countryside." In *The Church in Town and Countryside*, edited by Derek Baker, pp. 103–18. Repr. in Nelson, *Politics and Ritual in Early Medieval Europe*, pp. 75–90.

———. "Kingship and Empire." In *The Cambridge History of Medieval Political Thought, c. 350–c. 1450*, edited by J. H. Burns, pp. 210–51.

———. "The Lord's Anointed and the People's Choice: Carolingian Royal Ritual." In *Rituals of Royalty*, edited by David Cannadine and Simon Price, pp. 137–80.

———. "On the Limits of the Carolingian Renaissance." In *Renaissance and Renewal in Christian History*, edited by Derek Baker, pp. 51–69. Repr. in Nelson, *Politics and Ritual in Early Medieval Europe*, pp. 49–68.

———. "Perceptions du pouvoir chez les historiennes du haut moyen âge." In *La Femme au moyen-âge*, edited by Michel Rouche and Jean Heuclin, pp. 75–85.

———. *Politics and Ritual in Early Medieval Europe.* London, 1986.

———. "Symbols in Context: Rulers' Inauguration Rituals in Byzantium and the West in the Early Middle Ages." In *The Orthodox Churches and the West*, edited by Derek Baker, pp. 97–119. Repr. in Nelson, *Politics and Ritual in Early Medieval Europe*, pp. 259–81.

————. "Translating Images of Authority: The Christian Roman Emperors in the Carolingian World." In *Images of Authority*, edited by Mary Margaret MacKenzie and Charlotte Roueché, pp. 194–205.

NEUMAN DE VEGVAR, Carol. "The Origin of the Genoels-Elderen Ivories." *Gesta* 29 (1990): 8–30.

The New Grove Dictionary of Music and Musicians. 20 vols. London and Washington, 1980.

NICHOLS, Stephen G., ed. "The New Philology." *Speculum* 65 (1990): 1–108.

NOBLE, Thomas F. X. "John Damascene and the History of the Iconoclastic Controversy." In *Religion, Culture, and Society in the Early Middle Ages*, edited by Thomas F. X. Noble and John J. Contreni, pp. 95–116.

————. "Literacy and the Papal Government in Late Antiquity and the Early Middle Ages." In *The Uses of Literacy in Early Mediaeval Europe*, edited by Rosamond McKitterick, pp. 82–108.

————. "Louis the Pious and His Piety Reconsidered." *Revue belge de philologie et d'histoire* 58 (1980): 297–316.

————. *The Republic of St. Peter: The Birth of the Papal State, 680–825.* Philadelphia, 1984.

NOBLE, Thomas F. X., and John J. Contreni, eds. *Religion, Culture, and Society in the Early Middle Ages: Studies in Honor of Richard E. Sullivan.* Studies in Medieval Culture 23. Kalamazoo, Mich., 1987.

NORBERG, Dag. "A quelle époque a-t-on cessé de parler latin en Gaule?" *Annales: Economies, sociétés, civilisations* 21 (1966): 346–56.

————. "La Développement du Latin en Italie de Saint Grégoire le Grand à Paul Diacre." In *Caratteri del secolo VII in Occidente*, 2:485–503, 519–37.

————. "Latin scolaire et latin vivant." *Archivum Latinitatis Medii Aevi (Bulletin du Cange)* 40 (1977): 51–63.

————. *Manuel pratique du latin médiéval.* Collection connaissance des langues 4. Paris, 1968.

————, ed. *L'Oeuvre poétique de Paulin d'Aquilée: Edition critique avec introduction et commentaire.* Kungl. Vitterhets Historie och Antikvitets Akademien Hanlingar, Filogisk-filosofiska serien 18. Stockholm, 1979.

NORDEN, Eduard. *Die antike Kunstprosa vom VI. Jahrhundert vor Christus bis in die Zeit der Renaissance.* Leipzig, 1898.

NORTHALL, Ray-Harris, and Thomas D. Cravens, eds. *Linguistic Studies in Medieval Spanish.* Madison, Wis., 1991.

NOVICK, Peter. *That Noble Dream: The "Objectivity Question" and the American Historical Profession.* Cambridge and New York, 1988.

OELSNER, Ludwig. *Jahrbücher des fränkischen Reiches unter König Pippin.* Leipzig, 1871.

OEXLE, Otto Gerhard. *Forschungen zu monastischen und geistlichen Gemeinschaften im westfränkischen Bereich: Bestandteil des Quellenwertes "Societas et Fraternitas."* Münstersche Mittelalter-Schriften 31. Munich, 1978.

————. "Die Karolinger und die Stadt des heiligen Arnulf." *Frühmittelalterliche Studien* 1 (1967): 250–364.

————. "Les Moines d'occident et la vie politique et sociale dans le haut moyen âge." *Revue bénédictine* 103 (1993): 255–72.

OHNSORGE, Werner. "Orthodoxus Imperator: Vom religiösen Motiven für das Kaisertum Karls des Grossen." In Ohnsorge, *Abendland und Byzanz: Gesammelte Aufsätze zur Geschichte der byzantinisch-abendländischen Beziehungen und des Kaisertums*, pp. 64–78. Darmstadt, 1958.

O'MEARA, John J. *Eriugena*. Oxford, 1988.

O'MEARA, John J., and Ludwig Bieler, eds. *The Mind of Eriugena: Papers of a Colloquium, Dublin, 14–18 July 1970*. Dublin, 1973.

ONG, Walter J. *The Presence of the Word: Some Prolegomena for Cultural and Religious History*. New Haven, Conn., 1967.

OSTROGORSKY, Georg. "Rom und Byzanz im Kampf um die Bilderverehrung." *Seminarium Kondakovianum* 6 (1933): 73–87.

OTTEN, Willemien. *The Anthropology of Johannes Scottus Eriugena*. Brill Studies in Intellectual History 20. Leiden, 1991.

OZANAM, A. F. *La Civilisation chrétienne chez les Francs: Recherches sur l'histoire ecclésiastique, politique et littéraire des temps mérovingiennes, et sur le règne de Charlemagne*. Paris, 1849; 6th ed., 1893.

PACAUT, Marcel. *La Paupaté, des origines au concile de Trente*. Grandes études historiques. Paris, 1976.

PAGDEN, Anthony. "Rethinking the Linguistic Turn: Current Anxieties in Intellectual History." *Journal of the History of Ideas* 49 (1988): 519–29.

PALMER, Bryan D. *Descent into Discourse: The Reification of Language and the Writing of Social History*. Critical Perspectives on the Past. Philadelphia, 1990.

PANOFSKY, Erwin. *Renaissance and Renascences in Western Art*. Stockholm, 1960.

PARTNER, Nancy F., ed. "Studying Medieval Women: Sex, Gender, Feminism." *Speculum* 68 (1993): 305–471. Republished as *Studying Medieval Women: Sex, Gender, Femininism* (Cambridge, Mass., 1994).

PATTERSON, Lee. *Negotiating the Past: The Historical Understanding of Medieval Literature*. Madison, Wis., 1987.

PATZELT, Erna. *Die karolingische Renaissance*. Vienna, 1924; 2nd ed. unchanged, Graz, 1965.

PAUL, Jacques. *L'Eglise et la culture en occident, IXe–XIIe siècles*. 2 vols. Nouvelle Clio, L'histoire et ses problèmes 15, 15 bis. Paris, 1986.

PAXTON, Frederick S. *Christianizing Death: The Creation of a Ritual Process in Early Medieval Europe*. Ithaca, N.Y., 1990.

PELIKAN, Jaroslav. *The Christian Tradition: A History of the Development of Doctrine*. Vol. 3: *The Growth of Medieval Theology (600–1300)*. Chicago and London, 1978.

PÉRÈS, Marcel. "Rémi et la musique." In *L'Ecole carolingienne d'Auxerre de*

Murethach à Rémi, 830–908, edited by Dominique Iogna-Prat, Colette Jeudy, and Guy Lobrichon, pp. 435–42.

PERI, Vittorio. "La pentarchià: Istituzione ecclesiale (IV–VII sec.) e teoria canonico-teologia." In *Bisanzio, Roma e l'Italia*, 1:209–311.

PETRI, Franz, ed. *Siedlung, Sprache und Bevölkerungsstruktur in Frankenreich*. Wege der Forschung 49. Darmstadt, 1973.

PFAFF, Richard. *Medieval Latin Liturgy: A Select Bibliography*. Toronto Medieval Bibliographies 9. Toronto, 1982.

PFISTER, J. C. *Geschichte der Teutschen*. 5 vols. Hamburg, 1829.

PHILLIPS, Nancy. "Classical and Late Latin Sources for Ninth-Century Treatises on Music." In *Music Theory and Its Sources*, edited by A. Barbera, pp. 100–135.

PIRENNE, Henri. *Mahomet et Charlemagne*. Paris, 1937. Published in English as *Mohammed and Charlemagne*, translated by Bernard Maill (London, 1939).

PIZARRO, Joaquin Martinez. *A Rhetoric of the Scene: Dramatic Narrative in the Early Middle Ages*. Toronto, 1989.

POGGIASPALLA, Ferminio. *La vita comune del clero dalle origini alla riforma gregoriana*. Uomini et dottrina 14. Rome, 1968.

PORCHER, Jean. "La peinture provinciale." In *Karl der Grosse: Lebenswerk und Nachleben*, edited by Wolfgang Braunfels, et al., 3:54–73.

POSTER, Mark. *The Mode of Information: Poststructuralism and Social Context*. Chicago, 1990.

POULIN, J.-C. *L'Idéal de la sainteté dans l'Aquitaine carolingienne*. Quebec, 1975.

POWERS, Harold. "Mode." In *The New Grove Dictionary of Music and Musicians*, 12:373–84.

PRINZ, Friedrich. "Der fränkische Episkopat zwischen Merowinger- und Karolingerzeit." In *Nascita dell'Europa ed Europa carolingia*, 1:101–46.

———. *Frühes Mönchtum im Frankenreich: Kultur und Gesellschaft in Gallien, den Rheinlanden und Bayern am Beispiel der monastischen Entwicklung (4. bis 8. Jahrhundert)*. 2nd ed. Munich, 1988.

———. "Grundzüge der Entfaltung des abendländischen Mönchtums bis zu Karl dem Grossen." *Studien und Mitteilungen zur Geschichte des Benediktiner-Ordens und seiner Zweige* 102 (1991): 209–30.

———. "Kirchen und Klöster als literarische Auftraggeber." In *Committenti e produzione artistico-letteraria nell'alto medioevo occidentale*, 2:759–90.

———. *Klerus und Krieg im früheren Mittelalter: Untersuchungen zur Rolle der Kirche beim Aufbau der Königsherrschaft*. Monographien zur Geschichte des Mittelalters 2. Stuttgart, 1971.

———, ed. *Herrschaft und Kirche: Beiträge zur Entstehung und Wirkungsweise episkopaler und monastischer Organisationsformen*. Monographien zur Geschichte des Mittelalters 33. Stuttgart, 1988.

———, ed. *Mönchtum und Gesellschaft im Frühmittelalter*. Wege der Forschung 312. Darmstadt, 1976.

I problemi della civiltà carolingia. Settimane 1. Spoleto, 1954.

I problemi dell'occidente nel secolo VIII. 2 vols. Settimane 20. Spoleto, 1973.

QUADRI, Riccardo. Introduction to *I Collectanea di Eirico di Auxerre*, edited by Quadri, pp. 3–28. Spicilegium Friburgense 11. Freiburg, 1966.

QUASTEN, Johannes, and Angelo DiBerardino, eds. *Patrology*. Vol. 4: *The Golden Age of Patristic Literature*. Translated by Placid Solari. Utrecht, 1960; Westminster, Md., 1986.

RABB, Theodore K., and Robert I. Rotberg, eds. *The New History, the 1980s, and Beyond: Studies in Interdisciplinary History*. Princeton, N.J., 1982.

RADER, Melvin. *Marx's Interpretation of History*. New York, 1979.

RÄDLE, Fidel. *Studien zu Smaragd von Saint-Mihiel*. Medium Aevum, philologisches Studien 29. Munich, 1974.

RAND, E. K. *A Survey of the Manuscripts of Tours*. 2 vols. Mediaeval Academy of America Publications 3. Cambridge, Mass., 1929.

RANDSBORG, Klaus. *The First Millennium A.D. in Europe and the Mediterranean: An Archaeological Survey*. Cambridge and New York, 1991.

RANKIN, Susan. "Carolingian Music." In *Carolingian Culture*, edited by Rosamond McKitterick, pp. 274–316.

REGENOS, Graydon W., trans. *The Letters of Lupus of Ferrières*. The Hague, 1966.

RESNICK, Irven M. "*Risus Monasticus*: Laughter and Medieval Monastic Culture." *Revue bénédictine* 97 (1987): 90–100.

REUTER, Timothy, ed. *The Greatest Englishman: Essays on St. Boniface and the Church at Crediton*. Exeter, 1980.

——, ed. *The Medieval Nobility: Studies on the Ruling Classes of France and Germany from the Sixth to the Twelfth Century*. Europe in the Middle Ages 14. Amsterdam, 1978.

REYNOLDS, Roger. "Divine Office." In *Dictionary of the Middle Ages*, 4:221–31.

RICE, Eugene F., Jr. *Saint Jerome in the Renaissance*. Baltimore, Md., 1985.

RICHÉ, Pierre. "Les Bibliothèques de trois aristocrates laïcs carolingiens." *Le Moyen Age* 69 (1963): 87–104.

——. *Les Carolingiens: Une famille qui fit l'Europe*. Paris, 1983. Published in English as *The Carolingians: A Family Who Forged Europe*, translated by Michael Idomir Allen (Philadelphia, 1993).

——. *Ecoles et enseignement dans le haut moyen âge: Fin du Ve siècle–milieu du XIe siècle*. 2nd ed. Paris, 1989. The 1st ed. was published under the title *Les écoles et l'enseignement dans l'occident chrétien de la fin de Ve siècle au milieu du XI siècle*, Collection historique (Paris, 1979).

——. *Education et culture dans l'occident barbare, 6e–8e siècles*. 3rd ed. Paris 1973. Published in English as *Education and Culture in the Barbarian West, Sixth through Eighth Centuries*, translated by John J. Contreni (Columbia, S.C., 1976).

————. "Epilogo." In *La cultura antica nell'occidente latino dal VII all'XI secolo*, 2:929–47.

————. *Gerbert d'Aurillac, le pape de l'an mil*. Paris, 1987.

————. "Recherches sur l'instruction des laïcs du IXe au XII siècle." *Cahiers de civilisation médiévale* 5 (1962): 175–82.

————. "Le Renouveau culturel à la cour de Pépin III." *Francia* 2 (1974): 59–70.

————. "Trésors et collections d'aristocrates laïques carolingiens." *Cahiers archéologiques* 22 (1972): 39–46.

————. *La Vie quotidienne dans l'empire carolingien*. 2nd ed. Paris, 1979. First ed. published in English as *Daily Life in the World of Charlemagne*, translated by Jo Ann McNamara, The Middle Ages (Philadelphia, 1978).

RICHÉ, Pierre, and Guy Lobrichon, eds. *Le Moyen Age et la Bible*. Bible de Tous les Temps 4. Paris, 1984.

RICHTER, Michael. "A quelle époque a-t-on cessé parler latin en Gaul? A propos d'une question mal posée." *Annales: Economies, sociétés, civilisations* 38 (1983): 439–48.

————. "Die Sprachenpolitik Karls des Grossen." *Sprachenwissenschaft* 7 (1982): 412–37.

RICKERT, Franz. *Studien zum Ashburnham Pentateuch (Paris, Bibl. Nat. NAL. 2334)*. Bonn, 1986.

RIGBY, S. H. *Marxism and History: A Critical Introduction*. Manchester, 1987.

RISSEL, Marie. *Rezeption antiker und patristischer Wissenschaft bei Hrabanus Maurus: Studien zur karolingischen Geistesgeschichte*. Lateinische Sprache und Literatur des Mittelalters 7. Bern and Frankfurt, 1976.

ROBERTSON, Giles, and George Henderson, eds. *Studies in Memory of David Talbot Rice*. Edinburgh, 1975.

ROBERTSON, William. *Progress of Society in Europe: A Historical Outline from the Subversion of the Roman Empire to the Beginning of the Sixteenth Century*. Edited by Felix Gilbert. Classic European Historians. Chicago, 1972.

ROBINSON, Fred C. "Syntactical Glosses in Latin Manuscripts of Anglo-Saxon Provenance." *Speculum* 48 (1973): 443–75.

Roma e l'età carolingia: Atti delle giornate di studio, 3–8 maggio 1976. A cura della Istituto di storia dell'arte dell'Università di Roma. Rome, 1976.

RÖNNAU, Klaus. *Die Tropen zum Gloria in excelsis Deo*. Wiesbaden, 1967.

ROSANVALLON, Pierre. *Le Moment Guizot*. Bibliothèque des sciences humaines. Paris, 1985.

ROSENBAUM, Elizabeth. "The Evangelist Portraits of the Ada School and Their Models." *Art Bulletin* 38 (1955): 81–90.

ROUCHE, Michel. "The Carolingian Renewal." In *The Cambridge Illustrated History of the Middle Ages*, vol. 1: *350–950*, pp. 416–73.

ROUCHE, Michel, and Jean Heuclin, eds. *La Femme au moyen âge*. Mauberge, 1990.

RUDNICK, Ulrich. *Das System des Johannes Scottus Eriugena: Eine theologisch-*

philosophische Studie zu seinem Werk. Saarbrücker theologische Forschungen 2. Frankfurt, 1990.

RUNCIMAN, Steven. "The Empress Irene the Athenian." In *Medieval Women*, edited by Derek Baker, pp. 101–18.

RUNYAN, William McKinley, ed. *Psychology and Historical Interpretation*. New York and Oxford, 1988.

RUSSELL, James C. *The Germanization of Early Medieval Christianity: A Sociohistorical Approach to Religious Transformation*. New York and Oxford, 1994.

SAHAS, Daniel J. *Icon and Logos: Sources in Eighth-Century Iconoclasm*. Toronto Medieval Texts and Translations 4. Toronto, 1986.

Saint Chrodegang. Communications présentés au colloque tenu à Metz à l'occasion du XIIe centenaire de sa mort. Metz, 1967.

St. Kilian: 1300 Jahre Martyrium des Frankenapostel. Würzburger Diözesangeschichtsblätter 51. Würzburg, 1989.

SANDMANN, Mechthild. "Wirkungsbereich fuldische Mönche." In *Die Klostergemeinschaft von Fulda im früheren Mittelalter*, edited by Karl Schmid, vol. 2, pt. 2, pp. 692–791.

Santi e demoni nell'alto medioevo occidentale (secoli V–XI). 2 vols. Settimane 36. Spoleto, 1989.

SAUSSURE, Ferdinand de. *Cours de linguistique générale*. Edited by Tullio de Mauro. Paris, 1972. Published in English as *Course in General Linguistics*, translated by Roy Harris (London, 1983).

SAVIGNI, R. *Giona di Orléans, una ecclesiologia carolingia*. Bologna, 1989.

SCHÄFERDIECK, Knut, ed. *Die Kirche des früheren Mittelalters*. Kirchengeschichte als Missionsgeschichte, edited by H. Frohnes, et al. Vol. 2, pt. 1. Munich, 1978.

SCHALLER, Dieter. "Der Dichter des *Carmen de conversione Saxonum*." In *Tradition und Wertung*, edited by Günter Bernt, Fidel Rädle, and Gabriel Silagi, pp. 27–45.

SCHATZ, Klaus. "Oecuménicité du concile et structure de l'église à Nicée II et dans les *Livres carolins*." In *Nicée II, 787–1987*, edited by F. Boespflug and N. Lossky, pp. 263–70.

SCHEIBE, Friedrich-Carl. "Alcuin und die Admonitio Generalis." *Deutsches Archiv für Erforschung des Mittelalters* 14 (1958): 221–29.

SCHEIBELREITER, Georg. *Der Bischof in merowingischer Zeit*. Veröffentlichungen des Instituts für österreichischen Geschichtsforschung 27. Vienna, Cologne, and Graz, 1983.

SCHIEDER, Theodor, ed. *Handbuch der europäischen Geschichte*. Vol. 1: *Europa im Wandel von der Antike zum Mittelalter*. Edited by Theodor Schieffer. Stuttgart, 1976.

SCHIEFFER, Rudolf. "Ludwig 'der Fromme': Zur Entstehung eines karolingischen Herrscherbeinamen." *Frühmittelalterliche Studien* 16 (1982): 58–73.

————, ed. *Beiträge zur Geschichte des Regnum Francorum*. Referat beim wissenschaftlichen Colloquium zum 75. Geburtstag von Eugen Ewig am 28. Mai 1988. Beihefte der Francia 22. Sigmaringen, 1990.

SCHIEFFER, Theodor. *Winfrid-Bonifatius und die christliche Grundlegung Europas*. Freiburg im Breisgau, 1954.

SCHLAGER, Karlheinz. "Alleluia I: Latin Rite." In *The New Grove Dictionary of Music and Musicians*, 1:269–74.

————. *Alleluia-Melodien I (bis 1000)*. Monumenta Monodica Medii Aevi 7. Kassel and New York, 1968.

————. *Thematischer Katalog der ältesten Alleluia-Melodien aus Handschriften des 10. und 11. Jahrhunderts*. Erlanger Arbeiten zur Musikwissenschaft 2. Munich, 1965.

SCHMANDT, Walter. *Studien zu den Libri Carolini*. Mainz, 1966.

SCHMID, Alfred A., ed. *Riforma religiosa e arti nell'epoca Carolingia*. Atti del XXIV congresso internazionale di storia dell'arte, Bologna, sett. 1979. Bologna, 1983.

SCHMID, Karl, ed. *Die Klostergemeinschaft von Fulda im früheren Mittelalter*. 3 vols. Münstersche Mittelalter-Schriften 8. Munich, 1978.

SCHMID, Karl, and Otto Gerhard Oexle. "Voraussetzung und Wirkung des Gebetsbundes von Attigny." *Francia* 2 (1974): 71–122.

SCHMID, Karl, and Joachim Wollasch, eds. *Memoria: Der geschichtliche Zeugniswert des liturgischer Gedenkens im Mittelalter*. Munich, 1984.

SCHMIDT, Kurt Dietrich, and Ernst Wolf, eds. *Die Kirche in ihrer Geschichte: Ein Handbuch*. Vol. 2: Lieferung E: *Geschichte des Frühmittelalters und der Germanenmission*, by Gert Haendler. Göttingen, 1961.

SCHMIDT, Roderich. "Zur Geschichte des fränkischen Königsthrons." *Frühmittelalterliche Studien* 2 (1968): 45–66.

SCHMITZ, Philibert. *Histoire de l'ordre de Saint Benoît*. 7 vols. Maredsous, 1941–56; 2nd ed. of vols. 1–2, 1948.

SCHNEIDER, Friedrich. *Die neueren Anschauungen der deutschen Historiker über die deutsche Kaiserpolitik des Mittelalters and die mit ihr verbundene Ostpolitik*. 6th ed. Weimar, 1943.

SCHNEIDER, Gerhard. *Erzbischof Fulco von Reims (883–900) und das Frankenreich*. Münchener Beiträge zur Mediävistik und Renaissance-Forschung 14. Munich, 1973.

SCHNITZLER, Hermann. "Das Kuppelmosaik der aachener Pfalzkapelle." *Aachener Kunstblätter* 29 (1964): 17–44.

SCHNÜRER, Gustave. *L'Eglise et la civilisation au moyen âge*. Translated by Française de G. Castella. 3 vols. Paris, 1933–38.

SCHÖNWALDER, Karen. *Historiker und Politiker: Geschichtswissenschaft im Nationalsozialismus*. Historische Studien 9. Frankfurt, 1992.

SCHRADE, H., "Zum Kuppelmosaik der aachener Pfalzkapelle." *Aachener Kunstblätter* 30 (1965): 25–37.

SCHRAMM. Percy Ernst. *Die deutschen Kaiser und Könige in Bildern ihrer Zeit 751–1190*. Edited by Florentine Mütherich. Rev. ed. Munich, 1983.

———. *Kaiser, Könige und Päpste: Gesammelte Aufsätze zur Geschichte des Mittelalters*. 4 vols. Stuttgart, 1968–71.

SCHRAMM, Percy Ernst, and Florentine Mütherich. *Denkmale der deutschen Könige und Kaiser*. Veröffentlichungen des Zentralinstituts für Kunstsgeschichte in München 2. Munich, 1962.

SCHREINER, K. "Führertum, Rasse, Reich: Wissenschaft von der Geschichte nach der nationalsozialistischen Machterergreifung." In *Wissenschaft im dritten Reich*, edited by Peter Lundgreen, pp. 163–252.

SCHREINER, Peter. "Der byzantinische Bilderstreit: Kritische Analyse der zeitgenössischen Meinungen und Urteil der Nachwelt bis heute." In *Bisanzio, Roma e l'Italia nell'alto medioevo*, 1:319–407.

SCHRIMPF, Gangolf. *Das Werk des Johannes Scottus Eriugena im Rahmen des Wissenschaftsverständnisses seiner Zeit: Einführung zu Periphyseon*. Beiträge zur Geschichte der Philosophie und Theologie des Mittelalters, new ser., 23. Münster, 1982.

———. "Zur Frage der Authentizität unserer Texte von Johannes Scottus' 'Annotationes in Martianum.'" In *The Mind of Eriugena*, edited by John J. O'Meara and Ludwig Bieler, pp. 125–39.

SCHUBERT, Hans von. *Geschichte der christlichen Kirche im Frühmittelalter*. Tübingen, 1921.

SCHULZE, Hans K. "Reichsaristokratie, Stammesadel und fränkische Freiheit: Neuere Forschungen zur frühmittelalterlichen Sozialgeschichte." *Historische Zeitschrift* 227 (1978): 353–73.

SCHÜSSLER, Heinz Joachim. "Die fränkische Reichsteilung von Vieux-Poitiers (742) und die Reform der Kirche in den Teilreichen Karlmanns und Pippins: Zu den Grenzen der Wirksamkeit des Bonifatius." *Francia* 13 (1985): 47–112.

La scuola nell'occidente latino dell'alto medioevo. 2 vols. Settimane 19. Spoleto, 1972.

Il secolo di ferro: Mito e realtà dal sec. X. 2 vols. Settimane 38. Spoleto, 1991.

Segni e riti nella chiesa altomedievale occidentale. 2 vols. Settimane 33. Spoleto, 1987.

SELLIN, Volker. "Mentalität und Mentalitätgeschichte." *Historische Zeitschrift* 241 (1985): 555–98.

SEMMLER, Josef. "Benedictus II: Una regula—una consuetudo." In *Benedictine Culture*, edited by W. Lourdaux and D. Verhelst, pp. 1–49.

———. "Benediktinische Reform und kaiserliches Privileg: Zur Frage des institutionellen Zusammenschlusses der Klöster um Benedikt von Aniane." In *Institutionen und Geschichte*, edited by Gert Melville, pp. 259–93.

———. "Episcopi potestas und karolingische Klosterpolitik." In *Mönchtum, Episkopat und Adel zur Gründungszeit des Klosters Reichenau*, edited by Arno Borst, pp. 305–95.

————. "Karl der Grosse und das fränkische Mönchtum." In *Karl der Grosse: Lebenswerk und Nachleben*, edited by Wolfgang Braunfels, et al., 2:255–89.

————. "Le Monachisme occidental du VIIIe au Xe siècle: Formation et réformation." *Revue bénédictine* 103 (1993): 68–89.

————. "Mönche und Kanoniker im Frankenreich Pippins III. und Karls des Grossen." In *Untersuchungen zu Kloster und Stift*, pp. 78–111.

————. "Pippin III. und die fränkischen Klöster." *Francia* 3 (1975): 88–146.

————. "Le Souverain occidental et les communautés religieuses du IXe au début du XIe siècle." *Byzantion* 61 (1991): 44–70.

SEMMLER, Josef, and A. E. Verhulst. "Les Statuts d'Adalhard de Corbie de l'an 822." *Le Moyen Age* 68 (1962): 91–123, 233–69.

SHAW, William H. *Marx's Theory of History*. Stanford, Calif., 1978.

SHEILS, W. J., and Diana Wood, eds. *Women in the Church*. Studies in Church History 27. Oxford, 1990.

SIEBEN, Hermann Josef. *Das Konzilsidee der alten Kirche*. Konziliengeschichte, edited by Walter Brandmüller, Reihe B, Untersuchungen. Paderborn, Munich, and Vienna, 1979.

SIEGRIST, Theodor. *Herrscherbild und Weltsicht bei Notker Balbulus: Untersuchungen zu den Gesta Karoli*. Geist und Werk der Zeiten: Arbeiten aus den historischen Seminar der Universität Zurich 8. Zurich, 1963.

SIMPSON, Dean. Introduction to *Sedulii Scotti collectaneum miscellaneum*, edited by Simpson, pp. ix–xxxiii. CC cont. med. 67. Turnhout, 1988.

SMALLEY, Beryl. *The Study of the Bible in the Middle Ages*. 3rd ed. Oxford, 1983; repr., Oxford, 1984.

SMITH, Lesley, and Benedicta Ward, eds. *Intellectual Life in the Middle Ages: Essays Presented to Margaret Gibson*. London and Rio Grande, Ohio, 1992.

SMITS VAN WAESBERGHE, Joseph. *Musikerziehung: Lehre und Theorie der Musik im Mittelalter*. Musikgeschichte in Bildern 3, 3. Leipzig, 1969.

————. "Notation." In *Die Musik in Geschichte und Gegenwart* 9, cols. 1625–26.

————. "Zur ursprünglichen Vortragsweise der Prosulen, Sequenzen, und Organa." In *Bericht über den siebenten internationalen musikwissenschaftlichen Kongress, Köln 1958*, pp. 251–54. Kassel, 1959.

SOT, Michel. *Un Historien et son église: Flodoard de Reims*. Paris, 1993.

————, ed. *Haut moyen âge: Culture, éducation, et société: Etudes offertes à Pierre Riché*. Centre de recherche sur l'antiquité et le haut moyen âge de l'Université Paris X-Nanterre. Le Garenne-Colombes, 1990.

SPECK, Paul. "Ikonoklasmus und die Anfänge der makedonischen Renaissance." In *Poikila Byzantina* 4 (Varia 1), pp. 175–210. Bonn, 1984.

————. *Kaiser Konstantin VI*. 2 vols. Munich, 1978.

————. "Weitere Überlegungen und Untersuchungen über die Ursprünge der byzantinischen Renaissance." In *Poikila Byzantina* 6 (Varia 2), pp. 253–83. Bonn, 1987.

STÄBLEIN, Bruno. "Einführung." In *Die Gesänge des altrömischen Graduale Vat.*

lat. 5319, edited by Stäblein and Margareta Landwehr-Melnicki, pp. 1*–
164*. Monumenta Monodica Medii Aevi 2. Kassel, 1968.

———. "Gloria in excelsis Deo." In *Die Musik in Geschichte und Gegenwart* 5,
cols. 302–20.

———. *Hymnen I: Die mittelalterlichen Hymnenmelodien des Abendlandes.* Monumenta Monodica Medii Aevi 1. Kassel, 1956.

STANNARD, D. E. *Shrinking History: On Freud and the Failure of Psychohistory.*
New York, 1980.

STAUBACH, Nikolaus. "'Cultus divinus' und karolingische Reform." *Frühmittelalterliche Studien* 18 (1984): 546–81.

———. "'Das grossen Kaisers kleiner Sohn': Zum Bild Ludwigs des Frommen
in der älteren deutschen Geschichtsforschung." In *Charlemagne's Heir*, edited
by Peter Godman and Roger Collins, pp. 701–21.

STEGMÜLLER, Friedrich. *Repertorium Biblicum Medii Aevi.* 7 vols. Madrid,
1950–61.

STEINER, Ruth. "Hymn." In *The New Grove Dictionary of Music and Musicians*,
8:173–87.

———. "Trope (i) 3: Introit Tropes." In *The New Grove Dictionary of Music and
Musicians*, 19:178.

STERN, Henri. *Le Calendrier de 354: Etude sur son texte et ses illustrations.*
Bibliothèque archéologique et historique 55. Paris, 1953.

STEVENS, John. *Words and Music: Song, Narrative, Dance, and Drama, 1050–
1350.* Cambridge, 1986.

STEVENS, Wesley M. *Bede's Scientific Achievement: The Jarrow Lecture, 1985.*
Jarrow, 1985.

———. "Compotistica et Astronomica in the Fulda School." In *Saints, Scholars,
and Heroes*, edited by Margot H. King and Wesley M. Stevens, 1:27–63.

———. Introduction to *Rabani Mogontiacensis episcopi De Computo*, edited by
Stevens, pp. 165–97. CC cont. med. 44. Turnhout, 1979.

———. "Walahfrid Strabo—a Student at Fulda." In *Historical Papers 1971 of the
Canadian Historical Association*, edited by J. Atherton, pp. 13–20. Ottawa,
1972.

STIENON, Jacques. "Quelques réflexions sur les moines et la création artistique
dans l'occident du haut moyen âge (VIIIe–XIe siècle)." *Revue bénédictine* 103
(1993): 153–68.

STOCLET, Alain J. *Autour de Fulrad de Saint-Denis (v. 710–784).* Ecole pratique
des hautes études. Sciences historiques et philologiques, ser. 5: Hautes études
médiévales et modernes 72. Geneva and Paris, 1993.

———. "La 'Clausula de unctione Pippini regis': Mises en point et nouvelles
hypothèses." *Francia* 8 (1980): 1–42.

———. "Le *De civitate dei* de St. Augustin: Sa diffusion avant 900 d'après les
caractères externes des manuscrits antérieur à cette date et les catalogues
contemporains." *Recherches augustiniennes* 19 (1984): 185–209.

STOCK, Brian. *The Implications of Literacy: Written Language and Models of Interpretation in the Eleventh and Twelfth Centuries.* Princeton, N.J., 1983.

———. *Listening for the Past: On the Uses of the Past.* Parallax: Re-visions of Culture and Society. Baltimore, Md., and London, 1990.

STOIANOVICH, Traian. *French Historical Method: The Annales Paradigm.* Ithaca, N.Y., and London, 1976.

La storiografia altomedievale. 2 vols. Settimane 17. Spoleto, 1970.

STRAW, Carole. *Gregory the Great: Perfection in Imperfection.* Transformation of the Classical Heritage 14. Berkeley, Los Angeles, and London, 1988.

SULLIVAN, Richard E. "The Carolingian Age: Reflections on Its Place in the History of the Middle Ages." *Speculum* 64 (1989): 267–306.

———. "Changing Perspectives on the Concept of the Middle Ages." *Centennial Review* 28 (1984): 77–99. Reprinted in Sullivan, *Speaking for Clio*, pp. 152–69.

———. *Christian Missionary Activity in the Early Middle Ages.* Variorum Collected Studies Series CS431. Aldershot, England, 1994.

———. *Heirs of the Roman Empire.* Ithaca, N.Y., 1961.

———. *Speaking for Clio.* Kirksville, Mo., 1991.

SZABÓ-BECHSTEIN, Brigitte. *Libertas Ecclesiae: Eine Schlüsselbegriff des Investiturstreits und seine Vorgeschichte, 4.–11. Jahrhundert.* Studi Gregoriani 12. Rome, 1985.

SZÖVÉRFFY, Joseph. *Die Annalen der lateinischen Hymnendichtung: Ein Handbuch.* Vol. 1: *Die lateinischen Hymnen bis zum Ende des XI. Jahrhunderts.* Die lyrischen Dichtung des Mittelalters. Berlin, 1964.

Testo e immagine nell'alto medioevo. 2 vols. Settimane 41. Spoleto, 1994.

THIEL, Matthias. *Grundlagen und Gestalt der Hebräischkenntnisse des frühen Mittelalters.* Biblioteca degli "Studi Medievali" 4. Spoleto, 1973.

THOMAS, Heinz. "Frenkisk: Zur Geschichte von *theodicus* und *teutonicus* im 9. Jahrhunderts." In *Beiträge zu Geschichte des Regnum Francorum*, edited by Rudolf Schieffer, pp. 67–95. Referat beim wissenschaftlichen Colloquium zum 75. Geburtstag von Eugen Ewig am 28. Mai 1988. Beihefte der Francia 22. Sigmaringen, 1990.

THORPE, Lewis, trans. *Einhard and Notker the Stammerer: Two Lives of Charlemagne.* Baltimore, Md., 1969.

TOEWS, John E. "Intellectual History after the Linguistic Turn: The Autonomy of Meaning and the Irreducibility of Experience." *American Historical Review* 92 (1987): 879–907.

TRAILL, D. A. *Walahfrid Strabo's "Visio Wettini": Text, Translation, and Commentary.* Lateinische Sprache und Literatur des Mittelalters 2. Berne and Frankfurt, 1974.

TRAUBE, Ludwig. *Einleitung in die lateinische Philologie des Mittelalters.* Edited by Paul Lehmann. In Traube, *Vorlesung und Abhandlungen*, edited by Franz Boll, vol. 2. Munich, 1911.

TREADGOLD, Warren. *The Byzantine Revival, 780–842.* Stanford, Calif., 1988.

————. "The Empress Irene's Preparation for the Seventh Ecumenical Council." *Patristic and Byzantine Review* 7 (1988): 49–58.

————, ed. *Renaissances before the Renaissance: Cultural Revivals of Late Antiquity and the Middle Ages.* Stanford, Calif., 1984.

TREITINGER, Otto. *Die oströmische Kaiser- und Reichsidee nach ihrer Gestaltung im höfischen Zeremoniell.* 2nd ed. Darmstadt, 1956.

TREITLER, Leo. "The Early History of Music Writing in the West." *Journal of the American Musicological Society* 35 (1982): 237–79.

————. "Reading and Singing: On the Genesis of Occidental Music-Writing." *Early Music History* 4 (1984): 135–208.

TREITLER, Leo, Kenneth Levy, and David Hughes. "Communications." *Journal of the American Musicological Society* 41 (1988): 566–79.

TROMPF, G. W. "The Concept of the Carolingian Renaissance." *Journal of the History of Ideas* 34 (1973): 3–26.

ULLMANN, Walter. *The Carolingian Renaissance and the Idea of Kingship: The Birkbeck Lectures, 1968–1969.* London, 1969.

————. *The Growth of Papal Government in the Middle Ages: A Study in the Ideological Relation of Clerical to Lay Power.* 3rd ed. London, 1970.

Untersuchungen zu Kloster und Stift. Veröffentlichungen des Max-Planck-Instituts für Geschichte 68. Göttingen, 1980.

VAN DER HORST, Koert, and Jacobus H. A. Engelbregt, eds. *Utrecht-Psalter: Vollständige Faksimile Ausgabe in Originalformat der Handscrift 32 aus dem Besitz der Bibliotheek der Rijksuniversiteit te Utrecht.* Graz, 1984.

VAN UYTFANGHE, Mark. "Histoire du latin, protohistoire des langues romanes et histoire de la communication: A propos d'un recueil d'études, et avec quelques observations préliminaires sur le débat intellectuel entre pensée structurale et pensée historique." *Francia* 11 (1983): 579–613.

VAUCHEZ, André. *La Spiritualité du moyen âge occidental: VIIIe–XIIe siècles.* Collection SUP. Paris, 1975. Published in English as *The Spirituality of the Medieval West: From the Eighth to the Twelfth Century,* translated by Colette Friedlander, Cistercian Studies Series 145 (Kalamazoo, Mich., 1993).

VIERHAUS, Rudolf, and Manfred Botzenhart, eds. *Dauer und Wandel der Geschichte: Aspekte europäischer Vergangenheit: Festgabe für Kurt von Rauner.* Neue münstersche Beiträge zur Geschichtsforschung. Münster, 1966.

VINAY, Gustavo. "Letteratura antica e letteratura latina altomedievale." In *La cultura antica nell'occidente latino dal VII all'XI secolo,* 1:511–40.

VOGEL, Cyrille. "Les Echanges liturgiques entre Rome et les pays francs jusqu'à l'époque de Charlemagne." In *La chiesa nei regni dall'Europa occidentale e i loro rapporti con Roma sino all'800,* 1:185–295.

————. "Les Motifs de la romanisation du culte sous Pépin le Bref (751–768) et Charlemagne (774–814)." In *Culto cristiano,* pp. 13–41.

VOIGT, Karl. *Die karolingische Klosterpolitik und die Niedergang des west-fränkischen Königtums: Laienäbte und Klosterinhaber.* Kirchenrechtliche Abhandlungen 90–91. Stuttgart, 1917; repr., Amsterdam, 1965.

VOLBACH, Wolfgang Fritz. *Early Christian Art*. Translated by Christopher Ligota. New York, [1962].

——. *Elfenbeinarbeiten der Spätantike und des frühen Mittelalters*. 3rd ed. Mainz, 1976.

VOLLMANN-PROFE, Gisela. *Kommentar zu Otfrids Evangelienbuch*. Bonn, 1976.

VOLTAIRE. *Annales de l'empire depuis Charlemagne*. In *Oeuvres complètes de Voltaire*, vol. 13. New ed. Paris, 1878.

——. *Essai sur les moeurs et l'ésprit des nations*. In *Ouevres complètes de Voltaire*, vols. 12–13. New ed. Paris, 1878.

VON DEN STEINEN, Wolfram. "Die Anfänge der Sequenzendichtung." *Zeitschrift für Schweizerische Kirchengeschichte* 40 (1946): 190–212, 241–68; 41 (1947): 19–48, 122–62.

——. "Entstehungsgeschichte der Libri Carolini." *Quellen und Forschungen aus italienischen Archiven und Bibliotheken* 21 (1929–30): 1–93.

——. "Karl der Grosse und die Libri Carolini: Die tironischen Noten zum Codex." *Neues Archiv* 49 (1931): 207–80.

——. "Karl und die Dichter." In *Karl der Grosse: Lebenswerk und Nachleben*, edited by Wolfgang Braunfels, et al., 2:63–94.

——. "Der Neubeginn." In *Karl der Grosse: Lebenswerk und Nachleben*, edited by Wolfgang Braunfels, et al., 2:9–27.

VON EUW, Anton. "Studien zu den Elfenbeinarbeiten der Hofschule Karls des Grossen." *Aachener Kunstblätter* 34 (1967): 36–60.

VON EUW, Anton, and Peter Schreiner, eds. *Kaiserin Theophanu: Begegnung des Ostens und Westens um die Wende des ersten Jahrtausends*. 2 vols. Cologne, 1991.

VYKOUKAL, E. "Les Examens du clergé paroissial à l'époque carolingienne." *Revue d'histoire ecclésiastique* 14 (1913): 81–96.

WAGNER, David L., ed. *The Seven Liberal Arts in the Middle Ages*. Bloomington, Ind., 1983.

WALLACE-HADRILL, J. M. *The Barbarian West, 400–1000*. London, 1952.

——. *Early Germanic Kingship in England and on the Continent*. Oxford, 1971.

——. *The Frankish Church*. Oxford History of the Christian Church. Oxford, 1983.

WALLACH, Luitpold. *Alcuin and Charlemagne: Studies in Carolingian History and Literature*. Cornell Studies in Classical Philology 32. Ithaca, N.Y., 1959; repr., 1968.

——. "Charlemagne's *De litteris colendis* and Alcuin." In Wallach, *Alcuin and Charlemagne*, pp. 198–226.

——. *Diplomatic Studies in Latin and Greek Documents from the Carolingian Age*. Ithaca, N.Y., 1977.

WALTER, L. K. *St. Kilian: Schrifttums-Verzeichnis zu Martyrium und Kult des Frankenapostel und zur Gründung des Bistums Würzburg*. Würzburger Diözesengeschichtsblätter 51, Ergänzungsband. Würzburg, 1989.

WARD, Elizabeth. "Agobard of Lyons and Paschasius Radbertus as Critics of the Empress Judith." In *Women in the Church*, edited by W. J. Sheils and Diana Wood, pp. 15–25.

———. "Caesar's Wife: The Career of the Empress Judith, 819–829." In *Charlemagne's Heir*, edited by Peter Godman and Roger Collins, pp. 205–27.

WATTENBACH, Wilhelm, Wilhelm Levison, and Heinz Löwe. *Deutschlands Geschichtsquellen im Mittelalter: Vorzeit und Karolinger*. 5 vols. and Beiheft. Weimar, 1952–73.

WEAKLAND, Rembert. "The Compositions of Hucbald." *Etudes grégoriennes* 3 (1959): 155–62.

———. "Hucbald as Musician and Theorist." *Musical Quarterly* 42 (1956): 66–84.

WEINRICH, Lorenz. *Wala, Graf, Mönch und Rebell: Die Biographie eines Karolingers*. Historische Studien 386. Lübeck, 1963.

WEITZMANN, Kurt. *Late Antique and Early Christian Book Illustration*. New York, 1977.

———. *Studies in Classical and Byzantine Manuscript Illumination*. Edited by Herbert L. Kessler. Chicago, 1971.

———. "A Tabula Odysseaca." *American Journal of Archaeology* 45 (1941): 166–81. Repr. in Weitzmann, *Studies in Classical and Byzantine Manuscript Illumination*, pp. 1–19.

———, ed. *Age of Spirituality: Late Antique and Early Christian Art, Third to Seventh Century*. New York, 1979.

WEMPLE, Suzanne F. *Women in Frankish Society: Marriage and the Cloister, 500 to 900*. Philadelphia, 1981.

WENTZEL, Hans. "Der Bergkristall mit der Geschichte der Susanna." *Pantheon* 28 (1970): 365–72.

WERNER, Joachim, and Eugen Ewig, eds. *Von der Spätantike zum frühen Mittelalter: Aktuelle Probleme in historischer und archäologischer Sicht*. Vorträge und Forschungen 25. Sigmaringen, 1979.

WERNER, Karl Ferdinand. "Du nouveau sur un vieux thème: Les Origines de la 'noblesse' et de la 'chevalerie.'" In *Comptes rendus des séances de l'Academie des inscriptions et belles-lettres, Paris, 1985*, pp. 186–200. Paris, 1986.

———. "*Hludowicus Augustus*: Gouverner l'empire chrétien—idées et realités." In *Charlemagne's Heir*, edited by Peter Godman and Roger Collins, pp. 3–123.

———. *Das NS-Geschichtsbild und die deutsche Geschichtswissenschaft*. Stuttgart, 1957.

WETHERLY, Paul, ed. *Marx's Theory of History: The Contemporary Debate*. Avebury Series in Philosophy. Aldershot, England, and Brookfield, Vt., 1992.

WHITE, Hayden. *Metahistory: The Historical Imagination in Nineteenth-Century Europe*. Baltimore, Md., 1973.

———. *Tropics of Discourse: Essays in Cultural Criticism*. Baltimore, Md., 1978.

WICKERSHEIMER, Ernest. *Les Manuscrits latins de médecine du haut moyen âge dans les bibliothèques de France.* Paris, 1966.

WICKHAM, Chris. "The Other Transition: From the Ancient World to Feudalism." *Past and Present* 103 (1984): 3–36.

WIEDEMANN, Walter. *Untersuchungen zu dem frühmittelalterlichen medizinischen Briefbuch des Codex Bruxelliensis 3701–3715.* Berlin, 1976.

WIELAND, Gernot. "The Glossed Manuscript: Classbook or Library Book?" *Anglo-Saxon England* 14 (1985): 153–73.

———. "Latin Lemma—Latin Gloss: The Stepchild of Glossologists." *Mittellateinisches Jahrbuch* 19 (1984): 91–99.

WILLIAMS, Schafer. *Codices Pseudo-Isidoriani: A Palaeographico-Historical Study.* Monumenta Iuris Canonica, Series C, 3. New York, 1971.

WILMART, André. "La Lettre philosophique d'Altmann et son contexte littéraire." *Archives d'histoire doctrinale et littéraire du moyen âge* 3 (1928): 285–319.

WOHLMUTH, Josef, ed. *Streit um das Bild: Das zweite Konzil von Nicäa (787) in ökumenischer Perspektive.* Studium universale 9. Bonn, 1989.

WOLF, G. "Grifos Erbe, die Einsetzung König Childerichs III. und der Kampf um die Macht: Zugleich Bemerkungen zur karolingischen 'Hofhistoriographie.'" *Archiv für Diplomatik, Schriftgeschichte, Siegel- und Wappenkunde* 38 (1992): 1–16.

WOLFF, Philippe. *Les Origines linguistiques de l'Europe occidentale.* Univers des connaissances 63. Paris, 1970. Published in English as *Western Languages, A.D. 100–1500*, translated by Frances Partridge, World University Library (New York, 1971).

WOLLASCH, Joachim. *Mönchtum des Mittelalters zwischen Kirche und Welt.* Münstersche Mittelalter-Schriften 7. Munich, 1972.

———. "Zu den persönlichen Notizen des Heiricus von S. Germain d'Auxerre." *Deutsches Archiv für Erforschung des Mittelalters* 15 (1959): 211–26.

WOOD, Diana, ed. *The Church and the Arts.* Studies in Church History 28. Oxford, 1992.

WRIGHT, Roger. *Late Latin and Early Romance in Spain and Carolingian France.* ARCA Classical and Medieval Texts, Papers and Monographs 8. Liverpool, 1982.

———. "On Editing 'Latin' Texts Written by Romance Speakers." In *Linguistic Studies in Medieval Spanish*, edited by Ray-Harris Northall and Thomas D. Cravens, pp. 191–208.

YUDKIN, Jeremy. *Music in Medieval Europe.* Englewood Cliffs, N.J., 1989.

ZIELINSKI, Herbert. "Die Kloster- und Kirchengründungen der Karolinger." In *Beiträge zu Geschichte und Struktur der mittelalterlichen Germania Sacra*, edited by Irene Crusius, pp. 95–134.

Contributors

John J. Contreni (Ph.D., Michigan State University) is head of the Department of History at Purdue University. His research centers on education during the Carolingian period, with particular emphasis on Carolingian school texts and manuscripts. He has written on the cathedral school of Laon (*The Cathedral School of Laon from 850 to 930: Its Manuscripts and Masters* [1978]); the role of Irish masters (especially John Scottus) in Carolingian culture; the significance of biblical studies; the place of grammar, medicine, and law in the curriculum; and the relationship between social and political goals and the world of learning in the Carolingian realms. A collection of his essays, *Carolingian Learning, Masters, and Manuscripts*, was published in 1992.

Richard L. Crocker (Ph.D., Yale University) has recently retired after having taught in the Department of Music at the University of California, Berkeley, for thirty years. With the assistance of a Guggenheim fellowship, he published a major study entitled *The Early Medieval Sequence* (1977). He was the coeditor, with David Hiley, of *The Early Middle Ages to 1300* for the *New Oxford History of Music* (1990), contributing chapters on Gregorian and medieval chant and French and English polyphony. He has also published numerous articles on ancient and medieval music and is now working on a book on Gregorian chant.

David Ganz (Ph.D., Oxford University) teaches in the Department of Classics at the University of North Carolina at Chapel Hill, specializing in the teaching of medieval Latin and Latin paleography. In addition to numerous articles dealing with Carolingian cultural life, he has recently published *Corbie in the Carolingian Renaissance* (1990), the research for which was supported by the Alexander von Humboldt Foundation.

Bernice M. Kaczynski　(Ph.D., Yale University) is a member of the Department of History at McMaster University, Hamilton, Ontario, and an associate member of the Centre for Medieval Studies, University of Toronto. She is the author of *Greek in the Carolingian Age: The St. Gall Manuscripts* (1988), and of numerous other studies on language and literacy in the Middle Ages.

Lawrence Nees　(Ph.D., Harvard University) is a professor in the Department of Art History at the University of Delaware, where he has taught since 1978. His primary area of research has been early medieval art, especially in the eighth and ninth centuries, in both Byzantium and western Europe. His publications include *From Justinian to Charlemagne: European Art, 565–787* (1985); *The Gundohinus Gospels* (1987); and *A Tainted Mantle: Hercules and the Classical Tradition at the Carolingian Court* (1991). Works in progress include a summary catalogue of some Frankish illuminated manuscripts and a study of sculptural tombs and thrones in the eleventh and twelfth centuries.

Thomas F. X. Noble　(Ph.D., Michigan State University) has taught at Michigan State University, Albion College, Texas Tech University, and, since 1980, in the Department of History at the University of Virginia. In 1984 he published *The Republic of St. Peter: The Birth of the Papal State, 680–825* (1984). He has coedited *Religion, Culture, and Society in the Early Middle Ages: Studies in Honor of Richard E. Sullivan* (1987) and *Soldiers of Christ: Saints and Saints' Lives from Late Antiquity and the Early Middle Ages* (1994). He has also published more than twenty articles and a hundred reviews. He is currently finishing a book entitled *Images and the Carolingians: Discourses on Tradition, Order, and Worship*.

Richard E. Sullivan　(Ph.D., University of Illinois) is Professor Emeritus at Michigan State University, where he taught in the Department of History from 1954. His books include *Heirs of the Roman Empire* (1960); *Aix-la-Chapelle in the Age of Charlemagne* (1965); *Speaking for Clio* (1991); and *Christian Missionary Activity in the Early Middle Ages* (1994). He coauthored *A Short History of Western Civilization* (1960), now in its eighth edition. He has also published numerous articles on early medieval history in various scholarly journals. In 1993 he was elected a fellow of the Medieval Academy of America.

Index of Manuscripts Cited

Index